Divine Envy, Jealousy, and Vengefulness in Ancient Israel and Greece

This book is the first in-depth comparative analysis of envy, jealousy, and vengefulness experienced by divine personalities in the Hebrew Bible and ancient Greek texts, including the functions served by attributing negative emotions and traits to one's gods.

Readers are informed about the vigorous debates concerning the nature of emotion, a field with rapidly growing interest, including the specific emotions of envy, jealousy, and vengefulness. The book charts the complex, multi-faceted presentation of divine beings in the Hebrew Bible and ancient Greek literature, including their negative emotions. While the detailed readings of key biblical and Greek texts can stand on their own, Lasine's comparative analyses allow readers to appreciate the uniqueness of each tradition. Finally, examining the functions served by envisioning one's God or gods as jealous, envious, and vengeful offers readers a fresh perspective on biblical theology and the ways in which Greek poets and dramatists imagined the nature of their deities.

Divine Envy, Jealousy, and Vengefulness in Ancient Israel and Greece is intended for biblical, classical, and literary scholars, as well as the general reader interested in the Hebrew Bible and/or ancient Greek literature.

Stuart Lasine is Professor Emeritus of Religion at Wichita State University, USA. He is the author of *Knowing Kings: Knowledge, Power and Narcissism in the Hebrew Bible*, *Weighing Hearts: Character, Judgment, and the Ethics of Reading the Bible*, and *Jonah and the Human Condition*.

Divine Envy, Jealousy, and Vengefulness in Ancient Israel and Greece

Stuart Lasine

LONDON AND NEW YORK

First published 2023
by Routledge
4 Park Square, Milton Park, Abingdon, Oxon OX14 4RN

and by Routledge
605 Third Avenue, New York, NY 10158

Routledge is an imprint of the Taylor & Francis Group, an informa business

© 2023 Stuart Lasine

The right of Stuart Lasine to be identified as author of this work has been asserted in accordance with sections 77 and 78 of the Copyright, Designs and Patents Act 1988.

All rights reserved. No part of this book may be reprinted or reproduced or utilised in any form or by any electronic, mechanical, or other means, now known or hereafter invented, including photocopying and recording, or in any information storage or retrieval system, without permission in writing from the publishers.

Trademark notice: Product or corporate names may be trademarks or registered trademarks, and are used only for identification and explanation without intent to infringe.

British Library Cataloguing-in-Publication Data
A catalogue record for this book is available from the British Library

ISBN: 978-1-032-26179-9 (hbk)
ISBN: 978-1-032-26327-4 (pbk)
ISBN: 978-1-003-28774-2 (ebk)

DOI: 10.4324/b23212

Typeset in Times New Roman
by Apex CoVantage, LLC

Contents

Preface viii
List of abbreviations xi

1 Introduction: theories and methods 1

1. *Studying emotions 1*
   a. *Studying emotions in general 1*
   b. *Studying emotions in literary texts 4*
2. *Characterizing "envy" and "jealousy" 6*
3. *Theoretical views concerning revenge and its relation to envy 8*
4. *The functions of anthropomorphic and anthropopathic deities 10*

2 Divine envy, jealousy, and vengeance in ancient Israel and Greece 18

1. *Are Yahweh and the Greek gods "persons" with coherent personalities? 18*
2. *Biblical and Greek understandings of divine jealousy and envy 22*
3. *Divine vengeance and its relation to envy and jealousy in biblical and Greek texts 24*
   a. *Divine vengeance and wrath in biblical texts 24*
   b. *Indignation, vengeance, and divine jealousy in ancient Greek texts 28*
      (1) Nemesis, *envy, and vengeance 28*
      (2) Revenge and justice in Euripides' Hecuba *32*

3 Yahweh as a jealous and envious God 44

1. *The seeming impossibility of Yahweh experiencing envy 44*

2. Is Yahweh envious of his human creatures? 45
   a. The charge that Yahweh was envious of Adam and Eve 45
   b. Does Yahweh envy the best of his human creatures? 46
   c. Yahweh as both jealous and envious in relation
      to other gods 47
3. Yahweh's envy in relation to his narcissism 49
   a. Psychological approaches to the relationship between
      envy and narcissism 49
   b. Yahweh's narcissism and its relation to envy and
      attachment anxiety 51
   c. The charge that Yahweh is sadistic at times 53
   d. The charge that Yahweh's behavior is sometimes immature
      or infantile 56

4 Jealousy for Yahweh and divine vengeance   62

1. The three figures who are called "jealous for Yahweh" 62
   a. Phinehas 62
   b. Elijah 64
   c. Jehu 66
2. Moses the infanticidal avenger in Numbers 31 70
   a. Moses in Num 31:17–18 and Pharaoh in Exod 1:22 71
   b. Moses' alteration of Yahweh's call for vengeance 72
   c. Calls for mass slaughter in Num 31:17–18 and Judg
      21:10–12 72
   d. Vengeance and the "battle" in Num 31:7–8 74
   e. Numbers 31 and the Bible's presentation of Moses 74
3. Divine and human motivation for vengeance in the
   Samson story 77

5 Divine envy and vengeance in Homer and Herodotus' *Histories*   85

1. Hera and divine envy in Homer and the Homeric Hymn
   to Apollo 85
2. Advice about divine envy and revenge in Herodotus 90
3. Avengers and the divine in Herodotus 95
4. Conclusions on divine envy and vengeance
   in Herodotus 98

6 Divine envy and vengeance in Greek tragedy   104

1. Envy and vengeance in Aeschylus' Persians 104
   a. Explaining defeat: divine phthonos 104

b. *Explaining defeat:* hybris, *failed vengeance,*
      and divine punishment 105
   c. *Conclusions on Xerxes' defeat 107*
2. *Envy and Vengeance in Sophocles'* Oedipus Tyrannus *108*
   a. *Divine emotion and agency in* Oedipus Tyrannus *and*
      Ajax *108*
   b. *Oedipus as avenger and target of divine vengeance 112*
   c. *Herodotus' Adrastus and Sophocles' Oedipus 116*
   d. *Conclusions 117*
3. *Envy and Revenge in Euripides'* Hippolytus *118*
   a. *Is Aphrodite's revenge against Hippolytus motivated*
      by phthonos*? 118*
   b. *What motivates Phaedra's accusation that Hippolytus*
      raped her? 121
4. *Envy and revenge in Euripides'* Bacchae *123*
   a. *Is Dionysus' punishment of Pentheus motivated*
      by phthonos*? 124*
   b. *Is Pentheus shown to be irremediably stubborn*
      and reckless? 125
   c. *Dionysus' character in the* Bacchae *127*
   d. *Is Dionysus' vengeance excessive? 128*

7 Comparing divine vengeance and envy in Hebrew and Greek texts 136

1. *Comparing varieties of divine vengeance 136*
   a. *Deities directly taking vengeance 136*
   b. *Deities indirectly taking vengeance 142*
2. *Comparing divine envy and jealousy in biblical*
   and Greek texts 147

8 The functions of divine imperfection 153

1. *"Who would pray to such a deity"? 153*
2. *Divine perfection and Yahweh's imperfections 155*
3. *Conclusion 157*

Bibliography 161
Index of ancient sources 182
Index of authors 196

Preface

Figure 1 Family photo.

A few years ago my younger sister sent me a photo of herself as a baby on our mother's lap. At their left is 4-year-old Stuart, looking askance at the duo (Figure 1). Shortly before the picture arrived, I had been writing about an older child's envy of a younger sibling or fellow nursling, a phenomenon described by thinkers from St. Augustine to Freud and Lacan. In the older child's eyes, the infant and its mother form an image of closed completeness and unity, a unity from which the elder sibling is excluded. One look at this picture and I realized that I too had been acutely aware of both jealousy and envy at a very early age.

While this study does explore the nature and functions of jealousy and envy among human beings, my focus is on divine envy and jealousy as they manifest themselves in ancient Hebrew and Greek literature. In the Hebrew Bible, one does not have to hunt for examples of divine jealousy; the biblical God names himself "Jealous." I will argue that Yahweh also shows signs of envy. This is most evident in his attitude toward the "other gods" who repeatedly attract Yahweh's followers, in spite of his insistence that those "no-gods" are unreal and powerless and that there is no God but himself. Greek deities are also capable of exhibiting various forms of divine envy and jealousy, although there is no consensus among classicists about the nature and extent of divine envy in works by Homer, Herodotus, and the Greek tragedians. In both biblical and Greek writings, divine envy often arouses the gods' anger and a desire for vengeance. The relationship among envy, jealousy, and vengefulness is an essential component of this investigation.

While I will employ tools from other disciplines when I engage with these texts, this is fundamentally a comparative literary study. The reason that I chose to compare biblical and Greek writings is that, in my opinion, these bodies of work offer the most complete and nuanced portraits of human and divine personalities produced in the ancient Mediterranean and Near East.

In Chapter 1, I begin by charting recent developments in emotion theory. I then narrow my focus to the emotions of envy and jealousy. Examining jealousy and envy also requires that we consider the relationship between these emotions and revenge, including the disposition of vengefulness. I will survey different views of this relationship, along with associated variables such as narcissism and attachment patterns. The chapter concludes by examining the possible functions served by envisioning one's deity or deities as both anthropomorphic and anthropopathic.

Chapter 2 examines scholarly opinion about the envy, jealousy, and revenge exhibited by the anthropopathic gods of ancient Israel and Greece. Opinions range from Yahweh's jealousy having nothing to do with the envy of the Greek gods to there being a close correspondence between the Hebrew and Greek terms for jealousy and envy. Next I analyze specific examples of divine envy and vengeance in biblical and Greek literature. In Chapter 3 I discuss the ways in which these aspects of Yahweh's complex but coherent personality have been praised, condemned, or explained away by theologians and other commentators over the centuries.

In Chapters 4–6 I provide detailed analyses of biblical and Greek works in which divine envy and vengefulness play a significant role. In addition to passages which highlight the deities' emotions and direct actions, I will consider cases in which humans seek vengeance on their deities' behalf by punishing those whom they perceive as having provoked the gods' jealousy. This will allow us to observe how divine jealousy, envy, and vengeance are understood in a polytheistic context as well as the ostensibly monotheistic context of biblical Israel. Chapter 7 summarizes the most important results of the preceding comparative analyses, including the most significant similarities and differences we have discovered along the way. The comparisons also include biblical and Greek texts we did not discuss earlier.

x *Preface*

My final chapter asks what functions are served by envisioning one's deities as envious, jealous and/or vengeful. Why assign them dispositional traits which are generally considered to be among the more unpleasant aspects of human psychology? In short, why portray one's god or gods as imperfect?

I would like to thank Professor Michiel van Veldhuizen for his insightful and very helpful comments on the first draft of this study. I would also like to express my gratitude to Amy Davis-Poynter and Marcia Adams for guiding me through the Routledge publication process. Finally, I want to thank my wife, Rannfrid Lasine Thelle, for putting up with me as I hid in my study throughout the COVID-19 pandemic, working on this book.

Abbreviations

AB	Anchor Bible
ABD	*Anchor Bible Dictionary*. Edited by D. N. Freedman. 6 vols. New York, 1992
Ag.	Aeschylus, *Agamemnon*
Ag. Nic.	Demosthenes, *Against Nicostratus*
Aj.	Sophocles, *Ajax*
AjPh	*The American Journal of Philology*
Am. J. Psychoanal.	*The American Journal of Psychoanalysis*
Am. J. Psychother.	*American Journal of Psychotherapy*
Andr.	Euripides, *Andromache*
ANE	Ancient Near East/Eastern
Ant.	Josephus, *Jewish Antiquities*
Antiq. Class.	*L'Antiquité Classique*
Ap.	Plato, *Apology*
Apoc. Ab.	*Apocalypse of Abraham*
ApOTC	Apollos Old Testament Commentary
ATD	Das Alte Testament Deutsch
'*Abod. Zar.*	'*Abodah Zarah*
b.	Babylonian Talmud
Bacch.	Euripides, *Bacchae*
BASP	*Basic and Applied Social Psychology*
BibInt	*Biblical Interpretation*
BICS	*Bulletin of the Institute of Classical Studies*
BJS	Brown Judaic Studies
BMCR	*Bryn Mawr Classical Review*
Br. J. Med Psychol.	*British Journal of Medical Psychology*
CA	*Current Anthropology*
CBQ	*Catholic Biblical Quarterly*
CJ	*Classical Journal*
CJP	*Canadian Journal of Psychoanalysis*
ClAnt	*Classical Antiquity*
Cogn. Psychol	*Cognitive Psychology*
Cogn. Sci.	*Cognitive Science*

ColbyQ	*Colby Quarterly*
Conf.	Augustine, *Confessions*
Contra Gal.	Julian, *Against the Galilaeans*
CPh	*Classical Philology*
CQ	*Classical Quarterly*
CW	*Classical World*
Dev. Psychopathol.	*Development and Psychopathology*
Disc.	Epictetus, *Discourses*
DSM	*Diagnostic and Statistical Manual of Mental Disorders*
DtrH	Deuteronomistic History
ECC	Eerdmans Critical Commentary
EJPR	*European Journal for Philosophy of Religion*
EJST	*European Journal of Social Theory*
EMC/CV	*Echos du Monde Classique/Classical Views*
Eos	*Eos: commentarii Societatis Philologae Polonorum*
Erud. Repub. Lett.	*Erudition and the Republic of Letters*
Eth. Eud.	Aristotle, *Eudemian Ethics*
Eth. Nic.	Aristotle, *Nicomachian Ethics*
ETL	*Ephemerides Theologicae Lovanienses*
Eur. J. Pers.	*European Journal of Personality*
Eur. J. Soc. Theory	*European Journal of Social Theory*
Eur Psychol	*European Psychologist*
FOTL	Forms of the Old Testament Literature
Fr.	Fragment
G&R	*Greece & Rome*
Gen. Rab.	*Genesis Rabbah*
GRBS	*Greek, Roman, and Byzantine Studies*
GW	Freud, *Gesammelte Werke*. Anna Freud, ed. London, 1940–
HAR	*Hebrew Annual Review*
HB	Hebrew Bible
HCOT	Historical Commentary on the Old Testament
Heb.	Hebrew
Hec.	Euripides, *Hecuba*
HF	Euripides, *Heracles* (*Hercules Furens*)
Hipp.	Euripides, *Hippolytus*
Hist.	Herodotus, *Histories*
HS	*Hebrew Studies*
HTR	*Harvard Theological Review*
Hum. Dev.	*Human Development*
h. Ap.	*Homeric Hymn to Apollo*
IBC	Interpretation: A Bible Commentary for Teaching and Preaching
ICC	International Critical Commentary
IJP	*International Journal of Psycho-Analysis*

Il.	Homer, *Iliad*
Int	*Interpretation*
Isthm.	Pindar, *Isthmian Odes*
J Clin Psychol: IS	*Journal of Clinical Psychology: In Session*
JAOS	*Journal of the American Oriental Society*
J. Adolesc.	*Journal of Adolescence*
JBL	*Journal of Biblical Literature*
JCS	*Journal of Cuneiform Studies*
JEP:LMC	*Journal of Experimental Psychology: Learning, Memory and Cognition*
JHS	*The Journal of Hellenic Studies*
JNES	*Journal of Near Eastern Studies*
JNSL	*Journal of Northwest Semitic languages*
JPC	*The Journal of Pastoral Care*
J Pers	*Journal of Personality*
J Pers Soc Psychol	*Journal of Personality and Social Psychology*
J. Philos	*The Journal of Philosophy*
JPS	Jewish Publication Society of America Version
J. Psychol.	*Journal of Psychology*
JQR	*Jewish Quarterly Review*
J Relig Health	*Journal of Religion and Health*
J. Res. Pers.	*Journal of Research in Personality*
JSOT	*Journal for the Study of the Old Testament*
JSRNC	*Journal for the Study of Religion, Nature & Culture*
JSSR	*Journal for the Scientific Study of Religion*
KatBl	*Katechetische Blätter: Zeitschrift für religiöses Lernen in Schule und Gemeinde*
L.A.E.	*The Life of Adam and Eve*
Lam. Rab.	*Lamentations Rabbah*
LCL	Loeb Classical Library
Lev. Rab.	*Leviticus Rabbah*
LHBOTS	Library of Hebrew Bible/Old Testament Studies
ll.	lines
Lr.	Shakespeare, *King Lear*
LXX	Septuagint (the Greek Old Testament)
Ly.	Plato, *Lysis*
Metaph.	Aristotle, *Metaphysics*
Midr. Tanḥ	*Midrash Tanḥuma*
Moses	Philo, *On the Life of Moses*
MT	Masoretic Text (of the Hebrew Bible)
NAC	New American Commentary
NCBC	New Century Bible Commentary
Nem.	Pindar, *Nemean Odes*
NIB	*The New Interpreter's Bible*. Nashville: Abingdon, 1994–
NICOT	New International Commentary on the Old Testament

xiv *Abbreviations*

NIBCOT	New International Biblical Commentary on the Old Testament
Num. Rab.	*Numbers Rabbah*
Od.	Homer, *Odyssey*
OT	Sophocles, *Oedipus Tyrannus*
OTL	Old Testament Library
OTE	Old Testament Essays
OtSt	*Oudtestamentische Studiën*
PCPS	*Proceedings of the Cambridge Philological Society*
Pers.	Aeschylus, *Persians*
Pers. Relatsh.	*Personal Relationships*
Pers. Soc. Psychol. Bull.	*Personality and Social Psychology Bulletin*
Perspect. Psychol. Sci.	*Perspectives on Psychological Science*
Phil.	Sophocles, *Philoctetes*
Proof.	*Prooftexts: A Journal of Jewish Literary History*
Psychiatr. Ann.	*Psychiatric Annals*
Psychoanal. Psychol.	*Psychoanalytic Psychology*
Psychol. Bull.	*Psychological Bulletin*
Psychol. Rev.	*Psychological Review*
Psychother. Res.	*Psychotherapy Research*
Pyth.	Pindar, *Pythian Odes*
qted.	quoted
Resp.	Plato, *Republic*
RevQ	*Revue de Qumran*
Rh.	Aristotle, *Rhetoric*
RhM	*Rheinisches Museum für Philologie*
SBL	Society of Biblical Literature
SemeiaSt	Semeia Studies
SJOT	*Scandinavian Journal of the Old Testament*
S. *'Olam Rab.*	*Seder 'Olam Rabbah*
TAPA	*Transactions of the American Philological Association*
Theog.	Hesiod, *Theogony*
Ti.	Plato, *Timaeus*
TOTC	Tyndale Old Testament Commentaries
Trach.	Sophocles, *Trachiniae*
UCPCP	*University of California Publications in Classical Philology*
VT	*Vetus Testamentum*
VTSup	Supplements to Vetus Testamentum
Yebam.	*Yebamot*
WBC	Word Biblical Commentary
WBCom	Westminster Bible Companion
WD	Hesiod, *Works and Days*
WUNT	Wissenschaftliche Untersuchungen zum Neuen Testament
ZAW	*Zeitschrift für die alttestamentliche Wissenschaft*

1 Introduction
Theories and methods

1. Studying emotions

Before we can explore the intricacies of divine envy and jealousy, several preliminary tasks must be undertaken. First I will survey different views on the nature of emotion and ask how we go about analyzing the emotional experiences of others in daily life, as well as characters in textual worlds. I will then ask how "envy" and "jealousy" have been described by scholars in various disciplines, including the ways in which envy and jealousy differ from one another. Next I will examine theoretical views on vengeance and revenge, as well as their relation to envy. The chapter concludes by considering various theories concerning the functions of gods who are imagined by their worshipers to be anthropomorphic and anthropopathic.

a. Studying emotions in general

Whether emotions are universal or culturally determined continues to be debated.[1] Some investigators stress the biological universality of what Ekman calls "basic emotions" (1992; 1999, 45–60), while others reject the universality of basic emotions, if not the concept of basic emotions itself (e.g., Wierzbicka 1999, 168–72; Colombetti 2014, 26–52; cf. Cairns 2019b, 4). Wierzbicka does leave open the possibility of "emotional universals" (1999, 273–307). Colombetti points out that "arguments from cross-cultural linguistic differences do not undermine the claim (supported by empirical evidence) that some organismic features recur reliably across cultures and languages in comparable situations" (2014, 31).[2] Other specific aspects of emotional experience have also been deemed "largely universal."[3] In the literary texts we will be examining, the characters themselves sometimes assume that specific emotions are universal.[4]

The role of cognition in emotional episodes has also been vigorously debated. The most extreme example of the purely cognitive view of emotion is Robert Solomon's assertion that passions *are* judgments (1993, viii, 125–32). Solomon insists that an emotion "is not a feeling (or a set of feelings), but an interpretation" (1984, 248). In fact, "the feelings no more constitute or define the emotion than an army of fleas constitutes a homeless dog" (1993, 97).[5]

DOI: 10.4324/b23212-1

A number of scholars in different fields have warned that dichotomies such as cognition-emotion, nature-culture, and mind-body are both reductive and misleading (e.g., Leavitt 1996, 515–17; Colombetti 2014, xiv–xvii). Biology and culture both play a role in lived experience and the interpretation of emotions, as many scholars on both sides of this debate freely admit (Ekman 1992, 550; Wierzbicka 1999, 2; cf. Cairns 2004, 12). While Wierzbicka stresses the lexical differences among words designating emotions in different cultures, she readily admits that there is "no real conflict between the view that human feelings can . . . have a biological dimension and the view that they are 'socially constructed' and have a cultural dimension" (1999, 306).

Speaking from an evolutionary standpoint, Ekman asserts "that the primary function of emotion is to mobilize the organism to deal quickly with important interpersonal encounters, prepared to do so by what types of activity have been adaptive in the past" (1999, 46).[6] While the protective function of emotion is clearly important, humans experiencing emotions do not always "deal quickly" with perceived threats, because human emotions involve more than protecting the individual (or group) from sudden life-threatening crises. As Shaviro (2016, 1) points out, emotions themselves can be dysfunctional and dangerous. For example, envy and jealousy may be triggered by a threat to an individual's self-image and feeling of worth. As long as the individual remains in the situation which evokes these emotions, they may last indefinitely or intensify. In extreme cases, these feelings are not only maladaptive but life-threatening as well.

There are a number of universal features of human existence which call for protective responses from individuals. However, the forms these responses will take may vary according to one's culture, one's situation within that culture, and one's personality. Among the negative factors which have been most consistently cited as basic to the human condition are ephemerality, mutability, frailty, contingency, vulnerability, lack of control, the need to labor, and, at the most fundamental level, mortality.[7] Our awareness of our evanescence and vulnerability is itself a key aspect of the human situation, although we may work hard to obscure that awareness—and the emotions which that awareness might prompt.

Also relevant to our investigation is the question posed by classicist Michael Halleran (1992): "while it is unquestionably true that our categories are not the same as the Greeks', just how different are they?"[8] In another study I discussed the various answers given to this question by scholars in a variety of fields (Lasine 2012, 24–55). Among those which emphasize difference, the classicist and poet Ruth Padel advises that it is difficult, but rewarding, to think of the ancient Greeks as "astoundingly alien from ourselves"; it is we, not they, who are "the cultural oddity" (1992, 10, 35).[9] Among classicists of earlier generations, Fränkel (1951, 108) asserts that "the homeric person actually had a different structure from that with which we are acquainted today." Snell (1975, 7) warns that because Homer's works speak to us and strongly move us, we can easily overlook how fundamentally different everything is from what we are accustomed to. Snell argues that in the early period consciousness of the "character" of an individual person is

Introduction 3

lacking, as are self-awareness, genuine reflection, and a *Geist* or soul (1975, 10, 18, 27–28).

Other classical scholars disagree. Williams argues that "in important ways, we are, in our ethical situation, more like human beings in antiquity than any Western people have been in the meantime" (1993, 166).[10] Redfield (1975, 20–22) focuses on "Homeric social psychology" and suggests that we may be "more like Homer's Achilles than we like to think."[11] Momigliano (1985, 89) contends that "Greek and Roman historians talked about individuals in a manner which is not distant from our own." And while Pelling (1990b, 249) concedes that the Greeks may not have felt their emotions quite as we do, he adds that "such imaginative cultural leaps may not be different in type from those we make every day in seeking to engage sympathetically with people of different ages, cultures, and moral or religious values."

I agree with those classicists who conclude that while ancient literary works are different from modern literature, their "human intelligibility" allows them to seem familiar to us (Halliwell 1990, 34–35; Pelling 1990b, 254). Halliwell contends that we have to presuppose certain fundamental factors in human experience or there will be no basis on which to identify and comprehend significant cultural traits and distinctions in the interpretation of character. In reference to the Homeric poems, Williams argues that we could not view Homer as speaking of human actions if we did not find in his characters' words a notion of intention, as well as beliefs, desires, and purposes, which seem constitutive of the notion of human action (1993, 33–34).

Scholars from other disciplines concur. Linguist Frank Palmer (1992, 235, 241) believes that the products of high culture are "universal" in the sense of showing certain constancies in human nature that different people can recognize. Taylor (1989, 111–12) grants that there is "some truth in the idea that people always are selves, . . . [and] have shared a very similar sense of 'me' and 'mine.'" Geertz concedes that "some conception of what a human individual is . . . is, so far as I can see, universal" (1983, 59).

Among biblical scholars, Sandmel believes that people have been "basically the same . . . at least for the past four thousand years" (1972, 30). He is referring to basic human emotions. Sandmel *does* concede that some "habits of mind" differ among peoples. Thus, "the Hebrew mind" has a "bent for the concrete," has humor as one of its "facets," does not distinguish between history and non-history, and has an "elasticity" which "we" moderns lack (1972, 31, 33, 38, 42). Many biblicists do not acknowledge even this degree of basic "sameness" between the ancient Israelites and people today. Di Vito argues that the "notion of 'self' reflected in biblical literature presents a striking contrast to modernity" in several respects. These include the lack of "a true center for the person" and the absence of "hidden depths." In addition, "the boundaries that mark personal identity [are] extremely permeable" (1997, 59–61, 66).[12]

In the case of the Hebrew Bible, viewing the characters as fundamentally alien to ourselves goes against the grain of the text's narrative rhetoric. Characters are presented to us as our "relatives," that is, our ancestors. In that sense, the Hebrew Bible is the "family album" of the target audiences (see Lasine 2012, 53–55).

b. Studying emotions in literary texts

It is indisputable that the Hebrew and Greek terms for specific emotions are not entirely coextensive with the words for those emotions in modern Western languages. Fortunately, there is often significant overlap between the behaviors denoted by such terms and the situations which are found to evoke those emotions. Therefore, we cannot draw conclusions solely on the basis of whether a particular emotion word is present or absent in a given text. Kutter (2018, 59–60) points to the Typhon scene in the *Homeric Hymn to Apollo* (*h. Ap*. 300–69) as an example of Hera experiencing jealousy and envy, even though it is not "marked" by the Greek terms for those emotions.[13] In the Hebrew Bible, characters such as Cain[14] and the "false mother" in the Solomon's judgment story[15] are almost always assumed to be experiencing envy, even though Hebrew terms for envy are not present.

In addition, literary characters sometimes interpret another character's word or behavior as being driven by a specific emotion. For example, Scodel and Caston (2019, 112) point to Hector interpreting Andromache's tears as a sign that she is afraid for him in *Iliad* 6.484–87. They note that the narrator "does not signal whether Hector's interpretation of Andromache's feeling is entirely complete, but her feelings are basically legible."[16] There are a number of cases in the Hebrew Bible in which one character "reads" the emotion or mood of another. For example, the imprisoned Joseph views his fellow prisoners, the royal baker and cupbearer, as זעפים ("dejected" or "out of humor"). Joseph directly asks the moody persons about it and offers to help remove the cause of their faces being sad (פניכם רעים; Gen 40:7–8). A similar sequence of events occurs when King Artaxerxes interprets the expression on Nehemiah's face as indicative of "sadness of heart" (רע לב) and asks him about it (Neh 2:2–3). And while King Solomon does not attempt to read the emotion of the two prostitutes when they bring their dispute to him, he uses the threat of killing the living baby to trigger the deepest emotions of the two women, who then become totally "legible" (1 Kgs 3:23–27).[17]

Clearly, a purely lexical approach to studying emotions in literary texts is insufficient.[18] In order to analyze a literary personage's emotion, we must consider the situational factors which prompt the emotion (the "eliciting conditions"), the character's appraisal of the situation, any reported bodily sensations or "body language" triggered by the appraisal, and the character's words and actions in reaction to these stimuli.[19] At that point, the interpretive task is to "translate emotional communications from one idiom, context, language, or sociohistorical mode of understanding into another" (Lutz 1988, 8).

Many writers on emotions use the term "scripts" to denote the actions and situational factors which together constitute an emotional episode[20] or event. Cairns (2008, 46) describes a script as "a mini-narrative that will usually encompass (at least) the conditions in which emotion X occurs, the perceptions and appraisals of those conditions, and the responses (whether symptomatic, expressive, or pragmatic) that result." Cairns makes it clear that the term script "would be misleading if it suggested either the extreme dramaturgical model of the self according to which all emotional responses involve the conscious or unconscious assumption of a social role or that the 'actors' are somehow following a certain prescribed set of moves." Kaster (2003, 256) also employs the "script" metaphor but only as a convenient way to describe the features of an experienced emotion which are embedded in narrative. In this sense, the process of "emotion" is a "little narrative or dramatic script" (2005, 8; cf. 2003, 256–57).

Other scholars emphasize the dramaturgical connotation of the "script" metaphor,[21] at times in problematic fashion. For example, Wierzbicka includes a culture's "emotional scripts" in "its repertoire of 'cultural scripts'." The cultural scripts "implicitly (and sometimes explicitly) tell people what to feel, and what not to feel, and what to say and do, or not say and do, when they feel something" (1999, 34; 240). In this formulation, a culture's scripts dictate the actors' behavior as much as a dramatic script determines the cast's behavior—if the director does not allow the actors to improvise or ab-lib. This understanding of tightly scripted emotions and behavior overstates the degree to which most cultures are able enforce unanimity of feeling and response. Admittedly, legal collections in the Hebrew Bible do command members of the community to "love," or not "hate," or "fear" other people,[22] but biblical narratives and poetry make it clear that these dictates were not always heeded; they are even capable of being reversed.[23]

Averill and Tomkins both embrace the dramaturgical metaphor. Averill describes a person's emotional behavior and experiences as determined by his or her social role in a drama, in which "the plot is the cultural system." In order for the emotional actor to "perform [his] role adequately," he "must not only know his own part, and the parts of others, but he must also understand how the various roles relate to the plot (and subplots) of the play" (1980, 314–15). Tomkins distinguishes between the script produced by an individual and the script of the society. The individual creates the "plot of a life" by following his or her "rules for predicting, interpreting, responding to, and controlling a magnified set of scenes" (1978, 217). If the individual's society "is to endure as a coherent entity, its definition of situations must in some measure be constructed as an integral part of the shared scripts of its individuals" (1978, 218).[24] These formulations also overestimate the degree to which all members of a society (and its various subcultures) follow the "rules" of a society's supposed script, in order to advance the "plot" of this apparently never-ending social drama.

Whatever label one chooses to apply to emotional events involving ancient literary personages, evaluating their emotions is one aspect of the larger process of assessing the behavior and character of both "real people"[25] and literary personages. Elsewhere[26] I have employed insights from attribution theory and related branches of psychological research to examine the ways in which people evaluate and judge the behavior of others. In the modern West, this usually means basing our judgments on how we perceive others' character while ignoring the situational constraints to which the individuals (or groups) are exposed (see Chapter 2.1, below). Our judgments are influenced by our assumptions, expectations, values, and ideologies.

The Hebrew Bible includes many "round" characters[27] whose personalities are recognizable to modern Western readers, even if the terms used to describe their moods and actions differ in some respects from our own. Because people interpret literary characters in much the same way that they evaluate others in their quotidian worlds, this kind of investigation is warranted; in some cases it is even possible to identify complex characters as personality types (see Lasine 2012, 3–19, 115–43, 225–28).

As Scodel points out, literary characters also evaluate other characters in the same way that people ordinarily judge others in daily life. Speaking of Homer's *Iliad*, she notes that "the heroes, like real people in any real culture, evaluate themselves and others, anticipate and infer the judgements of others, seek to make their own evaluations prevail, moderate and compromise in endless adjustments" (2008, 157). To the extent that situations and social figurations promote specific modes of self-experience and determine character, a supposedly "modern" self-structure such as Elias's closed personality (*homo clausus*), which grew out of the need for masking and duplicity in European court society,[28] can also be found in an ancient narrative such as the Court History of King David (see Lasine 2001, 9–15, 93–140).

Critics who dismiss what they call "psychologizing" interpretations often fail to acknowledge that they themselves make psychological judgments (if not pseudo-medical diagnoses) about literary characters.[29] We all make judgments about characters. As critics, it is our obligation to do so in a rigorous manner, fully aware of the findings produced by social scientific research. Only when readers are given ample accounts of characters' behavior and directly quoted speech can we apply psychological insights in order to assess whether those characters possess specific robust personality traits and emotional dispositions. Information about the characters' thoughts, emotions, and interactions with others enhances the potential of such analyses. Fortunately, we are furnished with this depth of information about deities such as Yahweh and Hera, allowing us to investigate cases of envy, jealousy, and vengefulness in the gods' various textual appearances.[30]

2. Characterizing "envy" and "jealousy"

Psychologists who study envy do not agree about all aspects of this phenomenon. For example, some argue that envy is a specific emotion (see Harris and Salovey 2008, 337–38), while others hold that it is a situational label (White and Mullen 1989, 9–17, 39) or, like jealousy, a "blended" emotion which incorporates "basic-level emotions" such as anger, sadness, and fear (Sharpsteen 1991, 35–36). Some investigators contend that envy is a virtually universal or "pan-human" phenomenon, even though it can take different forms in different cultures and different periods within one culture (F. Foster 1972, 165; cf. Salovey and Rothman 1991, 282). Leahy also considers envy "a ubiquitous social emotion." He describes envy as a "status anxiety emotion that draws on a near universal positive evaluation of the importance of status across age groups, gender, social classes, and cultures" (2021, 418–19).

Certain social and political figurations are more likely to foster malicious envy and vengefulness than others. Cairns (2003, 241) notes that "envy is a problem where political equality is accompanied by social inequality." As Lindholm puts it, societies which are "prone to malicious envy are likely to be social formations that subscribe to an ideal of equality and an ethos of competitive individualism" (2008, 240). In order for envy to be accentuated, "there must be an absence of acceptable multiple pathways to success, a 'limited good' mentality, an agrarian mode of production, and a code of honor." In these circumstances, "the onus of defeat and inferiority rest solely on the individual, whose humiliation contributes to feelings of spiteful envy against the successful." Monarchical and patriarchal political figurations also leave ample room for destructive envy. Both the Bible and ancient Greek texts include numerous examples of malicious envy among humans, although my main focus in this study is on divine envy and therefore the ways in which each body of texts presents their deity or deities.

Scholars disagree about whether jealousy and envy are always negative or destructive emotional states. According to Cohen-Charash and Larson, "most researchers of envy agree it is an unpleasant emotion" (2017, 3; cf. Smith and Kim 2007, 47). Krizan and Johar (2012, 1418) call envy "the only unpleasant sin." Elliott goes further, asserting that "envy is always negative" (2016a, 91); in fact, it is "always evil and never virtuous" (2007, 346; cf. Kelly 2016, 61–62). F. Foster argues that envy is "a particularly dangerous and destructive emotion, since it implies hostility, which leads to aggression and violence capable of destroying societies" (1972, 165).

In contrast, Parrott (2002, 341–42) contends that "negative emotions" can still have positive "functional utility" if a number of conditions are met.[31] Henniger and Harris agree; negative social emotions such as jealousy and envy "create an impetus for behavior, which once engaged in helps alleviate [a] negative psychological state" (2014, 77). The "overarching goal" for enviers is to eliminate "the unfavorable comparison" between him- or herself and the person envied. This "may ultimately result in beneficial outcomes for the envier" (2014, 89; cf. 93).[32] Rentzsch and Gross (2015, 533) cite a number of studies in which envy is treated "as a beneficial trait that motivates striving to acquire the desired object." Other investigators argue that consumer envy is benign in a competitive market economy, functioning as a "needed spur to ambition" (see Belk 2008, 219–20; Schoeck 1987, 415–21). According to Lateiner, even Herodotus—who was well aware of the destructive effects of human and divine envy—believes that in nonautocratic governments envy promotes human freedom and fruitful diversity, because "the agonistic character of Greek institutions harnesses this energy [coming from envy]" (1991, 184).

There are more aspects of envy about which both ancient and modern observers do agree. Foremost among these is the fact that we envy people who are similar to ourselves (Harris and Salovey 2008, 339; Smith and Kim 2007, 48). Plato's Socrates declares that "what is most alike must necessarily be filled with envy, rivalry, and enmity (φθόνου τε καὶ φιλονικίας καὶ ἔχθρας) toward each other" (*Ly.* 215d; cf. Aristotle, *Rh.* 1386b). There is also widespread agreement that the envier wants to deprive the envied party of their perceived advantage, even if the envier does not desire that advantage him- or herself (see, e.g., Aristotle *Rh.* 1378b, 1387b; Parrott and Smith 1993, 906).[33] This is especially true if the envier views her situation as unfair or as a threat to her self-definition.[34]

Another oft-noted characteristic of envy is the envier's tendency to denigrate those whom they envy. Vidaillet points to research indicating that the denigration not only expresses aggression "but an attempt to expose the other and his or her limitations" (2008, 283; 2007, 1672–73). The envier perceives the envied person's advantage as "reflecting badly on the self" (Parrott 1991, 4). Derogating the envied rival "serves as a defense against the threat to the self as negative feelings about the self become projected onto the advantaged person" (Smith and Kim 2007, 54; cf. Schroeder 2005, 2032). However, in the process of degrading the opponent, the person experiencing such "malicious-spiteful hatred" may potentially weaken his or her position, thereby increasing their self-doubt (French 2001, 103).

It is important to keep in mind the distinction between envy and jealousy, especially because the two terms are often used synonymously in everyday parlance. Smith and Kim describe the key difference succinctly: "envy involves cases in which another person has what we want but cannot have, whereas jealousy involves the threat of losing someone to a rival" (2007, 49; cf. Parrott 1991, 4; F. Foster 1972, 168). In addition, envy and jealousy "may frequently co-occur." In fact, one "cause of conflation of envy and jealousy is the frequency of their co-occurrence" (Parrott 1991, 23; Parrott and Smith 1993, 907).[35] As we proceed we will encounter cases of such co-occurrence, particularly in reference to the biblical God.

3. Theoretical views concerning revenge and its relation to envy

Legal scholar Ken Levy argues that while many people repudiate revenge, often by citing the biblical admonition to "turn the other cheek" (Matt 5:39; Luke 6:29), the arguments against revenge are weak. Revenge does not always perpetuate a cycle of violence; in fact, it may not involve violence at all. Many "acts of private revenge . . . terminate the matter" (2014, 663–64). According to Levy, the "desire for revenge is rooted in the deeper, instinctive desire to maintain our supremely valued interests against unjustified and unexcused injury by others." Turning "the crime against the perpetrator helps to restore our sense of emotional equilibrium" (2014, 652, 654–56). In short, we should not "condemn revenge per se," but *"unjustified, misplaced, or excessive* revenge" (2014, 664). Solomon also believes that vengeance attempts to restore a kind of equilibrium. Vengeance is "the emotion of 'getting even,' putting the world back in balance." In fact, "to revenge oneself against evil . . . seems to lie at the very foundation of our sense of justice, indeed, of our very sense of ourselves" (1994, 305).[36] French agrees: "vengeance is the way of making things right, of restoring the balance to the scales of justice" (2001, 3).

In Milton's *Paradise Lost*, the "infernal Serpent" deceives the "Mother of Mankind" when his guile is "stirr'd up with Envy and Revenge" (1.34–36; Milton 1935, 9). It is not difficult to see how envy might lead to a desire for revenge.[37] According to Smith and Kim, "to the extent that it happens typically in envy, one can argue that a sense of injustice is a core feature of the experience of envy" (2007, 49). This feeling of having been treated unjustly, combined with the "hostile feelings typical of envy" (Smith 1991, 93; cf. 82), could give rise to a desire for revenge against the envied party. One may also prompt envy in others as a means of revenge. That is, individuals may attempt to "achieve something in order to evoke in their critics, rivals or relatives the impotent rage of envy" (Schoeck 1987, 417).

The relationship between envy and revenge is also acknowledged in theories of *ressentiment*. Leach (2008, 102) claims that Nietzsche's notion of *ressentiment* "includes all the elements considered central to envy," adding that this may be why a number of commentators view Nietzsche's account of *ressentiment* as a theory of envy. However, in the *Genealogy of Morality* Nietzsche mentions envy only once in connection with *ressentiment*, along with hatred, ill will, suspiciousness, grudging rancor (*Rancune*) and revenge (1887, 63). Nietzsche's focus is on revenge, more specifically, the ways in which "the priestly caste" gains "imaginary revenge" or "an act of the most spiritual revenge" against the knightly-aristocratic caste and its noble virtues (1887, 11–12, 16–20). This revenge is gained by devaluating all noble values and traits.[38]

While disparagement of the envied party is indeed characteristic of envy, Nietzsche does not say that the priests envied the knights for their health, power, or enjoyment of life or that they attempted to attain the desirable traits which they perceived to be in the possession of the hated enemy. In other words, he omits the essential dynamic of envy or leaves it to readers to make the connection. Instead, Nietzsche uses the metaphor of two castes "jealously" confronting one another. The only way for the priestly caste to "win" is by valorizing their own impotence and disparaging or marking as evil the *arete* of the knightly-aristocratic caste.[39]

Scheler attempts to develop and extend Nietzsche's concept of *ressentiment*, describing it as a kind of "psychological self-poisoning," an enduring emotional attitude which results from the systematically practiced repression of certain normal emotions and affects. This, in turn, results in a disposition to hold illusory values. The relevant emotions associated with *ressentiment* include revenge, hatred, malice, envy, the desire to disparage,[40] spite, and *Schadenfreude* (1955, 38, 41). Scheler stresses that the most important starting point for the formation of resentment is the "impulse for *revenge*" (1955, 38). Revenge reacts to an attack or injury, but not immediately; the impulse to get even is restrained, in part due to the aggrieved party's feeling of impotence. At this point Scheler focuses on the role of envy, which Nietzsche had left largely undiscussed. Scheler contends that the envious will not fall into *ressentiment* if they seek to acquire the envied property by means of work, exchange, crime, or force (1955, 41). *Ressentiment* only arises if the envious party believes that she or he is unable to act out their emotions due to weakness or fear.

One problem with Scheler's treatment is that his concept of "genuine envy" describes only a single sort of envy, which is often indistinguishable from his notion of *ressentiment* (see Kelly 2016, 52–53). Scheler argues that "envy" (*Neid*), in the ordinary sense of the word, emanates from a feeling of impotence when our striving for a piece of property is stymied because another person possesses the object (1955, 44). However, this feeling does not lead to genuine envy until it vents itself in an act of hatred or a hateful attitude toward the possessor of the object. The envious person is then able to experience the illusion that the possessor and the possession are the *cause* of our painful inability to possess the object (1955, 44–45). This contrasts with our earlier discussion of envy, which indicated that not every case of envy involves a feeling of impotence or hatred of the one envied. Nevertheless, the concept of *ressentiment* described by Nietzsche and Scheler underscores the relationship between envy and a desire for vengeance. This relationship has been confirmed by recent psychological studies. For example, Elshout and her team found that the "central emotions of vengeance were vindictive feelings, anger, humiliation, and envy" (2015, 507; cf. 517, 520).

4. The functions of anthropomorphic and anthropopathic deities

What functions are served by conceiving gods as humanlike, especially when those divinities are said to possess negative and destructive emotions such as jealousy, envy, rage, and a desire for revenge? Critiques of anthropomorphic deities go back as far as the philosopher Xenophanes (born ca. 570 BCE). Xenophanes famously remarks that if horses, oxen, or lions had hands and could draw, they would depict the gods as having bodies similar to their own (Fr. 15; Lesher 1992, 25). Xenophanes criticizes Homer and Hesiod for attributing to the gods actions which humans censure, citing theft, adultery, and mutual deceit (Fr. 11; Lesher 1992, 23). Lesher cautions that while Xenophanes does not explicitly mention the fact that humans envision the gods as "envious, jealous, or the source of undeserved sufferings," we should not conclude "that he was unaware of . . . these forms of wickedness" (1992, 84).[41]

Hume is one of the most influential modern thinkers to have asked why a culture would depict its deities as unjust and capable of negative emotions. He argues that the first ideas of religion are rooted in our "incessant hopes and fears" (2007, 38). Many "events of life" stem from our vulnerability, lack of control, and knowledge of our mortality. Hume stresses the urgency of our emotional reactions to the human condition, singling out anxiety, dread, and terror, as well as urgent desires for revenge as well as for food (2007, 39).

According to Hume, the urgent need to understand the causes of our perilous situation leads us to envision anthropomorphic gods: "while the passions are kept in perpetual alarm by an anxious expectation of the events, the imagination is equally employed in forming ideas of those powers on which we have so entire a dependence" (2007, 40). The reason that these powers are imagined to be human-like is the result of "an universal tendency amongst mankind to conceive all beings like themselves, and to transfer to every object those qualities with which they are familiarly acquainted." Thus, we "ascribe malice and good will to everything that hurts or pleases us" (2007, 40). And if a group envisions one god as their principal deity, and that deity is analogous to a human sovereign, the god's worshipers can "endeavor by every art to insinuate themselves into his favor; and supposing him to be pleased, like themselves, with praise and flattery, there is no eulogy or exaggeration which will be spared in their addresses to him" (Hume 2007, 53).[42] The goal of such flattery is to gain a modicum of control over the powerful forces which threaten them.

Hume finds it absurd that we transfer "human passions and infirmities to the deity, represent him as jealous and revengeful, capricious and partial" (2007, 41). He explains this philosophical "absurdity" by pointing to the "primary religion of mankind." The "dismal apprehensions" of people naturally lead them to imagine that the "invisible, unknown powers" possess the traits of "vengeance, severity, cruelty, and malice" (2007, 77). Paradoxically, "as men farther exalt their idea of their divinity, it is their notion of his power and knowledge only, not of his goodness, which is improved." In fact, "the higher the deity is exalted in power and knowledge, the lower . . . is he depressed in goodness and benevolence, whatever epithets of praise may be bestowed on him by his amazed adorers" (2007, 78–79). Hume does not consider the possibility that the contradictions and mysteries which characterize human life are better explained as caused by a deity who incorporates those contradictions rather than a philosophically perfect god which leaves unexplained the co-presence in our world of good and evil, life and death, beauty and horror.[43]

Like Hume, Freud contends that anthropomorphism in religion has its origin in the inability of humans to control their fate, predict their future, or fend off external threats. The elements resist our control; we are subject to earthquakes, floods, storms, illnesses, and, above all, the "painful riddle of death" (1948a, 336–37). Nature opposes us, "magnificent, brutal and merciless," forcing us to remain aware of our weakness and helplessness. Life is equally difficult to bear for individuals. The dictates of civilization (*Kultur*) require us to restrain ourselves, other people cause us pain, and unconquered nature—which we call destiny—adds to our injury (1948a, 337).

Naturally, humans' "severely threatened sense of self" longs for consolation; the "world and life must have their terror taken away" (1948a, 337–38). The first step in accomplishing this feat is to "anthropomorphize nature." Impersonal forces and destinies remain eternally alien to us. But if passions rage in the elements as they do in our own soul, then one can breathe again and feel oneself at home in the uncanny, allowing one to psychologically cope with one's aimless anxiety (1948a, 338). One is then no longer defenseless against the violent external "superhuman" forces.

Hume pointed to our tendency to flatter anthropomorphized powers. Freud stresses that we attempt to "coax, placate or bribe" such forces; by influencing them in this manner, we rob them of some of their power (1948a, 338). According to Freud, the gods serve a threefold function: "to ward off the terrors of nature, to reconcile one to the cruelty of fate—particularly as it manifests itself in death—and to make compensation for the suffering and privations which people have imposed upon them through living together in civilized society" (1948a, 339).

Freud likens helpless humans attempting to cope with overwhelming external forces to the situation of small children in relation to their parents (1948a, 338–39). When children reach adolescence and become aware that they can never do without protection against alien superior powers, they lend these powers the features of a father-figure and create for themselves gods before whom they are afraid and whom they seek to win over (1948a, 346).[44] Freud draws an analogy with present-day family relationships by pointing to the findings of psychoanalytic research. This research shows that a person's "personal relation to God depends upon his [sic] relation to his corporeal father" (1944, 177–79).[45]

Although Freud leaves room for people to have different understandings of a father-god based on their experience with their own human fathers, he gives all his attention to a father who is, in part, characterized by some of the same negative traits we are examining in this study. These include narcissism, a masterful nature, independence, sexual jealousy, intolerance, and godlike unconcern which can culminate in ruthlessness (e.g., 1940, 137–38, 151, 153, 217). The main function served by this father-god is the same as that of a small child's human father. The ambivalence a child feels for the father also remains, resulting in the child—and the adult worshiper—simultaneously experiencing fear and adulation toward the father's or paternal god's perceived power and autonomy. In terms of explaining the functions served by envisioning a god with negative traits, Freud's scenario is of limited value because his notion of fatherhood is so narrow, even in the context of the highly patriarchal society in which he lived and worked.

Recent psychological studies have confirmed the similarity between God concepts and images of a parent or both parents.[46] In fact, "the nature of relationships people report having with God often mirror the nature of relationships people report having with their parents" (Morewedge and Clear 2008, 183). For example, in the case of American female college students, mothers and fathers created a model of nurturance and power which contributed to seeing God as nurturing and powerful. Conversely, punishing and judging parents directly affected punishing and judging God images (J. Dickie et al. 2006, 57, 65–69).[47]

Other studies have examined the "particular personality dispositions" which subjects attribute to God, including "beliefs, desires, intentions, emotions, and perceptions" (Shtulman and Lindeman 2016, 637; cf. Barrett and Keil 1996, 221). In some of this research the focus is on "whether God is conceptualized as an attachment figure"; it has "therefore focused on attachment-related properties,[48] like whether God is comforting, controlling, distant, or wrathful" (Shtulman and Lindeman 2016, 636). Shtulman and Lindeman found that in three different cultural contexts it was "cognitively easier" to attribute psychological properties to God than to assign physiological properties to him.[49] They also concluded that "individuals with strong religious beliefs tended to attribute more anthropomorphic . . . properties to God than did individuals with weaker religious beliefs" (2016, 663).

Researchers such as Morewedge and Clear found that "believers perceiving God in anthropomorphic terms were more likely to judge violations of their religious doctrine to be morally unacceptable than believers not perceiving God in anthropomorphic terms" (2008, 182). They suggest that these believers "may perceive violations of their religious code to be offensive to God, because those violations defy the explicit requests of an entity akin to another person" (2008, 184). They summarize their findings by saying that "anthropomorphic God concepts appear to engender moral judgment among devout Christians" (2008, 188), but they do not ask whether those believers had parents who tended to be punishing and judging. Waytz and his team also conclude that people with anthropomorphic representations of the deity believe God to be "more judgmental than those with less anthropomorphic representations" (2010, 226).[50]

Another approach to divine anthropomorphism is suggested by anthropologist Stewart Guthrie. He argues that anthropomorphism is a perceptual strategy (1993, 38, 39–61, 91–121). We "typically find more agents than are really there . . . our default conception of these agents is as persons and centrally as humanlike minds, of which gods are one form" (2015, 288) Seeing the world as humanlike is a "good bet" (1993, 4). Our world is ambiguous and requires interpretation. Since our most significant possibilities are humanlike, viewing the world anthropomorphically can yield more in occasional big successes than it costs in frequent little failures (1993, 5; cf. 6, 189). In fact, Guthrie calls this a "Pascal's wager" strategy (1993, 4, 6, 45; 2015, 284). In essence, Guthrie is suggesting that anthropomorphism functions to protect humans from the possible dangers lurking in the surrounding world. In this sense, his approach is compatible with that of Hume and Freud when they suggest that by humanizing external forces we are able to negotiate with those forces as we might attempt to do with a powerful parent or monarch. Whether the passionate deities of the Hebrew Bible and ancient Greek writings can be "negotiated with" in this fashion is one of the issues I will address throughout this study.

Notes

1 See Lazarus 1999. For a more recent review with an emphasis on appraisal theory, see Giner-Sorolla 2019.
2 According to Schroer and Staubli (2007, 44), we are "physiologically comparable with our ancestors." Moreover, "the ten emotions which are today regarded as classic . . . are also described in ancient Near Eastern texts," including the Old Testament. What has changed is the "manner in which the feelings and affects are brought to expression, and how they are perceived and interpreted."
3 For example, Verduyn *et al.* conclude that the relation between the appraisal of an emotion-eliciting event and the duration of that emotion is "largely universal." However, they did find some evidence for variability in magnitude of response across the countries studied (2013, 481, 483, 492).
4 For example, in Euripides' *Andromache*, the Spartan Hermione tells "Asian" Andromache, the widow of the Trojan hero Hector, that "we do not live in our city by barbarian customs" (*Andr.* 243). Andromache replies, "what is a shameful thing there involves shame here" (244). In other words, the emotion of shame is the same in the

14 *Introduction*

two cultures. In the biblical context, the "hearts" of both Israelites and their Canaanite enemies "melt" (מסס) when they are greatly afraid (Deut 1:28; Josh 2:11; 5:1; 7:5; 14:8; cf. Isa 13:7; Nah 2:11). According to Kruger (2001, 78), this metaphor represents a "physiological effect" of the "basic emotion" of fear. In Chapter 3.2.b, below, we will encounter Otanes' belief that envy (φθόνος) is a universal emotion: "from the beginning envy is implanted in humanity" (Herodotus, *Hist*. 3.80).

5 For a definitive critique of Solomon's position from a philosophical standpoint, see Bergmann 1978, 201–208.
6 As noted by Colombetti, this coping function involves both emotion and cognition: "both cognition and emotion turn out to be instances of the relentless sense-making activity of the precarious living organism as it maintains itself via continuous processes of self-regulation and exchange with the environment" (2014, xvii).
7 Lasine 2019, 3–75, 114–32. Biblical and Greek conceptions of the human condition are compared on pp. 10–15 of that work.
8 Cf. Izre'el (2001, 135), who asks "are we indeed so different from these allegedly remote cultures [of ancient Mesopotamia]?" Izre'el's answer is that we are not at all remote from the ancients in most ways, including "in our understanding of human nature."
9 For Padel, another "core difference" between "us" and 5th c. Athenians is our tolerance for "extraordinary dissociations between what we think is inside us and what we imply is inside us when we speak of our feelings" (1992, 35). Padel (1992, 34) also suggests that there is likely a "profound chasm" between "our" approach to metaphor and that of pre-Aristotelian Greeks.
10 Williams assures his readers that he does not "want to deny the otherness of the Greek world" (1993, 2; cf. 4).
11 Redfield means this in the sense that "our lives could also be described as consisting of transparently socially conditioned speech and action" (1975, 22).
12 Other scholars contend that the Bible presents a radically new mode of consciousness (Alter 1981, 115; Geller 1996, 179; cf. Lasine 2012, 40–43).
13 See Chapter 5.1, below, for more on this scene.
14 For example, Cohen-Charash and Larson: "Cain murdered Abel out of envy, . . . Envy is . . . rebuked in the tenth commandment" (2017, 5; cf. Schimmel 2008, 20–21). Hamilton concludes that Cain exhibits both "unchecked envy and jealousy" (1990, 230). The situation in which Cain is placed by Yahweh almost seems designed to elicit the emotions of envy and vengefulness. Nevertheless, the role of envy here is not as clear-cut as it is when Joseph's brothers plan to kill or sell their father's favorite son. The narrator of Gen 37:11 tells us that the brothers envied Joseph; this predisposes readers to take their attempts to kill or sell Joseph as driven by envy, even though the brothers have other reasons to hate Joseph (see Gen 37:2, 5–10, 23). In contrast, readers who believe that Cain has been treated unfairly by Yahweh might conclude that envy is not the root cause of his killing his brother. If one views Cain as having a legitimate grievance against his divine father, one may view his anger and his "fallen" face as signs of moral outrage and dejection. From this perspective his murder of Abel could involve a displacement of his anger against Yahweh. Even Hamilton must concede that Cain is "understandably upset" after God's rejection of his offering. He believes that Cain is depressed and crestfallen in Gen 4:5–6, rather than angry (1990, 224). Also see Chapter 2, nn. 33–35, below.
15 On envy in the Solomon's judgment story, see Lasine 1989, 65, 70–72 and n. 18 in Chapter 5, below.
16 It would be shocking if Hector did not interpret Andromache's tears as fear for him and what would happen if he perished in battle. She has just told Hector that Achilles killed her father and brothers, so that Hector is now father, mother, and brother to her as well as her husband and sole protector (*Il*. 6.414–34). Hector responds by telling Andromache that Troy will fall, he will die, and she will be dragged away to become a slave (6.447–65).

17 See Lasine 1989, 65–66, 69–72.
18 Cf. Cairns 2008, 56–58; Sanders 2014, 5; Kutter 2018, 19–20.
19 See, for example, Cairns 2019b, 5; Kaster 2003, 256; Parrott 1991, 5.
20 Parrott (1991, 5) uses the term "episode" rather than script to describe individuals who are experiencing an emotion.
21 Kutter's definition of a script remains on a very general level: "Scripts are simply descriptions of situations that are commonly associated with a particular term," with the descriptions consisting "of general appraisals of situations" (2018, 20).
22 "Love" (אהב) other humans: Lev 19:18, 34; do not "hate" (שׂנא): Lev 19:17; do not "fear" (ירא): Num 14:9; Deut 1:21, 29; 3:2, 31:8. For a recent treatment of these emotions in the Hebrew Bible, see Mirguet 2016, 447–51.
23 For example, Joab accuses David of loving those who hate him and hating those who love him (2 Sam 19:7).
24 Tomkins, one of the founders of "affect theory," recalls that he developed "script theory" after having explored human motivation "by studying play writing and by writing plays." He claims that this approach followed from his "interest in the human drama and in human feelings" (1981, 306).
25 As noted by Leavitt, "in daily life we regularly entertain, and regularly impute to others, experiences that centrally and indissociably involve both meaning and feeling" (1996, 517).
26 Lasine 2012, 3–19, 214–52.
27 On "round" characters, see Chapter 2.1, below.
28 Elias's "*homo clausus*" is a "little world for himself," to whom every other person is likewise a *homo clausus* (1997, 52; cf. 1970, 128). Here the individual "I" is experienced as being shut off from everything outside like a hidden kernel in a shell. Elias posits transformation of the emotions, as well as the "armor of self-constraints" (2002, 408; cf. 409, 427–28), as the causes of this experience.
29 For examples, see Lasine 2012, 11–12, 56–89, 115–19; 2019, 80.
30 Biblical scholars have not yet produced the large number of sophisticated and disciplined studies of emotion which have been contributed by classicists, although the role of emotions in the Bible has received more attention in recent years (see Kruger 2015, 15–16). The current trend in biblical studies is to apply "affect theory" to biblical texts. According to Shaviro (2016, 2), "if emotions are personal experiences, then affects are the forces (perhaps the flows of energy) that precede, produce, and inform such experiences. Affect is pre-personal and presubjective," and "not necessarily conscious." Biblicists who apply affect theory to the Bible believe that it "enables biblical exegetes to consider the role of the reader's embodied experience as a tool for textual interpretation" (Cottrill 2014, 431). In his critique of the ways in which affect theory has been applied to the Bible and its readers, Moore claims that "contemporary theory . . . including affect theory—is postmethodological through and through"; in at least one case, affect theory is "post-poststructuralist" as well (2019, 187, 194). According to Moore (2019, 203–204, 207), "the biblical scholars whom Mirguet and Kurek-Chomycz [2016, 435] mainly have in mind when they write that 'emotions are in full bloom in biblical scholarship' have been seduced by the affective turn." Some of these scholars are "pastists," for whom "anachronism is a source of anxiety." Others are "presentists"; they evaluate "the past according to the values, standards, ambitions, and anxieties of a later 'present'." The affect that pervades their work is "the *joy* of anachronism."
31 Specifically, "these emotions must appear under the right circumstances, be expressed in ways that are productive in the current situation, be regulated so that their intensity and manifestations are appropriate, and be restrained under circumstances in which they are not helpful" (Parrott 2002, 341–42).
32 Like Parrott, Henniger and Harris concede that the outcomes of actions motivated by negative emotions are not always beneficial. For example, envy may "motivate people to harm individuals who have already obtained the target object" (2014, 89). From the

perspective of the person being envied, this outcome is not at all "beneficial"; for them, the envier's emotion remains totally negative. Henniger and Harris also admit that negative emotions may have some of their "most counterproductive effects . . . when people are overly concerned with perceived threats that likely do not exist in reality" (2014, 93).

33 The most extreme and nihilistic form of this feeling is expressed by Nietzsche's "*Welt-Vernichter*": "This person fails at something. Finally he shouts out in disgust: 'So may the whole world go under!' This repulsive feeling is the pinnacle of envy, which concludes that because I cannot have *something*, all the world should have *nothing*!" (1999b, 224).

34 See Smith 1991, 82; cf. 93; Most 2003, 127; Parrott 1991, 4, 23; Joseph *et al.* 2008, 245.

35 It is commonly asserted that jealousy is triangular, while envy only involves two people. However, the envier may desire the person whom the envied rival seems to possess, or at least want the rival not to possess this person. This may not be the only example of a triangular situation involving envy, as we shall see.

36 While many studies of vengeance use the terms "revenge" and "vengeance" synonymously (e.g., Elshout *et al.* 2015, 502 n. 1), other authors distinguish between the two. According to Uniacke (2000, 63), "revenge, as payback for an injury *qua* injury, and vengeance, as retaliation against an offense, are distinguishable and can be differentiated in terms of their accompanying emotions. The emotion that gives rise to the desire for revenge is resentment . . . the emotion appropriate to vengeance is moral indignation."

37 The same has been said of jealousy: "jealousy is often a kind of struggle against potential loss and contains a retributive desire for revenge on the betraying partner" (Ben-Ze'ev 2000, 301).

38 I leave aside here Nietzsche's notorious polemical application of this dynamic to Judaism and Christianity.

39 Nietzsche's "world annihilator" displays an extreme form of such *ressentiment*; see n. 33, above.

40 Scheler's list includes both *Neid* and *Scheelsucht*. Both denote envy, but Scheler (1955, 40) emphasizes that aspect of the obsolescent term *Scheelsucht* which refers to seeking to disparage the object of envy.

41 Lesher reminds us that "Xenophanes nowhere rejects anthropomorphic conceptions of the gods of any and all sorts." In fact, "what Xenophanes asserts in these remarks [Frs. 15 and 16] is not the complete *incomparability* of gods and men, but rather their complete *dissimilarity*" (1992, 94).

42 Even though many monarchs and other leaders show evidence of being narcissistic and envious (see Lasine 2001, 25–26, 191–97, 240–53; 2004, 132 n. 37), Hume's focus is not on the function of those traits, except insofar as those characteristics make it easier to influence the god's behavior by flattering the deity as one would a human king. In the *Dialogues Concerning Natural Religion*, the speaker Philo goes one step further, claiming that among the "human passions" attributed to the Deity is "one of the lowest . . . a restless appetite for applause" (1947, 226). This divine desire to be applauded brings to mind Yahweh's concern for his reputation and fame (on which see Glatt-Gilad 2002 and Chapter 3.3.b, below).

43 On this issue, see Chapter 8.3, below.

44 Freud was aware of this dynamic from an early date; in an undated handwritten note, he jotted down that "human beings cannot tolerate parentlessness and so they create for themselves a new parental couple from God and nature: [the] basis, [the] ultimate basis of religion [is] the infantile helplessness of human beings" (Grubrich-Simitis 1993, 149).

45 That God is "nothing other than" such a father is a point on which Freud insisted, from his early work on Leonardo to *Civilization and Its Discontents* and his final book on Moses and monotheistic religion (1943a, 195; 1948b, 431; 1950, 229).
46 See, for example, Barrett and Keil 1996, 221, Birky and Ball 1988, 136, Justice and Lambert 1986, 170–72. It is important to note that most of the research I cite in this section focuses solely on the attitudes of American college students.
47 Interestingly, for the male students, nurturing mothers were more responsible than fathers for viewing God as nurturing. Dickie and her team argue that "the initial attachment figure, most often the mother, exerts a powerful influence on developing God images, not only in the climate she creates but also directly in the qualities of power and punishing/judging that she exhibits, especially for sons." Nevertheless, "while mother is clearly the more important figure in creating young women's and especially young men's God concepts, . . . more of these young adults reported God being 'more like a male' and feeling closer to this male God" (2006, 68).
48 On attachment issues related to Yahweh, see Chapter 3.3b, below.
49 God is assumed to be male in these studies.
50 Waytz *et al.* also suggest that "religious systems that propose an omnipresent and judgmental God appear better able to enhance cooperation between group members, possibly because of the capacity for these gods to watch people's behavior at all times and serve as a constant source of social surveillance" (2010, 226). Waytz could have cited Qoh 10:20 to illustrate his point: "even in your conscious thoughts do not curse the king, and do not curse a rich man even in your bed chamber, for the birds of the sky will carry the voice, and a winged creature will report the matter." If an aura of omniscience is predicated of human kings, this is even more true of divine kings such as Yahweh. The same is true of Zeus, whose eye sees all things (Hesiod, *WD* 267). For the policies which Aristotle and others recommend that leaders put into place in order to gain panoptic knowledge, see Lasine 2001, 100–101. While Waytz views panoptic surveillance as a way of enhancing cooperation within a group, Hume argues that the terror caused by an all-seeing God forces believers to "be careful not to form expressly any sentiment of blame and disapprobation. All must be applause, ravishment, extacy" (2007, 78).

2 Divine envy, jealousy, and vengeance in ancient Israel and Greece

In this chapter I turn from theoretical views of negative emotions to specific portrayals of divine envy, jealousy, indignation, and vengefulness in biblical and Greek texts. I begin by asking whether the biblical God and Greek deities are depicted as coherent personalities in the texts we will examine. Next I outline the spectrum of opinion on whether there is significant similarity between divine envy in the Hebrew Bible and divine envy in ancient Greek texts. I then discuss the relationship between divine vengeance and envy in both contexts. The chapter concludes by analyzing specific examples of divine vengeance and jealousy in the two bodies of literature.

As we proceed, we should keep in mind that the ancient Greek texts we will be studying are not "holy scripture" or "sacred writings" in the same sense that the Hebrew Bible presents itself to readers and has later been regarded by believing communities (see, e.g., Muir 1985, 194; Easterling 1985, 35). Nevertheless, we cannot deny that Greek writings from Homer to the tragedians did have great religious significance in ancient Greek society. Herodotus famously declares that Homer and Hesiod gave the Greeks the gods' genealogy, titles, honors, competencies, and forms (*Hist.* 2.53). As Finley puts it, "it was only the cultural authority of the poets that preserved a measure of unity and coherence among the religious ideas and practices of Greek communities" in Herodotus' day (1985, xv). As for the Greek dramas we will be discussing, Sourvinou-Inwood argues that 5th-c. Greek audiences perceived tragedy "as a ritual performance" and that "the deities and other religious elements in the tragedies were perceived to be close to the "audience's religious realities" (2003, 1).

1. Are Yahweh and the Greek gods "persons" with coherent personalities?

Both classical and biblical scholars have claimed that the anthropomorphic deities they study are distinctive or special, although some of what each considers unique is actually shared by the other. Does their specialness include their being depicted as "persons," individuals with coherent and complex personalities?

Burkert contrasts the Greek pantheon to the "Near Eastern-Aegean *koine*." The "special character" of Greek anthropomorphism, and the Homeric gods in

DOI: 10.4324/b23212-2

particular, is that the "Greek gods are persons." In fact, this is their "defining characteristic" (1987, 182). The poets depict the deities as "human almost to the last detail" (1987, 183). This includes negative traits. Each god "has his dark and dangerous side." As examples Burkert cites Hera, Athena, Apollo, and Aphrodite (1987, 188), all of whom we will discuss later. One "can never be entirely sure of his gods," due to their "jealously [sic]" (1987, 189). Collectively, what "distinguish[es] the Greek/Homeric family of the gods is its compactness and clarity of organization." They "make up a highly differentiated and richly contrasted group" (1987, 218).

According to Fishbane, the Bible "resorts to myth" when it portrays the divine personality, as do "accounts of the lives of the gods in Mesopotamia or Greece." However, "the monotheistic myth of ancient Israel" has a "distinctive feature": its God "is a unity of traits found separately among the 'other gods,' and (in its view) of a higher order of magnitude" (1998, 93). The "vital aspects of the divine Person in relationship to Israel and the world" include "promise and purpose, requital and memory, wrath and mercy." Biblical anthropomorphism is characterized by "bold psychological and personal realism" (1998, 94). While Burkert acknowledges the Greek deities' dark and dangerous side, Fishbane does not mention either Yahweh's "dark side"[1] or his jealousy. However, it is unclear whether he would go as far as Muffs, who claims that the biblical God is "a paragon of human virtue, a kind of *Übermensch*," in comparison with one kind of "pagan" anthropomorphism (2005, 30).[2]

While Fishbane finds the distinctive feature of Yahweh's personality to be its "unity of traits," other scholars disagree. Noll claims that there are a "variety of Yahwehs within the Hebrew literature"; the divine personality has a "kaleidoscopic nature" (2001, 10). Miles begins with the historical assumption that Yahweh's character is the "fusion" of several "ancient Semitic divinities" that "nomadic" Israel "met in its wanderings" (1996, 13, 20, 72, 327, 401). Because this fusion "is inherently unstable" (1996, 197), God's character "is trapped within its contradictions," and clarity for readers disappears "beneath the welter of personalities and functions that are gathered together in him" (1996, 401, 408).

Similarly, Burkert's view of the Homeric gods as persons is not accepted by all classicists. According to Vernant, "the Greek gods are powers, not persons." They are "not individuals each with a particular single characteristic form and spiritual life" (1996, 108; cf. Pironti 2010, 113, 119). Vernant concedes that "Homer presents us with a Zeus who, as a figure, possesses a relative unity." However, in the "living religion of the Greeks" Zeus is "not in one single form but rather as many different Zeuses." At the same time, the pantheon as a whole is "an organized system implying definite relations between the various gods" (1996, 104). Within this framework, "each of these powers becomes distinct not in itself as an isolated object but by virtue of its relative position in the aggregate of forces" (1991, 273).[3]

Scholars such as Bremmer argue that we do not need to choose between the views expressed by Burkert and Vernant: "'power' and 'person' are two sides of the Greek gods which could both come to the fore at different times and in different contexts." The Greek poets tend to stress the personal side, while later on philosophers began to "promote the 'power' aspect of the divinities" (1999, 23).

Classicists have also noted other aspects of the personality-power distinction in Homer's works. Lattimore (1961, 54) observes that "the gods-as-persons of Homer" may also "represent projections of feelings or activities in the observed world." His example is Ares, who is both "a brutal and blustering character" and war, a force which "has no character at all." Gould points out that when a deity such as Apollo angrily avenges his favorites, such as the priest Chryses,[4] we are given "hints of a darker, altogether more uncanny aspect of divinity" (J. Gould 1985, 26–27). This invites comparison with Yahweh, whose dark side is increasingly noted by biblical scholars, as are his uncanny, and even demonic, actions.[5]

Redfield (1975, 75–76) distinguishes between the gods to whom Homer's audience prayed and offered sacrifice and the "literary gods" of epic. Most of the time "the gods of the epic are personalities, not impersonal potencies."[6] Kearns puts the difference this way: "perhaps the most general and far-reaching distinction between the Gods as they appear in the *Iliad* and the Gods as they were actually worshipped is the Iliadic conception of the Gods as precisely defined [humanlike] individuals." Where cult was concerned, however, "it was demonstrably normal to speak of 'a God' meaning the God of a particular sanctuary," so that we would have the Apollo of this place and of that place, each with different qualities and traditions and yet still Apollo" (2004, 61–62).

Even within the body of Greek poetry a specific deity may be presented in different ways. In that sense there are a number of "Heras" and "Athenas" in Greek literature. In Chapter 5.1 we will find that the portrayal of Hera in the *Iliad* is nuanced and multi-faceted. Yet the Hera of Euripides' *Heracles* is the incarnation of jealous vindictiveness (see Chapter 8.1, below). Similarly, the sometimes playful Athena of Homer's *Odyssey* is a far cry from the cruel and vindictive goddess of Sophocles' *Ajax*.[7]

In contrast, while different aspects of Yahweh's character are featured in different biblical narratives and poems, the Bible as a whole depicts Yahweh as a coherent individual who has a complex personality. Not all scholars agree with this conclusion. Noll contends that "most readers have been trained to read into the text a series of theological assumptions designed to harmonize the inconsistencies in divine portraiture" (2001, 17, 22). However, people do not have to be trained to smooth out seeming inconsistencies when they appraise someone's character; we do this as a matter of course. And, as I mentioned earlier, readers evaluate literary characters in many of the same ways that they judge people in daily life (see Lasine 2012, 3–19, 94–97, 218–28). People need to perceive others as possessing coherent and predictable character traits in order to negotiate their social world with economy and safety. In other words, "intolerance of ambiguity . . . serves a coping function" (Furnham 1995, 402). Many empirical studies indicate that readers do "attempt to maintain coherence at both a local and a global level" and experience difficulty when they read information which is inconsistent with a protagonist's already established characteristics (Albrecht and O'Brien 1993, 1066). In fact, when people are first exposed to others they "promptly appraise their character if provided even a modicum of morally relevant information about them" (Lupfer *et al.* 2000, 1363).

As a result, people (especially in modern Western cultures) often commit what has been called the "fundamental attribution error" (Gilbert and Malone 1995). This "error" involves explaining behavior in terms of a person's disposition and personality traits, even when evidence points to the situation being the cause of the behavior. This is true whether one is evaluating another individual in daily life or a literary character. This does not mean that an individual lacks a cohesive character when we perceive that person behaving in a way which seems to contradict the character we have attributed to them. Ordinary people *do* act "out of character" at times. Far from implying that they have no stable character, it means that we need to expand and nuance our understanding of that person. The same is true for literary characters; as E. M. Forster put it almost a century ago, "round" characters are those who are "capable of surprising in a convincing way" (1927, 118).

We must also keep in mind that the same person or literary character may be evaluated in very different ways by different perceivers or readers. A scene early in the 1947 film *A Double Life* offers an extreme example. Actor Anthony John bumps into two young female acquaintances on a street in Manhattan. They briefly chat, and after he leaves one woman says "What a darling!" at the same time as the other one says "Stinker!" They then look at one another in surprise and both say "What?!" As the movie proceeds it becomes clear that both are correct. When John is playing in a comedy, he is a "darling," but when acting in a drama, he is a "stinker." In this case, a person's situation dictates how that person behaves, and is perceived by others, at any given time. More commonly, differences in the ways individuals judge others are attributable to the perceivers' assumptions, expectations, values, and biases.

In scripture, Yahweh acts in a number of different ways and displays different traits in different situations. As Clines puts it, "Yahweh is a multi-faceted personality, complex and not entirely predictable" (1998, 503). In order to gauge the coherence of Yahweh's personality, one must take into account his behavior as Israel's father, spouse, and sovereign. In the biblical context, in each of these relationships the humans' role is to be totally obedient to the power and control of the divine partner. If that condition is met, the child/wife/subject can expect to receive care and protection from the dominant father, husband, or king. If not, the outcome will be the opposite.[8] We must also take into account Yahweh's assumptions about how a divine father, spouse, and king should be treated.[9] In addition, we must consider the ways in which Yahweh perceives himself, such as his self-characterization in Exod 34:6–7, which is followed by his announcement that his name is "Jealous" (34:14).

Also crucial are the various views of God's character given by different speakers within scripture. On rare occasions the narrator describes Yahweh's actions as an illustration of his compassionate, loyal, or gracious character (Gen 19:16; 39:21; 2 Kgs 13:23; cf. 2 Chr 7:6). More commonly prophets describe Yahweh's traits in their own voices; they may also quote Yahweh's self-descriptions. Finally, we must consider situations in which an important character gives a positive or negative opinion about Yahweh's attributes. For example, Abraham's assessment of God as judge of all the earth (Genesis 18) is vastly different from Job's opinion of God's justice in Job 3–31. A close examination of these perspectives on Yahweh's personality[10] suggests that the various portrayals of the biblical God constitute a coherent representation of a "round" character.

2. Biblical and Greek understandings of divine jealousy and envy

Many readers of ancient Hebrew and Greek texts have wondered whether Israel's "jealous God" is in any way analogous to the Greek deities who display *phthonos* (φθόνος), a term that can denote envy, jealousy, ill-will, or a begrudging attitude. As I noted in my preface, some authors insist that "the jealousy of Yahweh has nothing to do with the envy of the gods in Greek religion" (Bell 1994, 17 n. 101). According to Burkert, in polytheism "there is no jealous God as in the Judeo-Christian faith" (1987, 216; cf. 246, 318). De Ste. Croix (1977, 140) contends that the Greek "notion of the jealousy of the gods, their resentment at any extraordinary prosperity on the part of a mortal, ... is something quite different from the 'jealousy of Yahweh,'" because Yahweh's jealousy "is directed entirely against the worship or acknowledgement of other gods." In contrast, Ellis (2017, 8) asserts that the emotion denoted by Hebrew *qin'ah* (קנאה) and its cognates corresponds closely to Greek *phthonos* in many contexts.

These contrasting conclusions are based on the writers' assumptions about the meaning of *phthonos* and *qin'ah* in specific texts. For Bell, divine *phthonos* signals that "the gods wished to keep the εὐδαιμονία [good fortune, happiness, prosperity] to themselves" and "were jealous if things went too well for humankind" (1994, 17 n. 101).[11] In contrast, Burkert (1987, 216) claims that the Greek gods were not jealous; they simply did not like being "overlooked," in the sense that Artemis' devotee Hippolytus overlooks Aphrodite in Euripides' play.[12] In Chapter 3.2.c, I will ask how Yahweh could be envious of inferior—and allegedly nonexistent—beings. Classicist E. R. Dodds asks a similar question about ancient Greek deities: how could the "overmastering Power" of the Greek gods "be jealous of so poor a thing as Man?" Dodds' answer is that "the gods resent any success, any happiness, which might for a moment lift our mortality above its mortal status, and so encroach on their prerogative" (1968, 29). Here the gods jealously retain sole possession of immortality, a theme familiar from Akkadian texts such as *The Gilgamesh Epic* and *Adapa*, if not also from Genesis 3.[13]

For some classicists, divine envy is a primitive concept typical of archaic Greek thought, which gradually faded away and was replaced by more "advanced" theologies (e.g., Ellis 2017, 51; Lloyd-Jones 1983, 69; Lloyd 2013, 205, 221–22). Others find evidence that the idea perdured long after philosophers had declared that the divine was devoid of envy (e.g., Dover 1994, 77–78; Whitehead 2009, 330–32). Most extreme is Lanzillotta's contention that φθόνος θεῶν (divine envy/jealousy) "is in fact not envy at all," not even in Herodotus (2010, 78–79, 91).[14] He argues that "resorting" to "'envy' as a possible motivation" implies that "they were placing the gods and human beings on the same existential level," and that the gods "desired and were attracted to the nothingness of [ephemeral] human happiness" (2010, 80–81, 91).[15]

Commentators also have varying theories about the social functions served by divine envy in ancient Greece. According to Ostwald (1986, 137), the gods were "regarded as the guarantors of the stability of the social order." Since their displeasure disturbed the social order, it was in the state's interest to enforce divine worship, in order "to ensure that the public interest would suffer no harm by neglecting the gods." Such neglect might prompt the envy which can cause damage to the public. Thus, the "function of *phthonos* is to preserve the proper hierarchy in a society" (Konstan 2006, 121). In contrast, Cairns (2003, 249) stresses that divine *phthonos* serves "the interests of the mass." This "top-down jealousy" is "analogous to the jealousy of kings or tyrants towards their own inferiors," enforcing on "those who threaten the gods with rivalry an essential equality with their fellow mortals." This strategy also "contributes towards the tendency on the part of the mass to justify their negative emotions towards the elite."[16]

Other scholars view *phthonos* as one of the benefits of believing in anthropopathic gods. J. Gould (1985, 32) points out that *phthonos* is "an eminently human feeling, and a god who displays it is reassuringly intelligible in human terms." This approach recalls Hume's account of the tendency to imagine a humanlike deity whose nature would explain all the disasters and capriciousness that permeate human life and Freud's argument that humans tame the terror of nature by humanizing it (see Chapter 1.4, above). J. Gould notes that Herodotus' Solon not only calls the gods envious but disorderly; this acknowledges "the paradoxical coexistence of incompatible truths about human experience" (1985, 32). For Dover (1994, 77), the fact that "a touchy and malevolent jealousy was a conspicuous characteristic of the gods' attitude towards humanity" was needed to explain "the scale of human misfortune and the absence of any observable correlation between virtue and prosperity." As Eidinow puts it, narratives involving *phthonos* force readers "to contemplate . . . the terrible unreliability of divine behaviour; they express man's [*sic*] unbearably uncertain relationship with his gods" (2016, 231).

The notion that *phthonos* only applies to gods in an early "primitive" period is similar to the view that Yahweh's jealousy is typical of a "primitive" or "wild" stage in the development of Yahwism (e.g., Brueggemann 2000, 28; cf. 1997, 281–82). The claim that *phthonos* never meant envy in ancient Greek texts recalls some interpretations of Yahweh's jealousy. For example, Maimonides (*Guide*, I. 54; 1919, 77) asserts that when God acts in ways similar to human actions which originate in dispositions such as jealousy or anger, they are not the result of any divine emotion, "for he is above all defect."[17] That is, his jealousy isn't *really* jealousy.[18]

Finally, a person who evokes the Greek gods' envy is in just as much danger as those who provoke Yahweh's jealousy in biblical Israel. However, in Greece no god demands exclusive devotion from his or her devotees. For example, in Euripides' *Hippolytus*, Aphrodite feels no *phthonos* towards Hippolytus for his intense devotion to Artemis (*Hipp.* 20), but she punishes him severely for disdaining her cult. Greek gods do not demand exclusive devotion, but they do demand their fair share of acknowledgement and respect.

24   Ancient Israel and Greece

On the other hand, De Ste. Croix points to a difference between the two cultures when he observes that Yahweh's jealousy is fundamentally different from the Greek gods' envy because it is focused entirely on other gods (1977, 140). The difference is actually greater than he implies. De Ste. Croix does not acknowledge the power of divine jealousy and envy experienced by Yahweh as Israel's husband and father, as well as its meaning when it is viewed as part of Yahweh's emotional make-up as a whole.[19] In Greek religion there is no analogue to the metaphor of a possessive divine husband who becomes jealous and enraged when his followers (i.e., his "spouse") show interest in other deities.[20]

After we have engaged in close readings of a variety of biblical and Greek texts, we will be in a position to assess the various scholarly views outlined in this section and suggest other ways of comparing Hebrew and Greek perspectives on divine jealousy and envy.[21]

3. Divine vengeance and its relation to envy and jealousy in biblical and Greek texts

a. Divine vengeance and wrath in biblical texts

The connection between divine envy and vengeance is made clear in a number of biblical passages. Even people who have never read the Bible are familiar with the declaration "Vengeance is mine" (לי נקם; Deut 32:35).[22] In Ps 94:1 Yahweh is twice referred to as "God of vengeances" (אל-נקמות).[23] While the connection between Yahweh's vengeance (*naqam*) and his jealousy (*qin'ah*) is implicit in many passages, Peels (1995, 121) notes that the "word-pair נקם and קנאה" occurs only in Isa 59:17 and Nah 1:2. In the passage from Isaiah, Yahweh sees that there is "no man" to intercede and stop injustice. He then intervenes himself, having clothed himself with "garments of vengeance [as] clothing, and wrapped himself [in] jealousy/zeal as a cloak."

Nahum 1:2 is even more emphatic about the relationship between Yahweh's jealousy, vengeance and wrath: "God the jealous one (אל קנוא) and Yahweh the avenging one, Yahweh the avenging one and master [or possessor] of rage; Yahweh avenging to his adversaries and keeping wrath for his enemies." Nahum begins by naming Yahweh "the jealous one" and alludes to his vengeance (נקם) three times in v. 2. Yahweh's anger is mentioned five times in vv. 2–6.[24] In the book of Nahum, Yahweh's wrath, jealousy, and vengeance are uniquely directed against the "bloody city" of Nineveh (Nah 3:1) and the entire Assyrian empire, not his own people.[25]

The relationship between Yahweh's jealous vengeance and his concern for his reputation can be illustrated by comparing Psalm 79 and Joel 2. The speakers in the psalm have experienced the fall of Jerusalem and the destruction of its temple by the Babylonians. They ask Yahweh if he will remain angry forever, with his jealousy burning like fire (Ps 79:5). In other words, they accept the idea that Yahweh's jealous anger is the reason Jerusalem was devastated. At the same time, they realize that other nations might ask "where is their God?," assuming that

Judah's God had abandoned them. The lamenting community implores Yahweh to let the nations witness his vengeance against those who have shed the blood of his servants (Ps 79:10). This will restore his international reputation and image.[26] In Joel 2, Yahweh's priests and ministers also want their God to end their disgrace by preventing the peoples from jeering at them by asking "Where is their God?" Then Yahweh will be jealous for his land and compassionate toward his people (Joel 2:17–18). While in Psalm 79 Yahweh's jealous anger led to Jerusalem's fall, in Joel 2 his jealousy is protective and proprietary.

In Deut 32:43 Moses declares that Yahweh will "avenge (יקום) the blood of his servants, and return vengeance (ונקם ישיב) to his adversaries." In Jeremiah 50–51 Yahweh's anger, vengeance, and desire for payback are focused on the fall of Babylon. These oracles offer several perspectives on Yahweh's role in Babylon's demise. In Jer 50:41 the prophet declares that a people is coming from the north to attack the city (cf. 50:3, 9; 51:48), and "a great nation and many kings will be roused (יערו) from the remote parts of the earth." Yahweh is not explicitly credited for "rousing" these kings. In Jer 51:11, however, we are told that Yahweh has roused (העיר) the spirit of the kings of the Medes against Babylon. This constitutes Yahweh's vengeance, including vengeance for his temple, as fugitives from Babylon will declare in Zion (51:11; 50:28). Finally, in 51:1 Yahweh is quoted as saying that he himself is going to rouse (מעיר) a destructive wind (or spirit) against Babylon.

This distinction between Yahweh directly exacting vengeance and doing so through intermediaries is maintained through Jeremiah 50 and 51. Examples of his direct involvement include his setting a trap for Babylon (50:24), opening his armory (50:25), and stretching out his hand against the city (51:24). Yahweh's wrath is credited with Babylon becoming uninhabited (50:13). The city's fall is due to the "plan of Yahweh" (50:45). Jeremiah quotes Yahweh saying he will "take vengeance for you (ונקמתי את-נקמתך)," in part by employing his powers as creator, drying up Babylon's sea and making her fountain dry (51:36). This is the time of Yahweh's vengeance; he will "repay to her a recompense" (גמול הוא משלם לה; 51:6). In short, "Yahweh is a God of recompenses (אל גמלות); he will fully repay" (51:56; cf. 51:24).[27]

In other passages Yahweh is said to gain vengeance and give payback solely through the actions of others. In Jer 50:14 he calls upon "all of you who bend the bow" to attack Babylon, because she "has sinned against Yahweh." Here Yahweh's vengeance takes the form of the archers taking vengeance on Babylon, in the form of payback: "as she has done, do to her" (50:15; cf. 50:29). Rather than devastating the land of Babylon himself, Yahweh will send strangers to do so (51:2).[28]

The Bible also includes statements warning people not to take revenge or seek vengeance on their own. Before imploring listeners to love their neighbor as themselves, Lev 19:18 commands that one not "take vengeance, nor bear any grudge against the sons of your people." Proverbs 20:22 advises that we should not say "'I will repay evil'; wait for Yahweh and he will save you."

In some cases Yahweh gains vengeance through the actions of a human individual such as Jehu (2 Kgs 9:7)[29] or the Israelites as a whole (e.g., Ezek 25:14:

"I will set my vengeance on Edom by the hand of my people Israel"). He may even be perceived as exacting vengeance on behalf of a human being. For example, Jephthah's daughter tells her father that his victory over the Ammonites is a case of Yahweh having "done vengeance *for you* from your enemies" (Judg 11:36; emphasis added),[30] even though Jephthah sees himself as warring on behalf of Yahweh and Israel.[31] In other instances, Yahweh's vengeance is directed against his own people. Thus, after listing in detail the sins of Judah, Jeremiah repeatedly quotes Yahweh asking "Shall I not avenge myself on a nation such as this?" (Jer 5:9, 29; 9:8). Other reports make it difficult to determine whether vengeance is being gained by Yahweh, the Israelites, or both. My examples in the reminder of this section will indicate the complexity of divine vengeance in these and other instances.[32]

The first mention of divine vengeance in the Bible is in the story of Cain (Gen 4:1–15). After slaying his brother Abel, Yahweh tells Cain that he is cursed from the ground and will become a fugitive and wanderer in the earth (4:12). Cain answers that as a wanderer he will be hidden from Yahweh's face and all who find him will kill him (v. 14). Yahweh responds by announcing that "whoever slays Cain, vengeance will be taken (יֻקַּם) sevenfold" (v. 15).[33] In other words, Yahweh will become the protector and avenger of a man who murdered his brother.

Byron (2011, 106) finds God's response to be "unnerving." He believes that readers "would have been struck by the contradictory way in which Cain received protection from God while justice was denied to the murdered Abel." Leaving aside what might constitute justice (or divine compassion) in this situation, Yahweh did deny Abel the kind of protection from a would-be murderer that Cain now receives. Moreover, Yahweh may have generated Cain's animosity toward his brother in the first place by gazing upon Abel's offering but not Cain's, for no stated reason. Cain is commonly said to be jealous of Abel,[34] or of envying his brother's experience of the "friendly face of God" (von Rad 1981, 76). However, it is also possible that Cain experiences justifiable resentment at having been treated unfairly.[35]

When Yahweh sets his vengeance on Edom "by the hand of my people Israel," the Israelites will "do in Edom according to my anger and according to my fury," so that the Edomites will "know my vengeance" (Ezek 25:14). The reason for Yahweh's vengeance is that the Edomites have acted in revenge with vengeful vengeance[36] against the house of Judah, having scornful contempt in their souls (Ezek 25:12). In so doing, Edom incurred grievous guilt, triggering Yahweh's wrathful vengeance,[37] which will wipe out both human and animal life in the country (25:13). Ironically, Yahweh uses "my people Israel" as the instrument of his vengeance here shortly after having declared that he has been roused to take wrathful vengeance against his own people, specifically, the inhabitants of besieged Jerusalem and their sinful leaders (Ezek 24:8).[38]

Earlier I quoted the conclusion to the "Song of Moses," in which Yahweh states that he "returns vengeance to his adversaries" (Deut 32:43; cf. 32:41). As is the case in Ezek 25:14, Yahweh seeks vengeance on his—and Israel's—enemies shortly after his wrath has been aroused against Israel for its infidelity to him. The adversaries against whom Yahweh will now return vengeance had been used by Yahweh to punish Israel. That punishment is prompted by the Israelites making their God jealous with their "alien ones" (יקנאהו בזרים; Deut 32:16). Their preoccupation with "no-gods" leads Yahweh to make the Israelites jealous by afflicting his people with a "no-people," a "foolish nation" (Deut 32:16, 21).

Joshua 10 reports an event in which Yahweh, the Israelites, and their leader Joshua all participate "synergistically"[39] in achieving military vengeance over an Amorite coalition. In Josh 10:13 the narrator states that the sun and moon stood still "until the nation took vengeance (עד־יקם גוי) on its enemies."[40] By itself, this seems to highlight the role of the Israelite "nation" in the victory. However, the chapter as a whole stresses Yahweh's role in gaining this vengeance. In v. 8 Yahweh tells Joshua not to fear, for Yahweh has delivered the enemy into Joshua's hand. In v. 10 the narrator informs us that Yahweh inflicted a huge slaughter on the enemy at Gibeon. In the following verse, we are told that Yahweh threw down great stones on the fleeing enemy, killing more of them than the Israelites did with their swords. Yahweh's next action is in response to Joshua speaking to him before the eyes of all Israel. He[41] commands the sun and moon to stop their movement (v. 12). Yahweh performs this miracle, and the narrator concludes that this is a totally unique event, because Yahweh "listened to the voice of a man, because Yahweh fought for Israel" (v. 14). Thus, while the nation is said to have exacted vengeance, the key role in the battle is played by Yahweh, with assistance from both Joshua and his army.

Isaiah 59 provides an intriguing example of Yahweh expecting a human to act on his behalf in order to counter injustice and discovering that no one is enforcing justice: "he who departs from evil makes himself a prey. Yahweh saw it, and it was evil in his eyes that there was no justice. And he saw there was no man and was astounded (וישתומם) that there was no one interceding; then his own arm brought salvation to him, and his righteousness, it supported him" (Isa 59:15–16). Commentators have made a variety of suggestions concerning the kind of "man" whom Yahweh had expected to intercede. Whybray (1981, 226) understands Yahweh to be saying that there is no leader "willing and able to put things right," as Nehemiah will do later on.[42] Paul (2012, 508) believes that there is no man on whom Yahweh can rely; since the nation exists in a moral vacuum, there is no one to turn to for intercession. Blenkinsopp (2003, 197) argues that since Isa 59:15b-17 begins in the past tense, "the turning point has already come about" but "not through the agency of great figures on the international scene such as Cyrus." Finally, Niskanen (2014, 30) contends that Isa 59:15–16 implies that "there is not only no justice, nor a single person who acts justly, but not even someone to urge or encourage just action in another."[43] But if no one acts justly, how could there still be some who "depart from evil" (Isa 59:15), a quality also exhibited by God's favorite, Job (Job 1:1, 8; 2:3)?

In considering the kind of "man" Yahweh might have in mind in Isa 59:16 it is helpful to compare the striking passage in which a watchman asks for the identity of someone coming from Edom, whose garments are stained red as though he had been crushing wine grapes (Isa 63:1–2). Yahweh the divine warrior answers that he has trodden the wine trough alone, and "from the peoples there was no man with me." He trampled them in his wrath, and thereby defiled his garments with their "juice," that is, their blood (Isa 63:3). Yahweh goes on to explain that "the day of vengeance[44] was in my heart, and my year of redemption had come" (63:4). He reports that he "looked, and there was no one to help, and I was astonished (ואשתומם), and there was no one to give support, and my arm brought salvation to me and my own rage supported me" (63:5).[45] In this passage, when Yahweh remarks that there was no one with him he clearly means a helper or supporter.

The fact that Yahweh clothes himself in vengeance and jealousy in Isaiah 59 because there was "no man" implies that it is permissible for a human to enact justice, at least in some cases. The phrase "he saw that there was no man" in Isa 59:16 has reminded some readers of Moses in Exod 2:11–14.[46] When Moses "saw that there was no man" to intervene and save the beaten Hebrew, he did so himself. This intertextual allusion has raised the question whether the word "man" (איש) in these two passages refers to a "true man" who is ready to take action. One midrashic text has Moses looking for a man who would be jealous for Yahweh's name: "R. Yehudah said: he saw there was no one who would stand up and be jealous (יעמד ויקנא) for the name of the Holy One, . . . and kill him" (*Lev. Rab.* 32:4). According to Zivotofsky (1994, 261), the idea that Exod 2:12 and Isa 59:16 both refer to "a true man" is perhaps what inspired Hillel to advise "in a place where there are no men (אנשים), strive to be a man (איש)" (*Pirqe'Abot* 2.5; cf. Jacob 1942, 257).

As I mentioned earlier, when Yahweh goes on to exact vengeance, he dresses in battle garb, including "garments of vengeance." He even "wraps himself in jealousy as a robe" (Isa 59:17). The prophet then tells us that "according to deeds (גמלות), so will he repay, wrath to his adversaries, retribution (גמול) to his enemies," and "to the coastlands he will repay retribution (גמול)" (59:18). Peels (1995, 122–23) suggests that while vv. 17–19 initially cause one to think that Yahweh is targeting enemy nations, the main accent actually "falls upon the 'internal' vengeance of God," that is, vengeance against the "unconverted Israelites" who have become Yahweh's heathen-like enemies. His actions are driven by furious jealousy and a desire for vengeance. According to Niskanen (2014, 31), the threefold repetition of גמל (retribution, recompense) in v. 18 underscores the fact that this vengeance is a kind of "payback." In Chapter 4.3 we will witness repeated attempts at vengeful payback by the all-too-human Samson, whose revenge takes the form of "paying back with interest."

b. Indignation, vengeance, and divine jealousy in ancient Greek texts

(1) Nemesis, envy, and vengeance

In ancient Greek texts, jealousy and envy are also linked with indignation, vengeance, revenge, and retribution. Indignation (νέμεσις) is a key term associated with *phthonos* in Greek literature. According to Konstan (2006, 116), in Homer *nemesis* "is generally aroused at behavior that runs contrary to socially accepted norms." Ellis (2015, 93) concludes that the term "correspond[s] closely to English 'indignation,' expressing outrage at behaviour which a bystander would view as unacceptable." Sanders (2014, 51–52) believes that *nemesis* and the verb *nemesan* have several "scripts" in Homer. The first is "a hostile reaction to something that can be as strong as anger or merely a milder resentment." The second major script is "censure or blame (a meaning that *phthonos* can take in the classical period)." Sanders (2014, 52) notes two instances of censure in the *Odyssey* which relate most strongly to *phthonos*. In one case, Homer explicitly "couples *nemesis* with *phthonos*."[47] This is Penelope's "'begrudging refusal' at the bard singing the songs he wishes (*Od*. 1.346/350)." In these lines, Telemachus tells his mother Penelope not to begrudge (φθονέεις) Phemius singing of the Danaans' evil fate, adding that this is not a cause for indignation (νέμεσις).

Ellis (2015, 93) cautions that "given the paucity of attestations between early epic and fifth-century lyric there can be little certainty about the development of the term *nemesis*." Nevertheless, he concludes that "it seems likely that the emotional term *nemesis*, in the course of its abstraction to a divine or cosmic force, became associated with the limits of human fortune generally." In fact, "the idea of *nemesis* as the bringer of the misfortune inevitably associated with the mortal condition (rather than as punisher of crime, injustice, or arrogance) may also be present in Hesiod's description of Nemesis in the *Theogony* as simply 'a pain for mortal men' [*Theog*. 223]." Thus, from the human standpoint "the gods' insistence that humanity remain in an inferior position . . . looks less like 'righteous indignation' and more like the sign of a 'grudging' disposition" (2015, 94).

Ellis cites Pindaric epinician poetry to demonstrate "that *nemesis* (as a personification or process) can also refer to a different explanation of human suffering, unconcerned with 'guilt' and 'responsibility' and associated with (rather than opposed to) divine *phthonos*" (2015, 95). He points to Pindar's earliest ode, *Pythian* 10, to illustrate that "by the fifth century *nemesis*, like divine *phthonos*, was used to refer to the limitations of the mortal condition" (2015, 94). In this ode, the poet expresses the hope that his patron will meet no "envious reversals" (φρονεραῖς . . . μετατροπίαις) from the gods (*Pyth*. 10.20–21). Later Pindar mentions Perseus' visit to the Hyperboreans, the "sacred people" who are free from disease, ruinous old age, toil, and battles (*Pyth*. 10.41–42). For ordinary mortals, these are among the most distressing aspects of the human condition. Living as they do, the Hyperboreans avoid "severely-judging Nemesis" (ὑπέρδικον Νέμεσιν). The term ὑπέρδικος might seem to suggest that the Hyperboreans' realm affords them sanctuary from the severe judgment according to which humans grow old and infirm after a life of toil and battle. This judgment is not described as punishment for anything other than being human. The poet's hope is that his patron does not encounter reversals of fortune caused by divine envy. This implies that divine envy may be one aspect of the human condition that non-Hyperborean humans cannot completely avoid.

Konstan (2006, 115–16, 307 n. 5) contends that when forms of *nemesis* occur after the archaic period, they frequently describe the attitude of a deity or deities in contexts "that suggest fossilized locutions." Among the examples he cites are two lines in Sophocles' *Philoctetes*. In line 518 the Chorus attempt to convince their lord Neoptolemus to spoil the plans of his enemies the sons of Atreus by taking the suffering Philoctetes to his home rather than to Troy, where Philoctetes and his bow would cause the Trojans' downfall. By so doing, the Chorus argues, they will escape "the righteous anger of the gods" (τὰν θεῶν νέμεσιν), which might strike them if they ignored Philoctetes' plea for help. In line 602, Neoptolemus wonders why the sons of Atreus are seeking Philoctetes now, after casting him away so long ago. He asks if their actions might have been prompted by the gods' violent righteous anger (θεῶν βία καὶ νέμεσις),[48] which requites evil deeds.

Neither of these seemingly pious statements can be taken at face value. The Chorus and Neoptolemus are attempting to manipulate and deceive Philoctetes in order to steal the invincible bow which Heracles gave to Philoctetes, if not kidnap Philoctetes as well. As Schein puts it, the Chorus are "exploiting religious sentiment for their own advantage" (2013, 208). Neoptolemus does the same. He suggests that the gods may have decided to punish the Greek leaders for their mistreatment of Philoctetes, when in reality his appeal to divine retribution is designed to aid the sons of Atreus in committing more acts of injustice toward Philoctetes.

In contrast to these feigned appeals to divine *nemesis*, Philoctetes himself makes a genuinely pious appeal to divine *phthonos* later in the tragedy. When he hands over Heracles' bow—his sole means of killing game in order to survive—to his supposed friend Neoptolemus, he advises the young man to make obeisance to *phthonos*, so that it not become the cause of much painful toil for him, as it was for himself and Heracles before him (*Phil.* 776–78). As Kutter points out, Philoctetes is warning Neoptolemus to "avoid the *phthonos* that (Philoctetes implies) he himself has suffered" (2018, 187 n. 66). According to Kutter, Philoctetes believes the bow "attract[s] divine jealousy on account of its supernatural powers." The bow's supernatural powers—and its supreme value—make it inappropriate for mere mortals to possess.

Konstan (2006, 124) argues that "as an object of prayer, Phthonos acquires a human character, and one can appeal to it not to exercise the very emotion it names." Is this a case of full-blown anthropomorphic personification? Podlecki (1980, 74) notes that Nemesis, who has a shrine at Rhamnous, is recognized in cult. Because Phthonos is a "near-synonym of Nemesis, . . . it may be that he [Philoctetes] is personifying this abstraction as well." In contrast, Hogan believes that this is a case of the envy that prompts divine retribution being "substituted for the deity" (1991, 335). However one interprets this apparent personification of divine envy, what is most significant from a dramatic point of view is that Philoctetes shows himself to be genuinely humble and reverent to the gods, while the man he is addressing has used his evocation of divine *nemesis* as a ploy in his attempt to steal the object which, as he himself claimed, deserves obeisance as to a god (*Phil.* 657). Together, *Phil.* 518, 602, and 776 show that in this tragedy *nemesis* and *phthonos* are closely related, although the uses to which these terms are put differ greatly depending upon the integrity of the speaker who invokes them.

Aristotle also describes the relationship between *nemesis* and *phthonos*. In the *Rhetoric* he asserts that "one should . . . feel indignation at those who undeservedly do well. For what happens contrary to what is deserved is unjust, which is why we ascribe indignation (τὸ νεμεσᾶν) even to the gods."[49] While *phthonos*, like *nemesis*, is "a disturbing pain and . . . directed at doing well, it is not at someone undeserving of it, but at an equal and a similar" (1386b; cf. 1387a; Reeve 2018, 75). Unlike indignation, envy is a "base (φαῦλον) thing, characteristic of base individuals." The "base one, because of envy, is setting his neighbor up to not have [the good things]" (1388a; Reeve 2018, 79). In the *Nicomachean Ethics*, *nemesis* "is a mean between envy and spitefulness." The "indignant person (ὁ νεμεσητικὸς) is pained at those who fare well undeservedly; the envious person (ὁ φθονερὸς) exceeds him because he is pained at anyone's faring well[50]; the spiteful (ὁ ἐπιχαιρέκακος) is so deficient in feeling pain [at the misfortune of others] that he even delights in it" (*Eth. Nic.* 1108a-b; Bartlett and Collins 2012, 38).

Several scholars have noted that Aristotle's view of *nemesis* and its relation to *phthonos* differs from the contemporary norm. Cairns asserts that "the *nemesis* of the *Rhet* . . . does not wholly coincide with the ordinary sense of *nemesis* in ordinary Greek." In fact, "at some points it seems to represent what in the ordinary Greek of Aristotle's day might have been described as *phthonos*" (2003, 247 n. 42). Sanders (2014, 76) believes that Aristotle's analysis "differs significantly from contemporary usage" in another way, namely, "in his distinction between the immoral emotion *phthonos* and the moral emotion *to nemesan* (or *nemesis*)." Konstan (2006, 114–15) argues that the terms *nemesan* and *nemesis* were "archaic" and "old-fashioned" even by Aristotle's time, except in certain contexts. He concludes that "*nemesis* appears to overlap considerably with *phthonos* in classical Greek. Both terms represent an emotional response based on the judgment that a person, whether an equal or an inferior, is getting above himself" (2006, 122). Finally, Kutter observes that "by the fifth century, *phthonos* had begun to have an occasional moral aspect in certain contexts, thus aligning it more closely with Aristotle's concept of indignation than his own discussion would lead us to believe" (2018, 166).

As I mentioned earlier,[51] Uniacke argues that moral indignation is "the emotion appropriate to vengeance" (2000, 63). In some cases individuals attempt to gain vengeance (τιμωρία [*timōria*]; τίσις [*tisis*]) on behalf of the gods, or, in R. Parker's phrase, "'come to the god's aid'" (1983, 165).[52] Regarding ancient Greek culture in general, Mossman (1995, 169) notes that "in certain circumstances taking vengeance was positively considered a duty by the Greeks." Revenge can be "a necessary expression of private anger which goes hand in hand with public justice, as long as it remains within approved limits" and is not "disproportionate or indiscriminate" (1995, 170, 177).[53]

Revenge can be understood as an example of reciprocity in Greek life, as expressed in the oft-quoted maxim advising one to help one's friends and harm one's enemies.[54] In fact, a number of texts describe harming enemies as pleasurable. As the goddess Athena says to her favorite Odysseus in Sophocles' *Ajax*, "Isn't the sweetest laughter the laughter at enemies?" (*Aj.* 79; cf. 105). Thucydides cites the proverbial saying that nothing is more pleasant than revenge against enemies (7.68). Dover cites this statement as an example of "Greek frankness in admitting that revenge is enjoyable" (1994, 182–83, 191). Much earlier, Solon had prayed to the Muses to make him sweet to his friends and bitter to his enemies, respected by the former and dreaded by the latter (Fr. 13.5–6; Gerber 1999, 128–29). Even Aristotle concedes that getting revenge on enemies is not only noble and just but pleasant as well (*Rh.* 1367a20–22; 1370b28).

Herman (2006, 270–71, 278) argues that the maxim "help friends and harm enemies" had no more than a "negligible" effect upon Athenians' behavior, even in legal proceedings. However, the majority of classical scholars believe that personal revenge was an acceptable motive for prosecuting one's enemy in court. In a number of Athenian legal proceedings, the male prosecutor openly admits that revenge or vengeance is his motive (or one of his motives) for taking legal actions. For example, in his case against Nicostratus, Apollodorus begins by stating that he intends to exact vengeance (τιμωρεῖσθαι) because he has been "wronged and treated hybristically" (Demosthenes, *Ag. Nic.* 53.1).[55] Apollodorus insists that he is not acting as a sycophant, that is, someone who exploits "the institution of volunteer prosecution for the sake of financial gain" (Kucharski 2012, 190).

The accused might charge the speaker with sycophancy or "ignoble enmity." Ignoble enmity "is coupled with envy and spite, whereas 'good' forensic revenge is fuelled by sincere indignation at one's personal grievances and the defendant's public transgressions" (Kucharski 2012, 192). In the latter case, revenge and law enforcement are "synergistic forces" in the legal system. In contrast, Herman believes that 5th–4th c. Athenians "had deliberately purged their punitive system of the spirit of vengeance" (2006, 294).[56]

(2) Revenge and justice in Euripides' Hecuba

Euripides' *Hecuba* illustrates the major aspects of revenge and justice outlined previously. The play illustrates the importance of "helping friends and harming enemies," as well as the ways in which friends can transform themselves into enemies. The pleasure an avenger experiences after punishing his or her enemy is also on display in this drama. In addition, *Hecuba* features a case where personal revenge and judicial punishment go hand in hand. Finally, the tragedy hints at the role of the gods—and their *phthonos*—in human revenge.

This tragedy is set immediately after the Trojan war. The former Trojan queen Hecuba, now a slave, learns that her dead husband Priam's Thracian guest-friend Polymestor, who was supposed to protect Hecuba's only remaining son Polydorus from the Greek army, has instead murdered him. Polymestor's primary motive was greed (*Hec.* 25–27; cf. 775–76, 1245). Polymestor compounds his crime by dumping Polydorus' mutilated body into the sea. To exact revenge,[57] Hecuba uses Polymestor's greed to entice him and his sons into her tent, where a group of Trojan women are waiting. Together, Hecuba and these women kill the children and blind Polymestor, the "most accursed of men" (716; 890–1037).[58]

The violence of Hecuba's revenge has prompted a variety of responses from commentators over the centuries. Before we can evaluate this act of revenge, we must take into account the cultural context. When Hecuba first sees her son's mutilated corpse, she not only experiences intense grief, but shock at Polymestor's unholy and unjust violation of the crucial institution of *xenia* (guest-friendship; 715). As Belfiore points out, "*philoi* [friends] in a larger sense include suppliants and *xenoi*. . . . Suppliancy and *xenia* are initiated and maintained by reciprocation of favors" (1998, 140). Belfiore notes that Hecuba is a slave when we meet her because of the war started by her son Paris, "who violated his *xenia* relationship with Menelaus." When her *xenos* Polymestor kills her son, Hecuba realizes "that a *philos* has acted as an enemy" (1998, 158). Her revenge is reciprocal; she kills Polymestor while he is being "entertained as a *xenos* by her" (1998, 153, 158). Plato's Socrates warns against those who only seem to be friends but might in fact be bad people.[59] Hecuba had to learn this lesson the hard way.

Hecuba recognizes that she cannot avenge Polydorus' death (or the earlier death of her last remaining daughter),[60] without the help of her now-master, the Greek leader Agamemnon (*Hec.* 749–50). She repeatedly reminds Agamemnon that her son was killed by an untrustworthy *xenos* (774, 790, 803, 1216). Hecuba also stresses that violation of *xenia* rules is an affront to the gods, in part by referring to Polymestor's acts being "unholy" and "impious" (790, 792, 1234; cf. 715). These reminders are not lost on Agamemnon; he too calls Polymestor a host who has killed his *xenos*, an unholy act (781, 852, 1244–48). Hecuba also stresses the role of the gods and law in punishing violations of *xenia*, implying that in avenging the death of Polydorus she and Agamemnon would be enacting divine justice: "the gods have power and law (νόμος)[61] that rules over them: for by reason of law we believe in the gods and live by distinguishing between what is unjust and what is just" (799–801). Hecuba warns Agamemnon that if he allows offenders who murder guests to avoid punishment, then there will be no fairness in human life (803–805).

Although Agamemnon recognizes that the unholy guest-friend Polymestor deserves to be punished, he is still reluctant to act or to be seen as enabling Hecuba's revenge. Agamemnon fears that he might appear to his army to be harming his Thracian ally and aiding his enemy, the defeated Trojan queen (*Hec.* 850–58). However, Hecuba has provided Agamemnon with a rationale to act by referring to her dead son as Agamemnon's "affine," in this case, his brother-in-law (834), even though Polydorus' sister Cassandra shares Agamemnon's bed as a captive slave, not as a wife. Agamemnon agrees that if Polydorus is his kin, the matter of avenging his death is not the army's affair (859–60).

Next Hecuba assures Agamemnon that she will plot against Polymestor on her own, so that Agamemnon will not be an accomplice; if the Greeks do start an uproar after her act, all Agamemnon has to do is to keep the army away, without seeming to do so for Hecuba's sake (*Hec.* 869–74). Agamemnon then agrees to serve as judge in a court proceeding between her and Polymestor, admitting that it is crucial for both private citizens and the city as a whole that the bad be punished and the good succeed (902–904). From this point on, personal revenge and judicial punishment work together, as was the case with the historical legal proceedings I mentioned earlier.[62]

The trial scene takes place after Polymestor has been blinded and his sons killed. The plaintiff Polymestor speaks first. He admits that he killed Hecuba's son, but claims that he did so for a valid reason, namely, to prevent Polydorus from reaching adulthood and raising up Troy in order to gain revenge by plundering Thrace (*Hec.* 1136–44). As I will discuss in Chapter 4.2.a, biblical commentators have attributed a similar motive to Moses, when the prophet orders the mass infanticide of male Midianites in Numbers 31. Polymestor concludes his plea by claiming that his present sufferings are due to his having sought Agamemnon's favor (χάριν)[63] by killing his Trojan enemy (1174–75).

Hecuba responds by stressing that Polymestor had killed a *xenos* because of greed (*Hec.* 1205, 1216) and by telling Agamemnon that if he helped a *xenos* who was impious, untrustworthy, and unjust, Agamemnon too would appear evil (1233–35). Agamemnon then decides in favor of Hecuba, pointing out that killing one's *xenos* for his gold is not doing a favor for either himself or the Greeks in general (1244–45). Polymestor laments that he was defeated by a slave woman and has to pay the penalty to an inferior, Hecuba (1252–53). He asks the "villainous" Hecuba whether she rejoices at having treated him hybristically. Hecuba's response shows that she is another avenger who enjoyed her revenge: "should I not show delight, having vengeance on you?" (1257–58).

While Hecuba and Agamemnon both view themselves as acting on behalf of law and the gods, neither explicitly claims to be acting on behalf of divine envy or to be identifying with a god's envy. However, there are two passages early in the play which may allude to divine *phthonos*. In the first scene, Polydorus' ghost informs us that he had demanded of the underworld gods that his corpse be discovered, so that his mother could bury him properly (*Hec.* 49–50). He concludes the prologue by claiming that "some one of the gods is bringing ruin, counterbalancing your former success" (57–58). These lines remind the audience that one's prosperity can vanish at any moment, a view shared by some of the sages described by Herodotus (see Chapter 5.2, below). Segal (1993, 219) suggests that Polydorus' ghost may be appealing to "the traditional notion of the gods' envy" here, as though Hecuba were being punished for having been too successful.

The second passage which has been viewed as an allusion to divine envy is in a speech by Hecuba. In the past, Hecuba had accepted the supplication of the vulnerable Odysseus; now the former queen supplicates Odysseus, asking for a favor in return. That favor is to prevent the Greek army from sacrificing her daughter Polyxena to the dead hero Achilles. She reminds Odysseus that there is "jealous anger"[64] (φθόνος) at killing women whom the army did not kill earlier out of pity, when they tore the women away from their altars (288–90). The latter act is itself impious; killing them now would increase the army's culpability. This lends support for Battezzatto's view that "Hecuba does not state, but implies, that it is the gods who feel *phthonos*" in this passage (2018, 115).

We are now in a position to consider the propriety of Hecuba's revenge, as well as the related question of whether Hecuba's character degenerates after she decides on revenge. As I mentioned earlier, there is a wide spectrum of opinion on these issues. Heath concludes that there was "no adverse judgement of Hecuba's vengeance" in the sixteenth century [CE]; in fact, the horrific punishment of Polymestor and his sons fulfilled a "fundamental requirement of tragedy," namely, *atrocitas* (1987, 47–48). In contrast, seventeenth- and eighteenth-century critics censured horror and cruelty (1987, 51, 55). Heath finds broad areas of consensus in twentieth-century criticism of the play. Because almost all critics find Hecuba's vengeance to be "hideously and disproportionately cruel," there is "almost unvaried agreement" that her character has degenerated (1987, 62–63).

Heath himself does not agree. He points out that Hecuba's vengeance does not "evoke moral condemnation within the play" (1987, 65). In fact, "the judgements uttered within the play give every encouragement to Renaissance approval, none to modern disapproval, of Hecuba's actions" (1987, 65). Her "confidence in the gods and Nomos is justified by the event: Polymestor does suffer his deserved punishment." Heath concludes that "the sixteenth-century consensus about the play was in many respects preferable to our own consensus" (1987, 68). Heath acknowledges that he is not the only exception to the modern scholarly consensus (1987, 65). He finds that the "most radical and most persuasive" example is Meridor's 1978 analysis. While Meridor is well aware that many modern scholars regard Hecuba's vengeance "as an odious act of fury performed by a devilish creature," she argues that Euripides intended his audience to understand that in Hecuba's case "revenge was not only permissible but required" (1978, 28). Polymestor's punishment was "appropriate to the crime." Hecuba's revenge "was the last duty, and thus the only positive action left to Hecuba in the circumstances of her life" (1978, 34–35).

Since Meridor's and Heath's essays, critics have expressed a variety of opinions concerning Hecuba's revenge. Mossman lists many aspects of the play which prompt sympathy for Hecuba and moral approval of her revenge, but she also cautions us that "we should not be able to give our total approbation or condemnation to the actions of a major tragic heroine like Hecuba." Euripides has deliberately left ambiguities in order to set up "a complex moral problem for us" (1995, 203).

Scholars such as Gregory lean more on the side of approval of Hecuba's actions. She contends that "even when Hecuba makes Polymestor's children pay for their father's crimes, her revenge does not exceed the bounds prescribed by custom" (1999, xxxiii). Harris (2004, 142) also finds Hecuba's revenge to be justified and her anger "not delegitimized." He rejects the idea that her character has degenerated, and cautions us not to dismiss Mossman's view of Hecuba's moral ambiguity by regarding it "as the 1990s fashion." In fact, Mossman's view "seems just right." Similarly, Matthiessen (2010, 25) concludes that Euripides' contemporaries were in agreement with the form of Polymestor's punishment.[65] Finally, Zanotti argues that while Hecuba's revenge is "brutal," her "claim to revenge is valid . . . ethically coherent and deeply human." Moreover, Hecuba's "transformation does not mark her loss of humanity but rather her insistence on the value of the very human goods critics accuse her of abandoning: the *nomoi* of kinship and *philia*" (2019, 4).

Other recent studies do not view Hecuba's revenge so positively. For example, Segal views Hecuba and Clytemnestra as "vengeful, monstrous figures of violence." Hecuba is a "desperate suppliant" when attempting to save the life of her daughter Polyxena, but when she attempts to avenge her murdered son, her anger "soon takes its own direction into the realm of the demonic and the monstrous"

(1990, 119, 122). For Segal, "the most fearful metamorphosis of the play" is not Polymestor's prediction that Hecuba will be transformed into a dog with fiery red eyes (*Hec.* 1265) but her move "from just avenger to [Polymestor-like] monster (1990, 127).

When asking whether a fifth-century Athenian audience would find Hecuba's actions appropriate and acceptable, some commentators appeal to cases of violent revenge in Herodotus. For example, McHardy (2013, 40) claims that Hecuba is comparable to Herodotus' Pheretime in some respects. In Herodotus, Pheretime's excessively violent vengeance prompts divine *phthonos*, resulting in Pheretime suffering a horrid death (*Hist.* 4.205; see Chapter 5.3, below). Rather than explicitly accusing Hecuba of having provoked the gods in the same way that Pheretime did, McHardy focuses on alleged similarities between the two mothers while omitting crucial differences.[66]

More often commentators compare Hecuba's vengeance to that of Herodotus' Hermotimus (*Hist.* 8.104–106). As I will discuss in Chapter 5.3, Hermotimus was captured by enemies and sold to Panionius, a man who made a living by castrating and then selling young men. Hermotimus later becomes prosperous as King Xerxes' most honored eunuch. When he encounters Panionius again, Hermotimus acts friendly toward him, in order to be in a position to force Panionius to cut off the testicles of his four sons, who are then forced to do the same to their father. McHardy points to several plot similarities between this story and *Hecuba*. In both cases an apparent friend promises an enemy riches in order to lure the enemy and his sons into a position where the supposed friend can launch a revenge attack on the father and his sons. And in both "the revenge aims at replicating the damage originally inflicted on the avenger by his victim" (2013, 43). The damage is that both the family lines are doomed to end (2013, 44). We should add that Hecuba and Hermotimus both refer to their enemy or his deeds as "most unholy" (ἀνοσιωτάτον; *Hec.* 790, 792; *Hist.* 8.106).

A number of scholars conclude that the Athenian audience would find Hecuba's revenge to be acceptable. Mossman cites the Hermotimus narrative[67] in support of her conclusion that "killing the children of one's enemy as well as himself was not unusual or un-Greek" (1995, 188).[68] In contrast, Battezzato (2018, 16) finds appeals to Herodotus' Hermotimus narrative to be misdirected. While Hermotimus claims that his revenge was just and that "Herodotus does not explicitly condemn him," this "does not prove in any way that killing the children of one's enemy was a generally accepted practice." The infanticides are Hecuba's "weak point" (2018, 17).

Battezzato's comparison omits evidence of Herodotus' support for Hermotimus' revenge. Hermotimus not only claims that his revenge was just but that Panionius' crimes had caught the gods' attention so that their "just law" allowed Panionius to fall into Hermotimus' hands (*Hist.* 8.106). To say that Herodotus does "not explicitly condemn" Hermotimus is misleading, because the historian offers clear indications of support for this avenger. Herodotus, like Hermotimus, calls Panionius' practices "most unholy" (ἀνοσιωτάτων; 8.105). More importantly, when Herodotus comments that Panionius has been overtaken by τίσις *and* by Hermotimus (8.106), he affirms Hermotimus' actions.[69] As Romm puts it, by coming close "to personifying *tisis*," Herodotus "gives his assent to the moral Hermotimus himself draws from his remarkable revenge" (1998, 117).

Analyzing audience response to literary depictions of grisly punishments is a complex task, involving a variety of psychological and societal factors, discussion of which is beyond the scope of this study.[70] However, one observation by Joseph Carroll is helpful here: "fictional violence delineates extreme limits in human experience. . . . That is a kind of information for which we have evolved an adaptively functional need" (2012, 431). While Carroll does not cite *Hecuba*, he does note that "very few people" find it enjoyable to watch the gouging out of Gloucester's eyes in Shakespeare's *King Lear*. A brief look at these two plays reveals that the scene in *Lear* mirrors elements of *Hecuba* in topsy-turvy fashion. In *Hecuba* the host blinds the murderer of her son, who has abused *xenia* customs by killing his trusting guest out of greed. In *King Lear* the generous host Gloucester is the one betrayed and blinded by his wicked guests, King Lear's two daughters, Lear's son-in-law Cornwall, and Gloucester's son Edmund.[71] While they have betrayed both Gloucester and Lear, these power-hungry villains claim to have been betrayed by Gloucester, simply because he attempted to aid the legitimate king. In their eyes, blinding "the traitor Gloucester" (*Lr.* 3.7.22)—and enjoying doing so—is fitting revenge against their host.

It is not difficult to understand why viewers of this play are horrified (and perhaps fascinated)[72] by the prolonged on-stage blinding of this helpless old man.[73] While the host Hecuba blinds a man whose crimes merit his punishment (according to the majority of the commentators discussed previously), some readers find her action to be as disturbing or monstrous as the blinding committed by Gloucester's guests. In the end, what Peat says about this scene in *King Lear* applies equally to Hecuba's revenge: "the blinding [of Gloucester] brings home the harshest of realities: it forces us to acknowledge our capacity for cruelty and it also forces a radical reassessment of our ideas about justice; the justice we require for ourselves and desire for others" (Peat 1984, 107).

Later we will have occasion to ask whether readers of the Hebrew Bible are—or should be—horrified by biblical scenes of vengeful mass slaughter such as Moses' mass infanticide in Numbers 31 or individual atrocities such as the blinding of Samson (Judg 16:21; see Chapter 4.2 and 4.3, below). We will also have to deal with the fact that biblical scenes of mass killings sometimes provoke little or no emotional response from some readers—including commentators.

Notes

1 On Yahweh's "dark side," see Lasine 2010, 42–48, 56–57; 2016, 465, 472–75.
2 In contrast, M. Smith (2008, 179 n. 181) cites examples of "very poignant representations of deities" in the Akkadian *Atra-Ḫasīs* and *Ludlul bēl nēmeqi*. He concludes that "neither paradoxical representations of deities nor deeply moving portraits of deities constitute a unique feature of the biblical deity as such."
3 Pironti (2010, 130) argues that both the pantheon and individual deities display coherence: "the plurality of divine powers does not transform a pantheon into a disorganized

crowd. In the same manner, the polyvalence of a deity, both at the level of its spheres of intervention and in its modes of action, does not deprive a god or a goddess of any coherence or specificity."

4   On this scene in *Iliad* 1, see Chapter 7.1.a, below.
5   On the idea that Yahweh can act "demonically," see Volz 1924, 27–32; Lasine 2010, 42–48.
6   Redfield assumes that Homer's audience understood that they were being shown, for example, "not the Athena of cult, but the Athena of epic" (1975, 77).
7   On Athena in *Ajax*, see Chapter 6.2.a, below. Other deities are also depicted differently in various works. For example, Pironti notes that "Hesiod's Aphrodite is not identical to the Aphrodite in the *Iliad*" (2010, 119).
8   See Lasine 2002, 38–46; 2016, 474–75.
9   For example, in Mal 1:6 Yahweh declares that "'A son honors a father and a servant his master. And if I am a father, where is my honor? And if I am a master, where is my fear?'." In Malachi, one way in which Yahweh plans to treat the priests who have not honored and feared him properly is to "spread fecal matter on [their] faces" (2:3). On these verses, see Julia O'Brien 2008, 82, 85.
10 For an examination of each of these perspectives, see Lasine 2016, 467–75.
11 Ellis contends that divine envy focuses on specific types of humans: "in [Herodotus'] work and elsewhere in fifth century lyric, tragedy, and historiography, divine *phthonos* is associated with the reversal of fortune that meets successful monarchs and athletes who are particularly blessed . . . or with those who think or act in a conspicuously conceited or self-satisfied manner" (2015, 105).
12 On Aphrodite in *Hippolytus*, see Chapter 6.3.a, below.
13 On Genesis 3, see Chapter 3.2.a, below.
14 Lanzillotta believes that *phthonos* in some cases means avarice, not envy, and, more generally, denotes "the punishment that gods inflict on those who transcend human measures, the barriers that separate immortals from mortals" (2010, 79). On divine *phthonos* in Herodotus, see Chapter 5.2, below.
15 Both assumptions are open to objection. Predicating human emotions to deities is precisely what happens when one envisions a god anthropopathically, as in Greek texts and the Hebrew Bible. This assumes a similarity between the two types of beings in that respect, but without implying sameness of "level" in any sense. It merely implies that in order to explain the world in which we live we must imagine ourselves as ruled by beings whose behavior is analogous to that of envious and often unpredictable human rulers. This is part of the function of anthropomorphic deities, as I discussed in Chapter 1.4, above. Also see Chapter 8.3, below.
16 While punishing a hybristic leader might have dire consequences for the Greek people as a whole (e.g., by suffering a huge military defeat), the people in their entirety are not the primary target of such divine envy, as they are in the case of Yahweh's jealousy in the Bible. The monarch described by Herodotus' Otanes exhibits both *hybris* and envy (see *Hist.* 3.80 and Chapter 3.2.b, below).
17 In the *Mekilta* (*Baḥodesh*, 6; Lauterbach 1933, 244) God claims to be "above" jealousy: "I am ruler of my jealous anger" (אני שליט בקנאה), . . . jealousy has no power over me." Among modern scholars, MacKenzie (1955, 164–65) claims that "the word 'jealousy' must be stripped of emotional connotations" if it is to be applied to "supremely detached" decisions such as that made by Yahweh in Genesis 11. Similarly, when discussing Nahum 1 Peels remarks that "the root *qn'*, referring to God, has little to do with ordinary jealousy and everything to do with a zealous ardour for the maintenance and promotion of his own legal claims" (1955, 203–204).
18 It is often argued that anthropomorphisms and anthropopathisms are merely metaphors needed to be able to talk about God to human audiences. As a rabbinic dictum puts it, "the torah speaks in the language of human beings" (דברה תורה כלשון בני אדם); ordinary

Ancient Israel and Greece 39

humans are not perfect or capable of fathoming God's immutable essence. See Maimonides, *Guide* I, 26; 1919, 39; Sackson 2017, 109–10.
19 Yahweh's complex personality and his emotions will be discussed in Chapter 3, below. The violence of his spousal jealousy is evident in texts such as Hosea 1–3, Ezekiel 16, and Numbers 25, although Elliott (2007, 358) believes that "in Num. 25.11–13, . . . the stress on God's wrath against Israel and absence of any issue of possession or envious malice favors 'zeal' over 'jealousy.'" On divine jealousy in Numbers 25, see Chapter 4.1.a and 4.2.e, below. On Yahweh's behavior as an abusive husband in passages such as Hosea 1–2 and Ezekiel 16, see especially Julia O'Brien 2008, 31–48, 63–75. On Yahweh as abusive husband in Isaiah 54, see Goldingay 2001, 310–11.
20 Another difference is that in some Greek texts humans who exact violent revenge against wrongdoers, even on behalf of the gods, may prompt divine envy and punishment, while those who commit violence on behalf of Yahweh's jealousy, such as Phinehas, are rewarded rather than punished. We will examine specific cases of these situations in detail; see Chapters 4.1.a and 5.3, below.
21 These comparisons can be found in Chapter 7, below.
22 The full form is "vengeance is mine and repayment" (ושלם). The verb שָׁלֵם appears in the MT only here and in Isa 59:17–18, a passage which combines vengeance with divine jealousy. Mendenhall's influential argument that *naqam* denotes "vindication" rather than "vengeance" (1973, 69–104) has led commentators such as Milgrom to assert that "the rendering 'avenge' has hardly any basis in Scripture and none at all when the subject is God" (1990, 255). This a very comfortable theological position, but Mendenhall's conclusions have been forcefully refuted by Pitard, who affirms the traditional understanding that the term expresses vengeance, recompense, retribution, and revenge in various contexts (1982, 16–17).
23 In Jer 51:56 Yahweh is called "a God of recompenses" (or retributions; אל גמלות).
24 For more on this remarkable passage and its allusions to Exod 34:6–7, see Lasine 2019, 110–13.
25 Spronk (1997, 34) notes that "Nah. 1:1 is the only place where the jealousy of this אל קנוא is indicated as the root of his anger against the enemies of Israel."
26 Glatt-Gilad (2002, 66) points out that in Psalm 79 the speakers are concerned about "the effect of the current situation on God's reputation." The taunt "Where is their God?" shows that God's reputation has been "sullied." The "necessary antidote to this belittling of God's reputation is for God to exact his vengeance on these very nations who scorned him (v. 12)." This implies that one motive of Yahweh's vengeance against those who scorned him is concern for his "image."
27 Yahweh's direct action is also signaled by the formula, "Behold, I am against you" in Jer 50:31 and 51:25. Yahweh makes this declaration in Nah 2:14 and 3:5 as well, before detailing the direct actions he will perform against Nineveh. Apart from the books of Jeremiah and Nahum, this formula appears only in Ezekiel. Spronk (1997, 107) points out that the phrase is "known among OT [Old Testament] scholars as the '*Herausforderungsformel*,' in which YHWH calls forth his opponent for the deciding battle."
28 Other examples of Yahweh using foreign armies to attack his people are discussed in Chapter 7.1.b, below.
29 On Jehu, see Chapter 4.1.c, below.
30 Of course Jephthah's daughter may be describing the victory in the way which most honors her father. Her devotion to both Jephthah and Yahweh is amply demonstrated in the story. While I read her quoted speech in terms of her character as it is depicted in the narrative, Block (1999, 373) believes that it is the narrator's voice we are hearing when she speaks. Through the young woman "the narrator offers a theological interpretation of the battle," with *naqam* answering Jephthah's earlier declaration in v. 27 that Yahweh should decide the dispute between the warring parties.

40 Ancient Israel and Greece

31 In contrast, Jeremiah wants Yahweh to take vengeance for him on his persecutors (והנקם לי מרדפי), but Yahweh has so far failed to do so (Jer 15:15).

32 Not all reports of Yahweh destroying his (and Israel's) enemies employ the Hebrew key word for vengeance and revenge (*naqam*). A famous example is Exod 12:12, in which Yahweh announces that he will personally wipe out all first-born Egyptians and their animals in one night and execute judgments on all the gods of Egypt.

33 As noted by Peels (1995, 64; cf. 68–69), Yahweh's words here are "not directed to Cain but to everyone who listens ('anyone who kills Cain' rather than 'anyone who kills you')." On the ambiguities of the language employed in vv. 13 and 15, and the various ways in which Yahweh's statement has been construed over the centuries, see Byron 2011, 106–19. In Gen 4:24 Cain's descendant Lamech declares, "if Cain will be avenged sevenfold, then Lamech seventy-sevenfold!" Peels points out that "Cain is avenged, but Lamech avenges himself (1995, 66). For other perspectives on this verse, see Twersky 2017, 283–84 and Byron 2011, 107–108.

34 For example, Hamilton speaks of "unchecked envy and jealousy on Cain's part" (1990, 230). Twersky (2017, 282) goes further, claiming that "jealousy is Cain's most essential and key characteristic." After Cain's offering is ignored, we are told that he is "very angry" or "dejected, chagrined" (see Sasson 1990, 274–75 on the verb חרה in this and other passages) and that his "face fell." These descriptions have been variously interpreted. After Yahweh gives some pastoral counseling to Cain in vv. 6–7, we are told that Cain spoke to Abel, but in the Hebrew text we are not informed about what Cain said to his brother (v. 8). Clearly, Genesis 4 does not provide readers with an adequate basis for any conclusions about Cain's "essential and key characteristics" or robust personality traits.

35 Humphries understands Cain's emotions here as his "initial angry response to an unfair world," a world in which "Yahweh can and does have favorites for no apparent reason" (2001, 60). See Chapter 1, n. 14, above.

36 This is Block's felicitous rendering of בנקם נקם (1998, 23).

37 The root *naqam*, denoting vengeance and revenge, is a *Leitwort* in the oracles against Edom and Philistia in Ezek 25:12–17, appearing ten times; see, for example, Block 1998, 22–23.

38 An even more complex example is found in Numbers 31, after Moses transforms Yahweh's order to "avenge the vengeance of the children of Israel from the Midianites" into a command to go to war "to set the vengeance of Yahweh on Midian" (31:1–3). Numbers 31 is discussed in detail in Chapter 4.2, below.

39 To use Peels' apt term for this dynamic (1995, 88).

40 Peels (1995, 87, 89) argues that the subject of יקם is actually "he," that is, Joshua, and that גוי refers not to the nation of Israel, but to the "host" of "his [Joshua's] enemies."

41 The MT of v. 12 does not specify whether "he" refers to Yahweh or Joshua. The LXX has Joshua as the speaker.

42 Given leaders' failure to institute *mishpat* [justice], Goldingay finds it unlikely that the "man" to whom Yahweh is referring is a world (or community) leader whom he himself raised up, such as Cyrus or Nehemiah (2001, 334–35).

43 Verse 4 claims that "no one calls in righteousness and no one pleads in truth." This verse appears to refer to a specifically judicial setting.

44 The phrase "day of vengeance" is mentioned in Isa 34:8 and 61:2.

45 Later in the chapter Isaiah implores Yahweh to look down from his heavenly abode, asking "where are your jealous zeal (קנאתך), your powerful deeds, the agitation of your inward parts, and your compassion? They are held back from me" (Isa 63:15).

46 For example, Jacob 1942, 257: "The prophet [Isaiah] had the story of Moses and our verse before him, and he compares God's judgment with the behaviour of Moses." Cf. Greenberg 1969, 45 n. 1.

47 The other instance is "the suitors' anger at Odysseus' suggestion that he too try his bow" (*Od.* 21.285; Sanders 2014, 52). Here "envy/jealousy" is suggested by Homer's comment about the suitors' fear that Odysseus "might succeed where they did not."

48 On this reading of the phrase, see Schein 2013, 219.
49 Cf. *Eth. Eud.* 1233b: "what the ancients call 'indignation (*nemesis*)' is being pained at those who, contrary to worth, are doing badly or doing well, while rejoicing at those in accord with worth. That is why people think that Nemesis is actually a god" (Reeve 2021, 49).
50 Cf. *Eth. Eud.* 1220b: "the envious are pained even by the doing well of those who deserve to do well" (Reeve 2021, 19).
51 See Chapter 1 n. 36, above.
52 Examples of exacting vengeance on behalf of the gods will be discussed when we analyze Herodotus' Hermotimus later in this section and in Chapter 5.3. On Sophocles' Oedipus seeking vengeance on behalf of the gods, see Chapter 6.2.b, below.
53 Mossman (1995, 170) does acknowledge that "the same incident can be described very differently by opposing parties: one man's act of just retribution is another man's act of disproportionate revenge." In Chapter 5.3 I will discuss cases in which avengers such as Herodotus' Pheretime go beyond those limits.
54 For additional examples of this maxim in Greek writings, see Blundell 1991, 27; Knox 1961, 3–4; Herman 2006, 270–71 n. 40. Barlow (1998, 176) notes that reciprocity of benefits between friends is "part of the general code of behaviour 'helping friends and harming enemies.'" Plato argues that this maxim is inadequate as a definition of justice. In the *Republic*, Polymarchus cites Simonides, who defines justice as giving everyone their due. When pressed by Socrates, he claims that Simonides must have meant that justice is helping friends and harming enemies (*Resp.* 331e-332d). Socrates counters that one can have *seeming* friends who are actually bad and enemies who are good. In response, Polymarchus qualifies the maxim: one should only do good to one's friend if he or she really is good and harm only an evil enemy. Socrates does not accept this version either, since it is never just or right to harm anyone (335e).
55 In Euphiletus' defense speech after killing Eratosthenes, the speaker says that he committed the act for the sake of *timōria*, in accordance with the laws (Lysias 1.4; cf. Harris 1997, 365).
56 On Herman's idealized view of Athenian life and legal practice, his dismissal of significant counter-evidence from forensic oratory, and his refusal to admit evidence from Aristotle and Greek drama, see, for example, Christ 2007.
57 Only Hecuba uses forms of τιμωρεῖν (to exact revenge) in the play, and she does so six times (*Hec.* 749, 756, 789–90, 842–43, 882, 1258).
58 On Herodotus' account of the blinding of Euenius by misguided "avengers," see Chapter 5.3, below.
59 On this scene in the *Republic* see n. 54, above.
60 Hecuba's revenge is triggered by the treachery committed against her son. Hecuba's only remaining daughter Polyxena had died earlier in the play, after the ghost of Achilles demanded a prize gift. The demand is fulfilled by the sacrifice of Polyxena (*Hec.* 37–44, 177–437). Hecuba attempts to prevent her daughter's death by appealing to Odysseus as a supplicant, after he had supplicated her successfully in the past. Odysseus shows himself to be another bad *philos* by refusing her request.
61 I agree with those commentators who contend that Hecuba is using *nomos* (νόμος) to denote law, not "convention"; see, for example, Battezzato 2018, 177–79; Mitchell-Boyask 2010, 110.
62 Meridor (1978, 29–30) notes that several speakers (and the chorus) refer to perpetrators having to pay a just penalty for their misdeeds. They usually employ the expression δίκην διδόναι; on this term, see Chapter 5. n. 49, below. The repeated application of this expression to what is due to Hecuba seems "intended to represent 'Hecuba's Revenge' as an official act of justice" (Meridor 1978, 30). Battezzato (2018, 17) points out that "*Hecuba* is different from most other ancient revenge plays in that the revenge plot is followed by a judicial procedure assessing the justice of the revenge." Among extant tragedies, this sequence occurs only in *Hecuba* and Aeschylus' *Eumenides*.

63 Polymestor is anticipating a favor in return from Agamemnon. As Mitchell-Boyask observes, "*kharis* is almost reciprocity itself" (2010, 220).
64 This is Mitchell-Bayask's rendering of *phthonos* here (2010, 90). In contrast, Mossman (1995, 111) contends that *phthonos* merely means "it is wrong" here, that is, wrong to kill in cold blood women who were spared when the city was sacked.
65 In support of this conclusion, Matthiessen points out that an audience watching *Hecuba* hardly has the possibility of engaging with Polymestor's sons emotionally. It is as though the children are only introduced so that they may be killed. Their deaths serve to increase the suffering of Polymestor, because he has lost the heirs to his fortune. This in turn makes the extent of his punishment proportionate to the gravity of his crimes.
66 McHardy claims that Pheretime is motivated by "mother-love" and "constant concern" for her son Arcesilaus, and that Hecuba defeats Polymestor "for the sake of her beloved son." Yet in the *Histories* neither Pheretime nor Arcesilaus is described in terms of familial love; both act out of political self-interest. Moreover, Arcesilaus is not a young innocent boy like Polydorus; he is a power-hungry married man who has scorned the legacy of his father and committed atrocities (*Hist.* 4.162–64). And while Polydorus was certainly loved by Hecuba in Euripides' play, her desire to punish Polymestor is also motivated by Polymestor's unholy violation of *xenia* customs and his personal betrayal of her and her husband Priam. Finally, McHardy contrasts Hecuba with Pheretime by claiming that Hecuba "attacks *philoi* rather than political enemies" (2013, 40). While she acknowledges that Polymestor is a treacherous *philos*, McHardy still refers to "Hecuba's betrayal of her guest-friend Polymestor" while they are guests in her tent (2013, 42). I would suggest that Polymestor can no longer be classified as Hecuba's *xenos* once he has violated the rules of that institution in a sacrilegious manner and consequently cannot be said to have been betrayed by Hecuba. He betrayed her, and now she punishes him in a way which mirrors his criminal act.
67 Mossman (1995, 175–76, 188–89) also cites Herodotus' reports on Artayces (*Hist.* 9.120; cf. 7.33) and other texts in support of her view.
68 In addition to Mossman, Gregory and Matthiessen both cite the Hermotimus narrative to support their opinion that Hecuba's vengeance was appropriate (Gregory 1999, xxxiii n. 56; Matthiessen 2010, 25 n. 43). Like Heath, they note that within the play all the characters except Polymestor consider his punishment, and Agamemnon's court proceeding, appropriate. Matthiessen also cites the blinding of King Zedekiah in Jeremiah 39. Both Zedekiah and Polymestor witness the deaths of their sons before they are blinded (Jer 39:6–7, 52:10–11; 2 Kgs 25:7; *Hec.* 1160–72).
69 I therefore disagree with Mitchell-Boyask's criticism of Mossman, whom she accuses of "making far too much of lack of overt condemnation by Herodotus of the revenge of Hermotimus against Panionius . . . especially given Herodotus' mastery of irony" (1996). I detect no hint of irony in these statements by the historian.
70 Elsewhere I have argued that literature can function as a kind of "safe space" within which readers and theatre audiences can explore harsh realities and feel negative emotions without reacting as they would if they experienced these emotions in their daily lives (Lasine 2019, 63–64). In the present case, I would suggest that portraying the acts of violent revenge as having occurred in the distant past, or in an alien land, facilitates this process, allowing audiences to experience both horror and fascination without their reactions implying that similar emotions would trigger similar violence in their own behavior or that of their society as a whole.
71 Gloucester entreats his tormentors, saying "Good my friends, consider; you are my guests. Do me no foul play, friends . . . I am your host; with robber's hands my hospitable favours you should not ruffle thus" (*Lr.* 3.7.30–31, 39–41). It is Goneril who first mentions blinding Gloucester (3.7.5), but it is her sister Regan and her husband Cornwall who actually perpetrate the crime, with the tacit assent of Gloucester's son Edmund.

72 Peat (1984, 106) believes that "fascination and horror, . . . are the component parts of our response to the blinding." I doubt that all of "us" would admit to being fascinated by this scene.
73 At first only one of Gloucester's eyes is crushed (3.7.66–81). The audience has reason to hope that he will be able to retain his other eye, especially when Gloucester's servants attempt to stop the mutilation, but this hope is soon shown to be in vain.

3 Yahweh as a jealous and envious God

In this chapter I will ask whether Yahweh, the self-described jealous God (אל קנא; Exod 20:5),[1] also displays dispositional envy. I will begin by questioning the common assumption that it would be impossible for Yahweh to experience envy. Next, I will examine the charge that Yahweh is envious of the creatures he has made in his own image. Then I will analyze Yahweh's view of his seeming rivals, the "other gods (אלהים אחרים),"[2] and the strong negative and destructive emotions he expresses when his people bow down to these no-gods. The final sections discuss narcissism and associated traits as well as their relation to envy, both in general and as they apply to the biblical God's personality.

1. The seeming impossibility of Yahweh experiencing envy

At first glance the notion that the biblical God Yahweh could experience envy might seem far-fetched. For one thing, people envy those who are like themselves, but, as one psalmist puts it, "who is like Yahweh our God?" (Ps 113:5; cf. Exod 15:11). Envy is a rivalrous emotion, but who could be Yahweh's rival? The so-called "other gods" have no reality, according to many biblical speakers. Enviers often want something that another possesses, but Yahweh already possesses everything. To whom would he feel inferior?

Francis Bacon claims that "where there is no comparison, no envy; and therefore kings are not envied but by kings" (1985, 85). While most of the "other gods" ridiculed by Yahweh are not described as their worshippers' divine king,[3] Yahweh does not acknowledge even the existence of other deities, let alone their having regal status. He insists upon his incomparability, asking "to whom will you compare me, that I should be equal?" (Isa 40:25; 46:5). Moses, Isaiah, and speakers in Psalms make the same point (Deut 33:26; Isa 40:18; Ps 89:7). A number of other passages refer to Yahweh being "above all gods" (על-כל-אלהים).[4] If Bacon is correct, Yahweh should not be envious of any other being, divine or human, and no other beings should envy him.

In Job 41:3 Yahweh asks, "Who has confronted me that I should requite? Everything under heaven belongs to me."[5] We should therefore not be surprised if some scholars believe it to be "inconceivable that Jahweh might ever feel envy towards humans" (Most 2003, 125). Schroeder (2005, 2034) assumes the same

DOI: 10.4324/b23212-3

concerning Yahweh's attitude toward other gods: "the all powerful, all confident Yahweh could not conceivably be envious of Baal and the other false gods." For Elliott, attributing envy to Yahweh "would have been inconsistent with their sense of Yhwh's superiority and incomparability as well as of his generosity and liberality. Lacking peers of similar status, Yhwh stood without rival, with no possibility of feeling inferior by comparison" (2007, 362; cf. 2016b, 75). Yet we must ask whether assessing Yahweh's behavior in terms of what we might find "conceivable" and "consistent" prevents us from taking account of passages which suggest that Yahweh is indeed envious, not only of other gods, but also of certain humans.

2. Is Yahweh envious of his human creatures?

a. The charge that Yahweh was envious of Adam and Eve

Von Rad contends that divine envy is expressed in Genesis 3: "the serpent imputes envious intentions to God. It is the age-old notion of the envy of the deity, with which it casts suspicion on God's good command" (1981, 62; cf. Skinner 1930, 87–88, 94). The serpent's idea that Yahweh's prohibition was motivated by envy seems ironic in light of the later traditions which claim that it is the serpent who is envious of the human couple and eager to bring them down (e.g., Wis 2:24). In addition, if we are to predicate an emotional motive to Yahweh here, jealousy seems more likely than envy. From this perspective Yahweh would be forbidding the man and woman access to knowledge of good and evil because he wants to jealously retain that advantage for himself alone.

Is Yahweh exhibiting envy as well as jealousy in the Garden story, or in Genesis 1–3 as a whole? *The Life of Adam and Eve* points to one reason for divine envy in this story: "But since God knew this, that you would be like him, he begrudged (or envied; ἐφθόνησεν) you and said, 'Do not eat of it'" (*L.A.E.* 18:4; M. Johnson 1985, 279). The emperor Julian also believes that the Jews' God "must be called envious (βάσκανος)" because he did not want humans to become *too much* like himself: "when he saw that man had attained to a share of wisdom, that he might not, God said, taste of the tree of life, he cast him out of the garden, saying in so many words, 'Behold, Adam has become as one of us'" (*Contra Gal.* 93e; Wright 1923, 326–27). Julian concludes that God is both envious and jealous in this scene: "to refuse the knowledge of good and bad, which knowledge alone seems to give coherence to the mind of man; and lastly to be jealous (ζηλοτυπῆσαι) lest man should take of the tree of life and from mortal become immortal—this is to be grudging and envious (φθονεροῦ καὶ βασκάνου) overmuch" (*Contra Gal.* 94a; Wright 1923, 326–29).[6]

Yahweh wanted humans to be "in his image" and "likeness" (Gen 1:26; cf. 5:3), but too much similarity can trigger malicious envy.[7] According to Job 28, God prohibits human access to wisdom, his exclusive possession. In Gen 3:22–23 Yahweh evicts the couple from the garden to prevent them from attaining another of his exclusive rights: living forever. In terms of envy, the expulsion can be viewed as lowering the humans' status in order to remove anything enviable in their situation.[8]

It is not surprising that Julian would be unreceptive to the idea of a jealous deity who forbids humans from gaining access to knowledge of good and evil. The emperor was familiar with the Greek philosophical tradition of divine *aphthonia* (ἀφθονία), lack of envy.[9] Commenting on Plato's *Phaedrus* 247a, M. Dickie describes *aphthonia* as "the overflowing generosity of spirit" which leads the gods to allow humans to "participate with them in the knowledge that gave them their immortality" and thus be "willing to let [them] share in their immortality" (1993, 381). As Plato puts it in the *Timaeus*, the maker of the created world was good and therefore devoid of envy; he therefore desired that all should be as similar to himself as possible (*Ti.* 29e; cf. Aristotle *Metaph.* 983a).[10]

Among modern interpreters of Genesis 3, Nietzsche is most emphatic in predicating divine envy as the motive for evicting the primordial couple from Eden. For Nietzsche the key is God's "hellish fear of science." Creating humans was "God's greatest mistake," because he thereby "created a rival for himself." Once the couple has ingested the knowledge of good and evil, their acquisition of "science" makes them "like God." For God, science is the first sin, the seed of all sins, the original sin: "You shall not know" (1999a, 226–27).

b. Does Yahweh envy the best of his human creatures?

Herodotus' character Otanes warns the Persian elite about the dangers of monarchy. The king "is unaccountable and allowed to do what he wishes." Given this power, even the best of humans would be affected negatively: "*hybris* is bred in him by the good things he has, while from the beginning envy (φθόνος) is implanted in humanity. . . . Being satiated he does many reckless things, some from *hybris*, some from envy." Otanes concedes that "an absolute ruler (τύραννος) ought to be free of envy (ἄφθονον), having all good things," but the fact is that "he becomes the opposite of this in respect to his citizens: he envies the best who survive and live,[11] and is pleased by the worst of them" (Herodotus, *Hist.* 3.80).

In addition to envying the best of their subjects, Otanes' monarchs display signs of narcissism; if "you admire him moderately he is vexed that you do not pay court to him in a servile manner, but if you pay court to him in a servile manner he is vexed because you are a flatterer" (*Hist.* 3.80).[12] Ronningstam (2005, 91) points out that narcissistic individuals tend to be preoccupied with others' envy of them. This may be based, in part, on "a perception of other people's envy as a threat to [their] own self-esteem and grandiose self-experience, that is, a belief that others are going to criticize or destroy what one can do or have." In other words, narcissists know from their own experience that envying another involves wanting to harm and bring down the envied person. Therefore, if others envy and excessively flatter the monarch, this may mean that the enviers actually have hostile intentions toward him.[13]

The biblical God is also presented as a king. Job points to God's unaccountability, asking "Who can say to him, 'what are you doing'?" (Job 9:12; cf. Qoh 8:4 on unaccountable human kings). Does Yahweh envy the best of his subjects?[14] Elsewhere I have discussed how Yahweh's favorite humans include those who suffer so much from their divine king's attention that they wish to die or wish that they had never been born (see Lasine 2019, 35–44). These figures include Job and prophets such as Moses, Elijah, Jeremiah, and Jonah. These individuals are also the ones who most strenuously force God to account for his behavior toward them. Job goes so far as to claim that Yahweh tore him in his wrath and hatred (Job 16:9). Job is drawing a logical conclusion from his situation based on his correct assumption that Yahweh is responsible for that situation. So is it far-fetched to ask whether Yahweh might harbor a grudge against his favorite human because Job is *too* good? It is, after all, Yahweh who initiated Job's fall by bragging about Job's incomparable virtues to the *satan* (השטן; 1:8, 2:3)? No wonder Qoheleth advises his readers not to be too righteous or wise (Qoh 7:16)!

c. Yahweh as both jealous and envious in relation to other gods

Earlier I cited Elliott's position that it is impossible for Yahweh to have felt envy toward inferior beings, since he "stood without rival." Elliott then asks a crucial question: "what valued good enjoyed by another, moreover, could have been imagined as obtained at Yhwh's loss?" (2007, 362). If we do not exclude responses which might initially seem "inconceivable" or "inconsistent," the answer to this question should be obvious. The valued good is the love and loyalty of Israel, the people whom Yahweh views as his spouse, child, and subject. When Yahweh perceives that Israel has abandoned him for new "lovers," the other gods, he hardly seems "all confident." He views their disloyalty as monumental ingratitude for all he has done for them. His reaction is to direct violent fury against his wayward people and to fantasize about even greater devastation to come. These actions do not express "generosity and liberality." Given Yahweh's claims about being all powerful and without rival, such behavior might seem illogical, but viewed in terms of the psychology of envy, jealousy, and narcissism, it makes perfect sense.

Yahweh's continual denigration of other gods is further evidence of envy. Most emphatic are verses which claim that other deities are not gods at all. In Isa 41:21–24, 29 Yahweh challenges other gods to prove their potency by revealing the past and future and by doing good or evil. His conclusion: you are nothing and your work is less than nothing (v. 24). In Deut 32:17, 21 Moses sings that Jeshurun sacrificed to demons and new gods that were no gods, making Yahweh jealous and provoking him to anger with their idols. In Jer 2:5, Yahweh asks "what wrong did your fathers find in me that they walked after futility and became futile" (הבל; cf. Jer 2:11, 5:7; 2 Kgs 17:15). The implied answer is that Yahweh had done nothing to deserve being abandoned by his people.

In one remarkable midrash (*Lam. Rab.*, *Petichta* 24) Rachel tells God that she had actually formulated an intricate plan to help her sister Leah fool Jacob into thinking that he was sleeping with her, Rachel, and not Leah.[15] She then asks God that if she, who is made of dust and ashes, was not envious of her rival (לא קנאתי לצרה), why is he, the divine king, envious of false gods, so that his envy has led his children to be exiled or killed? Her argument rouses God's compassion, and he informs Rachel that, because of her, the exile will end (Neusner 1989, 78–79).

Rachel's point is clear: if human compassion is capable of conquering envy, the same should be true of the deity, especially when the object of his envy is not even real.[16]

The seeming absurdity of an all-powerful deity being envious of unreal rivals has also noted by commentators from the emperor Julian to modern researchers on idolatry. Earlier I mentioned that Julian finds the biblical God jealous, grudging, and envious in the Garden of Eden story. Elsewhere he points out that if God is jealous, "then against his will are all other gods worshipped." This raises two questions: "how is it that he did not himself restrain them, if he is so jealous and does not wish that the others should be worshipped, but only himself? Can it be that he was not able to do so?" (*Contra Gal*. 155d-e; Wright 1923, 362–63). When discussing a midrash which implies that God is jealous of insubstantial idols (*b. 'Abod. Zar*. 54b–55a), Halbertal and Margalit argue that Yahweh "has been placed in an untenable position: if he does not confront the idol this may be seen as a sign of his weakness while if he is jealous of it this is seen as a sign of the idol's importance." For these scholars, this conundrum "grasps the internal contradiction within the feeling of jealousy itself" (1992, 27).

Yahweh has no hesitation about calling himself a jealous God; in fact, he declares that his name is Jealous (יהוה קנא שמו; Exod 34:14). Passages such as Numbers 25, Hosea 1–3, and Ezekiel 16 are well-known examples of Yahweh acting as a jealous husband who is furious at his wife Israel's infidelity. The passages in Hosea and Ezekiel include grotesque revenge fantasies against his unfaithful and ungrateful spouse. In contrast, there is no clear example of Yahweh admitting that he is envious of his rivals for their having won Israel's devotion.[17]

According to Brueggemann (1997, 283), Yahweh will "brook no rival." Brueggemann is referring to the God of the first commandment, "who intends to be fully sovereign." This calls our attention to the fact that the three main analogies used for Yahweh's relationship with Israel are that of king, father, and husband. All three leave room for only one individual in that role. Even if his subjects seek to worship Yahweh along with another deity (see, e.g., 1 Kgs 18:21), Yahweh's self-definition is threatened. Most often he is said to react to this threat with jealous wrath, but other emotions are also triggered. Yahweh feels that he is being treated like a fool (or scorned; Deut 32:15; נבל), hated (שנא),[18] treated with contempt (נאץ),[19] or ignored by those who serve other gods and/or violate his statutes.[20] In Deut 32:15–17, 21 Yahweh adds that he will show the scoffers that to ignore him and his dictates is what truly makes one a fool (נבל), with deadly consequences. It is therefore fitting that Yahweh threatens to provoke Israel with a נבל nation.

Psalm 69 shows that Yahweh's followers can identify with their God's presumed experience of being disgraced or reviled. The speaker declares that he is suffering for Yahweh's sake[21]: "my jealousy (קנאת) for your house[22] has eaten me up and the revilings of your revilers (וחרפות חורפיך) have fallen upon me" (v. 10).[23] In other words, it is because Yahweh is being reviled that the speaker suffers the same humiliation.[24] The feeling of being reviled and disgraced is stressed throughout the poem; the *Leitwort* חרפה (*ḥerpah*) appears six times between vv. 8–21. The speaker does not specify how or why these individuals have reviled God.[25]

Nor does the psalm indicate whether Yahweh himself feels reviled. We only know that the speaker identifies so closely with his God that disgrace heaped upon the deity also falls upon his suffering zealot. In Num 25:11 Yahweh views Phinehas as having identified with his jealousy ("he was jealous with my jealousy among them").[26] In Psalm 69 the speaker identifies the disgrace he has experienced with the disgrace he claims was inflicted upon his God Yahweh.

In Exod 20:5 and Deut 5:9 Yahweh declares himself a jealous God and adds that he will punish three or four generations of those who "hate" him (cf. Deut 32:41). How should one understand "hating God" here?[27] In reference to Deut 5:9 Tigay notes that "it is unlikely that a polytheistic Israelite would literally hate, or even reject, the Lord; at worst one might worship Him together with other gods or ignore Him" (1996, 66). It is also unlikely that Jacob really "hated" Leah, but as the rejected/ignored party it is understandable that she would *feel* that he hated her (Gen 29:33; cf. 29:31). Given Yahweh's emotional makeup as displayed in the Hebrew Bible, he too might feel hated by anyone who ignores him or worships other gods along with him. He wants to be unique and the sole object of his wife's, children's, and subjects' attention and worship.

The term "practical atheism" is often applied to passages such as Ps 14:1, in which the fool (נבל) says in his heart that "'there is no God'" (אין אלהים), leading to them acting abominably.[28] In several passages (Pss 10; 53; Prov 30:8–9), denying the existence of God is also paralleled with doing evil. Not doing good is paralleled with not seeking after God. This, in turn, implies that they are ignorant fools. Some commentators assume that the wicked in Psalm 10 do not actually "say in their heart" that there is no God; rather, that is the author's way of communicating that these exploiters act *as though* they believed there was no God, although their actual assumption is that God will not notice or care about their evil actions.

Yahweh *does* notice and react with strong emotion to his creatures ignoring him. In Deut 29:18–19 Yahweh imagines an individual who would stubbornly follow the dictates of his own heart,[29] triggering Yahweh's jealousy and obliterative punishment. This individual's heart is turning away from Yahweh toward other gods. The apostate assumes that he will be able to avoid Yahweh's covenant curses. Yahweh's reference to his jealousy in Deut 29:19 suggests that when Yahweh becomes incensed after being ignored, he is reacting as though he has failed to jealously keep his audience's total attention. The passage as a whole alerts potential perpetrators that they cannot succeed in avoiding Yahweh's attention or the violent actions which Yahweh is willing to take in defense of his prerogatives.

3. Yahweh's envy in relation to his narcissism

a. Psychological approaches to the relationship between envy and narcissism

In his *Moralia in Job* (ca. 590 CE) Gregory the Great suggests a relationship between envy and what we now call narcissism. The seven principal vices (the so-called "seven deadly sins") are the "progeny" of pride. The "first offspring . . .

is vain glory, and this . . . presently begets envy." Because vainglory seeks "the power of an empty name, it feels envy against any one else being able to obtain it." From envy springs "exultation at the misfortunes of a neighbor, and affliction at his prosperity." The more that the mind is "pierced by the inward wound of envy," the more envy also generates anger (1850, 490). Given that vainglory denotes ostentatious pride in one's real or imagined achievements, its kinship with narcissism is evident. As DeYoung points out, "vainglorious practices can lead to lying to ourselves; this, in turn, could "be motivated by blinding narcissistic tendencies—a version of prideful vainglory" (2014, 72–73).

Echoing Gregory's reference to envy as an "inward wound," some modern researchers call envy a "narcissistic wound" (e.g., Smith *et al.* 2008a, 296). Envy is also one of the diagnostic criteria for narcissistic personality disorder (NPD) in recent editions of the *Diagnostic and Statistical Manual of Mental Disorders* (*DSM*). The individual with NPD "is often envious of others or believes that others are envious of him or her" (2013, 670). Clinicians such as A. Cooper believe that *DSM* "inadequately emphasizes the role of envy as part of the unconscious core of the disorder." Narcissists not only envy "the good qualities they detect in others, . . . but also most often denigrate" them (2000, 70–71; cf. Berke 1988, 74). We have already noted that denigration of others is frequent among the envious (see Chapter 1.2, above). Envy may lead the narcissist to "react with contempt toward the envied person and to project envy onto others" (Smith *et al.* 2008a, 296). As Berke puts it, "the quality of hurt . . . seeks discharge by omnipotent self-inflation and other-denigration" (1988, 74; cf. Lasine 2012, 133–34).[30]

Recent research on the relationship between narcissism and envy has shown that dispositional envy feelings are strongest among those who are termed "vulnerable" or "covert" narcissists (Neufeld and Johnson 2016, 693; cf. Krizan and Johar 2012, 1440). According to Neufeld and Johnson, "vulnerable narcissism entail[s] unique and marked susceptibility to dispositional envy feelings, which, in turn, promot[e] stronger feelings of envy toward an advantaged rival." The "Achilles' heel" of these narcissists is that "seemingly positive beliefs about worthiness and deservingness set the stage for situational experiences of deprivation and envy" (2016, 693).

Another, more fundamental, cause of narcissism accompanied by envy has its origins in infancy and early childhood. According to Freud (1946, 157–58), affectionate parents act toward their child as though he or she is not subject to the necessities which dominate life, like illness, death, and restrictions on our will. For Freud (1943b, 232 n. 1) and Ferenczi (1950, 218–19), the fetus in the womb enjoys self-sufficiency, omnipotence, and "blissful isolation," like a chick in the egg. After the infant is born, parents attempt to recreate the child's supposed pre-natal feeling of inviolability by serving as adoring courtiers to what Freud calls "His Majesty the Baby," in order to revive their own lost feelings of completeness in the mirror of their little prince or princess (Freud 1946, 157–58; cf. Lasine 2002, 36–38).[31]

While most of us lose this presumed feeling of "infantile omnipotence" as we mature, Vidaillet (2008, 283) notes that "envious people cannot renounce omnipotence." He cites Lacan's reference to a famous observation made by St. Augustine: "I myself have seen and experienced an infant jealous (*zelantem*): it could not speak and became pale and cast bitter looks on its fellow-nursling" (*Conf.* 1.7.11; Augustine 1995, 34). Commenting on this passage, Lacan writes that "what the small child, or whoever, *envies* is not at all necessarily what he might want. . . . Who can say that the child who looks at his younger brother still needs to be at the breast? Everyone knows that envy is usually aroused by the possession of goods which would be of no use to the person who is envious of them, . . . Such is true envy—the envy that makes the subject pale before the image of a completeness closed upon itself" (2018, 116).

What the older sibling envies is the infant's imagined sense of closed completeness or unity.[32] As Freud points out in reference to Goethe and a few of his own patients, this envy can lead the older child to express hostility toward the new baby by symbolically or "magically" ridding himself of the rival, for example, by throwing objects such as the mother's crockery out the window (1947a, 15–26).[33] As noted by Vidaillet, "it is when he can see that another is usurping his own place in the relation with the mother that the child apprehends for the first time what he is deprived of and experiences an unbearable loss"; what he or she has lost is "the image of himself as complete and omnipotent," and is left with "the feeling of no longer existing" (2007, 1680–81; cf. Freud 1940, 133).

The adult narcissist attempts to become complete in him- or herself, in part by inviting the adoring gaze of as many people as possible. The role of ruler lends itself to this strategy. As Freud points out, "the leader himself does not need to love anyone else, he may possess a masterful nature (*Herrennatur*), absolutely narcissistic, . . . self-reliant and autonomous" (1940, 138).

Narcissism can also be associated with high attachment anxiety. According to Besser and Priel (2009, 306; cf. 308), "attachment anxiety, . . . seems to predispose a person to, or to accompany, covert narcissism." As Smolewska and Dion (2005, 65) point out, "anxiety attachment reflects a proneness to anxiety and vigilance concerning rejection and abandonment by others . . . covert narcissists might have particular difficulty regulating their emotions and behavior in the context of attachment relationships and perhaps interpersonal relationships generally." Rohmann and her team state the problem more dramatically: "feelings of vulnerability that are fuelled by narcissism seem to function like a matchstick which ignites anxious attachment" (2012, 285).[34]

Recent research indicates that some individuals lessen attachment anxiety by maintaining emotional distance from their attachment figure, whom they distrust. This strategy of "dismissive avoidance" is associated with both malicious envy and grandiose narcissism. Dismissive avoidants "see themselves in a positive way but see others negatively," and are therefore more likely to attempt "pulling down the envied person." (Baumel and Berant 2015, 2–3, 7–8).

b. Yahweh's narcissism and its relation to envy and attachment anxiety

Elsewhere I have argued that the predominant mode of divine narcissism in the Hebrew Bible involves Yahweh the parent using his human children as a mirror (Lasine 2002, 36–43; cf. 2001, 208–16, 261–63). Psychologists such as Winnicott argue that the human child "needs [maternal] hate to hate" (1958, 201–202; cf. Benjamin 1988, 212). From this perspective, Yahweh's demand for total love (Deut 6:5) is an example of enforced idealization which precludes his children from experiencing the kind of hate needed to make love authentic. And we have already noted how much Yahweh hates to be hated, and how violently he returns that perceived hatred.

The jealous God of Israel is "self-originate," "without mother [and] without father," as the *Apocalypse of Abraham* puts it.[35] Nor does the biblical God have a wife. Like the depictions of Yahweh as a lone father who uses his children as mirrors, and as a king whose prophets portray him as a glorious lone warrior (Isa 63:1–6; Hab 3:3–12; cf. Judg 5:4–5), this aspect of Yahweh's aloneness also suggests the narcissistic desire to make the self absolute and omnipotent. Based on her experience with her patients, psychoanalyst Jessica Benjamin gives this desire a voice: "I want to affect you, but I want nothing you do to affect me; I am who I am" (1995, 36; 1988, 32). According to Benjamin, narcissistic omnipotence is exhibited by the insistence on being one ("everyone is identical to me") and all alone ("there's nothing outside of me that I don't control"; 1995, 36).[36]

At the same time, narcissists are *never* self-sufficient, no matter how much they might claim to be. Viewing Yahweh as a narcissist highlights his need for others. And it is precisely in his behavior as father and husband that Yahweh most clearly displays this neediness. Yet as we have seen, Yahweh's special human children and his wife Israel still run away in order to cling to other gods who are false foster parents (Jer 2:26–28) or impotent lovers (Hos 2:7), in spite of all the gifts which Yahweh claims to have given them. For that reason alone, Yahweh can never rest supremely secure, indifferent to his children and his unreal rivals.

As noted earlier, some theorists stress that the envier views the person envied as being free from envy. This reinforces the envier's fantasy that the envied person, with his or her perceived advantage, must be complete as a "closed unity." The envier, especially if she or he tends to be narcissistic, desires to destroy the perceived completeness of the envied one. In Yahweh's case, the other gods must be shown not only to be powerless but vacuous and lifeless. In short, they must be denigrated into darkness. In contrast, the advocates of other gods give no sign of wanting to denigrate Yahweh or to deny his existence. To take one famous example, it is not the prophets of Baal who ask for a contest on Mt. Carmel or who seek to ridicule Yahweh or his prophet, as Elijah ridicules them and their god (1 Kgs 18:20–38).[37]

Biblical narrators rarely tell their readers why the Israelites keep being attracted to other gods. One exception involves the conversation between the Judeans and the prophet Jeremiah after the fall of Jerusalem. According to the prophet's opponents, when they made offerings to the "queen of heaven" they had peace and prosperity (Jer 44:17–19; cf. 7:18). Since they ceased to do so, in obedience to the recent cult reforms, they have experienced deprivation, war, and famine. Jeremiah then delivers Yahweh's rebuttal to the people's reasoning. It was their sins against Yahweh and his laws which caused the war and the resulting devastation. And the same will now happen to the refugees in Egypt because of their continued infidelity to him (44:20–27).

In other cases in which the Israelites point to the benefits of worshipping other gods, Yahweh offers a convenient explanation. For example, in Hosea 2 Yahweh quotes his adulterous wife Israel saying that she will go after her "lovers" who give her bread, water, wool, flax, oil, and drink (2:7). Yahweh replies that it was he who had given her grain, wine, oil, silver, and gold which she used for Baal, although she did not know it (v. 10). To punish her, Yahweh will take back these goods. When Israel then seeks her lovers, she will not find them. That will convince her that she was better off with her "first husband" (v. 9). Similarly, in Deut 13:2–4 Moses concedes the possibility that a prophet might perform a wonder or predict a sign which comes to pass, demonstrating the power of unnamed "other gods." But he immediately invalidates this demonstration, explaining that such occurrences are actually loyalty tests arranged by Yahweh himself.

King Yahweh's insistence that his deeds as conqueror and miracle-worker be broadcast over the world, and his horror that his name might be profaned,[38] take on new significance when we consider that narcissists have a pressing need for the adulation of others. While Yahweh's renown certainly serves an important "public relations" function, it is also conducive to reinforcing whatever narcissistic tendencies this divine king might already possess. After viewing the presentation of Yahweh's personality through a psychological optic, it becomes clear that theologians who discuss Yahweh's personality are responding to his envy and narcissism even if they do not employ these terms. For example, Brueggemann (1997, 293) claims that "the terms jealous and jealousy . . . refer to Yahweh's . . . singular preoccupation with self." Even his "jealousy for Israel, when it evokes a defense of Israel, is in the service of Yahweh's self-regard" (1997, 294). In short, "Yahweh's self-regard is massive in its claim, strident in its expectation, and ominous in its potential" (1997, 296).

As for the connection between abandonment anxiety and narcissism, the Hebrew Bible includes many examples of Yahweh exhibiting "vigilance concerning rejection and abandonment by others" (Smolewska and Dion 2005, 65), which make it a challenge for him to regulate his emotions and behavior. The books of Deuteronomy and Jeremiah include a number of occasions on which Yahweh declares that he has been, or will be, abandoned or forsaken by his people.[39] Other prophets quote Yahweh lamenting that he and his *torah* have been forgotten by the people.[40] Other speakers declare that the people have abandoned Yahweh or his covenant.[41] We also find the claim (at times made by Yahweh himself) that Yahweh has abandoned and/or forgotten his people,[42] as well as statements declaring that Yahweh will *not* abandon his people or forget the ancestral covenant.[43]

c. The charge that Yahweh is sadistic at times

Several biblical scholars have described the God of the book of Job as sadistic.[44] Noting that readers are informed of Job's innocence in the prologue, Pope asks "why the devilish sadistic experiment to see if he [Job] had a breaking point?"

(1965, lxix). Newsom points out that for Job, the language of psalmic prayer refers to a divine-human relationship which has a "fundamentally sadistic structure" (2009, 137). And Levenson suggests that God attacks Job in chapters 38–41 not for Job's "belief that God can be sadistic, . . . but for his insolence in expressing it" (1988, 155).

Genesis 22 has also been cited as an example of divine sadism. God tests Abraham by commanding him to kill his only child, for no stated reason. According to Gunn and Fewell (1993, 98), in Genesis 22 God is, "at the very best . . . simply unfathomable," but "at the worst, . . . deranged and sadistic." Similarly, Armstrong admits that "a deity who asks for such an extreme demonstration of devotion can seem cruel and sadistic" (1997, 67–68). Humphreys considers God "savage" in this narrative (2001, 138–44). The test itself has been called "monstrous," "unthinkable," "horrible," and "gruesome" (Crenshaw 1984, 13–14; Boström 2000, 58).

If the biblical God is sadistic in such cases, does that make his worshipers masochistic? A number of theorists have linked masochism with religion—at least in part—as a response to basic aspects of the human condition. As Charmé puts it, masochism provides "a means of dealing with such universal experiences as powerlessness, helplessness, and guilt" (1983, 232, 221; cf. Fromm 1994, 17, 37, 150–53, 169). In the present context, the question is whether masochism is one of the ways in which people in the Hebrew Bible are shown to cope with the challenges presented by their life-world, a world which is governed by their divine master Yahweh. Charmé believes that "the acceptance of suffering as punishment is a deep-seated biblical idea." As an example he cites Ezekiel 16, which portrays "Yahweh as a jealous husband who is punishing his wife (Israel) with a beating" (1983, 225).

For Berger, religiosity can involve both sadism and masochism. The "attitude of masochism" is "an intensification of this self-denying surrender to society," one which is "of particular interest in connection with religion" (1969, 22–23, 55). Berger contends that the masochist requires "a sadistic counterpart." Unlike human counterparts who cannot play the role of master for long, "the sadistic god . . . remains invulnerable, infinite, immortal by definition" (1969, 57). Such a god can succeed in being "absolutely dominating, self-affirming, and self-sufficient." While a human sadistic counterpart might succeed "in becoming something of a credible master for awhile, he remains vulnerable, limited, mortal."

Berger believes that "the Book of Job presents us with the, as it were, pure form of religious masochism *vis-à-vis* the biblical God" (1969, 74–75). He supports this contention by pointing to only two verses out of the book's forty-two chapters, in translations which do not reflect what those verses say in the MT. Berger's versions of Job 13:15 and 42:6 have Job saying that he will trust God even if God slew him, and that he repents because he "abhors himself." In these translations,[45] it does sound as if the book of Job has translated "the problem of theodicy into the problem of anthropodicy" (Berger 1969, 78). Crenshaw seems to read Job 42:6 in this fashion when he refers to "the masochistic response of Job, so prevalent in the Judeo-Christian world" (1983, 128–29).

Patrick (1979, 281 n. 56) rejects Berger's reading of Job. He believes that "the book of Job, to the contrary, rejects the masochism of Job's companions, in favor of the right of humans to protest the decrees of the Almighty." Since Job refuses to follow his friends in declaring themselves guilty in order to justify God's actions, Patrick's point is well taken. While a full analysis of the book of Job is beyond the scope of this study, I would suggest that if any speakers in the book display a masochistic attitude, it is Job's friends, not Job himself. It is they who justify God by claiming that humans are impure maggots who drink iniquity like water.[46] In contrast, Job holds fast to his integrity to the very end of the book.[47]

If the views of Charmé, Berger, and Fromm have any applicability to the Hebrew Bible, it is only for worshipers of Yahweh who are already masochistic. Charmé (1983, 225) notes that masochists frequently pair off with narcissistic, jealous, and punitive partners, and cites Yahweh as a jealous husband. In Berger's version of the master-slave dynamic, the divine partner is the sadistic counterpart to the masochistic self, invulnerable, infinite, and immortal. This meets the needs of the masochist, who finds happiness in believing that he or she is nothing and the master is everything (1969, 56; cf. Sacher-Masoch 1980, 63). As Fromm puts it, a masochistic person strives to get rid of the individual self with all its shortcomings, risks, and unbearable aloneness (1994, 153). By submitting to the masterful authoritarian god, a masochistic believer is saved from the final responsibility for his or her fate. Masochists are fortunate in this regard, because narcissistic and envious individuals who are prone to rage may welcome the opportunity to portray themselves as perfect, masterful, and self-sufficient, and therefore worthy of others' submission and adoration.

A link between masochism and narcissism has also been described by researchers in psychology and psychiatry, although they rarely apply their findings to religion.[48] For example, A. Cooper (2009, 904) concludes that "masochism and narcissism are developmentally, functionally, and clinically intertwined." Cooper believes that "masochistic traits develop as an attempt to repair the painful memories of early child experience that are an unavoidable concomitant of narcissistic development" (2009, 905). In other words, masochism is not self-destructive, but a "self-protective" defense mechanism (D. Shapiro 2002, 343). A. Cooper points out that for masochists, "any sense of continuing safety through the maintenance of an attachment to an object of power and control becomes the primary pleasure need" (2009, 911).

Does Yahweh, as an "object of power and control," actually exhibit the kind of sadistic behavior often associated with narcissism and envy? It is clear that Yahweh does *not* want his human subjects to be "nothing," in Berger's sense. If his subjects were nothing, they could not acknowledge his mastery and his claim to their exclusive devotion.[49] Yahweh does not always approve of adherents who are passive and masochistic. In fact, he seems to appreciate those followers who are most independent-minded, assertive, and persistent in opposing his plans, such as Abraham, Moses, Elijah, Jonah, and Job. And while Yahweh wants other *gods* to be "nothing," his behavior reveals that he considers them to be enviably attractive to his subjects and thus a real danger to his self-image.

Few would dispute that various biblical passages could be adduced to support the idea that Yahweh's followers abase themselves before their God in a fashion which could be construed as masochistic, if readers conclude that their abasement is undeserved or that Yahweh did not show himself to be a reliable covenant partner (Pss 13:2–3; 44:10–27; 89:39–52; Hab 1:13–17). Of course, many biblical speakers admit that they have committed sins or been disloyal to their God (e.g., Pss 41:5; 90:7–8; 106:6; Lam 3:42). To use Berger's terms, the people have chosen to become submerged in the nomos provided by Yahweh's covenant. They therefore accept that they deserve their suffering, although they may protest the duration of the punishment by asking Yahweh how long his wrath and/or jealousy will continue (e.g., Ps 79:5, 9; Lam 3:42–50, 5:20), or by begging God to restore them (e.g., Pss 60:3; 80:4, 20).[50]

Acts of Yahweh which readers might find overly harsh or unfair could also be cited as evidence of sadism. For example, in 1 Sam 2:25 the sinful Hophni and Phinehas do not listen to the warnings of their father Eli because "Yahweh was pleased (חפץ)[51] to kill them." On the other hand, when 1 Sam 2:25 is viewed together with two passages in Ezekiel, Yahweh's pleasure at the death of Eli's sons seems to be an exception to a non-sadistic rule. There Yahweh asks, "do I take any kind of pleasure at all (החפץ אחפץ) that the wicked should die?" and declares "I have no pleasure (אחפץ) in the death of one who dies" (Ezek 18:23, 32).

We also cannot ignore the many passages in which Yahweh professes his paternal love and compassion for his human children and for his spouse Israel. On these occasions, Yahweh is "a protective and caring parent who is always reliable and always available" when needed (Kaufman 1981, 67). The problem is that Yahweh is *not* always a reliable "safe haven" for his people (on this issue, see Lasine 2019, 52–56, 60). In addition, one might question the extreme harshness with which father Yahweh sometimes punishes his wayward son or spouse Israel. Clearly, the divine portrait presented by the biblical authors is complex and multi-faceted. However, the problematic aspects of Yahweh's behavior can often be attributed to the very emotions and traits we have been highlighting: jealousy, envy, vengefulness, and narcissism.

d. The charge that Yahweh's behavior is sometimes immature or infantile

In his "psychohistory" of the Jewish people, Gonen (2005, 7) claims that "it behooves us to compare the infant's behavior to that of mighty Yahweh." From "the recesses of their unconscious thoughts and dim feelings [the Israelites] drew out an image of vulnerability and of a tenacious infantile reaching out for the security and soothing impact of a transitional object." The vulnerable God Yahweh's "transitional object" is the Jewish people.[52] Similarly, Jung's portrayal of Yahweh in his *Answer to Job* has been described as the depiction of an "immature know-it-all" (Dohe 2016, 203).[53] Can such characterizations of the biblical God hold up under scrutiny? If Yahweh exhibits signs of dispositional envy and narcissism, does that have any bearing on whether he is presented as a mature adult?

Modern Western personality theorists[54] take the capacity for self-extension, the ability to engage in compassionate and intimate relationships with others, increasing impulse control, and emotional security as hallmarks of maturity. Enright *et al.* argue that the lowest level of maturity grants forgiveness only after revenge has been taken (1989, 96, 106–108; cf. Enright 1994, 65). Other psychologists contend that maturity requires that individuals come to terms with their mortality (Kastenbaum 2000, 105; cf. Freud 1944, 114).[55] Cultural critic Neil Postman adds that in a fully literate culture, self-restraint and delayed gratification are required for one to "earn adulthood" (1994, 76–77, 88). Finally, Stearns examines a twentieth-century American tradition which views jealousy as indicative of "childish selfishness and immaturity" (2013, 18, 23; cf. Gale 1969, 178).[56]

These understandings of maturity all stem from modern Western notions of desirable adult traits. Within the Hebrew Bible itself, we can add that unrestrained or impulsive anger is associated with immaturity, especially in wisdom literature (e.g., Prov 22:24–25; 27:4; 29:11, 22; Qoh 7:9; Ps 37:8). In the book of Job, young Elihu is introduced to us as "angry" four times in four verses (Job 32:2–5); he is "bursting" to speak, like new wineskins that have no way to vent pressure (32:19). While there is no consensus among scholars on whether Elihu is shown to be a brash fool, it is unlikely that many readers would judge him a mature individual.

Does Yahweh display emotional security, impulse control, self-restraint, and the ability to engage in compassionate and intimate relations with his human children and his wife Israel? There is ample evidence to indicate that we can answer in the affirmative in some cases. Whether he consistently and reliably acts in this fashion is another matter. The occasions on which Yahweh acts out of jealousy, envy, and rage in defense of his self-image frequently fail to illustrate the emotional control, self-restraint, and compassion which are usually associated with maturity.

Notes

1 Cf. Exod 34:14; Deut 4:24, 6:15. Yahweh may be jealous *for* something, such as his holy name (Ezek 39:25), Jerusalem (Zech 1:14), Zion (Zech 1:14, 8:2), or his people (Isa 26:11; cf. 9:6). He may also be jealous *against* his enemies (Isa 42:13; Ezek 36:5–6), his wayward people (Deut 29:19, 32:16, 21; 1 Kgs 14:22; Ezek 5:13, 16:38, 23:25), or all the inhabitants of the earth (Zeph 1:17–18; 3:8). In almost all these cases, Yahweh's jealousy is mentioned along with his fury and wrath; on some occasions Yahweh speaks of "the fire of my jealousy" and "the fire of my wrath" (Ezek 36:5, 38:19; Zeph 1:17, 3:8; cf. Ps 79:5). In the HB, the noun קנאה may also denote envy but only in reference to human beings (e.g., Qoh 4:4 and 9:6).

2 Apart from Exod 20:3; 23:13 and Hos 3:1, the phrase אלהים אחרים is found in Deuteronomy, the DtrH, and Jeremiah; see Weinfeld 1972, 320–21.

3 The "queen of heaven" is a notable exception; see Jeremiah 7; 44 and Section 3.3.b, below.

4 1 Chr 16:25; Pss 95:3; 96:4; 97:9; cf. Ps 135:5.

5 Clines (2011, 1162) believes that this verse envisages "an encounter, not with Yahweh but with Leviathan." However, the idea that everything belongs to Yahweh is expressed in a number of verses; see, for example, Deut 10:14; Ezek 18:4; Ps 24:1; Ps 50:10–12. Cf. Num 16:5; Deut 1:17; 1 Chr 29:16; Ps 22:28.

58 Yahweh as a jealous and envious God

6 Satan, in Twain's satirical *Letters from the Earth*, is even more emphatic: "jealousy is . . . the blood and bone of his [the biblical God's] disposition, it is the basis of his character. . . . The fear that if Adam and Eve ate of the fruit of the Tree of Knowledge they would 'be as gods' so fired his jealousy that . . . he could not treat those poor creatures either fairly or charitably, . . . a wild nightmare of vengefulness has possessed him ever since" (1996, 238).

7 Elsewhere I have discussed Yahweh's desire for his human "children" to mirror their divine father in ways which gratify his narcissism. See Lasine 2002, 37–43 and Sections 3.3.a and 3.3.b, below.

8 Did God view Adam's transgression as an act of ingratitude or betrayal? If so, Adam's expulsion could be seen as motivated by Yahweh's righteous indignation rather than by divine envy. Other commentators suggest that the expulsion is actually a case of divine benevolence; humans becoming immortal after such a fateful act of disobedience would do them more harm than good (see, e.g., von Rad 1981, 70).

9 Not all Greeks agreed with Plato and others that the gods cannot be envious. For example, Lesher (1992, 84) cautions readers not be assume "that Xenophanes was . . . unaware of a whole variety of ways in which men supposed that the gods could be envious, jealous, or the sources of undeserved sufferings. . . . But these forms of wickedness are not explicitly mentioned."

10 Also compare Epictetus, *Disc.* 2.19.26: "the soul of a man who wants to be of one mind with God, . . . never to be angry, never to be envious (μὴ φθονῆσαι), never to be jealous (μὴ ζηλοτυπῆσαι)" (Hard 2014, 120).

11 Lateiner suggests that the reason a tyrant envies good men their existence is because "their lives reproach his habits" (1991, 168). In other words, the good threaten the tyrant's self-definition, in the sense discussed earlier.

12 Cf. this description of one modern tyrant from Humphrey Slater's novel *The Heretics*: "it seemed almost . . . as if Stalin simultaneously demanded and hated the sycophancy of absolute obedience" (1947, 204).

13 F. Foster (1972, 168) notes that if the possessor of an advantage realizes that he is envied, and views "this envy as a realistic threat to a valued possession," he or she may also experience jealousy.

14 In general, Yahweh's jealousy is aroused by the behavior of his people as a whole, not by actions performed by individuals. This is in contrast to the *phthonos* of the Greek gods, which is usually prompted by individuals' hybristic actions, excessive good fortune, or "big thoughts." It is perhaps worth noting that the Hebrew term קנאה is not employed by the narrators who report the envious actions of Aaron and Miriam toward Moses in Num 12 or those of Korah and his cohort in Num 16, although קנא *is* used in the allusion to the Korah story in Ps 106:16. Nor does the word appear in the reports of royal apostasy committed by kings such as Solomon and Ahab. The LXX of 1 Kgs 14:22 is one exception; here the evil acts of Solomon's son Rehoboam provoke the Lord's jealousy (παρεζήλωσεν). However, in the MT of this verse it is general apostasy among the people of Judah which is said to call forth Yahweh's jealousy.

15 For the biblical version of the story, see Gen 29:20–26.

16 Stern (1992, 163) describes this narrative as "reverting to the anthropomorphic paradox." In an "ironic reversal of *imitatio dei* that we might call *imitatio hominis*, it is the model of *human* behavior to which God now turns in submitting to Rachel's example."

17 According to Ben-Ze'ev (2000, 313), one "way of reducing jealousy is to attribute the mate's preference to some flaw in the mate and not in oneself. In this way God's jealous attitude toward the people of Israel can be explained. God's jealousy does not express his inferiority, but the flaws of the people of Israel. Hence, God is described in the Bible as being jealous, but not envious." Feeling envious does not always mean that the envier is conscious of feeling inferior to the one he or she envies. One may merely feel undervalued or unfairly ranked below a rival. We will continue to find evidence that the biblical God is presented as envious as well as jealous.

18 Those who "hate" Yahweh are mentioned in Exod 20:5; Num 10:35 (where Moses refers to those who hate Yahweh); Deut 5:9; 7:10; 32:41; Pss 81:16, 83:3; 139:20–21.
19 Other cases of Yahweh interpreting others as having treated him with contempt or having despised him, using נאץ, include Num 14:11, 23; 16:30; Jer 23:17; Isa 5:24; cf. Ps 10:3; Ps 74:18.
20 For example, Exod 20:5; Deut 31:20; Ps 10:3–4, 11, 13; Ps 53:2.
21 Or "because of you" (עליך); cf. Jer 15:15 and Ps 44:23.
22 This is usually assumed to be a reference to the Temple (e.g., Hossfeld and Zenger 2005, 178–80; Goldingay 2007, 343–44).
23 Other examples of those who revile or disgrace Yahweh can be found in Pss 74:22; 79:12.
24 Hossfeld and Zenger (2005, 180) understand the speaker's point to be that "because these influential people ridicule Yhwh by their speech and actions, something the petitioner apparently accuses them of doing, they now (consequently, from their standpoint) ridicule this 'zealot' for Yhwh as well." Taken literally, v. 10 does more than "apparently" accuse them.
25 In addition, the speaker does not directly address the reason for his enemies' actions against him. Those who hate him "for no reason" are many and/or mighty (עצמ; v. 5) and include those who sit at the city gate talking about him and drunks who sing about him (v. 13).
26 On this passage, see Chapter 4.1.a, below.
27 Other references to hating God include Num 10:35; Deut 7:10; Pss 81:16; 139:21; 2 Chr 19:2.
28 For example, Crenshaw 2005, 27–43; Kraus 1993, 197, 221. In Ps 94:7 the evil ones say that "Yahweh will not see" their sinful and criminal actions (cf. Ps 10:11; Ezek 8:12, 9:9).
29 Weinfeld (1972, 105–106) takes כי in the sense of "since" here ("*since* I walk in the stubbornness"). Thus understood, the verse is akin to ironic quotations which satirize idolaters (see Lasine 1992, 139–42). In this instance, the narrator quotes the perpetrator stating that his self-assurance is really blind "stubbornness" (cf. Jer 18:12; see Weinfeld 1972, 340 for examples). This is of course the narrator's opinion, not the evildoer's, unless the latter understands "stubbornness of heart" to imply strength. Lundbom (2013, 810) takes כי in the concessive sense ("even though") here, adding that "a person will not likely speak thus about himself, particularly with שְׁרִרוּת ('stubbornness') being an irksome type of self-reliance."
30 Baranger (1991, 111) defines a narcissistic wound as "everything that reduces the self-regard of the ego or its feeling of being loved by valued objects." It can be accompanied by "feelings of lack and helplessness" (Grinberg 1991, 100).
31 As Maurer points out, "if the parents are jealous gods, unpredictable, predominantly wrathful, or if they do not answer wailing prayers for help, the child is caught in a double bind as he [*sic*] doubles his efforts to please them, more fearful than most that he will lose even that which he has" (1966, 38). The narcissistic injury caused by such parenting can result in the child becoming envious of others whom he or she perceives to have a closed unity with their parent. From this point of view, a parent who imitates a god's jealousy leads to a dysfunctional familial unit.
32 One photographic illustration of this situation is the picture of my younger sister and myself (Figure 1), discussed in the preface to this book.
33 In the Goethe essay Freud calls the older sibling's emotion "jealousy" (*Eifersucht*). When he refers to this phenomenon again in his book on group psychology, he speaks of the older child's initial "envy" of the new arrival (*Neid*; 1940, 132–33).
34 On the relationship between narcissism and sadism, see Section 3.3.c, below.
35 *Apoc. Ab.* 17:9–10; Rubinkiewicz 1983, 697; cf. Lasine 2002, 47–50.
36 According to Freud, narcissism on the part of a paternal leader serves a vital function. Freud notes that group members identify with the same leader who becomes their ego

60 Yahweh as a jealous and envious God

ideal. This social figuration allows them to view themselves as equals to each other in their shared focus on the leader. It also transforms individuals' original feelings of envy toward each other into a public spirit which allows them to identify with one another in their adulation of the leader (1940, 132–35). All are therefore equal. In short, this is the benefit the group receives for focusing on the same ruler. For Freud, that leader will have narcissistic traits (see Chapter 1.4, above). In fact, this group dynamic *requires* a narcissistic leader, quite apart from possible patterning of the leader on the dominant traits of a father or husband in a highly patriarchal culture. That is, the people need their leader to seem godlike, in the sense of invulnerable, self-sufficient, universally adored, and fascinating, all qualities which narcissists—including narcissistic leaders—want to project.

37 Another partial example is the Pharaoh's response when Moses relays Yahweh's demand to let his people go, so that they can hold a pilgrimage feast to him in the wilderness (Exod 5:1). Pharaoh asks, "who is Yahweh?" Why should he, Pharaoh, do what this Israelite god demands? The Pharaoh then adds, "I do not know Yahweh." In other words, he does not recognize this god or its authority (5:2). This is still a far cry from Elijah's coarse mocking of Baal on Mt. Carmel.

38 See Glatt-Gilad 2002, 69–74.

39 Deut 28:20; 31:16; Jer 1:16; 2:13; 5:7; 5:19; 9:12; 16:11; 19:4.

40 Hos 2:15; 4:6; 13:6; Isa 65:11; Jer 2:32; 13:25; 18:15; cf. 23:27.

41 Abandoned: Isa 1:4, cf. v. 28; 65:11; Jer 2:17, 19; 17:13; 22:9; 2 Chr 24:20. Forgotten: Hos 8:14; Isa 17:10; Deut 8:14; cf. 4:23; 6:12; 8:19; Jer 3:21.

42 Both abandoned and forgotten: Lam 5:20; Isa 49:14 (according to Zion); in Isa 49:15 Yahweh insists that he can no more forget them than a woman can forget the nursing son of her womb. Forgotten: Hos 4:6; cf. Deut 31:17. Abandoned: Deut 31:17; 2 Chr 12:5; 15:2; 24:20 (in these cases, it is because the people abandoned Yahweh that he abandons them); Ezek 8:12; 9:9; Isa 54:7.

43 Deut 4:31; cf. Isa 41:17; 42:16.

44 The Hera of Euripides' *Heracles* has also been described as sadistic; see, for example, Stróżyński 2013, 237–38.

45 The first is Job 13:15, which Berger quotes in the *qere* (what is recited), not the *ketib* (what is written). The *kere* has "though he slay me, yet I will trust in him," while the MT has "behold, he slays me, I have no hope." The masochistic attitude is illustrated only by the recited version, which functions to tame Job's far from masochistic stance. In 42:6, Job does not say "I abhor myself," as Berger has it; the word "myself" does not appear in the verse. The verb אמאס has no object; a number of scholars translate "I submit," "I reject" or "I retract" (see Clines 2011, 1207–1208, 1218–20; Habel 1985, 575–76, 582). In effect, Job is giving up his legal suit against Yahweh; see n. 47, below.

46 Job 4:17–19; 15:14–16; 25:4–6; see Lasine 1988, 30–38. Newsom, citing Berger, argues that Eliphaz and Bildad embrace "the masochistic perspective of human corruptibility" (2009, 143).

47 See Lasine 2001, 182–89; 2012, 188–89. Admittedly, Job's recantation in 42:6 means that he has dropped his "class-action suit" against God for his indifference to—and thereby his injustice toward—the many innocent sufferers about whom Job has become increasingly aware. However, having heard God's speeches from the whirlwind, Job may have concluded that it is futile to reason with a God who is interested only in power and unquestioning obedience.

48 See, for example, Stolorow 1975, 442; Rosegrant 2012, 935; Hibbard 1992, 502; Békés *et al.* 2018, 477, 479–80.

49 This is one aspect of the problem of intersubjectivity described by Hegel in the master-slave section of his *Phenomenology* (1952, 146–50).

50 Lam 3:30 could easily strike a reader as the description of a masochistic gesture. The speaker has been advising that one should patiently wait for Yahweh's help with

hopefulness. The one waiting should offer his cheek to the one striking him, and be filled with disgrace (v. 30), thereby voluntarily increasing his humiliation. However, the speaker does not say that the recipient of this blow will experience a feeling of voluptuous humiliation.

51 חפץ indicates pleasure or desire, for example, in 1 Kgs 5:8, 10; 9:11; 10:13.
52 For a critique of Gonen's project, and particularly his use of psychological concepts (including Winnicott's notion of "transitional objects"), see Cohen 2007, 397–98.
53 At the beginning of *Answer to Job*, Jung refers to testimonies prior to the writing of Job which give "a contradictory picture of Yahweh." These testimonies depict "a God who knew no moderation in his emotions and suffered precisely from this lack of moderation. He himself admitted that he was eaten up with rage and jealousy and that this knowledge was painful to him" (1969, 365). As we discussed earlier, Yahweh does characterize himself as jealous in the HB, but he is hardly admitting that he is being "eaten up" with rage and jealousy, let alone that he finds the knowledge that he is being eaten up to be painful. It is his people's abandoning him which is painful to Yahweh.
54 For example, Allport 1961, 275–307; Helson and Wink 1987, 531; Josefsson *et al.* 2013, 713.
55 Yahweh is of course immortal. However, studies have shown that childhood fears of abandonment can develop into mortality fear once the child has become old enough to understand the irreversibility of death. See Lasine 2019, 69 n. 23, 99–102, 110.
56 Henniger and Harris (2015, 303) observe that among the subjects of their study "the likelihood of envying certain domains shifted across the life span." With age (and therefore with maturity?) "scholastic success, social success, looks, and romantic success were less envied, whereas money was more envied with age."

4 Jealousy for Yahweh and divine vengeance

In this chapter I begin by focusing on the three biblical figures who are said to be—or who describe themselves as—jealous for Yahweh: the priest Phinehas, the prophet Elijah, and king Jehu. All three seem to identify with Yahweh's emotion of outrage against his unfaithful spouse Israel and with his tendency to kill humans when jealousy drives him to do so (e.g., Deut 29:19; 32:16, 21; Ezek 16:38). To that extent, their actions reveal their interpretation of Yahweh's jealousy. Nevertheless, all three act on their own authority when they slay their victims. Next I turn to Moses, who, while never said to be jealous for Yahweh, orders a vengeful slaughter which far exceeds the carnage perpetrated by Phinehas, Elijah, and Jehu. This act is the eradication of all Midianite male children. The chapter concludes with an analysis of Samson's revenge against the Philistines and Yahweh's role in the violence committed by this Nazarite judge.

1. The three figures who are called "jealous for Yahweh"

a. Phinehas

The only mention of Aaron's grandson Phinehas prior to Numbers 25 is the birth notice in Exod 6:25. Numbers 25 begins by reporting that Israel settled in Shittim. In Num 21:25, 31 readers had been informed that Israel settled in the Amorite city of Heshbon and its "daughters," that is, the nearby towns and villages. This is all we know about Israelite settlement in the region when we reach Numbers 25. This chapter tells us only one thing about the quotidian activities of the Israelites and the attitudes of the native people toward their occupiers: "the people began to commit adultery with the daughters of Moab" (25:1). The people accept the women's invitation to the sacrifices of their gods, where they eat and bow down to those gods (v. 2). This violates Yahweh's earlier warning not to bow down to any other god, lest the Israelites accept invitations to attend the sacrifices of those gods and then eat the sacrifice (Exod 34:14–16). Exod 34:14 is also the verse in which Yahweh declares that his name is Jealous. When Exod 34:14–16 and Num 25:1–2 are read together, we should expect the Israelites' behavior in Shittim to trigger a major manifestation of divine jealousy and wrath.

DOI: 10.4324/b23212-4

This is especially true since the chapter presents both figurative and literal examples of Yahweh's spouse Israel being unfaithful to her divine husband. Milgrom (1990, 212) asserts that Num 25:1 is "the only place in the Bible where this verb [זנה] in its literal sense takes a masculine subject." The verb *zanah* can denote "playing the whore," fornicating, or committing adultery. In Num 25:1 it is the figurative sense of *zanah* which seems intended, not the literal;[1] the male Israelites are unfaithful to their "husband" Yahweh by consorting with the Moabite gods.

The Israelites attaching or yoking themselves (הנצמדים) to the Baal of Peor in this manner makes Yahweh understandably angry (Num 25:3–5). He responds by ordering Moses to hold the leaders responsible for the apostasy. Moses is commanded to impale the leaders of the people (literally, the "heads") before the sun, in order to turn away Yahweh's wrath (v. 4). Moses then alters Yahweh's order, telling one group of leaders, the judges, to kill all their men who have yoked themselves to the Baal of Peor (v. 5). Instead of the leaders being responsible for their followers, now each individual follower who is guilty of infidelity to Yahweh is to be killed. As far as we know, neither order is actually carried out, because Zimri, an Israelite male, brings to the community a prominent[2] Midianite woman named Cozbi, while the Israelites are all weeping at the tent of meeting (v. 6). The weeping implies that a plague has already begun. Later we learn that twenty-four thousand people died from the plague (25:9).

It is at this point that the priest Phinehas makes his entry into the story. When he sees Zimri and Cozbi arrive, he picks up his spear and follows them into what is apparently a tent-chamber (Num 25:7–8). Inside, the couple are engaging in what seems to be a literal case of sexual infidelity to Yahweh. Phinehas then kills the two *in flagrante delicto* (25:8). One thrust of his spear suffices to kill both. Since the weapon stabs Cozbi through the belly (קבתה), Milgrom concludes that the pair were skewered through their genitals (1990, 215).[3] In short, Phinehas acts like a jealous husband who returns home to find his wife in bed with another man and reaches for his weapon of choice.

Phinehas' action turns away Yahweh's wrath and halts the plague (Num 25:8, 11). The priest's thoughts, words, and emotions are not reported by the narrator. His motivation for the killings is left unstated. Yahweh seems to deduce Phinehas' emotions from his act of violence. Yahweh, Israel's betrayed husband, lauds and rewards the priest for killing the couple, because Phinehas was "jealous with my jealousy among them" (בקנאו את-קנאתי בתוכם; 25:11). Yahweh identifies with what he perceives to be Phinehas' identification with his feeling of jealousy, even though Phinehas acted without being told to do so by Yahweh. Yahweh does not tell Phinehas how he views the executions. It is Moses to whom God gives this information. Ironically, the prophet Moses is never said to be jealous for Yahweh.[4]

The final biblical allusion to this incident occurs in Ps 106:30. This verse minimizes the violence of Phinehas' act, saying only that Phinehas stood and "intervened" (or "rendered judgment"; ויפלל), resulting in the plague being restrained.[5] Phinehas is also mentioned in Num 31:6. There we learn that he accompanied the troops as a priest when they attacked the Midianites. While the mere mention of his name could remind readers of Phinehas' earlier jealousy for Yahweh, the Hebrew term for jealousy and envy (*qin'ah*) does not appear in Numbers 31. It is actually Phinehas' father Eleazar who conducts all priestly business in the remainder of this chapter. Nevertheless, later ancient traditions (e.g., Philo *Moses* 1.56; Josephus *Ant.* 4.159) and some modern scholars make Phinehas the leader or commander in chief in the ensuing military victory, rather than Moses or Moses' designated replacement Joshua (see n. 47, below).

While there is no quoted speech from Phinehas in either Numbers 25 or 31, he does speak as part of a group voice in Josh 22:16–20, in a speech which includes an allusion to the incident at Peor. Phinehas and ten leaders, one from each tribe, are sent to the tribes of Reuben, Gad, and the half-tribe of Manasseh to implore them not to rebel against Yahweh when they settle in the Transjordan. Finally, in Judg 20:27–28 Phinehas is standing by the ark when the Israelites address a question to Yahweh. Yahweh himself is said to answer; nothing is mentioned about Phinehas voicing that answer. In short, Phinehas remains a "flat" character throughout the Hebrew Bible.

Although Phinehas never states that he is jealous for Yahweh, his actions at Peor are reported in a book in which envy and jealousy are repeatedly mentioned as destructive emotions, from the ordeal on behalf of the jealous husband in Numbers 5, to Joshua's perceived jealousy for Moses' sake in Num 11:28–29, to the Phinehas episode and its aftermath. While forms of the root *qn'* are absent in Numbers 12 and 16, these chapters also focus on human envy and resentment. Moses' siblings and his first-cousin Korah all resent and envy Moses' position as leader. Korah and his company even project their own envy onto Moses when they accuse him of jealously hoarding power at their expense.

b. Elijah

Elijah twice tells Yahweh that he has been "very jealous for Yahweh" (קנא קנאתי ליהוה; 1 Kgs 19:10, 14). It is important to examine these statements in context. After the prophet flees following Jezebel's death threat, he journeys south to Horeb for forty days on the strength of two angel-served meals (1 Kgs 19:1–8). Ensconced in a cave, Yahweh asks him what he is doing there. Elijah begins his answer by proclaiming that he has been very jealous for Yahweh.

Surprisingly, Elijah's answer does not mention the previous actions which might be viewed as illustrating this jealousy, such as his demonstration of Yahweh's power in contrast to the impotence of Baal (1 Kgs 18:20–39). The contest on Mt. Carmel is not something which Yahweh told Elijah to arrange; it is entirely Elijah's doing. Nevertheless, when Elijah calls upon Yahweh to demonstrate that he is God in Israel, and that he, Elijah, is Yahweh's servant, Yahweh backs him up by producing "fire of Yahweh" to miraculously consume the burnt offering (1 Kgs 18:36–38). Nor does Elijah illustrate his jealousy for Yahweh by pointing to his singlehanded slaughter of four hundred and fifty Baal prophets after the contest (1 Kgs 18:40), an action about which Yahweh makes no comment, either positive or negative.

Instead of citing these actions, Elijah explains his presence at Horeb by listing a series of Israel's alleged sins: "the people of Israel have abandoned your covenant, torn down your altars, and slain your prophets with the sword, and I, I alone, am left, and they seek my life to take it" (1 Kgs 19:10). These charges cannot be taken at face value. Elijah makes it seem as though his flight from Jezebel has been tantamount to being expelled by his community, even though he had succeeded in prompting his audience to unanimously affirm Yahweh (and presumably himself) at Mt. Carmel (1 Kgs 18:39; cf. v. 36). Moreover, Yahweh reminds Elijah that around seven thousand Israelites have not bent their knee to Baal (19:18). Elijah's charge that the Israelites have "torn down" Yahweh's altars (1 Kgs 19:14) is usually validated by referring to the destroyed altar on Carmel repaired by Elijah (1 Kgs 18:30). However, in 1 Kgs 18:31–32 Elijah builds a new altar rather than repairing an old one. Moreover, the Carmel mountain range may have marked the border between Israel and Tyre during this period, raising the question whether the altar repaired in 18:30 was for Yahweh, and, if so, whether this was an appropriate cult site (see Lasine 2012, 128–29). As for prophets being killed, it is the Sidonian Jezebel, not the Israelites, who sought to cut off the prophets of Yahweh, including Elijah.

Finally, Elijah's claim that he is the only prophet left, and that the Israelites are still trying to kill him, is patently false. Elijah had already made this claim before "all the people" on Mt. Carmel, pointing out that he was there as the lone Yahweh prophet facing four hundred and fifty Baal prophets (18:22). Yet Elijah is not the only prophet left. We know about the hundred prophets whom Obadiah saved from Ahab and Jezebel, and we know that Elijah knows, because Obadiah told him (18:13; cf. v. 4). Chapters 20 and 22 drive the point home by showing other prophets who act loyally and courageously on Yahweh's behalf. But in Elijah's eyes, the situation in 19:10 is a case of all against one, just as it was on Mt. Carmel.[6]

Yahweh's response to Elijah's complaints is to grant the prophet a theophanic vision, culminating with the "voice of thin silence" (19:11–12). Apparently Yahweh was not satisfied with Elijah's stated reasons for being in Horeb, because he again asks Elijah what he is doing there (v. 13). The theophany seems to have had no effect on the prophet, since he answers by listing the same series of grievances that he expressed earlier (v. 14). This time Yahweh replies not with a theophany but with specific instructions detailing what Elijah should do up north (vv. 15–18). These tasks include the "anointing" of two kings, the Aramean Hazael and the Israelite Jehu, as well as the anointing of Elijah's replacement Elisha (19:15–18). Yet Elijah does not end up accomplishing any of these tasks.[7]

Viewed in context, Elijah's repeated claim to have been very jealous for Yahweh is difficult to detach from his perceived victimhood and his expressions of self-pity. Elijah is admittedly a very complex character. Elsewhere I have offered a detailed examination of Elijah's character and the ways his character has been construed over the centuries (Lasine 2004; 2012, 115–43). For our present purposes, it is sufficient to conclude that Elijah's perception of himself as very jealous for Yahweh must be evaluated in terms of a given reader's assessment of the prophet's personality and trustworthiness.

c. Jehu

Jehu, like Elijah, refers to himself as jealous for Yahweh. He does so before engaging in an activity that he considers illustrative of such jealousy, while Elijah asserts that he has been jealous for Yahweh in the past. Jehu makes this declaration to Jehonadab, while Elijah does so to Yahweh himself. The two zealots kill large numbers of people both before and after declaring themselves jealous for Yahweh. In terms of the themes of this study, the Jehu story has an extra dimension. He, unlike Phinehas and Elijah, is explicitly given a mission of vengeance by a prophet of God. After discussing Jehu as jealous for Yahweh, I will therefore consider Jehu as an avenger.

In 2 Kgs 10:15 Jehu encounters Jehonadab son of Rechab. After exchanging greetings Jehu asks "is your heart straight (or right) as my heart with your heart?" Jehonadab answers with one word, the only word he utters in the Bible: יש ("it is").[8] Readers are not told about any previous relationship between the two men. In effect, Jehu is asking Jehonadab "are you with me or against me?" As G. Jones (1984, 468) points out, "Jehonadab in associating himself with Jehu was giving a sign of his allegiance to the one who had established himself on the throne." Given that Jehu has just slaughtered the last group of people he met on his journey, without any prophetic mandate to do so (2 Kgs 10:12–14), it would seem prudent for Jehonadab to affirm that Jehu is the legitimate king, no matter what his actual political views might be.

Jehu proceeds to invite Jehonadab to come with him and observe his jealousy for Yahweh (2 Kgs 10:16). Sweeney (2007, 338) contends that "the enigmatic Jehonadab . . . plays a key role" in 2 Kings 10, "particularly since he is identified as a zealous supporter of YHWH." Sweeney adds that in Jeremiah 35 "the Rekabite house represents an idealized form of YHWH worship." Both of these claims are false. No jealousy or zeal for Yahweh is predicated of Jehonadab in 2 Kings 10; he merely witnesses two cases of Jehu's mass killings without reacting in any way, as far as we are told.[9] Jeremiah 35 does call Jehonadab founder of the Rechabite clan, but it does not equate the Rechabites' abstinence from wine and farming, or their preference for living in tents, with ideal Yahwistic worship. The point being made in that chapter is that the descendants of Jehonadab have obeyed their "father"[10] and followed the way of life dictated by him, whereas the way of life commanded by Israel's father Yahweh has not been followed by his child Israel.

It is nevertheless possible that Jehu views Jehonadab as a pious man in 2 Kings 10. If so, it would be in Jehu's interest to have such a person witness his brutal massacres, so that Jehonadab might confirm that the usurper's motivation was jealousy for Yahweh. Clearly, we must make a judgment concerning Jehu's sincerity and trustworthiness before we can decide whether his zealotry is the result of devotion to Yahweh or political expediency.

Before making that decision we should take into account Jehu's references to the prophet Elijah. After Jehu orders the execution of queen Jezebel and runs over her body with his chariot, he cites Yahweh's word about Jezebel which he spoke by his servant Elijah (2 Kgs 9:36–37), although he adds to what Elijah had said in 1 Kgs 21:23.[11] In 2 Kgs 10:10 Jehu informs the people of Samaria that Yahweh has done what he had spoke by his servant Elijah, presumably referring to the annihilation of Ahab's house, proclaimed by Elijah in 1 Kgs 21:21–22. In 2 Kgs 10:17 the narrator also mentions the word of Yahweh spoken to Elijah, just after Jehu has wiped out the remnant of Ahab's house in Samaria, the first mass killing observed by Jehonadab.[12]

Jehu is stressing that the predictions uttered by the prophet who was jealous for Yahweh are being fulfilled by the king who claims to be jealous for Yahweh. Is Jehu attempting to justify his violence by comparing himself to the violent prophet Elijah, who is never criticized by Yahweh even though he killed hundreds of people in 1 Kings 18 and 2 Kings 1? Fretheim (1999, 172) believes that it is the narrator who is presenting Jehu "as Elijah in royal robes." Long (1991, 134) focuses on the writer, who "provides a bit of alchemy" in 2 Kgs 10, turning a "ruthless rebel ... into king-zealot-for-Yahweh." Neither considers the possibility that Jehu himself is engaging in impression management by linking himself to Elijah. Long's skeptical reference to the writer's "alchemy" also casts doubt on the depth of Jehu's supposed jealousy for Yahweh.

From the character Jehu's point of view, claiming a motivation shared by the priest Phinehas and the prophet Elijah has another advantage: neither Phinehas nor Elijah requested permission from Yahweh before they engaged in multiple killings for which they were not criticized, let alone punished. Jehu also kills without requesting permission from Yahweh, slaughtering not only the relatives of Ahaziah but the worshippers of Baal. The young prophet in 2 Kgs 9:6–10 had said nothing about killing the followers of Baal. Elijah had also massacred prophets of Baal without Yahweh commanding it (1 Kgs 18:40). In 1 Kgs 19:17 Yahweh does order Elijah to anoint Hazael, adding that "he (or, "the one") who escapes from the sword of Hazael shall Jehu slay."[13] Jehu shows no awareness of this divine instruction to Elijah, no matter who is meant by "the one."

At the beginning of 2 Kings 9, Elisha calls one of the "sons of the prophets" and directs him to locate Jehu in Ramoth-Gilead, privately anoint Jehu as king of Israel, and then rush away (9:1–3). When the "young prophet"[14] (v. 4) is alone with Jehu, he delivers Elisha's message of anointment in slightly expanded form,[15] and then makes crucial additions: "you shall strike the house of Ahab your master, and I will avenge on Jezebel the blood of my servants the prophets, and the blood of all the servants of Yahweh" (v. 7). He then elaborates on the coming slaughter of Ahab's line and Jezebel, likening it to the fate of two previous northern royal houses, those of Jeroboam and Baasha (vv. 8–10).

The young prophet echoes Elijah's prediction that all members of Ahab's house who "urinate against the wall" will be cut off (2 Kgs 9:8; cf. 1 Kgs 21:21). These prophecies echo two earlier cases in which those urinating against the wall (משתין בקיר) are targeted, Ahijah's prophecy concerning Jeroboam's house (1 Kgs 14:10) and the narrator's report concerning the annihilation of Baasha's house (1 Kgs 16:11). All four of these passages also mention dogs eating at least one member of the doomed house. However, the young prophet in 2 Kgs 9:10 limits this punishment to Jezebel, not all males who are cut off in the city. He also omits that those who die in the country will be eaten by birds (contrast 1 Kgs 21:24; cf. 1 Kgs 14:11, 16:4). When Zimri fulfills the prophecy against the house of Baasha, he goes beyond the prophet Jehu's instructions by wiping out all of Baasha's friends as well as his kin (1 Kgs 16:11; cf. 16:2–4). One might argue that king Jehu does the same when he massacres all the relatives of Ahaziah who were visiting up north to inquire after the welfare (שלום) of the "sons" of the king and queen (2 Kgs 10:13–14).

The narrator gives us no indication that Jehu had any interest in becoming a usurper prior to the arrival of the young prophet. Nor is anything said about Jehu objecting to the state's religious policies prior to his announcement that he is jealous for Yahweh. By linking the extermination of Ahab's house to several previous divinely sanctioned slaughters, the young prophet's forecast allows the usurper Jehu to cement his position as ruler by eliminating all members of the previous regime in the name of divine vengeance. A usurper would realize the necessity of eradicating the members of the old ruling family without having to be told. What the young prophet provides is a pious excuse for doing what a canny usurper would do in any case.

The fact that these additions are so significant has led commentators to speculate on the young prophet's reliability. Some assume that Elisha must have provided the young man with the extra predictions; after all, Elijah also expanded what Yahweh told him to say when he delivered a key oracle to Ahab.[16] Others assume that because the "son of the prophets" is called "the young prophet," he is not merely a servant or admirer of Elisha but a prophet who is qualified to receive oracles directly from Yahweh, which must have occurred here (Rofé 1988, 82). Some of the rabbis identify the unnamed young prophet with Jonah ben Amittai, thereby ensuring his credibility (*S. 'Olam Rab.* 18–19; cf. *Gen. Rab.* 21.5). At the other end of the spectrum of opinion, Roncace (2020, 172) believes that the prophet was "not following his master's commands very carefully."[17] García-Treto (1992, 161) goes further, claiming that the young prophet "disobeys" his master Elisha "by adding to Elisha's terse message."[18]

In 1 Kgs 19:15–17 Yahweh had told Elijah to anoint Hazael and Jehu, adding that he who escapes from the sword of Hazael will be slain by Jehu, and he who escapes from Jehu's sword will be slain by Elisha. As mentioned earlier, Elijah anoints none of these three men. Elisha does not anoint Hazael either, but he is involved in the coup which allows Hazael to gain the throne of Aram, and go on to kill many Israelite men, women, children, and fetuses (2 Kgs 8:7–13). King Ben-Hadad of Aram sends Hazael to fetch the visiting Elisha. The king is ill and wants to know if he will recover from his sickness (8:7–9). Elisha's reply gives Hazael the idea of killing the bed-ridden king and taking over the monarchy, leading to the grisly deaths of many Israelites (vv. 10–12).

This story illustrates how indirect and convoluted the path from prophecy to fulfillment can become. This is true of 2 Kings 9–10 as well. There is no opening scene in which Yahweh tells Elisha to order one of his assistants to anoint Jehu, let alone send him on a mission of vengeance. Elisha gives no reason for directing the young prophet to rush and then flee immediately after anointing Jehu.[19] We have no guarantee that the assistant's additions emanate from

Yahweh or Elisha. The young prophet does not tell Jehu that he was sent by Elisha, and Jehu never mentions being anointed at the behest of Elisha (Rofé 1988, 82). Elijah has long ago left the earth, so he cannot confirm or disconfirm the accuracy of Jehu's memories of what Elijah had predicted. In 2 Kgs 9:25 Jehu asks his comrade Bidkar to recall Yahweh's words the day after Naboth was killed, but Bidkar does not confirm the correctness of Jehu's memory. He simply remains silent.[20]

The fact that the young prophet's words to Jehu remind readers of the obliteration of two preceding royal houses should not lead us to conclude that 2 Kings 9–10 simply adds one more example to the list. There is a crucial difference between this account and the reports of the destruction of the royal lines of Jeroboam and Baasha. In the earlier cases readers were given no details on how the destroyers Baasha and Zimri went about their violent tasks. Here we are given a detailed and vivid description of Jehu's bloody work, including his use of deceptive and manipulative tactics.[21] His aptitude as an assassin is clear, as is his alacrity at carrying out his mission. The extent of the annihilation is underscored by the narrator when he repeatedly reports that Jehu slaughtered his victims until none remained (שאר; 10:11, 14, 17). The details of the carnage wrought by Jehu make the loss of life more disturbing than the brief reports of Baasha's and Zimri's killings.[22]

There is another key difference between the account of Jehu's killings and those of Baasha and Zimri. Only Jehu is given a direct order from Yahweh's representative to wipe out the previous royal house. While prophets predict the extermination of Jeroboam's and Baasha's royal houses (1 Kgs 14:10–12; 16:1–4), neither Baasha nor Zimri is told by a representative of Yahweh to fulfill these prophecies. No reason is given for Baasha's conspiracy against Jeroboam's son Nadab (1 Kgs 15:27–28). Later Yahweh gives the prophet Jehu a speech aimed at Baasha: "I lifted you up from the dust and made you leader over my people Israel" (1 Kgs 16:2). Up to this point, the narrator had given no indication of divine influence on Baasha attaining the throne. Nor is there any indication that Baasha thought he was on a divine mission. He seems to be yet another usurper whose interest is served by eliminating the former ruling house. Similarly, the army officer Zimri is not told by Yahweh or one of his representatives to annihilate both Baasha's kinfolk and his friends (16:11). Since no motive is given for Zimri's act, it appears to be another case of political usurpation.[23]

A final difference between Jehu and the others deserves mention. Jehu is rewarded for his destructive work, while Baasha and Zimri are not. Yahweh tells king Jehu that he has acted well in doing what was right in Yahweh's eyes, according to all that was in Yahweh's heart, when he slaughtered the house of Ahab (2 Kgs 10:30). In contrast, Baasha has his own house eradicated because he did the slaughtering that Yahweh wanted done (ועל אשר-הכה אתו; 1 Kgs 16:7). Baasha is also condemned for not eliminating Jeroboam's cult. Of course Jehu did not remove this cult either, but far from having his family wiped out, four generations of Jehu's sons will sit on the throne (2 Kgs 10:30). Zimri, who eliminates Baasha's line, rules for only one week before committing suicide under duress

(1 Kgs 16:18). The reason given for his quick demise is his adherence to Jeroboam's cult, a practice he has in common with both Baasha and Jehu (16:19).

The in-depth description of Jehu's killings, and the contrasts between his fate and those of his fellow usurpers, may prompt readers to ask themselves if Jehu's violence is excessive and his reward unjust. Lamb (2007, 85) believes that "Jehu's zeal justifies his excessive violence." This statement concedes that the violence is "excessive." As noted above, Jehu's claim of jealousy for Yahweh might be *his* attempt to justify his violence, but it is not affirmed by Yahweh, the listener Jehonadab, or the narrator. Moreover, the narrator does not attempt to excuse Jehu's slaughter of Ahaziah's relatives by mentioning a divine command to kill them, or by calling all the relatives evil. The narrator simply reports the explanation given by Ahaziah's relatives, namely, that they are on their way to visit the northern royal family (2 Kgs 10:12–14). As Long (1991, 117) points out, the narrator relates these events in a "dispassionate" manner. Finally, the narrator does not attempt to portray Jehu's deception and slaughter of the Baal worshippers as commanded or foretold by Yahweh. Taken together, these features of the narrative increase the likelihood that some readers might find the violence of Jehu and his men to be excessive and, in some cases, unnecessary.

If Jehu is viewed as following the instructions given to Elijah in 1 Kgs 19: 16–17 and fulfilling Elijah's prophecies in 1 Kgs 21:21–24, it is difficult to see how his violence could be called "excessive" without calling Yahweh excessively violent. It is Yahweh who wants Ahab's house to be annihilated, as he had desired the obliteration of the houses of Jeroboam and Baasha. Is it possible for any amount of violence or revenge to be "excessive" if it is willed by a deity whose dignity and power are both infinite? As I will discuss in Chapter 5.3, some classical scholars believe that the Greek gods possess "the divine prerogative of excessively great vengeance" (S. Shapiro 1996, 353; cf. Mikalson 1991, 138–39). Humans who usurp this divine prerogative, even with the intention of punishing those who have offended the deity, will themselves be punished. Does Yahweh punish humans who indulge in excessive violence when avenging him? Jehu goes beyond his divine mandate to commit violent acts against Ahaziah's relatives and the Baal worshippers, but those acts are not condemned or punished by Yahweh. In the next section I will ask whether the same is true when Moses goes well beyond Yahweh's order to "to avenge the vengeance of the children of Israel from the Midianites" in Num 31:2.

2. Moses the infanticidal avenger in Numbers 31

Every son born (כל-הבן הילוד) you shall throw into the river and every daughter you shall let live.

(Exod 1:22)

Kill every male among the little children (כל-זכר בטף) . . . but all the female children (וכל הטף בנשים) . . . keep alive for yourselves.

(Num 31:17–18)

Jealousy for Yahweh and divine vengeance 71

Two similar infanticide orders given by two very different speakers: the Pharaoh of the oppression and the prophet Moses. Juxtaposing these verses highlights the unsettling fact that Moses, who had once been a target of a leader's infanticide order, issues an almost identical order when his own career as leader is at its end. In this section I ask why Yahweh's uniquely humble and trusted servant (Num 12:3, 7–8) would demand that male children be exterminated, a fate from which he himself had once been spared. After examining Exodus 1 and Numbers 31 in more detail, I will compare Moses' commands in Num 31:17–18 to the similar account of mass slaughter in Judg 21:10–12. The section concludes by viewing Moses' infanticide order in the context of Numbers 25 and Moses' career as a whole. While Moses never calls himself "jealous for Yahweh," and the narrator never characterizes him in that way, some commentators believe that Moses does exhibit such jealousy (if not envy of Phinehas as well). These suggestions will also be evaluated at the end of this section.

a. Moses in Num 31:17–18 and Pharaoh in Exod 1:22

In Numbers 31 Moses' intended victims are Midianite. Yahweh holds the Midianites responsible for Israel's committing apostasy with the "daughters of Moab" at Shittim (Num 25:1).[24] While many readers assume that Moses is merely executing Yahweh's verdict in Num 31:17–18,[25] Moses' directives are not presented as something Yahweh told him to announce. The prophet is expressing his own rage (ויקצף משה; v. 14). That Moses expands Yahweh's instructions concerning the Midianites (Num 25:17–18; 31:2) should not come as a surprise, since he had already changed the substance and principle of Yahweh's command to punish the heads of the people for the Peor affair (Num 25:4–5; see Section 1.a, above). As far back as Exod 8:5–9 (Heb.), Moses had improvised a self-promoting challenge to the Pharaoh without consulting Yahweh first.[26]

Surprisingly, Moses' directive to kill all male Midianite children is not mentioned in many modern commentaries on Numbers 31.[27] Consequently the disturbing parallel between Moses' command and that of the Pharaoh in Exod 1:22 goes unmentioned as well. Among ancient commentators, Josephus omits Moses' infanticide order (*Ant.* 4.162), while Philo insists that Moses actually showed *mercy* to both the girls and the boys (*Moses* 1.311).[28]

Adding to the startling nature of Moses' command is the fact that he gives no reason for the extermination of the captured male children. A number of scholars have suggested a plausible explanation: he is preventing a new generation from arising and exacting revenge.[29] Exodus 1–14 certainly illustrates the danger of allowing even one targeted child to survive.[30] So does the later story of Hadad the Edomite in 1 Kings 11. After having escaped David and Joab's extermination of Edomite males when he was a little boy (נער קטן), Hadad returns to Edom as an adult, becoming a adversary (שטן) to David's son Solomon (1 Kgs 11:14–22).[31]

In the case of the Pharaoh in Exodus 1, there is no need to speculate about motive. He tells his people that the Hebrew slaves are too many and too mighty for them.[32] He is afraid that if Egypt were attacked by a foreign power, the slaves might join the attack and then flee Egypt (Exod 1:9–10). The king says nothing about the Hebrew newborns growing up to rebel. His worst nightmare is the exodus, not "regime change" initiated by rebellious slaves. The Pharaoh does not command the killing of Hebrew male babies (vv. 16, 22) until after he has failed to weaken the slave population by increasing the harshness of their labor. He does not say whether the infanticide is a temporary measure or whether he intends to mate the spared Hebrew females with Egyptian males in order to produce a new generation of Egyptian slaves, as Calvin suggests (1852, 45).

In neither narrative are readers explicitly told that the slaughter of children is actually carried out. In Exodus 2, the only baby we hear of being put in the river is Moses himself. While Moses does not attribute his kill order to Yahweh in Num 31:17, as he had done earlier when he commanded the Levites to slay their family members and neighbors (Exod 32:27), the narrator gives us little reason to doubt that the Midianite children were slaughtered.[33]

b. Moses' alteration of Yahweh's call for vengeance

What did Yahweh actually tell Moses to do about the Midianites? In Num 31:2 Yahweh instructs Moses "to avenge the vengeance of (נקם נקמת) the children of Israel from the Midianites."[34] Moses then demands that the Israelites arm for war, "that they might be against Midian, to set the vengeance of Yahweh on Midian" (v. 3).[35] Both versions pick up on Yahweh's earlier directive at the end of Numbers 25: "show hostility (צרור) toward the Midianites and strike them" (25:17). There, and in Num 31:2, Yahweh leaves unspecified *how* they should show hostility and gain vengeance. Should they strike the Midianites with the intent of totally eradicating them or simply inflict a military defeat on them and then demand tribute?

In Num 25:18 Yahweh tells Moses that the Midianites had been "crafty" to Israel in the affair of Peor. He singles out the Midianites' "sister" Cozbi who was slain by Phinehas on the day of the plague. This also leaves room for interpretation. How were the Midianites "crafty"? Yahweh says nothing about Balaam playing a role in craftily causing the "adultery" at Shittim. Yet in Num 31:16 Moses blames the women as a group in the affair (רבד), because they committed infidelity against Yahweh at the word (רבד) of Balaam, which then caused the plague. As I mentioned earlier, Moses does not attempt to explain or justify his next order, which is to exterminate the male children. Together, Moses' commands in vv. 17–18 are designed to eradicate the Midianite people, or at least their national identity, since the virginal female captives will be assimilated into the Israelite community.[36] Ironically, Moses himself married the Midianite Zipporah, and the couple's two half-Midianite sons became part of the Israelite nation.

c. Calls for mass slaughter in Num 31:17–18 and Judg 21:10–12

The brutality of the measures taken by Moses in Num 31:17–18 is underscored when that mass killing is compared to the slaughter of fellow Israelites reported in Judg 21:10–12. Here the male adults and children of Jabesh-Gilead are killed, and the female virgins[37] are left alive to be given as slave-wives to Israelite men. When one views this massacre in the larger context of Judges 19–21, the narrator's attitude is clearly negative. In this travesty of a holy war, the avengers are punished when Yahweh twice permits them to go into battle, only to lose badly (Judg 20:18–25).[38]

After Yahweh finally allows the Israelites to nearly exterminate their brother tribe of Benjamin (Judg 20:46–48), the Israelites decide to regrow the population of their former enemy. They do so, in part, by exterminating the males of Jabesh-Gilead and giving the women to Benjaminite survivors, using the pretext that Jabesh had not participated in the earlier fratricidal war. The tribes had sworn not to wed their daughters to Benjaminites (Judg 21:1). Jabesh-Gilead is targeted as a source for Benjaminite brides because the town had apparently violated the assembly's "great oath" to kill those who did not participate in this enterprise (21:5). However, as Niditch points out, "no one seems to think of hunting down disloyal members of the league until the need for women becomes clear" (2011, 209). Non-participation is merely an excuse for mass murder, designed to solve a problem created by the tribes themselves (cf. Hackett 2004, 363). Ironically, the killings at Jabesh are motivated by a desire to save the very brother tribe which the other Israelites had almost exterminated in the third battle (Judg 20:46–48).

The parallels in language[39] between Num 31:17–18 and Judg 21:10–11 are important, because, once again, many readers tend to assume (as do the avengers) that Yahweh approves of this supposed holy war. The fact that the tribes use the verb *ḥaram* (חרם) to describe the slaughter in Judg 21:11 does not guarantee that this is a legitimate holy war.[40] The only other use of this verb against fellow Israelites concerns worshipping other gods in one of the cities which Yahweh has given to his people (Deut 13:13–16). No such personal affront to Yahweh's exclusive sovereignty had been committed by the citizens of Jabesh-Gilead, and Yahweh's jealous wrath is not mentioned in all of Judges 19–21. This is a time when every man does what is right in his own eyes, rather than what is right in Yahweh's eyes (Judg 21:25; cf. 17:6). The similarity between Moses' infanticide orders in Numbers 31 and the condemnable acts of violence at Jabesh-Gilead suggests that we have reason to question the morality and wisdom of Moses' actions against the Midianite women and children.[41] As K. Brown puts it, the comparison "is not flattering to Moses" (2015, 78).

Another case of mass slaughter which appears to be condemned by the author is reported in Genesis 34. In this scene, the duped and incapacitated males of Shechem are slaughtered (34:25), and their little children (כל-טפם) are appropriated by Jacob's sons, along with the women (v. 29). Jacob condemns the violent actions of his killer sons Simeon and Levi and later curses their wrath and cruelty (Gen 34:30; 49:5–7). Jacob's judgment would seem to reflect the author's view of this mass violence, especially because the "scattering" and "dissolution" Jacob predicts for the sons' descendants actually takes place (see, e.g., Hamilton 1995, 652). Nevertheless, some commentators believe that the narrator "seems to approve" of Simon and Levi's actions (Driver 1904, 307) or that the narrator may be "picturing Simeon and Levi as individuals of conscience and integrity," when contrasted with their brothers (Hamilton 1995, 371).

Carmichael compares Genesis 34 with Numbers 31, albeit in problematic fashion. He views Moses' death orders in Numbers 31 as a critique of Simeon and Levi. In the judgment of the Numbers narrator, the brothers were not violent enough; they should have killed the married women along with the men. Carmichael concedes that the Hivite women in Genesis 34 do not engage in seductive activity, as the Midianite women (allegedly) do in Numbers 31. He then claims, without evidence, that Dinah "made herself available to Shechem" and "becomes a seductress"! Consequently the Genesis narrator "suggests a negative evaluation" of Dinah (2012, 155–56). For Carmichael, "the judgment emerging from Numbers 31 is that Jacob should have shown a comparable ferocity in Genesis 34" (2012, 156).

d. Vengeance and the "battle" in Num 31:7–8

When Moses alters the divine command to "avenge the Israelites' vengeance" into a mission to "avenge Yahweh on the Midianites" (Num 31:2–3) he sets himself up as the agent of Yahweh's desire for vengeance and vindication. That goal is actually accomplished *before* Moses' infanticide order. How it was accomplished is not entirely clear. Num 31:7–8 does not exclude the possibility that the attack against the Midianites was actually a massacre of a people who had their guard down rather than a battle in which both sides were "large organized armies, within a clearly stratified society of priests, commanders, soldiers, and citizens," as Niditch assumes (1993b, 82). Noting that "details of the war are really non-existent here," Ashley observes that "the impression given is one surprise attack rather than a long war waged on many fronts" (1993, 589). Apart from an unmentioned miracle, what other reason could there be for the Israelites not suffering even one casualty (Num 31:49), while their enemy is totally annihilated?[42]

Another surprise attack on an unsuspecting foe is also reported in Judges, when the Danites annihilate the peaceful population of Laish, an isolated town whose inhabitants lived quietly and securely (Judg 18:7–10, 27–28). The Danites' action is not a case of vengeance; they simply wanted the land for themselves. They burned the existing town, rebuilt it, and named it after their ancestor Dan. Neither this act or the later eradication of the Jabesh-Gileadites is said to be approved by Yahweh.

e. Numbers 31 and the Bible's presentation of Moses

If we view Moses' commands in the context of the Bible's entire presentation of the prophet's character, we might gain another perspective on Moses' infanticide order. Yahweh intends Moses' orchestrating of vengeance against the Midianites to be the prophet's last official act before he is "gathered to his people" (Num 31:2). We have to go all the way back to Moses' first reported act as an adult to find the sole example of Moses engaging in violence against another person. Long before he is commissioned as Yahweh's prophet, Moses strikes an Egyptian who was striking a Hebrew (Exod 2:11–14). Once Moses reluctantly accepts that commission many years later, he has to endure the continual murmuring of his ungrateful followers as well as the envy of his siblings (Num 12:2) and first-cousin Korah (Num 16:1–3; cf. Ps 106:16), all of whom view Moses as hogging the spotlight.

In Num 20:12 Moses is informed by Yahweh that he will not be allowed to enter the land, because he struck the rock twice instead of speaking to it. After Moses and Aaron had gathered the assembly Moses declared "hear now, you rebels, shall we bring water for you out of this rock?" (20:10). These words, followed by Moses hitting the rock, certainly suggest anger,[43] but the narrator does not characterize it as jealous anger for Yahweh. What matters to Yahweh is that Moses and Aaron failed to sanctify him in the eyes of the people. As a result, Moses will not lead those people into Canaan.[44] In Num 25:3–4, 11 Yahweh's anger is turned back by an action which Yahweh *does* view as "jealousy" for himself, but the actor there is Phinehas, not Moses. Nor does the narrator mention jealousy for Yahweh playing a role in Moses' extermination order against Midianite children in Num 31:17, in spite of Moses' anger in v. 14.

Between Yahweh's verdict on Moses in Numbers 20 and the Peor crisis in chapter 25 the prophet's actions are largely unremarkable. Moses does direct the drama of Aaron's death and follow Yahweh's instructions to make the bronze serpent (Num 20:27–28; 21:8–9). However, he proves risk-averse when confronted with the Edomite threat immediately after Yahweh's judgment against him (Num 20:14–21). In chapter 21 "Israel" twice achieves important military victories without Moses even being mentioned (Num 21:1–3, 21–31). Nor does Moses appear in the book of Balaam (Numbers 22–24). In Num 25:5 Moses directs the judges to kill those who had yoked themselves to the Baal of Peor, but that command is not said to be carried out.

It is at this point that Moses' grand-nephew takes center stage, acting on his own to kill Zimri and his Midianite lover (25:7–8). Allison concludes that Phinehas "upstages" Moses in Numbers 25 (1993, 303 n. 28). Grossman argues that the story "undermines" Moses' authority; in fact, "Phinehas . . . fulfills Moses' role" here (2007, 54, 60). Grossman argues that Phinehas, overcome with zeal for God, had simply internalized what "his teacher" Moses "taught" when he came down from Sinai and ordered the slaughter of fellow Levites in Exodus 32.[45] Grossman also contends that Moses' instructions in Exod 32:26–27 illustrate "his zeal for God" (2007, 60).

Admittedly, Moses had experienced anger when he saw the calf and the dancing, according to Exod 32:19. However, the first specific object of his anger is Aaron. When Moses delivers what he claims is Yahweh's kill order to the Levites, nothing is said about Moses experiencing anger or jealousy for Yahweh. Yet Assmann contends that "Moses and the Levites act as *qana'im* in making themselves tools of God's jealousy" in the golden calf story (2011, 24). Leaving aside the fact that the root *qn'* is not used in Exodus 32, the Israelites have not abandoned Yahweh for a different god in the chapter; in other cases that is the sin which prompts Yahweh's jealous rage.[46] Nor does Moses mention "jealousy for Yahweh" when alluding to Exodus 32 in his blessing of Levi in Deut 33:9. In short, there is no evidence in Exodus 32 or later books that Moses—or the Levites who rallied to Yahweh's side—experienced "jealousy for Yahweh" when the Levites slaughtered their family members, friends, and neighbors.

Nor are there any indications in Numbers 25 or 31 that Moses views himself as being "upstaged" or "undermined" by Phinehas. Could Moses have been attempting to demonstrate *his own* jealousy for Yahweh when he issued his cruel new orders in Num 31:17–18? Could he have envied Phinehas for having been so richly rewarded when he is not even allowed to enter the promised land, in spite of all that he has had to endure as leader of the murmuring Israelites for forty years? These questions cannot be answered definitively since Moses and Phinehas are never said to interact directly. Nor does the narrator give us any information about Moses' reaction to Phinehas' deed in Numbers 25 or Phinehas' presence with the army in chapter 31. In Num 25:10–13 Yahweh tells Moses of the rewards he will give to Phinehas, but Moses' response to this news is not given.[47] In Numbers 31, Moses' only reported emotion is his anger at the army commanders for not completing the extermination of the Midianite males and non-virgin women.

On three occasions in Deuteronomy, Moses mentions Yahweh's verdict that he must die outside the land. In each case Moses blames the people for his plight and omits Yahweh's actual reason for that penalty.[48] He even appeals to Yahweh to reverse his decision, but the appeal is rejected (Deut 3:26). Moses does refer to the Peor incident in Deut 4:3, but he makes no mention of the "jealous" Phinehas or his deed.

In Num 11:29 Moses had chided Joshua for being jealous for Moses' sake.[49] While Moses is never said to be jealous for Yahweh or to envy Phinehas, the extreme violence he commands in Num 31:17–18 is very similar to the carnage caused by Phinehas, Elijah, and Jehu. Yet not even Moses' directing Israel's vengeance against the Midianites leads Yahweh to view him favorably enough to reverse his decision about the prophet's impending death. From this perspective, Moses had reason to be resentful of Yahweh's extravagant rewarding of Phinehas, although the narrator says nothing which indicates that this is the case.[50]

How do the events reported in Numbers 25 and 31 affect the biblical portrait of Moses as a whole? The narrator does not provide enough relevant information for readers to determine Moses' motivation for his infanticide command. Does that imply that his motivation is irrelevant? Considering that Moses is the most important human character in Exodus-Deuteronomy, it seems unwise to dismiss the question of his motivation simply because it is not plainly stated. This is particularly true if one regards the Hebrew Bible as ethical literature. While the biblical narrators present Moses as a public figure and give us little insight into his personal life, Moses' kill order is presented as a *personal* decision, which is without precedent and which violates the holy war laws which Moses will go on to announce in Deuteronomy 20. This means that Numbers 31 is crucial for our assessment of the prophet whom the Pentateuch describes as incomparable, both in terms of his intimate relationship with Yahweh and his "mighty hand" (Deut 34:10, 12; cf. Num 12:6–8).[51]

I began this section by noting Moses' echo of Pharaoh's infanticide order. This intertextual link suggests that Moses may have become Pharaoh-like near the end of his life.[52] Later on, the same will be true of king Solomon. However, while Solomon had been violating the laws for kingship for decades prior to his Pharaoh-like attempt to murder Jeroboam (1 Kgs 11:40; see Lasine 2001, 150–58), Moses had consistently enforced Yahweh's covenant laws and only acted like a murderous Pharaoh in his final official act. The encomium to Moses in the last verse of the Pentateuch praises him for "all the great terror (ולכל המורא הגדול) he did in the eyes of all Israel" (Deut 34:12).[53]

Sadly, the last "great terror" Moses performed as avenger in the Israelites' eyes—and now ours—is against the Midianite children in Numbers 31, a narrative which should terrify us, as it did Mark Twain. In Twain's *Letters from the Earth* (1996, 257–58), the visitor Satan observes that the biblical God is "totally without mercy—he, who is called the Fountain of Mercy. He slays, slays, slays! All the men, all the beasts, all the boys, all the babies; also all the women and all the girls, except those that have not been deflowered. . . . He makes no distinction between innocent and guilty."

In short, "there is nothing in either savage or civilized history that is more utterly complete, more remorselessly sweeping than the Father of Mercy's campaign among the Midianites."

Twain makes no mention of the fact that the worst of the slaughter was ordered by Moses, not Yahweh. Yet he, and the many scholars who attribute the infanticide to Yahweh, are not really wrong. Yahweh does not stop Moses from carrying out the slaughter. God may have stopped Abraham when he was about to kill his son Isaac (Gen 22:11–12), but he does not intervene when Moses—and the three figures who are "jealous for Yahweh"—carry out extrajudicial killings and mass slaughters, even when those slaughtered are little children.

3. Divine and human motivation for vengeance in the Samson story

The Samson narrative subtly intertwines the judge's own desire for revenge with Yahweh's intention of using Samson to provoke conflict with the Philistines. As early as Judg 13:5 Yahweh's angel tells Samson's mother that her yet unborn son will become a Nazirite from the womb and begin to deliver Israel from the hand of the Philistines. This chapter ends with the notice that Yahweh's "spirit" began to agitate (לפעמו) Samson.[54]

In the following chapter Samson seems guided solely by his passion for the Philistine woman he wants to marry, although the narrator alerts us that this was "from Yahweh," who was seeking an occasion from the Philistines (Judg 14:4). Yahweh's spirit again comes strongly upon Samson when he kills a young lion (14:5–6). We soon learn that this seemingly chance event helps to achieve Yahweh's goal of conflict with the Philistines. Later, Samson discovers that bees have made honey in the fallen lion's carcass and harvests some to eat with his parents (vv. 8–9). After crafting a riddle based on this event, Samson makes a bet about its meaning with his Philistine wedding guests. The guests fail to guess the meaning, so they coerce Samson's bride to betray him by obtaining the riddle's solution for

78 *Jealousy for Yahweh and divine vengeance*

them (vv. 12–17). Realizing what has happened, Samson tells the Philistines, "if you hadn't plowed with my heifer, you wouldn't have found out my riddle" (v. 18). Samson's double entendre likens the Philistines forcing his wife to reveal his secrets to their having committed adultery with her.[55] While Samson's statement and the situation would seem likely to trigger jealousy and anger, it is Yahweh's spirit (here mentioned for the third time) which motivates Samson's killing of thirty other Philistines to pay off the debt. Oddly, Samson is only said to become angry after he pays his debt (v. 19). In this scene personal revenge and the motivating force of Yahweh's spirit work together once again.

Judges 15 is dominated by Samson's desire to "get even" with the Philistines and their desire to do the same with him (Judg 15:3, 7, 9, 11). While Samson naively believes he can even the score and then quit (v. 3), the narrative makes clear that attempts at tit-for-tat revenge lead to an ever-increasing spiral of violence. In this case, increasing violence against the Philistines is Yahweh's professed goal. Samson expresses his personal motivation in terms of vengeance (נקם; 15:7; 16:28). When his fellow Israelites tie him up and hand him over to the Philistines, the narrator reports, for the fourth and last time, that Yahweh invests Samson with his spirit. This allows Samson to kill a thousand Philistines (15:14). The chapter concludes with Samson calling on Yahweh for help when he needs water, pointing out that "you have given this great deliverance by the hand of your servant" (15:18). Samson knows that his own desire for vengeance is at the same time a "deliverance" from the Philistines in his role as Yahweh's servant.

In Judges 16 Samson tells Delilah that he has been a Nazirite to God from his mother's womb and that he will lose his strength if his hair is cut (v. 17). Readers are not told whether Samson has been aware of his identity and mission from the start. Now in possession of Samson's crucial secret, Delilah has Samson sleep on her knees. A group of Philistines subdue him, for Yahweh "had departed from him" (v. 20). His enemies gouge out his eyes, bind him with bronze fetters, and force him to grind in the house of the prisoners (v. 21).

In Chapter 2.3.b.2 we discussed the blinding of Polymestor in Euripides' *Hecuba*, including the fact that some readers find Hecuba's action to be excessively brutal and horrific (although possibly fascinating as well, like the blinding of Gloucester in *King Lear*).[56] The blinded Polymestor has the opportunity to complain at length about having to suffer this degrading punishment. In contrast, the narrator of Judges 16 makes no mention of Samson's reaction to his blinding, or to his humiliating and emasculating work as a grinder.[57] Only later artists, such as Rembrandt, highlight the gory and horrifying aspects of this scene. Rembrandt's large painting *The Blinding of Samson* (1636) includes Delilah's reaction to the blinding, which combines "ecstatic fascination with cruelty" (Suthor 2018, 122).

Later the Philistines display their blinded enemy in a large building packed with people, including all the Philistine leaders. Samson has a boy lean him against the pillars of the immense structure and asks Yahweh to give him strength on this final occasion, so that this once he can be avenged (ואנקמה נקם) of the Philistines for one of his two eyes[58] and die along with them (Judg 16:28, 30). When the building collapses, approximately three thousand Philistines die with him. This scene illustrates the subtle interplay between Samson's need for personal revenge and his divinely ordered mission to deliver Israel. Once again Samson wants to avenge himself and then cease, in this case by dying (16:28; cf. 15:7). In effect he asks Yahweh to assist in his suicide and Yahweh complies.[59]

Thus, Samson enacts his ultimate personal revenge and Yahweh achieves his goal of having Samson inspire conflict with the Philistines, even though Israel is not completely "delivered" from Philistine oppression during Samson's judgeship. While Samson is never said to be "jealous for Yahweh," he does see himself as someone who has a mission from Yahweh. In several cases it is Yahweh's spirit which is said to move Samson, rather than specific emotions such as jealousy or rage. This is significant, in light of the fact that Prov 6:34 warns that "jealousy is the burning anger of a man (or husband; גבר) and he will not have compassion in the day of vengeance (ביום נקם)."[60] However, Samson *is* moved to slaughter his enemies singlehandedly, something which links this judge to the priest, the prophet, and the king whose jealousy for Yahweh leads them to engage in multiple killings.

Notes

1 While the Israelite Zimri and the Midianite Cozbi do seem to engage in intercourse in v. 8, it is not certain that there was general cohabitation between other Israelite males and Moabite or Midianite females. For other examples of *zanah* used in a figurative sense with a masculine subject, see Thelle 2015, 111 n. 15.
2 Numbers 25:15 describes Cozbi's father Zur as a tribal head; cf. Josh 13:21. In Num 31:8 he is listed as one of the five kings of Midian.
3 Reif argues against the ancient understanding that Phinehas struck her/them through their genitals. He renders Num 25:8 as "Following the Israelite into the shrine, he ran them both through, the Israelite and the woman in her shrine" (1971, 206). On the possible meanings of קבתה here, and the question of whether the couple were having intercourse as opposed to engaging in an act of sacrifice or celebration, see Levine 2000, 287–88.
4 See further in Section 2.e, below. In the golden calf crisis, Moses attempts to calm God's anger at the people in Exod 32:11–13 rather than becoming angry or jealous for Yahweh. Later on, when he sees the apostasy close up, he does become enraged (32:19).
5 ויפלל here is usually rendered "intervened" or "executed/rendered judgment." Muffs (1992, 41) translates "prayed," and over-concludes from this reading that "'And he prayed,'" means "with words, and not by the shedding of blood." The psalmist is "put off by the act of zealousness dripping with blood, and so replaces it with conversation, dialogue, and rational means of persuasion."
6 For a detailed discussion of each of these charges, and the various ways in which commentators have attempted to validate and justify Elijah's claims, see Lasine 2012, 120–30.
7 Some scholars (e.g., Montgomery and Gehman 1951, 316; Fretheim 1999, 110) assert that Elijah throwing his cloak over Elisha (v. 19) is symbolically equivalent to anointing him.
8 More precisely, this is Jehonadab's only directly quoted word. In Jer 35:6–10, the Rechabites cite the instructions which Jonadab the son of Rechab had given them.
9 Sweeney goes on to claim that Elijah "emphasizes his zealousness for YHWH much like Jehonadab," in spite of the fact that Jehonadab never speaks after his opening word of support for Jehu and does nothing which might demonstrate jealousy for Yahweh.

10 In Jeremiah 35 the Rechabites refer to "Jonadab the son of Rechab our father" or "Jonadab our father" three times (vv. 6, 8, 10); Yahweh and Jeremiah refer to "their/your father" four times (vv. 14–16, 18).
11 What Elijah says in that verse also adds to what Yahweh had told him to say in 1 Kgs 21:19. When Jehu characterizes Jezebel's activities in terms of "whoredom" and "sorceries" in 2 Kgs 9:22, is he voicing his own perspective on syncretism and Baal worship or is he appealing to what he assumes is a popular bias against Jezebel and her innovations?
12 Wray Beal (2020, 119) claims that Elijah is "named as the 'prophet of record' throughout" the Jehu narrative, citing 2 Kgs 9:25–26 along with the three verses I discuss here. However, Elijah is *not* named in 9:25–26. In fact, what Jehu quotes bears the most similarity to what Yahweh says *to* Elijah in 1 Kgs 21:19, not what Elijah adds to that message in 21:20–24. On the ways in which the prophecy in 2 Kgs 9:26 differs from that in 1 Kgs 21, see, e.g., Rofé 1988, 84–85. Hobbs (1985, 117) claims that 2 Kgs 9:26 "finds its closest parallel in Deut 32:43." The latter verse asserts that Yahweh "avenges the blood of his servants and returns vengeance on his adversaries." 2 Kings 9:26 does state that the victim will be "requited," but it is the young prophet's words in 2 Kgs 9:7 which echo the reference to "the blood of his servants" in Deut 32:43. On the latter verse, see Chapter 2.3.a, above.
13 Hazael is certainly not expected to target Israelite devotees of Baal.
14 הנער הנער הנביא, literally, "the youth, the youth, the prophet." Some scholars understand the second נער to denote "servant," a widely attested meaning of the word. The youth then becomes the servant, or attendant, of the prophet Elisha.
15 The young prophet adds a reference to Yahweh as "the God of Israel" and a description of Israel as "the people of Yahweh."
16 Wray Beal (2014, 374) takes the prophet's additions to Elisha's instructions as "an example of prophetic (re)interpretation for specific situations and times (something that Elijah had already demonstrated; see 1 Kgs 21:17–24)." According to Long (1991, 122), "Jehu improvises." The scene justifies the view that "within the story world prophets creatively applied their inspirations to changing circumstances" (1991, 119). The statements by Wray Beal and Long seem to confuse the *author* creatively adapting to and re-interpreting changing situations with the *character* doing so. There is no reason for the young prophet or Elijah to adjust the message they are to deliver, because nothing changes during the very short time between receiving their instructions and delivering their messages. On the complexity of Elijah's additions in 1 Kgs 21:17–24, see Lasine 2012, 71–73.
17 Roncace (2020, 172) finds this scenario "funny"; when this "over-eager young prophet who is on his first really big mission . . . gets his chance to speak, he's not going to make some one-sentence proclamation and exit stage left."
18 For a survey of other explanations of the discrepancy between the young prophet's words and those of Elisha, see Wray Beal 2007, 57–59.
19 In his instructions, Elisha uses the action verb בוא three times in different forms ("come . . . go in . . . bring"). The impression of haste makes it less likely that Elisha took the time to give the young man all the detailed instructions the youth enumerates in 2 Kgs 9:6–10. Wray Beal (2014, 373) believes that the prophet had to rush away since he is in á "potentially dangerous situation" at the battlefront. This seems unlikely, given that the soldiers he encounters are at ease, away from any fighting. One of Jehu's men asks why the young prophet, "this crazy man" (המשגע הזה), came to him (9:11). Later a watchman identifies a chariot driver as Jehu because he drives "crazily" (בשגעון; 9:20). Whether or not one agrees that these details are signs of humor or the "carnivalesque" (García-Treto 1992, 156–66), they certainly underscore the element of haste in the chapter.
20 Nelson (1987, 202) concedes that "to modern ears" the previously unmentioned oracle in 2 Kgs 9:26 "seems a bit too convenient, flavored strongly with pretext and

self-justification." He takes Bidkar to be "the needed second witness," so that "ancient readers probably would have accepted it as genuine without question." Nelson ignores the fact that Bidkar does not confirm Jehu's words. The modern-ancient distinction drawn by Nelson is also unhelpful. Many modern readers have taken Jehu's evocation of Yahweh's words at face value, and I find it likely that savvy and politically astute ancient hearers and readers would recognize Jehu's attempt at self-justification for what it is.

21 Jehu's commander, king Jehoram, refers to Jehu's treacherous deceit against him (מרמה; 2 Kgs 9:23). Readers familiar with Genesis might recall the blind Isaac telling Esau that his brother Jacob had come with מרמה to rob Esau of his father's death blessing (Gen 27:35). Later the narrator of Kings tells us that Jehu's call for a great sacrifice to Baal was done with deception (בעקבה; 2 Kgs 10:19). From the time of Jacob (whose name resembles the word for deception used in 10:19), deception—including deception leading to mass murder, as in Genesis 34—has largely gone uncriticized by Yahweh and the narrator, in spite of the object lesson given in Genesis 3 about the supposed penalties for trickery.

22 The same can be said of the brief sketch of Joshua's holy wars in Josh 10:28–40. In this passage we also hear repeatedly that none remained alive. The formulaic repetition of this fact may have a deadening effect on some readers, leaving only an abstract impression of unspeakable horror.

23 It is worth noting that Baasha and Zimri each attack the son of a former king who was strong and long-reigning. Each son rules for only two years before being assassinated (1 Kgs 15:25–27; 16:8–10). From a usurper's point of view, this is the safest time to make a coup attempt.

24 There is no consensus on the relationship between the terms "Moab" and "Midian." Mendenhall argues that the Midianites "formed part of the population ruled by the king of Moab . . . Moab is a political designation, while Midian is the designation of a social organization (tribe) which makes up an influential element of the state" (1973, 108, 164). Mendenhall (1992, 817) claims that in later biblical tradition "the term Midian has already become a geographical designation," citing 1 Kgs 11:18 as an example. Dumbrell (1975, 337) concludes that construing Midian "as a league and not as a land best explains the political enigma." Milgrom suggests that Numbers 25 "may reflect the period when Moab was part of a Midianite confederation . . . that embraced all of Transjordan as its protectorate" (1990, 78, 218).

25 For example, Steinberg calls the slaughter "divinely sanctioned genocide" (2018, 24). Admittedly Yahweh makes no attempt to alter or countermand the commands given by Moses in vv. 17–18; see Section 2.e, below.

26 Moses takes the initiative by offering the Pharaoh the opportunity to have "glory" over him by choosing when Moses should make supplication for the king and his people, so that the frog plague might end. When the Pharaoh says "tomorrow," Moses tells him that this will teach him that Yahweh is incomparable. It also shows the Pharaoh the power that Moses possesses as Yahweh's prophet. Yahweh backs Moses' play (v. 9), just as he will back Elijah when that prophet expands Yahweh's orders in a self-promoting way in 1 Kgs 18:1, 19–40.

27 For example, by Milgrom 1990, 259; Wenham 1981, 211. When discussing the prepubescent female children in v. 18, Levine (2000, 456) cites the parallel phrase about male children, but only to establish that these young girls are not yet virginal women; the cruelty of the male baby slaughter in v. 17 and its parallel in Exod 1:22 go undiscussed. Dozeman acknowledges that male children must be killed but says no more about it (1998, 247; cf. Budd 1984, 333). Instead, Dozeman notes that "verses 17–18 state the priestly law of booty in both a negative and a positive form." For Dozeman, the speaker "Moses" is merely the mouthpiece of the presumed priestly authors. In contrast, K. Brown (2015, 65–66) acknowledges the slaughter of male children in Num 31:17 *and* the parallel with Exod 1:22.

28 As Begg (2007, 104) puts it, "the two authors, in their different ways, dispose of the problem posed by Moses' disturbing order to execute the boys."
29 For example, Gray 1906, 422 ("in order to secure the extinction of Midian"); Ashley 1993, 595; Mbuwayesango 2019, 85; Niditch 1993a, 51.
30 Pitkänen (2018, 187) hints at the Exodus parallel with Numbers 31 when he suggests that if the Midianite boys in Numbers 31 had been allowed to live "they would be likely to . . . cause problems sooner or later," adding "cf. Moses himself in Ex 1ff."
31 The violence in Edom reported in 1 Kings 11 is occasionally written off as a reference to the battle described in 2 Samuel 8. However, 2 Sam 8:14 clearly states that Edom became a vassal of Israel and that David put garrisons there. Even if Edom later rebelled, the rules of engagement in Deut 20:13–14 dictate that the Israelites not kill women and little ones (הנשים והטף), among whom would be the "little boy" Hadad in 1 Kgs 11:17. 1 Kings 11 is describing a systematic genocide complete with mass graves, not a series of battles. As Mulder puts it (1998, 569), "for a period of no less than 6 months, Joab and 'all Israel,' went on a horrendous rampage in Edom."
32 This is also the Moabite king Balak's root fear in Num 22:3, 6. While Balak and Moabites play no role in Numbers 25 or 31, Balaam is mentioned among the slain in Num 31:8, and Moses uses him as part of his excuse for ordering more slaughter (31:16).
33 Admittedly, the fact that "Midianites" are described as populous and powerful later on (Judges 6–7) implies that Moses' extermination program was not completely successful.
34 Could this unusual phrasing imply that Yahweh wants Israel to avenge their having been tricked by Midian into sinning, which caused Yahweh to exact vengeance on his people in the form of the plague at Shittim? K. Brown argues that Yahweh is ordering Moses to "seek the vindication [or redress] of the Israelites from the Midianites" (2015, 74), but he does not explain why the imperative נְקֹם implies "seeking."
35 Steinberg explains Moses' anger in v. 14 as caused by the troops' failure to kill all the Midianites "as Moses had originally commanded" (2018, 24). The anger reported in v. 14 might help to explain Moses' kill orders in vv. 17–18, but his "original" command in v. 3 directs his men to "go against Midian," not to eradicate all Midianites.
36 As Steinberg points out, these virgins "are socially dead through assimilation as wives and slaves, often through rape or forced impregnation . . . the physical survival of the Midianite virgins comes at the cost of the killing of their past, an erasure of their earlier identities in all its forms" (2018, 25).
37 According to an understandably controversial (and disturbing) interpretation of Numbers 31 and Judges 21 in *b. Yebam.* 60b, females "who have not known man" refers to girls who are merely capable of having intercourse, that is, those above the age of three years and one day.
38 The tribes ask Yahweh who should go up first against Benjamin, and then should we go again, instead of first asking whether *or not* they should attack their brother tribe (Judg 20:18, 23). Clearly they had already decided to attack before asking for direction from Yahweh. On their third attempt they ask Yahweh the correct question and Yahweh grants them victory. Yet afterwards the tribes seem dumbfounded, asking Yahweh why a tribe is now lacking in Israel (Judg 21:3), as though they were oblivious to the fact that their own actions explain why this has occurred.
39 For example, וכל-זכר in Num 31:17 and Judg 21:11; משכב-זכר . . . ידעת אשה-וכל in Num 31:17 and Judg 21:11; אשר לא-ידעו משכב זכר in Num 31:18 and אשר לא-ידעה איש למשכב זכר in Judg 21:12. K. Brown (2015, 77–78) lists other similarities between Numbers 31 and Judges 21. However, he omits one difference: in Numbers 31 the males of an entire people are to be eradicated for allegedly having caused widespread sinning among Israelite males, while in Judges 21 the Israelite males of only one town are to be killed, allegedly for not participating in an ill-conceived fratricidal war.

40 According to Beldman, "most commentators agree that the Israelites had twisted the law [regarding holy war] in a most troubling and absurd manner" (2017, 95; cf. McCann 2011, 135–36) Wenham assumes that the "participation of Phinehas [in Numbers 31] shows that this is a holy war . . . carried out in obedience to the divine command" (Wenham 1981, 211; cf. Organ 2001, 210). This ignores two key facts. First, the war is carried out in obedience to *Moses'* commands in Num 31:3, 16–18, not Yahweh's command. Second, the Israelites do not follow the holy war laws of Deuteronomy 20 in their destruction of the Midianites (on this, see K. Brown 2015, 75–78).

41 As for the slaughter of children, in the vision report in Ezekiel 9 Yahweh goes far beyond the orders given by humans in Genesis 34, Numbers 31, and Judges 21. He tells six leaders of Jerusalem to slaughter all those who have not been marked as innocent, including "the old man, the virgin, the little children (טף), and women" (Ezek 9:6).

42 After the battle against the five kings in Joshua 10, we are told that "all the people returned to the camp to Joshua at Makkedah in peace" (v. 21), a statement which is often taken to mean that the Israelites suffered no casualties.

43 Moses is explicitly said to be angry in the following verses: Exod 11:8; 16:20; 32:19 (in Moses' retelling of the golden calf fiasco in Deut 9:17 he omits his anger); Lev 10:16; Num 16:15 and Num 31:14. Sommer (1999, 604 n. 5) views Moses as angry in Num 11:10–12, although words for anger are absent. Since we are told that the situation was evil in the eyes of Moses, and Moses himself tells Yahweh that he has acted evilly toward his servant (vv. 10–11), there is certainly reason to attribute anger to Moses here. Finally, 4 Maccabees follows Numbers in reporting that Moses was angry at Dathan and Abiram; however, in Maccabees Moses controls his anger through his powers of reason (Num 16:12–16; 4 Macc 2:17).

44 Is Moses punished for displaying too much autonomy and for overidentifying with Yahweh's role? If so, that could imply that Yahweh viewed Moses as going beyond proper human limitations, which, in the ancient Greek context, could trigger divine envy and jealousy. Some rabbinic commentators suggest that by asking "Are *we* to get water . . . ?" instead of asking "Is *he* [God] to get water?" Moses was giving credit to himself (and Aaron) rather than to God, an act which could indeed imply *hybris* on Moses' part (see, e.g., Milgrom 1990, 451–52; Kok 1997, 112).

45 Grossman incorrectly claims that in Exodus 32 the Levites are "to kill all those who had 'made sport' with women." It is also highly misleading to state that "Moses takes vigorous action against the sinners; despite a direct command, Moses is able to intuit the divine will through his own initiative" (2007, 60). Moses tells the Levites, who came to Yahweh's side, to kill their family members, friends and neighbors (who will primarily be Levites). As I have argued elsewhere (Lasine 1994, 206–14), this scene records a voluntary sacrifice on the part of the Levites, not a punishment of three thousand "sinners" who had supposedly "made sport" with Moabite women. Moreover, the fact that the narrator does not record Yahweh instructing Moses to send out the Levites does not necessarily imply that Moses opening declaration "Thus says Yahweh" is a case of Moses "intuiting" Yahweh's will.

46 The calf is a way of representing Yahweh or his footstool. The following day Aaron declares a festival to Yahweh, not to a different deity.

47 One feature shared by Exod 32:29 and Num 25:13 is that in both cases Levite killers are rewarded with priestly blessings. According to Philo, Moses himself wanted to reward Phinehas for his actions at Shittim: "When the purging was completed, Moses sought how to give to the high priest's son, who had been the first to rush to the defence, such reward as he deserved for his heroism. But he was forestalled by God" (*Moses* 1.55; Colson 1966, 435). In Philo, Moses proceeds to appoint Phinehas commander-in-chief (*Moses* 1.56). According to Feldman, this makes Philo's Phinehas "parallel in rank with Moses himself" (2002, 322). Numbers 31 itself does not focus on any single commander-in-chief. Given Phinehas' key role in Numbers 25 it would

84 *Jealousy for Yahweh and divine vengeance*

have been surprising if Phinehas did not accompany the army on its mission of vengeance on Yahweh's behalf. However, Phinehas' presence seems largely symbolic; see Section 1.a, above.
48 Deut 1:37; 3:23–28; 4:21–22; cf. Num 20:12; 27:14.
49 Apparently Moses does not jealously guard his status as the only prophet as Elijah seems to do (see Section 1.b, above).
50 If Moses *were* embittered and splenetic about the way Yahweh had treated him, it is not inconceivable for him to have had a "what have I got to lose?" attitude when he unleashed his rage and resentment by exterminating the Midianite boys. Such a Moses figure would of course lose all claim to our sympathy.
51 Kirsch (1999, 10) believes that in Num 31:14–18 "the emancipator is also the exterminator, although the blood-thirsty and ruthless nature of Moses is almost never spoken out loud." Although Moses' commands in Num 31:16–18 are definitely ruthless, that does not necessarily mean that Moses' "nature," that is, his defining character traits, include "bloodthirstiness" and "ruthlessness."
52 Is the biblical Moses therefore akin to African leaders such as Robert Mugabe and Frederick Chiluba, who were initially viewed as Moses-like liberators by their peoples, only to be considered "Pharaohs" by their opponents later on? See Langston 2006, 70–71, 88, 152.
53 The phrase "מוראים גדלים/מורא גדול" normally alludes to the terror[s] which *Yahweh* inflicts upon the Egyptians in order to demonstrate his power and prompt the exodus (e.g., Deut 4:34; 26:8; Jer 32:21; cf. Deut 10:21).
54 One Talmudic text understands the verb פעם in this verse as implying that the spirit "struck" Samson in the way that a clapper vibrates a bell (*b. Sotah* 9b).
55 According to Suetonius, the Roman emperor Augustus often committed adultery with the wives of his adversaries in order to gain information (*Life of Augustus* § 69; Edwards 2000, 79). In Judges, the Philistines do not even have to sleep with Samson's bride in order for them to learn his secrets. Interestingly, Augustus also instituted laws to make adultery a serious criminal offense. One of the consequences of this legislation may have been a reduction in the kind of adulterous "pillow talk" from which he himself had benefitted.
56 On blinding and revenge in Herodotus' Euenius narrative, see Chapter 5.3, below.
57 On this degrading form of punishment in Judges 16, the LXX of Jer 52:11 (in which king Zedekiah is blinded and taken to "the house of the mill"), and various Mesopotamian texts, see van der Toorn 1986, 248–50. Van der Toorn points out that Samson and other prisoners of war are degraded by doing work normally done by women and slaves.
58 Most English translations have Samson asking for revenge for both of his eyes, but the Hebrew is more accurately rendered "for one of my two eyes"; see Webb 2012, 408–409.
59 On whether Samson's death qualifies as suicide, see Lasine 2019, 43–44 n. 62.
60 Prov 27:4 asserts that jealousy (and/or envy) is even harder to bear than anger: "wrath is cruel and anger a flood, but who can stand before jealousy (קנאה)?"

5 Divine envy and vengeance in Homer and Herodotus' *Histories*

In the next two chapters I will discuss examples of divine envy and vengeance in Herodotus' *Histories* and several Greek tragedies. It is usually assumed that there is less evidence of divine envy in works written prior to Herodotus and Pindar. In fact, Walcot "fail[s] to detect in the Homeric poems anything comparable to the concept of divine envy associated with Herodotus, Aeschylus or Pindar in the fifth century B.C." (1978, 22–23; cf. Lanzillotta 2010, 87).[1] Garvie agrees: "in Homer there is "very little sense, if any, that the gods in general resented human success" (2009, xxvi).[2] These generalizations are a bit misleading. There are significant examples of divine envy in Homer's *Odyssey*. I will therefore begin this chapter by discussing these Odyssean passages and the characterization of the jealous goddess Hera in the *Iliad* and the *Homeric Hymn to Apollo*. I will then turn to divine (and human) envy and revenge in Herodotus.

1. Hera and divine envy in Homer and the *Homeric Hymn to Apollo*

To denote envy Homer usually employs the verb *agamai* rather than *phthoneō*.[3] Menelaus speculates that "the god himself" must have been envious (ἀγάσσεσθαι) of Odysseus and therefore prevented his return home (*Od.* 4.181–82). The goddess Calypso calls the gods merciless and supremely jealous (ζηλήμονες)[4] because they are resentful toward (ἀγάασθε) female deities who publicly have human male bedfellows (5.118–20). She also cites the gods' begrudging (ἠγάασθε) the goddess Eos loving the human hunter Orion, which led to Artemis killing Orion (5.121–24). Alcinous, king of the seafaring Phaeacians, believes that Poseidon bears a grudge (ἀγάσασθαι) against his people because they keep convoys safe (8.565–66). Finally, Penelope complains that the gods' envy (ἀγάσαντο) prevented her and Odysseus from being together from their youthful vigor to the threshold of old age (23.210–12). Clearly, a variety of human and divine speakers in *The Odyssey* interpret specific events and divine attitudes in terms of the gods' envy and resentment of human excellence, success, and happiness.[5]

While scholars such as Dodds contend that, unlike the *Odyssey*, "the *Iliad* ignores . . . the idea of divine *phthonos* or jealousy" (1968, 30), we cannot overlook the fact that a major character in the *Iliad* has been viewed as the quintessence

DOI: 10.4324/b23212-5

of divine envy and vengefulness. For some commentators, the goddess Hera is the stereotypical jealous wife and a resentful, vindictive virago. In fact, "Hera is *phthonos* itself" (Clay 1972, 60)[6] and a "paradigm of *zêlotupia*"[7] (Konstan 2006, 416). For Clay, Hera embodies *phthonos* because she is "jealous of any commerce . . . between her husband and mortal women." Konstan argues that Hera's personality is characterized by *zêlotupia* due to her "peevish reaction to the philandering of her husband, Zeus"; her behavior "brands her as a truculent spoilsport" (2006, 228, 232).[8]

Other scholars do not regard Hera as the incarnation of divine jealousy and envy but still view her as characteristically jealous and vengeful, if not comical as well. For example, Burkert believes that Hera becomes "almost a comic figure" in Homer. As Zeus' wife "she is more a model of jealously [*sic*] and marital strife than of connubial affection." And in the *Iliad*, she is "*the* quarrelsome, jealous wife, . . . dangerous, malicious, and implacable in her rage" (1987, 132–34; emphasis added). According to Joan O'Brien (1991, 122), Homer chose Hera as "his symbol of demonic rage." Hera not only "remains committed to a demonic hatred" but exhibits "brutal caprice towards friend and foe alike" (1991, 107). Her "unremitting lust for vengeance" is an "obsession" (1991, 106, 110). Her "only value" is revenge, "the only weapon available to the isolated and embittered." In short, Hera is "psychotic" (1991, 112, 124).

These evaluations of Hera in the *Iliad* tend to omit that Homer also shows us *why* Hera is often described as jealous, envious, and vengeful. This can be demonstrated by taking a closer look at key scenes in which Hera takes part, including those in which she interacts with her husband Zeus and her son Hephaestus. Hera's conversation with Zeus at the beginning of Book 4 is a good starting point, since it sheds light on Clay's assertion that Hera is "*phthonos* itself." The verb *phthoneō* appears only twice in the *Iliad*, both in a speech by Hera: "I will not stand up for these [cities] against you, nor yet begrudge (μεγαίρω) you. Yet if even so I bear malice (φθονέω) and would not have you destroy them, in malice (φθονέουσ') I will accomplish nothing, since you are far stronger" (*Il*. 4.54–56; Lattimore 1961, 114).

Taking this scene as an example, Walcot (1978, 26) argues that "the verb *phthonein* can be used by Homer when it means not much more than 'to be unwilling'," but he nevertheless translates φθονέω here with "I am jealous." Eidinow (2016, 222) agrees that Hera is expressing unwillingness but in a context in which Hera is being forced to unwillingly give a gift. She believes that in Homer *phthoneō* is "used to describe the darker emotions associated with the dynamics of giving and receiving gifts: feelings of resentment and anger."

Whether Homer's Hera is shown to be envious, jealous, and/or resentful, as is often asserted, does not depend upon the nuances of *phthoneō* in its two Iliadic appearances. What counts is Hera's behavior in specific situations. The situation in Book 4 is orchestrated by Zeus. He attempts to provoke his wife into becoming angry by addressing her with heart-cutting (κερτομίοις) malicious words (*Il*. 4.5–6). He mocks Hera and Athene for sitting in the assembly instead of aiding Menelaus, while Aphrodite stands by her man Paris in the fighting. Zeus then proposes that the gods reach a peaceful conclusion to the hostilities, one which saves Troy but still allows Menelaus to retrieve Helen (4.14–19).

Both goddesses become extremely angry at Zeus' speech, but only Hera speaks out. She does not want her efforts on behalf of the Achaians to have been in vain. Zeus can save Troy, but the other gods will not approve (*Il*. 4.25–29). Zeus retorts by wondering what the Trojans have done to her that justifies Hera's animosity toward them. He tells his wife that her anger could only be sated if she could walk through Troy and eat Priam and his sons raw (4.34–36). Zeus concludes by telling Hera that she can do as she pleases, but if he later decides to lay waste one of Hera's favorite cities, she should not stand in his way (4.40–43).[9]

It is at this point that Hera makes the speech in which she agrees not to begrudge Zeus these cities, even though she feels jealous about (or objects to, or balks at) the situation, because she knows that her husband is much stronger than she. At the same time, Hera reminds Zeus that she too is a god, and of the same race as he; in fact, she is first among Cronos' daughters, since she is the eldest of her sisters and wife of lordly Zeus. She then suggests that they give way to one another (*Il*. 4.58–62). Later, Hera again reminds Zeus of her high status when they have a brief round of squabbling with each other (18.356–68). When evaluating Hera's jealousy, envy and resentment, we will need to keep in mind her pride at her high status, as well as her awareness that she is not powerful enough to carry through any ambitious plans of which Zeus does not approve.

The first example of Zeus and Hera's interaction occurs toward the end of Book 1. This scene indicates that Hera faces a very real threat of violence from her husband when she objects to his actions. It also displays the tenacity with which Hera expresses her strong opinions to her husband in spite of his threats. The situation is triggered when Achilles' divine mother Thetis asks Zeus to strengthen the Trojan side in the war until the Achaians show respect to her son, whom Agamemnon has dishonored by taking Achilles' rightful prize (*Il*. 1.503–10). Thetis' request greatly disturbs Zeus, because it will put him in conflict with Hera, who constantly reproaches him for aiding the Trojans (1.517–21; cf. 5.893).

Zeus agrees to help Thetis but asks her to go away, for fear that Hera will notice theme plotting together (*Il*. 1.522–23). Zeus' fear is well-founded; Hera does see them together. She chides her husband for not sharing his plans with her. In response Zeus tells Hera not to probe or question him, because anything he decides to do apart from the other gods is his secret alone (1.536–50). Hera replies that he can think whatever he likes; she rightly suspects that he has granted Thetis' request. As Synodinou (1987, 13) points out, in this scene "Hera succeeds in exposing, in front of the other gods, Zeus' inadequacy to conceal his activities from her, in spite of his confidence that he can do so."

Zeus counters by telling Hera that she will accomplish nothing with her suspicions but to alienate him, and, he adds ominously, that will make things worse for her (*Il*. 1.560–63). He then makes it unmistakably clear that he is indeed threatening his wife. If Hera does not sit down and remain quiet, none of the gods will be able to protect her when he comes and lays his invincible hands upon her. The fact that this threat frightens Hera shows that she takes her husband seriously (1.565–68).

In Books 14 and 15 we learn that Hera has good reason to be frightened. She famously seduces Zeus and puts him to sleep in order to allow Poseidon to further aid the Achaians (*Il.* 14.153–360). When Zeus awakens and sees the wounded Hector on the battlefield, he immediately threatens to whip Hera with the lash and reminds her of the time when he did torture her. Zeus hung her from on high, with two anvils slung on her feet and an unbreakable chain of gold around her hands. She hung there in the air and none of the gods could intervene and set her free. If one tried to free her, Zeus flung that deity down to earth (15.18–25).[10] The memory and threat succeed in frightening Hera once again (15.34). When she returns to Olympus, the goddess Themis sees her and remarks that Hera appears to have been terrified. Themis correctly guesses that Hera's husband Zeus has frightened her (15.90–91).[11]

These are not the only examples of Zeus threatening violence or acting violently against other gods. In Book 8 he again threatens Athene and Hera with violence after they decide to fight on the Achaian side in order to counter Zeus' aid to the Trojan Hector. On this occasion it is Athene who criticizes Zeus in harsh terms (*Il.* 8.350–96). When the goddesses prepare their chariots and weapons, Zeus sees them and sends the messenger Iris to them with a warning. If they do not stop, Zeus will hurl them from their chariots so violently that even after ten years they will not have fully recovered from his lightning strike (8.397–431). His message also makes it clear that he is more angry at Athene than at Hera, because Hera habitually opposes his commands (8.407–408, 423–24). Later Zeus adds that if the goddesses had been struck in their chariots, they could never return to Olympus (8.455–56). After this last threat, angry Athene remains silent but Hera cannot contain her anger and speaks out, as was the case in Book 4.[12]

The epic also includes other examples of Zeus' potential for violence against fellow deities. For example, Hypnos once helped Hera to put Zeus to sleep so that Hera could thwart Heracles. When Zeus awakened in anger, he flung the gods around the halls, and Hypnos narrowly avoided being thrown down into the sea (*Il.* 14.249–61). A scene in Book 1 is particularly germane here. After Hera has become frightened by her husband's threat, her son Hephaestus speaks to the assembled gods on behalf of his "beloved mother" (1.572; cf. 587), in order to render her comforting service. He urges Hera to have patience and endure the situation, because Zeus is strong enough to hurl the other gods out of their places (1.572–89). Hephaestus then reminds his mother how he had tried to help her in the past, only to have Zeus grab his foot and throw him down to earth (1.590–94).[13] In addition to illustrating Zeus' violence, this speech reminds us that Hera is also a mother, one who—in this scene—is said to be loved by her son. Yet we later learn that Hera has also thrown Hephaestus from Olympus in the past. In Book 18 Hephaestus recalls his "dog-faced mother"[14] causing his fall because she wanted to hide him due to his lameness (18.394–99).

Together, these episodes demonstrate that Homer's Hera is more than a caricature of a jealous, vindictive wife. She is a proud and powerful individual who is fully conscious of her high status in Olympian society. Yet her husband makes it difficult, if not impossible, for her to carry out her own plans if he disapproves of them. His advantage is superior power and the threat to use his power against her.

Commentators such as Sissa and Detienne (2000, 105) believe that Zeus' "amorous infidelities [do] not bother her," even when Zeus lists seven examples of his infidelity to Hera just before he is about to sleep with her. He even mentions the sons five of these females bore to him (*Il.* 14.317–28). I find difficult to believe that Hera is indifferent to Zeus' affairs. Hera has not engaged in any extramarital affairs. Apart from Hephaestus, whose relationship to Zeus is left uncertain,[15] the most important child Hera bears to Zeus is Ares, whom Zeus calls the "most hateful" of the gods (5.890). Yet in the seduction scene Zeus feels comfortable mentioning his extramarital relationships to his wife. He even tells Hera that she arouses him more now that in the past, when Hera knows that she has only had this effect due to the help of Aphrodite; it is not something prompted by her beauty alone. Given Hera's personality as she is portrayed throughout the *Iliad*, it is likely that she feels both humiliated and outraged when Zeus enumerates his amours. Even before she begins plotting to seduce him in this scene, we are told that Zeus is "loathsome" in her eyes (14.158).

Given the repeated threats of physical violence from her husband, Synodinou (1987, 13) has good reason to view Hera in these scenes as an example of an "oppressed woman who, although not lacking in ambitions and in abilities to carry them out, . . . has each time to face the violence of her all-powerful husband and to submit to it." Synodinou argues that this "makes it easier to assess some of the strong characterizations attributed to Hera, as, for instance, hostility, scheming, frustration, resentment, bitterness, vindictiveness." In fact, "it seems difficult to expect something different from someone who is repeatedly humiliated and who not only cannot fulfil her own plans but . . . is forced to renounce them and to act against them" (1987, 22).

Clearly, we do not have to cite the judgment of Paris story (in which Aphrodite is chosen over Hera and Athene) in order to explain Hera's frustration and bitterness in the *Iliad*, even though Homer does mention the judgment briefly in *Il.* 24.25–30.[16] Nor do we need to view Hera in terms of P. Slater's theory concerning Greek male fear of "whole women" (1992, 66) such as Hera in order to demonstrate that Homer presents Hera as more than a two-dimensional representation of "*phthonos* itself."

In contrast, later portrayals of Hera seem to offer support for the idea that Hera represents "*phthonos* itself." For example, in the *Homeric Hymn to Apollo* the poet explicitly attributes envy[17] to Hera when the goddess attempts to prevent Leto from giving birth to Apollo (*h. Ap.* 100). In a later scene, it is the emotion of anger which is explicitly highlighted. This scene culminates in the birth of Hera's monstrous son Typhon (*h. Ap.* 307, 309, 331). Hera also makes it clear that she feels the emotions of shame and dishonor due to the infirmities of her son Hephaestus. Her lack of maternal affection toward her son is so great that she attempts to dispose of Hephaestus permanently by throwing him into the sea (*h. Ap.* 317).

In the Typhon episode, Hera insists on her rights as Zeus' lawful wife and resents that Zeus has had children without her participation (*h. Ap.* 323–25). Hera's attempt to right the balance by having another child without Zeus produces only the destructive monster Typhon. Her hope that her new child would excel Zeus in strength implies a wish to destroy her husband as Zeus destroyed his father Cronos, replacing Zeus with the son whom she created without her husband's involvement (*h. Ap.* 325–30). When Typhon is born and proves to be unlike both gods and humans, to whom he is a cruel "plague," she immediately rids herself of her new son by giving him to the dragon who will later be killed by Apollo (*h. Ap.* 356–62).

In both episodes it is Hera's perception of her situation and her awareness of her august queenly status (πότνια; *h. Ap.* 309) which motivate her anger and resentment. These emotions have been viewed as the result of envy, if not jealousy as well. Kutter argues that the ζηλοσύνη experienced by Hera in the Leto scene is not merely jealousy. Hera also feels "envy over the fact that Leto is about to have a "blameless and mighty" son while Hera herself does not" (2018, 58). The same is true in the Typhon scene: "Hera is jealous because Zeus has procreated without her, proving that their relationship does not have the exclusivity she would like." According to Kutter, envy adds to Hera's frustration, "on the grounds that Zeus has produced a child who is distinguished . . . while she herself has failed to produce a comparable child" (2018, 59).

Miller goes further, asserting that "Hera's *phthonos*" is on display in both scenes, even though the term *phthonos* does not appear in the hymn. He accuses Hera of engaging in "malicious envy" in the Leto episode; in the Typhon episode, "the depth and ferocity of Hera's malice are laid bare" (1986, 45, 87). Miller does not believe that Hera's actions are motivated by what she perceives as the infringement of her rights as Zeus' lawful wife. Underlying her "ostensible indignation at undeserved injury" are "congenital spite and malice" (1986, 109–10).[18] Leaving aside the notion that Hera's maliciousness is "congenital," the depiction of the goddess in this hymn is much closer to the Hera of Euripides' *Heracles* than the more complex and less unsympathetic Hera of *The Iliad*, as I will discuss in Chapter 8.1, below.

2. Advice about divine envy and revenge in Herodotus

In Herodotus' *Histories* four speakers give good advice which involves the crucial factor of divine envy. Solon speaks to the Lydian king Croesus (*Hist.* 1.32), Amasis advises Polycrates, ruler of Samos (3.40), Artabanus counsels the Persian king Xerxes (7.10, 46), and Themistocles addresses an audience of Athenians (8.109). In addition, Herodotus himself points to the role of divine *phthonos* in the hideous death of Pheretime, an overly violent avenger (4.205).

In the *Histories* excessive human revenge is not the only trigger for divine envy. It can also be prompted by individuals who rise beyond the norm of human achievement or glory or who have had nothing but success in their lives. Amasis warns Polycrates that the latter's continual good fortune and success might arouse the envy and jealousy[19] of the divine (τὸ θεῖον; *Hist.* 3.40).[20] Amasis' statement seems to be based on the fact that he had never heard of someone whose totally good fortune did not end evilly, destroyed root and branch (πρόρριζος; 3.40). This echoes Solon's earlier warning to Croesus that "the god (ὁ θεὸς) promises fortune to many people and then overturns them root and branch" (1.32). Solon pulls no punches when it comes to divine envy: "the divine is entirely envious and disturbing (φθονερόν τε καὶ ταραχῶδες) to us" (1.32). According to Grene (1988, 25), this is a point about which "Herodotus is quite definite."

In these cases, great good fortune—apart from how that success was achieved—prompts destructive divine envy. Speakers later in the *Histories* agree. Artabanus tells his nephew King Xerxes that "the god loves to bring low all things of surpassing greatness."[21] When, for example, a large army is totally destroyed by a smaller one, the cause may be the envious and jealous god (ὁ θεὸς φθονήσας) sending panic or thunderbolts among them, "for the god permits no one to think big (φθονέειν μέγα)[22] except for himself" (*Hist.* 7.10). Later Artabanus interprets the brevity and wretchedness of human life as another illustration of divine envy: "therein is the god discovered to be envious (φθονερὸς); for he gives us but a taste of the sweetness of life" (7.46; Herodotus 1988, 486), an attitude which some readers have found to be present in Genesis 3. Finally, Themistocles claims that "the gods and the heroes" who brought the Greeks victory over the Persians "begrudged (or were envious; ἐφθόνησαν) that Asia and Europe be ruled by one man, especially one like Xerxes, who is "unholy and reckless" (8.109).[23]

Do these wise advisors practice what they preach? Solon is presented as an unimpeachable source of wisdom. Assessing Artabanus is also a straightforward matter. On several occasions he offers sagacious and prudent advice to his brother Darius and nephew Xerxes, even when doing so may anger the king (e.g., *Hist.* 4.83; 7.10, 46). Artabanus is bold enough to counter the advice given by all of Xerxes' other counselors (7.10–11). He is not described as having character flaws, such as Themistocles' talent for manipulation and deception or his insatiable desire for wealth (8.4–5, 108–10, 112). Themistocles is an extremely complex character; Herodotus also provides ample evidence of Themistocles' intelligence and persuasive powers, which lead to the Greeks' victory over the Persians (7.143–44; 8.57–63, 75–80, 83). His achievements give weight to his evocation of divine *phthonos*, even though his aim in this speech is to deceive his Athenian audience (8.109–10).[24]

Evaluating the Egyptian king Amasis is also a complex matter. He is highly successful, not merely for a short period but through the entire forty-four years of his rule (*Hist.* 3.10). Egypt is very prosperous under his leadership. Amasis even promulgates a new and excellent law which Solon later copies and imposes on the Athenians (2.177). Amasis dies a natural death.[25] Herodotus notes that no great adversity happened to Amasis in all that time (3.10).

The ways in which Amasis is different from most tyrants in Herodotus show him to be laudable.[26] For example, when Amasis takes over as king he is not initially accorded due respect because he is not from a distinguished noble family. Amasis wins over the people because he is clever and not senselessly arrogant

(*Hist.* 2.172).[27] When he is criticized for not performing like a serious-minded king all day long, preferring to drink and joke with his companions after finishing his official duties,[28] Amasis responds that giving each part of one's personality its due makes one more flexible and stable.[29] Not doing so can make one so tense that one becomes mad or moronic (2.173–74). In other words, Amasis is not interested in appearing magnificent and pompous, which, from Herodotus' point of view, is to his credit.[30]

The individuals who receive wise advice about divine *phthonos* tend to be morally complex. Far from appreciating Solon's advice to look at how things come out in the end before counting someone blessed, the super-wealthy Croesus simply concludes that Solon is "stupid" (ἀμαθής) for not acknowledging Croesus' present blessedness (*Hist.* 1.33). Only after Croesus is captured by Cyrus and about to be burned alive on a pyre does he realize the truth of Solon's advice (1.86).[31] After calling out Solon's name three times, Cyrus asks who Croesus was calling on. When Croesus summarizes Solon's views, Cyrus fears the retribution for what he is doing to Croesus and orders the fire stopped, with no success. Croesus then prays to Apollo who rescues him by sending a violent storm. This convinces Cyrus that Croesus is "loved of god and a good man" (1.86–87).

Herodotus also reports other actions by Croesus, some of which are laudable and others which are not. Croesus unsuccessfully attempts to avoid fulfillment of a prophetic dream which informs him that his son Atys will be killed by iron spearpoint (*Hist.* 1.34–42).[32] Herodotus speculates that the divine *nemesis*[33] which led to Atys' death was caused by Croesus' belief that he was the most blessed among humans (1.34). Later Croesus misinterprets an oracle which states that if he makes war on the Persians he will destroy a mighty empire (1.53, 71). This turns out to be his own kingdom.

On the positive side, Croesus takes pity on the man who unintentionally killed Atys, pointing out that "some god" was the cause, a god who predicted this (*Hist.* 1.45). After escaping his chains when placed on a burning pyre after his defeat by Cyrus, Croesus faults Apollo for being disloyal to him after he had made so many offerings to the god. But when the Pythia explains that Croesus had to pay for a sin of his ancestor, and that Apollo had done all he could to aid Croesus, Croesus accepts that the fault had been his own and not the god's (1.90–91). Croesus becomes an advisor to his captor Cyrus, who appreciates the captive's good advice (1.88–89; cf. 1.155–56). In his final advice to Cyrus, Croesus observes that his own sufferings have been a harsh teacher for him. He then gives the Persian king the Solonian advice that all human matters are a wheel, and as it turns it never suffers the same men to be happy forever (1.207). In this instance Croesus is similar to Artabanus in displaying the courage to give advice which is contrary to that of all the other royal advisors. And unlike Artabanus, Croesus is successful in persuading the king to change his mind (1.208).[34]

Polycrates has great success as a ruler and becomes Amasis' guest-friend. On the other hand, he violates his power-sharing agreement with his brothers, exiling one and killing the other (*Hist.* 2.182; 3.39). He is also foolishly fond of money (3.123).[35] The fact that Polycrates was the first of the Greeks who contrived to master the sea (3.122) is, for scholars such as Gammie (1986, 190), indicative of *hybris*. As I mentioned earlier, Amasis warns Polycrates that his great success might trigger divine *phthonos*. Amasis then advises Polycrates to decide what was of the very most value to him—which, if lost, would cost him the greatest mental anguish (ἄλγησις)—and then throw it away where it will never be seen among humans. If that attempt does not change the pattern of his success, he should repeat the process (3.40). Polycrates decides on discarding his signet ring and publicly throws it into the sea (3.41).

Scholars such as Romm (1998, 69–70) applaud Polycrates' attempt to heed Amasis' advice. Romm believes that "Polycrates seems to deserve his sufferings even less than Croesus did." He concludes that "the iron laws of *tisis* and *phthonos* become despotic when they punish even those who try earnestly to obey them." Van der Veen (1993, 436) disagrees. He notes that when Polycrates was deciding what to give up (*Hist.* 4.31), he looked for "what he would *probably* be most *annoyed* to lose." In other words, "'suffering' (ἀλγεῖν) has been changed into 'annoyance' (ἀσᾶσθαι)." In addition, Polycrates has changed Amasis' reference to what was most valuable to Polycrates into what "among his treasures" would annoy him most to lose (van der Veen 1993, 436). Thus, Polycrates "tries to soften the pain needed to neutralize divine envy, and so does not neutralize it at all, as is evident from the bare fact that his ring is returned to him" (1993, 440). According to van der Veen, what Polycrates *actually* values most is power, and that he did not give up (1993, 442–43). Nor does he attempt to repeat the process of surrendering what he valued, as Amasis recommended (1993, 436 n. 10; 451–52). Therefore, "Polycrates is responsible for the fact that φθόνος has not been neutralized" (1993, 448).

However one interprets Polycrates' single attempt to follow Amasis' advice, his downfall is eventually caused by an individual who has no redeeming qualities. While Amasis warns Polycrates of the divinity's envy, it is human envy which leads to Polycrates' demise. The Persian Oroetes has never seen Polycrates, let alone suffered any offence from him, yet he yearns to do something "impious" (οὐκ ὁσίου) to him. The reason is that a Persian colleague had reproached Oroetes for not having conquered Samos, whose ruler is Polycrates. Oroetes decides to take vengeance not on his colleague for taunting him, but on Polycrates, to whom he has been made to appear inferior (*Hist.* 3.120). Oroetes then tricks Polycrates into trusting him by appealing to Polycrates' avarice.[36] Oroetes ultimately murders Polycrates "in a manner not fit to be told," before crucifying him (3.121–25). While the term *phthonos* does not appear in this account, Oroetes clearly feels diminished in his worth in comparison with the successful Polycrates and wishes to destroy him, presumably in order to recover his feeling of self-worth. This emotional dynamic is characteristic of malicious envy.[37]

Oroetes' evil actions continue after the killing of Polycrates. He commits a number of murders[38] and "all kinds of hybristically violent deeds" (ἐξύβρισε παντοῖα; *Hist.* 3.126). Darius finally orders his death for having openly committed unendurably hybristic acts (3.127). After Oroetes is executed, Herodotus comments that personified *tisis* (vengeance, retribution) "pursued" Oroetes for Polycrates

(3.128; cf. 3.126), just as the historian concludes that a seemingly personified vengeance—and Hermotimus—overtook Panionius (8.106; see Chapter 2.3.b.2, above).

Like the other figures just discussed, Herodotus' Xerxes is not a one-dimensional character. Admittedly, he is best known for nefarious deeds such as his order to whip and fetter the Hellespont (*Hist.* 7.35) and his illicit and destructive passion for his brother's wife and daughter (9.108–13). After Xerxes proposes gaining vengeance and requital against the Athenians (7.8), Artabanus becomes the lone voice arguing against the campaign, in part because of divine *phthonos* (7.10). Xerxes then becomes furious, calling his uncle "craven and spiritless" (κακῷ καὶ ἀθύμῳ; 7.11). Yet after thinking it over during the night, Xerxes is magnanimous enough to make a public apology to his counselors, attributing his initial reaction to his youthful impetuosity boiling over (7.13).[39] Later Xerxes and his uncle share a moment of pity for short-lived, suffering humans, with Artabanus again invoking the enviousness of "the god" (7.46).

Later Xerxes is also grateful for the wise advice of another counselor, Artemisia, queen of Halicarnassus. Although her advice does not involve divine envy, Artemisia's interactions with Xerxes reveal much about the personality of the king. Herodotus introduces Artemisia by calling attention to the fact that she, a Dorian Greek, chooses to become an ally of the Persian king, contributing five excellent ships to his expedition against Greece. Herodotus marvels (θῶμα) not only because Artemisia is a woman, but because she has retained control of her husband's tyranny after his death, even though she has a son, a young man old enough to serve in the military.[40] Most surprisingly, she joins Xerxes without being compelled to do so, motivated by her courageous spirit and "manliness" (ἀνδρηίης). Herodotus completes this initial sketch of Artemisia by noting that she offers the king better advice than any of his other allies (*Hist.* 7.99).

Artemisia's courage and manliness are on display when she first offers Xerxes good advice. The king's cousin Mardonius has solicited the counsel of all the advisors. Like Croesus and Artabanus before her, Artemisia's opinion is contrary to all the other counselors. She offers her "true opinion," which is that Xerxes not fight the Greeks at sea. She goes so far as to compare the Greek males' superior fighting skills at sea to that of the Persian males: the Greek men are stronger "as men are stronger than women" (*Hist.* 8.68). We can gauge Artemisia's boldness here by the reaction of those who learn that she counseled Xerxes not to fight at sea. Those who admire her worry that she will suffer misfortune because of her opinion. Those who resent and envy her because of the high esteem in which she is held are glad about her advice, thinking that she will be killed. But contrary to both groups' expectations Xerxes is delighted by Artemisia's opinion. Before this he had considered her to be someone of serious merit; now he praises her much more (8.69).

When Herodotus reports the ensuing sea battle at Salamis, he pays special attention to Artemisia's deeds, which give her even more esteem and influence with the king. When Artemisia's ship is being pursued by an Attic vessel, and she is unable to escape due to being hemmed in by other ships allied with Xerxes,

Artemisia purposely rams one of the allied vessels, sinking it. Herodotus makes it clear that he is unsure whether Artemisia did this because she had had a quarrel with the king of the Calyndians, whose vessel she rammed. In other words, Herodotus cannot determine whether Artemisia acted out of revenge, whether she did it intentionally, or whether this particular ship fell in her way by chance or luck (κατὰ τύχην; *Hist.* 8.87). In any case, she had the good luck (εὐτυχίη)[41] to gain doubly by what she had done. First, the captain of the pursuing Attic ship concludes that Artemisia's vessel is Greek, or is commanded by a former Persian ally who has joined the Greeks (8.87). Second, Xerxes is informed that Artemisia has sunk an enemy ship, prompting him to echo Artemisia's own gendered judgment prior to the battle: "my men have become women, and my women men" (8.88).[42]

After the devastating loss at Salamis Xerxes must decide whether to stay and attack the Greeks with his land army or go back to Persia. The king's trust in Artemisia is demonstrated when Xerxes includes her among the counselors with whom he will consider the better course of action. Artemisia's special status is highlighted when the king tells all the others to leave, including his spear-bearing bodyguard (*Hist.* 8.101).[43] Artemesia advises Xerxes to return home, which pleases the king because this is exactly what he wants to do. In Herodotus' opinion, Xerxes is so full of dread that he would not have remained at the battlefront even if all the counselors had advised that he remain. Herodotus does not ask whether Artemisia might have been aware of the king's state of mind and told him what she knew he wanted to hear.[44]

Together, the episodes involving Artemisia show that Xerxes is far more than a stereotypical tyrant.[45] Contrary to the expectations of both Artemisia's friends and her envious enemies, the king is not furious with her for having given advice contrary to that of all his other counselors; in fact, he is delighted with her. While his even greater esteem for her later is the result of an erroneous report of her performance in the sea battle at Salamis, Herodotus is calling our attention to her great luck rather than to fact that Xerxes' praise of her is based on faulty military intelligence. Finally, the fact that Xerxes holds an unusual private meeting with Artemisia—in spite of the fact that she is a woman and a Greek—also speaks well of the king's character.[46]

3. Avengers and the divine in Herodotus

Among those who receive advice about divine envy, two go on to seek revenge against their enemies. Croesus wants to avenge himself (τίσασθαι) against Cyrus on behalf of his brother-in-law (*Hist.* 1.73), and Xerxes wants vengeance and retribution (τιμωρίην τε καὶ τίσιν) against the Athenians for what they did to his father Darius and the Persians (7.8).[47] Both fail. In this section I will focus on cases in which vengeance is the actors' primary motive.

My first example is a report in which humans attempt to vindicate a deity or enact retribution on a god's behalf (*Hist.* 9.93–94).[48] In Apollonia on the Ionic Gulf there is one flock which is sacred to the Sun. The most highly regarded of the citizens guard the flock. When this story takes place, Euenius is the guard chosen for that year. He falls asleep, and as a result wolves kill about sixty of the flock. The Apollonians find him guilty in court and sentence him to lose his eyes. The gods are not happy with the townspeople's act and cause the land—and sheep—to become infertile. Through prophets, the Apollonians learn that the gods consider their action against Euenius to have been unjust, because the gods themselves sent the wolves. As a result the gods will continue to avenge (τιμωρέοντες) Euenius until the citizens give reparation or pay the penalty to him.[49] Euenius himself is to decide what reparation he finds just. Afterwards the gods will give Euenius a gift so valuable that all humankind will consider him blessed for possessing it (9.93).

After hearing these oracles the townspeople deceive Euenius. A group of citizens approach Euenius without sharing the oracles with him. They ask him what requital he would choose if the people promise him restitution. Euenius names two farms and the finest house in the city. When Euenius learns about the oracle he becomes angry, because he realizes that he has been tricked (*Hist.* 9.94). In this case, while the gods avenge the wrong done by the human avengers to their victim, those who roused the gods' vengeance are not made to suffer personally, either for their blinding of Euenius or for the later deception of their victim. Neither divine wrath nor divine *phthonos* is mentioned. However, the gods keep their promise to give Euenius an impressive gift. This is the gift of prophecy, for which Euenius becomes famous (9.94).

Hermotimus is probably the clearest case of an avenger in Herodotus whose personal revenge also becomes a case of divine retribution, even if he is not said to view himself as an agent of the divine. As I mentioned in Chapter 2.3.b.2, as a youth Hermotimus had been taken captive and sold to Panionius, a man who earns his living through "the most unholy practices" (ἔργων ἀνοσιωτάτων), namely, castrating and selling beautiful boys. Hermotimus is later in a position of power that allows him to achieve vengeance against his tormentor. He deceives Panionius and his four sons in order to put Panionius in a position where he is forced to castrate his sons, after which the sons are compelled to castrate their father. Before he inflicts this punishment, Hermotimus tells Panionius that he must have thought that his wicked deeds would escape the gods' notice, but their just law has brought him into Hermotimus' hands (*Hist.* 8.106). If Panionius did assume that his crimes would go unnoticed by the gods, he made the same mistake as the biblical sinners who believe that God does not see them (see Pss 10:3–6, 11; 14:1; 94:6–7; Isa 29:15; Ezek 8:12; 9:9).

Herodotus begins this story by commenting that Hermotimus "achieved the greatest vengeance (μεγίστη τίσις) for being wronged than anyone we know" (*Hist.* 8.105). He ends the tale with another comment: "This, then, was the way in which Panionius was overtaken by τίσις at the hands of Hermotimus" (8.106). Hermotimus' personal revenge is also the gods' revenge for Panionius' unholy deeds. In this instance of extremely violent vengeance there is no divine reprisal against the avenger. In fact, Hermotimus views himself as a knowing agent of divine justice (8.106). He does not mention divine jealousy or envy, but three paragraphs later divine *phthonos* is brought to readers' attention when Themistocles becomes the last authoritative voice in the *Histories* to point to the dangers of incurring divine *phthonos* (8.109).

Finally, Herodotus' account of Pheretime and her son offers an example of how excessive revenge can prompt divine envy and exceptionally severe punishment. This part of Cyrene's turbulent political history begins when Pheretime's son Arcesilaus refuses to maintain the tripartite form of government to which his dead father had agreed. Arcesilaus demands all the rights and royal domains that his father Battus had possessed prior to the partition of the government (*Hist.* 4.161–62). Arcesilaus fails in his power grab and flees to Samos, and Pheretime flees to Cyprus. Arcesilaus puts together an armed force and gains control of the government in Cyrene and seeks vengeance against the opponents responsible for his exile (4.162–64). After he burns some of his Cyrenaean adversaries who had fled to a great tower, Arcesilaus realizes that an oracle he had received but forgotten has come to pass in a way unfavorable to himself. He therefore flees to Barca, where some Cyrenaean exiles kill him (4.164).[50]

It is Arcesilaus' death which prompts his mother Pheretime's revenge. She goes as a suppliant to Aryandes, viceroy of Egypt, exhorting him to avenge her (*Hist.* 4.165). Aryandes takes pity on her and sends an armed Persian force to Barca (4.165–67, 200). The invaders demand the surrender of those guilty of Arcesilaus' murder but the Barcaeans refuse, since all citizens of Barca claim that they are guilty of this act. Pheretime's forces then trick the Barcaeans into leaving their city and allowing in those who had been besieging them. When the city is taken, those Barcaeans who are "most guilty" are handed over to Pheretime, who has them impaled on the city walls. Their women's breasts are cut off and set around the wall. Pheretime gives the remainder of the offending citizenry to her Persian soldiers as booty. Those Barcaeans who had no share of the murder are then given control of the city (4.200–202).

Shortly thereafter Herodotus informs his audience that the avenger Pheretime did not end her life well. After she had avenged herself on the Barcaeans she goes back to Egypt and dies badly. While she is still alive she breeds worms in herself. Herodotus then offers the moral of this story in his own voice: "vengeful acts that are exceedingly violent are for the gods a cause of envy (or resentment; ἐπίφθονοι) against humans (*Hist.* 4.205).

Herodotus' assessment is straightforward and clear. However, there is still much to point out. Readers are not told whether the gods would have approved of Pheretime's actions—or would have even taken notice of them—if her vengeance had not been so bloody. She was not said to be acting as an agent of the gods in punishing the Barcaeans so harshly. And the son whom she was avenging had not been shown to be an innocent victim in any sense. In fact, this series of events began when Arcesilaus rejects the peaceable solution accepted by his father, for the sake of increasing his wealth and power. Moreover, the Cyrenaean exiles in Barca have some justification for executing Arcesilaus, given his brutal treatment of his opponents earlier.

Commentators on this narrative tend to focus on the fact that "the *timoriai* [vengeful actions] of the gods are never 'excessively violent' (as devastating as they may seem)" (Munson 2001, 187). Pheretime's problem is that she "had assumed the divine prerogative of excessively great vengeance" (S. Shapiro 1996, 353; cf. Chiasson 2016, 48). Mossman argues that Pheretime punished "a community, rather than individuals." Such "lack of discrimination in punishment is usually a characteristic of divine vengeance, like the plague in *Oedipus Tyrannus*" (1995, 175).[51] However, *all* the Barcaeans claim responsibility for the killing as a "community," because they had all suffered much ill-treatment from Arcesilaus (*Hist.* 4.167).[52]

4. Conclusions on divine envy and vengeance in Herodotus

Is human success or great prosperity—as in the cases of Croesus and Polycrates—enough to trigger divine *phthonos*, even without the prosperous person having committed any acts of violence or impiety? Herodotus' Solon certainly seems to think so when he declares that "the god promises fortune to many people and then overturns them root and branch," and "the divine is entirely envious and disturbing to us" (*Hist.* 1.32). A number of scholars conclude that Herodotus "does in fact agree with the views expressed by his character Solon" (S. Shapiro 1996, 349; cf. Romm 1998, 61)." Lateiner (1991, 196) is a bit more cautious. He notes that the concept of "an *immoral and divine jealousy*" is endorsed not only by Solon but the three other advisors as well. Since all "four individuals . . . are credited with perspicacity, . . . it is unlikely that Herodotus rejects it."

For most commentators the issue is more complicated than this implies. Some argue that the wise advisors Solon, Amasis, and Artabanus seek to warn their powerful advisees of danger from envious deities "without giving offence" by accusing the rulers of wrongdoing or *hybris* (Cairns 1996, 22; cf. Munson 2001, 185). In other words, the advisors are being "tactful" (Pelling 2006, 106; Chiasson 2016, 48–49). In addition, Herodotus has a number of different types of explanation, of which divine envy is merely one. Romm (1998, 65–66) points to the "principle of *tisis*, or payback," which has "stronger ethical force" than *phthonos*. Greatness, "by its very nature," disrupts "the Solonic balance in the world of human affairs" and invites "the wrath of a spiteful deity *and* the retribution of injured justice." For Lateiner "the principle of 'evening out' or retribution (τίσις) . . . promotes equipoise *through* divine envy" (1991, 193, 195; emphasis added).[53] Here *phthonos* and *tisis* are tools used to restore cosmic balance.

Asserting that greatness itself disrupts the world's balance and that retribution helps to reestablish that balance is not to say that great success is a moral failing which merits divine vengeance. Chiasson describes "the new and distinctive element" in the Herodotean Solon's portrayal of deity as "his explicit articulation of the idea that divinity resents and disrupts extraordinary human success as encroaching or threatening to encroach upon divine prerogative" (2016, 48). While Chiasson does not mention any intention to encroach on the part of the successful person, his characterization of Solon's view makes human greatness into more of a moral transgression. As discussed earlier, Pheretime demonstrates that excessive revenge can also constitute a usurpation of a divine prerogative, one which prompts divine envy and devastating punishment; it too disrupts cosmic balance. Lateiner notes that Oroetes' unjustified retribution against Polycrates also creates a serious imbalance. His "capture of Polycrates is 'unholy' because . . . he had no reason to seek *tisis*." The nature of things "encourages the restoration of balance" (1991, 203).

These interpretations of Herodotus' Solon still leave room for a person to unintentionally exceed human limits for success, but still encounter divine envy and punishment. How, after all, is an individual to know when his or her success has exceeded proper human limits (S. Shapiro 1996, 353)? According to Munson (2001, 187), when Herodotus himself asserts that Pheretime's violent revenge has caused divine envy against her, he is joining "the Solonian notion of divine envy of human power to that of divine anger against wrongdoing," as Themistocles does when speaking to the Athenians later. She concludes that "many *timoriai* [acts of vengeance] of the *Histories*, with *or without* ulterior motives, are equivalent to *adikiai* [acts of injustice], and as such they are vulnerable to divine punishment" (2001, 188; emphasis added). It is therefore the responsibility of the avenger to know when her or his act of violence becomes excessive, and therefore unjust.

Finally, Cairns offers another way of determining whether an extraordinarily successful person has become culpable by indulging in excess. This is the person's attitude. If "a person's success does antagonize the gods, he [*sic*] has failed to be cautious, to exhibit the proper attitude of mind" (1996, 20). Divine resentment is caused either by the individual's failure to manifest the correct attitude (to recognize the gulf between human and divine prosperity, as well as the role of the gods in human achievement)," or by "his active adoption of the wrong attitude (deliberate rejection of mortal limits, . . .)." The target of divine *phthonos* "has failed (by commission or omission) to recognize the boundary which separates his *timê* [honor] from that of the gods" (1996, 20–21). Thus, when Solon advises Croesus and Amasis counsels Polycrates, "the emphasis is more on the need to manifest the proper attitude in success than on the notion that success in itself provokes the gods to envy" (1996, 21).[54]

In sum, while many scholars claim that Herodotus agrees with Solon's pronouncements on divine envy and resentment of human success, they usually go on to argue that the humans in question have said or done something wrong which justifies the gods' destructive actions against them. The lingering question is whether such arguments are motivated by a need on the part of interpreters to avoid the conclusion that Herodotus and his wise advisors view the gods as possessing destructive human emotions, emotions which might lead them to topple an extraordinarily successful individual "for no reason," as the biblical Yahweh admits that he has done with Job (חנם; Job 2:3).

Notes

1 Walcot contends that the Greek gods "needed" to feel envy only when there were "mortal men whose powers might seem to approach those of the gods themselves, and such men became known in the Greek world when the Greeks encountered for the first time eastern potentates" (1978, 31; 36). At that point, "kings became rivals and not the protegés of the gods as they are in the *Iliad*."

2 Garvie notes that "the verb φθονέω occurs in Homer only ten times . . ., and never in the context of a god's attitude to a human being" (2009, xxvi). For a survey of the eight occasions on which this verb appears in *The Odyssey* in the context of gift-giving and receiving, see Eidinow 2016, 218–22.
3 See Sanders (2014, 50) for a discussion of ἄγαμαι, a "Homeric term that dies out after the early Archaic period." He classifies the relevant occurrences in *The Odyssey* as following the "script" of "censuring resentment." On Telemachus using the verb φθονέω when telling his mother Penelope not to begrudge the singer giving pleasure by singing of the Danaans' evil fate (*Od.* 1.346), see Chapter 1.3, above.
4 Sanders (2014, 48) concludes that *zêlêmôn* "means something more like begrudging or censure" here.
5 Walcot (1978, 25–26) does acknowledge these references to the gods' envy, but he downplays their significance: "throughout the Homeric poems, we hear of the envy of the gods merely in vague statements" which "do not add up to anything like a theory of divine envy directed against the powerful."
6 Clay makes this comment when investigating why Plato's Socrates describes the city's *phthonos* against him by comparing himself with Achilles. In the *Iliad* Achilles had compared himself to Heracles (*Ap.* 28a-d; *Il.* 18.117–19). Achilles declares that fate (μοῖρα) and Hera's "troublesome wrath" (ἀργαλέος χόλος) brought him down (*Il.* 18.119).
7 The term *zêlotupia* first appears in the 4th c. BCE (Sanders 2014, 49, 164–65). It is usually translated as "jealousy," "rivalry," or "envy." To Konstan (2006, 223), "the Stoics' conception of *zêlotupia* seems more like malice or spite than jealousy, nastier even than envy."
8 Konstan believes that Hera's "principal preoccupation" is not "Zeus's philandering as such," but "the status of her children" (2006, 229).
9 Reinhardt considers Hera's hatred to be "puzzling, uncanny, outrageous" in this scene (1960, 29). Hera's animosity is not so puzzling when ones takes into account the situation into which her husband has placed her.
10 The precise occasion for this punishment is left vague, although Zeus does remark that he felt agony for Heracles. P. Jones draws the general conclusion that "Zeus is referring to the punishment he meted out to Hera for her treatment of Heracles" (2003, 213). Postlethwaite is more specific: "the occasion was the previous sacking of Troy by Heracles, son of Zeus, who on his return journey was blown off course by Hera" (2000, 195).
11 I disagree with Whitman's view that Zeus' threat of punishment (and mention of previous punishment), is "simply . . . a piece of rather grim domestic discipline, but well deserved and, . . . more of a cause for merriment than for concern" because the victim Hera is immortal (1970, 42). In Homer the emotions predicated of the gods are not reported in a way which prompts readers to conclude that the suffering they express is not *really* suffering to them (or, in this case, that Hera's fright and terror are not experienced as real by her). If one is dead one cannot feel pain (I assume), but being deathless does not necessarily mean that pain does not hurt Homer's immortals.
12 In fact, *Il.* 8.459–61 repeats 4.22–24 verbatim.
13 The event to which Hephaestus alludes is left vague; see Scodel 2009, 148–49.
14 This term (κυνώπιδος) is often rendered "bitch-faced." Helen applies it to herself twice (*Il.* 3.180; *Od.* 4.145) and Hephaestus applies it to his spouse Aphrodite once (*Od.* 8.319). Achilles also insults Agamemnon with this word (*Il.* 1.159).
15 It is difficult to explain Hera's ambivalence toward her son Hephaestus in the *Iliad* without determining whether his father is Zeus. It is unclear whether Homer's readers and hearers would assume that Zeus is Hephaestus' father, as Stanford (1967, 340) believes is the case in *Od.* 8.318, or that Hera produced Hephaestus parthenogenetically, as in Hesiod (*Theog.* 924–28). In the latter tradition it is envy and anger which

lead Hera to birth Hephaestus by herself, after Zeus had created the impressive goddess Athena without Hera playing a role in the birth. As I will discuss shortly, the *Homeric Hymn to Apollo* explains Hera's negative feelings toward Hephaestus by having her tell the assembled gods that her son's weakness and shriveled feet were "a shame and disgrace" for *her* (*h. Ap.* 317).

16 For theories about Homer's reason for mentioning the judgment story only at the end of the epic—and then only briefly—see Chapter 7.1.a, below.
17 The poet uses the *hapax* ζηλοσύνη here. Sanders (2014, 48) suggests that the term refers to an emotion similar to "begrudging envy."
18 It is not difficult to imagine that the mother of a deformed or dead baby might envy the mother of a healthy baby. Nor is it difficult to imagine that this envy would become so malicious and spiteful that the envious mother would attempt to destroy the other mother or her healthy child. This is what occurs in the story of Solomon's judgment (1 Kgs 3:16–28); the mother of the dead baby wants the live baby destroyed even when she is offered the living baby by its birth mother (see Lasine 1989, 65–66, 71–72).
19 In these contexts, *phthonos* includes elements of jealousy (the god seeking to retain sole possession of his or her prerogatives) and envy (the desire to bring down those who are viewed as rivals of the god, by becoming too much like the deity).
20 On Herodotus' abstract references to gods and the divine in general, see Chapter 7.1.a, below.
21 Earlier Periander had acted in a manner similar to the gods when he took Thrasybulus' advice and cut down the most outstanding of his citizens (*Hist.* 5.92). For a comparison of the supposedly wicked kings Periander and Ahab, see Lasine 2012, 171–82.
22 On the problem of "thinking big" and having "big thoughts" in Sophocles' *Ajax* and Euripides' *Hippolytus*, see Chapter 6.2.a and 6.3.a, below.
23 Later the Athenians echo Themistocles' reference to "the gods and the heroes" when telling Alexander of Macedon why they will not make an agreement with Xerxes (*Hist.* 8.143).
24 On the character and reliability of Herodotus' Themistocles, see, e.g., Romm 1998, 187–89; Zali 2013, 466, 473–80.
25 However, Cambyses later attempts to desecrate Amasis' embalmed remains (*Hist.* 3.16).
26 Gammie notes that "no really negative traditions have been recorded at all" concerning Amasis (1986, 176; cf. 189). He adds that in Amasis' case "the historian refrains from drawing heavily on a list of negative stereotypical traits of a monarch" (1986, 182; cf. van der Veen 1993, 449).
27 Amasis does so in unique fashion, taking a golden footbath and making a divine image from it. When the people show reverence to the image, Amasis informs them that the Egyptians used to vomit and relieve themselves in this gold when it was a mere footbath. Now they revere it, and so should they also honor Amasis, who was once a man of the people but is now their monarch (*Hist.* 2.172). Ironically, this speech recalls biblical idol parodies, but in those cases, readers are to disdain images made from the same piece of wood that they had used to warm themselves (e.g., Isa 44:9–20) rather than to honor those images.
28 Amasis has also been criticized by scholars such as Romm, particularly for his response to the demand made by Apries' messenger. When Amasis is summoned to the royal court his reply is merely a fart (*Hist.* 2.162). In Romm's reading, Amasis is nothing more than "a somewhat shallow 'good-time' Charlie" who turns back "to his frat-boy ways" after completing the day's official business (1998, 61, 165)!
29 Van der Veen (1993, 449) concludes that for Amasis "life is more than being a king"; power and its splendor do not blind him to possible dangers.
30 On the negative side, Amasis does lead a rebellion against king Apries, but Apries is shown to be cruel, impulsive, and so unpopular that his people rebel against him (*Hist.*

2.161–62). And when Apries is captured by Amasis, he is treated well by his successor (2.169). In terms of Amasis' character, we are told that before he became king he sometimes stole from others. However, he admits as much later on, by maintaining only the shrines of the gods whose oracles had convicted him of being a thief; these oracles he took to be truthful (2.174).

31 Lattimore points to the fact that "Croesus is wise only after the event, when he has suffered," and concludes that "fallen kings drop their delusions with their power" (1939, 31).

32 This story is discussed in more detail, and compared with the situation of Sophocles' Oedipus, in Chapter 6.2.c, below.

33 *Nemesis*, which appears only here in Herodotus, is usually taken to denote "righteous indignation" in this passage. Ellis (2015, 95) contends that "like Pindar and Hesiod and unlike Homer and Aristotle," Herodotus "does not use *nemesis* as an emotional term." On *nemesis* and its relation to *phthonos*, see Chapter 2.3.b.1, above.

34 Xerxes is initially very angry at his uncle's advice, but he soon recognizes the wisdom of Artabanus' position. However, prophetic dreams force the king to change his mind again. When Artabanus has the same dream vision as his nephew, he too renounces his original advice (*Hist.* 7.10–18).

35 Herodotus gives no information about what might have led Polycrates to take action against his brothers. For all we know, these actions could have been driven by *Realpolitik*, as is the case when the biblical Solomon orders the death of his brother Adonijah and the exile of the priest Abiathar (1 Kgs 1–2).

36 Herodotus also claims that there was no end to Themistocles' greed (*Hist.* 8.112).

37 Herodotus himself states that Oroetes wants to kill Polycrates because the Samian ruler had unknowingly been used by the Persian colleague to sully Oroetes' reputation (*Hist.* 3.120). However, this does not alter the fact that the emotional process described by the historian is characteristic of envy. Later Themistocles, who himself expresses a belief in divine envy, is verbally attacked by an Athenian enemy named Timodemus, who was "mad with envy" (φθόνῳ καταμαργέων) against Themistocles (8.125).

38 Among Oroetes' victims are the colleague who originally taunted him for not conquering Samos, as well as that colleague's son (*Hist.* 3.126).

39 Xerxes and Artabanus then experience terrifying dream visions which convince them that they must invade Greece after all. On the implications of having a youthful ruler in *Persians*, *Hippolytus*, and *Bacchae*, see Chapter 6.1.b, 6.3.a and 6.4.b, below.

40 As How and Wells put it, she "had a son of an age to serve . . . and might have stayed at home to safeguard her throne" (1912, 164). The son is called a νεανίης here. This term is also employed by Euripides to describe the young, militaristic Pentheus in *The Bacchae* (974), a play we will discuss in Chapter 6.4. On Theseus as a νεανίης in Euripides' *Suppliant Women*, see Strauss 1993, 114–15.

41 According to Munson (1988, 105–106), "*tychē* in Herodotus often clearly indicates the divine influence that man [*sic*] does not comprehend by reason, as when an outcome cannot be interpreted as the logical consequence of a good or bad decision or as an appropriate retribution for a moral or immoral action."

42 Gender also plays a role when the Athenians offer a ten thousand drachma reward for the capture of Artemisia, because it was so terrible and strange (δεινὸν) that a woman has engaged in war against Athens (*Hist.* 8.93).

43 While this unusual private meeting shows how much Xerxes trusts and respects Artemisia, not all readers may agree with Romm that the scene indicates "something touching . . . about the affinity of these two characters" (1998, 172).

44 A final sign of Xerxes' trust in Artemisia is the fact that after thanking her for her advice, he entrusts her to take to Ephesus the bastard sons who have accompanied him to the front (*Hist.* 8.103). These sons will be guarded by Hermotimus (8.104), whose enactment of divine vengeance against his enemy I will describe in the next section.

45 On the senses in which Xerxes does, and does not, resemble the conventional portrait of a tyrant, see Gammie 1986, 183–85.
46 Artemisia's advice to Xerxes is given from a Persian perspective. However, as Munson points out (1988, 97–101, 103–104), Artemisia's own character, including her aggressiveness, freedom of speech, and her actions motivated by self-interest, are typical of Athenians, and the Athenian advisor Themistocles in particular. For the differences between the ways in which Persians and Greeks deliberate in these scenes, see Pelling 2006, 110–12.
47 I might also mention Oroetes wanting to achieve retribution (τίσασθαι) against Polycrates, a man he had never even met (*Hist.* 3.120).
48 Thucydides (1.127) offers an example of a group (the Spartans) who claim that an action they propose is motivated by their desire to avenge the gods. In reality, their proposal is motivated by self-interest.
49 Lateiner (1980, 30) notes that "the most common idiom in Herodotus to express the concept of 'paying a penalty' or 'making amends' is the metaphor δίκας (or δίκην) διδόναι." In the Euenius narrative, "the concept of δίκη [justice, order, judgment, penalty] is central"; in fact, "the root appears seven times in one paragraph" (1980, 30 n. 5).
50 Cf. the biblical Abimelech, who attempts to burn a tower into which the citizens of Thebez have fled, only to have his skull fractured by a millstone dropped by a woman from the roof of the tower (Judg 9:50–54).
51 Mossman (1995, 175) believes that Herodotus' "choice of the word ἐπίφθονος ('grudged') ... may imply that Pheretima has usurped divine authority."
52 Whether Mossman's analogy of the plague in *Oedipus* is relevant here will become clear when we study envy and revenge in that play; see Chapter 6.2, below.
53 Lateiner also mentions three other modes of explanation employed by Herodotus: fate, divine influence and "down-to-earth" historicist political analysis (1991, 197–204).
54 Cairns concedes that Solon, Amasis, and Artabanus are "suggesting that the gods have a tendency to perceive offence where none is intended," implying that "divine resentment is sometimes excessive and unjustified." However, he views this as a result of the advisors avoiding the need to tell their advisees that they may be guilty of *hybris*. Cairns adds that "the gods themselves believe their *phthonos* to be justified, and the author or the reader can always endorse this interpretation" (1996, 22).

6 Divine envy and vengeance in Greek tragedy

The tragedies I will examine in this chapter illustrate a variety of attitudes toward envy and revenge on the part of both gods and humans.[1] In several plays individual gods appear on stage. In others, occurrences are attributed to "the gods" or *daimōnes* in general. In some cases deities who have an active on-stage role attribute their actions to a desire for vengeance. The protagonists may also see themselves as an ally of the gods in exacting revenge. In one case, different speakers within the drama attribute the protagonist's defeat to one of several causes, including divine envy, punishment, or excessive revenge. In three tragedies the main characters' youth contributes to their suffering or death, while in the other tragedies mature individuals experience disaster and feel hated by one or more deities. Scholars also have varying opinions about the role of envy and revenge in each play, as well as the roles played by gods in the tragedies. A few argue that a deity's hostility toward the protagonist in a given tragedy is motivated by envy, even when *phthonos* and other terms for envy do not appear in the text.

1. Envy and vengeance in Aeschylus' *Persians*

a. Explaining defeat: divine phthonos

The two major speeches in *Persians* attribute the victory of the Greeks over the Persians to different causes. The first explanation is offered by the Persian Messenger, who "thinks like a Greek" (Garvie 2009, 177).[2] He views the disaster as the work of some unidentified spirit or deity (δαίμων; *Pers.* 345).[3] According to the Messenger, Xerxes is unaware that the "envy of the gods" (τὸν θεῶν φθόνον) is at work against him (362). Garvie notes that the Messenger does not explain Xerxes' defeat in terms of punishment for *hybris*; he "says merely that the δαίμων was not impartial, and that the gods favored Athens" (2009, 178). However, the Messenger also refers to the divinity who caused the defeat as a "vengeful spirit (ἀλάστωρ) or evil *daimōn*" (*Pers.* 354; cf. 345–47).

The Messenger observes that Xerxes was unable to understand the cunning of the Greeks (*Pers.* 362–63). He does not suggest that the gods blinded Xerxes to the Greek's trickery, although earlier the chorus had asked, "what mortal man can avoid being cunningly deceived by god?" (93).[4] The Messenger also points

DOI: 10.4324/b23212-6

out that Xerxes did not know what the gods were about to do and was ill-informed about what was about to occur (373, 454). He does not attribute Xerxes' failures of understanding to arrogance, inflated self-importance, or *hybris*.

The Messenger's eyewitness testimony leaves an impression of authority and credibility. The Queen herself tells Darius that the Messenger's account is indisputably correct (*Pers.* 738), as the chorus had predicted it would be (246–48).[5] Can the same be said of the Messenger's "theology," including his mention of divine *phthonos*? Within the play, the Messenger is not alone in attributing events to an unnamed divine being, referred to either as a *daimōn* or a god. In fact, all the characters and the chorus make "multiple references ... to a nameless *daimōn* with malevolent intent towards the Persians" (Hall 2007, 15).[6] On the other hand, the Messenger is the only character to appeal to divine envy (*Pers.* 362). Garvie contends that while "this is the only occurrence in the play of the word *phthonos*," the "idea underlies the whole of the first half of the play" (2009, 186).

We get a glimpse of the Messenger's personal attitude toward the divine when he relates how the retreating troops crossed the sacred river Strymon (*Pers.* 495–512). "God" had caused the river to freeze out of season (495–96). Those who "up until then had considered the gods to be of no account"[7] called on Earth and Sky with prayers (497–500). In modern parlance, they demonstrated that "there are no atheists in foxholes." When the soldiers who had called to the gods many times finished, they began crossing the frozen river. Only those who had crossed quickly, such as the Messenger, survived (500–12). According to Hall (2007, 145), the implication may be that the soldiers "stupidly wasted valuable time on praying." The Messenger does not say whether he himself had offered any prayers, but the fact that he was one of the few survivors suggests that he did not join in the protracted prayers of the formerly godless soldiers. This does not imply that he himself holds the gods to be of no account; in fact, he consistently sees the hand of the divine in these events. But it does imply that he puts pragmatism and self-help above passively requesting divine aid when urgent action is called for.

b. Explaining defeat: hybris, *failed vengeance, and divine punishment*

The second major speech offers a very different perspective on the Persians' humiliating defeat. The ghost of Xerxes' father Darius attributes the Persians' defeat and suffering to *hybris* committed by his son Xerxes and the Persian soldiers in Greece. If the Messenger "thinks like a Greek," Darius' "theological views could not sound more Greek if he tried" (Hall 2007, 164). When Darius appears he asks the chorus what new evil is afflicting the Persians. When they cannot overcome their fear in order to answer, Darius observes that "calamities to which humans are subject happen to mortals" (*Pers.* 706), or, in Hall's rendition (2007, 158), "it is the human condition that calamities happen to men." Calamities arise for mortals from both sea and land, and the longer one lives, the more true this is (*Pers.* 707–708).

This non-judgmental attitude toward disaster does not last long. Once the Queen informs Darius' ghost that his son Xerxes has led their armed forces to

106 Envy and vengeance in Greek tragedy

Athens where they were destroyed, Darius condemns his wretched son for his "foolish attempt" (*Pers.* 716–19). At first Darius surmises that some mighty *daimōn* came upon Xerxes so that he was not able to think clearly (725), a suggestion which accords with the explanations offered by speakers earlier in the play. When Atossa gives the ghost more details of the defeat, Darius' criticisms of his son become sharper. Xerxes' haste brought about the premature fulfillment of previous oracles, for when one is hasty, god assists (742).[8] Xerxes' failure to understand is due in part to "his youthful rashness" (744). Even more seriously, "although only a mortal, he supposed, without good counsel, that he could prevail over all the gods, including Poseidon." Darius wonders whether "a disease of the mind" (νόσος φρενῶν) has affected his son (749–51). Then the royal ghost accuses young Xerxes of thinking young thoughts and not remembering his father's orders and instructions (783).[9]

Later Darius' ghost informs the chorus that few of the Persian forces now in Greece will return. What god had decreed in his oracles will come to pass (*Pers.* 801). It is at this point that Darius makes his most severe moral judgments. Xerxes is deluded by empty hopes. The troops he left behind "have in store to suffer their highest evil as requital (ἄποινα) for their *hybris* and god-denying (κἀθέων) arrogance" (804–808). The most glaring example is that when they reached Greece, they stole images of gods, burned temples, and destroyed altars and shrines (809–13). So what they are about to suffer at Plataea and elsewhere is caused by their misdeeds. This will show future generations that "a mortal must not think thoughts which are excessive" (ὑπέρφευ . . . φρονεῖν; 820). When *hybris* "has flowered," it "bears as its fruit a crop of infatuation and doom (ἄτης)" and reaps a harvest of lamentation (820–22). Darius then reminds the chorus that Zeus is a chastiser (or "punisher"; κολαστής) of overweening prideful thoughts and a severe corrector (827–28). Therefore one should "cease from offending the gods through overweening rashness" (829–31).

At first glance, Darius' credibility as an authoritative moral judge seems indisputable. The chorus refers to this "Sousa-born god of the Persians" as "like the gods in counsel" and "godlike" (*Pers.* 642, 654, 857). His queen says that he lived his life "like a god" (710–11). Darius himself states that he has some power among the underworld gods (690–91). Perhaps most importantly, Darius has prophetic knowledge of the upcoming disasters.

On the other hand, the original audience would be aware that the play presents an idealized Darius. As noted by Kantzios (2004, 13), the historical Darius, like the son he posthumously condemns, attempted to bridge a body of water in a war, attacked Greece to punish Athens, and returned to Asia empty-handed after a defeat at Marathon. Kantzios concludes that "the credibility of [Darius'] words is undermined by the audience's knowledge of him." Garvie (2009, xxxi) also finds evidence that Darius' authority is "slightly undermined," not because his presentation is unhistorical but because of "his surprising final words, in which this great king reveals that his wealth has done him no good in the underworld." Winnington-Ingram notes another factor: after the ghost's departure, "it is as though Darius had never spoken" (1973, 217; cf. Garvie 2009, xxx).[10]

Although this might seem to diminish Darius' authority as a speaker, Fisher argues that it is "unreasonable to conclude from the evident failure of Atossa, the Chorus, and Xerxes to adopt [Darius'] views in their entirety that they would carry little weight with the audience" (1992, 261).

Before asking whether the audience must choose between the perspectives of the Messenger and Darius' ghost, it is worth noting that Atossa also offers a unique perspective on the Persian disasters. After hearing a good portion of the Messenger's report, she castigates the "abhorrent *daimōn*" which has "deceived the wits of the Persians" (*Pers.* 472–73). Then she laments that "the vengeance (τιμωρίαν) my son gained from famous Athens was bitter and the barbarians whom Marathon destroyed were not enough." While "he thought he would achieve retribution (ἀντίποινα) for them," he ended up bringing upon himself many troubles (474–77). In other words, Xerxes' attempt at excessive and ill-considered revenge resulted in divinely inspired disaster.

Earlier I discussed the case of Pheretime's excessive revenge against her enemies, about which Herodotus comments, "vengeful acts that are excessively violent are for the gods a cause of envy against humans" (*Hist.* 4.205). While queen Atossa does not follow the Messenger in citing divine envy as a factor in Persia's defeat or anticipate Darius' judgment of *hybris* against her son, she does suggest that excessive revenge is a factor which is itself sufficient to explain Persia's divinely inspired catastrophe.

c. Conclusions on Xerxes' defeat

We are now in position to ask whether we should view the humiliating defeat of Xerxes and his troops through the optic provided by the Messenger, Darius' ghost, or Queen Atossa. Can all three explanations be taken as authoritative? Garvie (2009, xxv) reduces our choice to two options: "the *hybris* view we may describe as the moral explanation, the *phthonos* theory as the amoral explanation of human suffering." Leaving aside for the moment whether the Messenger's viewpoint should be characterized as "amoral," a number of commentators give most weight to Darius' charge that his son—and his armed forces—have committed hybristic acts. In fact, "the amoral *phthonos* view has usually been labelled more primitive than the supposedly more advanced moral explanation of suffering" (Garvie 2009, xxv).

While Fisher does not call the Messenger's view "primitive," he does regard Darius' interpretations as authoritative. He finds it "plausible" to "grant some extra authority to the ghost over the other characters," not least because his opinions are "propounded so effectively by [an] impressive, god-like, ex-King" (1992, 261). Fisher characterizes Darius' views as "essentially 'Solonian' doctrine" and contrasts his position "with the vaguer notions of the jealousy of unnamed gods, unfairly and deceitfully attacking the wealth and power of the Persians, expressed earlier in the play by Atossa, the Messenger, and the Chorus." Yet only the Messenger mentions divine *phthonos*, and he does not label the gods "unfair." Fisher notes the "tension between the ideas of Zeus' punishment of human *hybris* and godless and excessive thoughts and those of the more irrational jealousy of the gods" (1992, 261). Yet if divine jealousy is a realistic way of expressing the changes of fortune which humans may undergo during their lifetime, it is not necessarily "irrational" any more than it is necessarily primitive.

Scholars such as Broadhead do not believe that we must choose between these explanatory schemata. Commenting on Darius' words in *Pers*. 821–22, Broadhead notes that "*hybris* is the child of impiety . . . for it deludes a man into the belief that he can overrule the divine will. . . . He thus incurs the jealousy of the gods . . ., who send upon him a blindness or infatuation (ἄτη)" (1960, 205). Impiety leads to hybristic delusions of grandeur, and this leads to divine jealousy, which leads to divine infatuation of the offender. Of course Darius himself does not invoke divine *phthonos* in his speeches. In effect, Broadhead has incorporated the idea of divine jealousy and envy into an overarching moral scheme.

In contrast, Garvie believes that "Aeschylus has left us to choose" between the amoral perspective of the Messenger and Darius' moral viewpoint (2009, xxxi). Garvie himself seems to favor the supposedly amoral view. He observes that "the amoral *phthonos* view has usually been labelled more primitive" by those who want to believe that the good are always rewarded and the impious are always punished. The problem is that "in terms of human experience it would be hard to prove that [the amoral view] is less true" (2009, xxv)[11] Garvie points out that "in every culture and every age there must have been a tension between the hope that only bad people will suffer, and the more realistic understanding that suffering is not necessarily the result of bad behaviour" (2009, xxvii).[12] In short, Darius' view fails as theodicy and the Messenger's view is a more realistic depiction of how good and evil are dispensed by the gods.[13]

The *Persians* as a whole makes it clear that Persia's defeat is the result of Xerxes' poor leadership. The king's failures include intellectual errors, impious actions, and miscalculations caused by his excessive grandiosity. The audience may hope that divine vengeance is always motivated by such egregious errors, but ordinary observers such as the Messenger offer no assurance that this will always be the case. "Stuff happens" and divine envy also happens. We can only hope that a godlike apparition will arise from Hades to assure us that the suffering we are experiencing or witnessing is both appropriate and just.

2. Envy and Vengeance in Sophocles' *Oedipus Tyrannus*

a. Divine emotion and agency in Oedipus Tyrannus and Ajax

According to Lloyd-Jones (1983, 122), in *Oedipus Tyrannus* the god Apollo "loathes the race of Laius." On three occasions Oedipus exclaims that he is hated by the gods and *daimōnes* (*OT* 816; 1345–46; 1518). While Oedipus feels that he is the recipient of divine hatred, none of the gods—including Apollo—expresses any emotion toward Oedipus in the play, let alone *phthonos*, wrath, or loathing. When Oedipus realizes that he has slain King Laius, and that he must still avoid his supposed birth parents in Corinth, he asks whether someone would not judge rightly if they concluded that some savage *daimōn* did this to him (828).[14] Earlier, when Oedipus first suspects that he might be the regicide, he asks Zeus what he has willed to do to him (738). This is the only time that Oedipus mentions Zeus by name. All the other occasions on which he names a specific god it is Apollo, usually in relation to one of the oracles which Oedipus has received from the Pythia in Delphi.[15]

The process by which Oedipus comes to the conclusion that he is hated by the gods can be traced by following the usage of the term *daimōn* in the play.[16] In the opening scene, the old priest of Zeus tells Oedipus that he and the other supplicants do not consider the king "equal to the gods," but they do consider him first among men in "dealings with *daimōnes*" (*OT* 31–34). After Creon reports Apollo's command to exact vengeance against the killers of former king Laius, Oedipus declares that he will be the "ally" (σύμμαχος) of the god in taking vengeance (106–107, 135–36). Later he tells the chorus that he will be an ally to both the *daimōn* and the murder victim (244–45; cf. 274–75).[17] All that changes after Oedipus learns that he is not only a polluted regicide (828), but a patricide who has committed incest with his own mother. When the chorus asks him which *daimōn* leapt against him in his "ill-daimoned fate" (δυσδαίμονι μοίρᾳ; 1301–1303; cf. 1330), Oedipus replies that it was Apollo (1330–31). At this point he considers himself the most utterly abominable and god-hated mortal (1345–46; cf. 1518).

Commentators do not agree about the extent of Apollo's involvement in Oedipus' downfall. J. Gould contends that this is a play "in which *no* god is seen to be active and no motivation given for Oedipus' destruction" (1985, 32; emphasis added). Segal (2001, 53) acknowledges the "supernatural elements" in the play, including Apollo, the plague, the oracles, and Tiresias' prophetic knowledge, but adds that "the play does not label any of these as the certain causes of suffering." He suggests that the "mysterious agent Oedipus calls 'Apollo' and modern interpreters call 'fate'" is possibly "something in the structure of reality itself," which "lies behind this innocent suffering" (2001, 61).[18] Winnington-Ingram (1980, 178) claims that "Apollo is divine foreknowledge of what is destined to happen." He then asks if Apollo is "also an agent? Or is Oedipus under an illusion?" His answer is that if it is an illusion, it is one "under which generations of readers have suffered. It is, surely, impossible to read the play without feeling that, in some more or less incomprehensible way, Apollo is at work."

Kovacs is more emphatic about Apollo being "at 'work'" in the play. He repeatedly asserts that Apollo "engineers" Oedipus' downfall (2009, 360, 361, 362). Specifically, "in the case of the parricide and incest Apollo creates a situation where Oedipus, a free agent acting on the information available to him, unwittingly carried out Apollo's designs" (2009, 359). In short, "Apollo tricked him" (Kovacs 2019, 109). Although Oedipus' actions are all "perfectly free" in the play, Apollo manipulates him by withholding information from him at critical moments and supplying it "where it will be most misleading" (2009, 360; cf. 2019, 111). Kovacs also cites Tiresias' words in *OT* 376–77: "it is not your fate (μοῖρα) to fall through me. Apollo is enough. To bring this about (or, to exact revenge; ἐκπρᾶξαι) is his concern" (2009, 362 n. 9).[19] Finally, Kovacs notes that

Sophocles says nothing explicit about "why Apollo contrives disaster for Oedipus." Kovacs believes that the answer is implicit: Sophocles, like Aeschylus and Euripides, "leaves Laius the option of having no child" (2009, 366).

The idea that Apollo "engineers" and "contrives" Oedipus' fall is problematic, as is Cairns' view that the prophecies from Delphi are "projects of divine intention," not merely "objects of divine knowledge" (2013b, 136). Apollo is not present in the play as an agent who consciously manipulates situations, and thereby people such as Oedipus. Apollo is not a character in the sense that the character Yahweh manipulates the situation of the Pharaoh in Exodus 7–14 or his favorite human Job, or in the sense that Aphrodite and Dionysus manipulate the humans who have offended them in Euripides' *Hippolytus* or *Bacchae*.

The sense is which Apollo is not a "character" in this play becomes most clear when we compare Apollo in *Oedipus Tyrannus* with Athena in Sophocles' *Ajax*. In *Ajax*, the chief deity makes an appearance in the prologue, conversing with her favorite human Odysseus as well as with the mad Ajax.[20] Sophocles shows Athena's feelings toward Ajax here; later, other characters tell us that those feelings are "anger" and "wrath." In the prologue Athena takes pleasure in humiliating and laughing at Ajax in the presence of Odysseus. She even instructs Odysseus to proclaim Ajax's diseased mind to all the Argives (*Aj.* 68), in order to further humiliate him and strip him of his honor. She then taunts the mad Ajax by calling herself his ally (90).[21] Ajax then hopes that Athena will always stand by him as an ally, as she has done that day (116–17). His madness is so great that he considers his greatest enemy his supporter.

After Ajax departs, Athena calls Odysseus' attention to her divine power. She is capable of transforming a man with Ajax's forethought and ability for timely action into a wretch who enacts his vengeance against the Greeks by slaughtering and torturing helpless animals. The scene ends with Athena warning Odysseus not to utter an arrogant word against the gods or be puffed up with pride, for the gods love[22] the self-controlled and abhor the wicked (*Aj.* 127–33).

Many commentators have had no difficulty in describing Athena's personality and attitude in this scene. Stanford (1968, 108) calls her "savagely vindictive." For Kennedy (2009, 113) she is not only cruel, but "relishes in her cruelty." Others view her as "toying cruelly" with Ajax (Finglass 2011, 135; Esposito 2010b, 196). Hogan highlights her "malice" and "malevolence" (1991, 179–83). In short, Athena's animosity toward Ajax is nearly impossible to miss. While Knox (1961, 6) also acknowledges that the goddess is "vengeful and fierce," he believes that she is merely "the traditional morality personified, in all its fierce simplicity." By traditional morality, Knox means the maxim directing one to aid one's friends and harm one's enemies.[23] Therefore, even her "merciless delight" in humiliating Ajax is "natural and right" (1961, 7). As we discussed in Chapter 2.3.b.1, to Athena "the sweetest laughter [is] the laughter at enemies" (*Aj.* 79; cf. Knox 1961, 8).

The audience must wait until later in the play to learn that Athena's malevolence toward Ajax involves more than his intention to wipe out the entire Greek army.[24] Ajax is the first character to label Athena's emotional attitude toward him as anger. This occurs after his fit of madness has subsided. Athena, the fierce-eyed unconquered goddess, has destroyed him with her maltreatment (*Aj.* 401–402, 450); he therefore seeks to escape "the heavy anger (μῆνιν βαρεῖαν) of the goddess" (655).[25] A short time later a messenger arrives. He informs the chorus that Ajax's half-brother Teucer has arrived, only to meet the abuse of the army who are furious with Ajax. The prophet Calchas had told Teucer to keep Ajax in his tent that entire day, because for during this day "the anger (μῆνις) of divine Athena" will harass him (756–57).

What is the source of this anger? Ajax, although of human birth, did not "think in accordance with human thoughts" (*Aj.* 760–61). Calchas offers two concrete examples. When Ajax left home he showed himself to be without sense by ignoring his father's advice to seek victory with the help of god. Instead he boasted that even a worthless man can be victorious with a god's help, so he intended to win glory without that help (762–69). Later, during the fight, Athena urges him on, but he answers the goddess with "words terrible and shameful to be spoken," telling her to stand beside the other Greeks, because no enemy could break through where he was located (774–75). With boastful words such as these Ajax wins for himself the "implacable anger (ἀστεργῆ ... ὀργήν) of the goddess." Calchas repeats the reason: Ajax was "not thinking in accordance with human thoughts" (776–77). While commentators disagree on whether Ajax's "thinking big" constitutes *hybris*,[26] his transgression of human limitations is sufficient to explain Athena's anger, especially because Ajax rejects her personal offer of aid.[27]

The character of the chief deity in these plays could hardly be more different. Apollo makes no appearance on stage and converses with no one. Apollo is never shown to hate Oedipus, even though Oedipus feels hated by the gods. While the prophet Calchas tells the chorus that Athena is angry at Ajax, and explains why she is angry, the prophet Tiresias never says that Apollo is angry at Oedipus. Tiresias does say that Apollo is sufficient for Oedipus' fate (μοῖρα) to occur (*OT* 376–77).[28] Apollo and fate are almost synonymous here; the prophet does not say that Apollo has a personal animus against Oedipus, as Athena does for Ajax.

While Oedipus has reason to believe that he can be an "ally" of the god in ferreting out the polluting killer—which he does succeed in doing—it takes a bout of madness for Ajax to believe that Athena could be his ally after he has refused her help and advice. Athena is the full and direct cause of Ajax attacking the animals in a fit of madness, while Apollo cannot be said to "cause" actions such as Oedipus' self-blinding in such an unproblematic sense. Among the other differences between the two situations, I will mention only that Ajax has incurred the wrath of Athena for intentional acts which he foolishly committed, while Oedipus' deplorable fate, although known to Apollo's ministers, is not punishment or revenge for any intentional bad act committed by the king.

As Tiresias points out, Oedipus' destiny is inexorably fixed; the oracles emanating from Delphi are the means by which that fate comes to pass. To use Winnington-Ingram's phrase, Apollo "presides over the process" (1980, 178), but he does so only in an abstract and inscrutable fashion.[29] Hogan notes that while "Apollo predicted murder and incest and later called for the apprehension of the polluted murderer," it is "not true ... that Apollo caused the murder or incest, or in any tangible way tempted or beguiled Oedipus to those crimes" (1991, 71). There is certainly no hint of "beguiling" going on. Nor must we conclude that Apollo "caused" the murder or incest.[30] The oracles helped to set up situations in which an individual with Oedipus' personality would react in the manner that he does.

b. Oedipus as avenger and target of divine vengeance

When Creon returns from Delphi early in the play, he announces that they have been commanded to exact vengeance (τιμωρεῖν), with force, on the murderers of King Laius and drive out the pollution which has ravaged Thebes (*OT* 96–99, 106–107). Mossman (1995, 173) notes that "τιμωρεῖν is used of the action needed to remove the pollution three times in under forty lines: 107, 136, 140." In line 136, Oedipus declares himself an ally in obtaining just vengeance for his land and the god. In line 140, he speculates that the killer might want to use the same avenging hand against him,[31] so that capturing the assassin is in his own self-interest.

In this tragedy, the avenger and his target are one and the same. As an avenger Oedipus shows himself to be completely devoted to discovering the identity of the perpetrator, and then exiling or executing him. He does not care what happens to him, as long as the city can be saved (e.g., *OT* 443, 1065, 1170). When Tiresias refuses to reveal what he knows about the killer, Oedipus is shocked and infuriated.[32] He views this as an act of disloyalty and betrayal which will destroy the city (322–23, 330–31). Oedipus is aware that monarchs are vulnerable to harem conspiracies, coups d'état, and assassination attempts, especially from those closest to them.[33] These dangers increase during periods of social crisis, such as the plague in Thebes (see Segal 2001, 84). Given the situation and the vulnerabilities of kingship, it is not surprising that Oedipus immediately suspects the prophet of having been hired by Creon in order to engage in a conspiracy against the sitting monarch (*OT* 378).

It is at this point that Oedipus brings up the envy faced by rulers such as himself, and the danger presented by malicious envy. He laments the "much-envied[34] life" (τῷ πολυζήλῳ βίῳ) of a *tyrannos*, especially how much envy and resentment (*phthonos*) are stored up, or fostered, against him (*OT* 380–82).[35] Jumping to the conclusion that Creon envies Oedipus' status as king, Oedipus accuses his brother in law—his "trusted friend from the beginning"—of creeping against him by stealth in order to depose him (385–89). According to Oedipus, Creon's means to that end involves the profit-loving and deceitful beggar-priest Tiresias.

When Creon learns of Oedipus' accusations against him, he confronts the king and defends himself. After reminding Oedipus that he had allowed Creon and his sister Jocasta to share in power (*OT* 579–82), Creon asks Oedipus to consider the reasons why it would be irrational for him to crave his brother-in-law's throne. He begins by asking whether anyone would choose to rule in fear instead of sleeping peacefully, if he already had power and could act like a king. Anyone who is of sound mind (or, temperate; σωφρονεῖν) would agree with him (584–89). That kings must remain wakeful and vigilant—both to watch out for the welfare of their people and to defend themselves from assassination—is a fact attested in many ancient and modern texts, including historical records.[36] Creon points out that he can gain all from Oedipus without such fear; if he were the ruler, he would have to do much under constraint (590–91). Now everyone welcomes him and greets him kindly. Those who want something from the king seek out Creon, for their success depends upon his political influence (596–98). No one who thinks well would become evil, that is, become a traitor (600).

Many commentators are far from impressed by Creon and his defense speech. For Dawe (2006, 124–25) Creon is sententious; his "essentially second-rate nature ... becomes more and more clear with each facile argument." For Blondell (2002, 112) the speech "reveals some less appealing aspects of Kreon's character ... he is essentially unheroic and scarcely admirable." Knox (1971, 87–90) emphasizes that the speech is "a masterpiece of the new sophistic rhetoric," including clichés typical of Athenian defense speeches such as those by Aeschines and Antiphon. Segal (2001, 85) finds Creon to be reasonable but "a little pedantic."[37]

Creon's rhetorical style does resemble the techniques typical of the period. And similar examples of "arguments from probability" are not difficult to find. Hogan (1991, 47) cites Euripides' *Hippolytus* 1002–1035 and Herodotus *Hist.* 5.106. Like Creon, Hippolytus argues that it is more enjoyable to have political power without the dangers involved in being the ruler. And Herodotus' Histiaeus defends himself from the charge of having worked against king Darius' interests by pointing out that he lacks nothing at the royal court, so what would be his motivation to act in a way which would harm the king? However, while Histiaeus succeeds in convincing Darius of his innocence, he does so by deceiving the king (*Hist.* 5.107), for he *was* guilty of the charges against him. This is not the case with Creon.

The *Oedipus Tyrannus* as a whole makes it clear that Creon is not guilty of any conspiracy against Oedipus. While the style of Creon's defense may be typical of the period, that does not mean that Creon is being insincere or disingenuous. In fact, his defense is remarkably candid. He makes no secret about enjoying his privileged position as a man of great political influence, without all the cares and dangers of being the king. In addition to being vulnerable to attack by disloyal family members or rival cliques, monarchs are dependent upon information-givers to supply them with news about any goings-on which might threaten their safety.[38] As a courtier, Creon is in a much better position to be "in the know" than the king himself. This puts him in a position to control the flow of information which reaches the king. Creon does not abuse that position, as does Haman in the biblical book of Esther (Esth 2:8–9). In addition, Creon makes no effort to block Oedipus' access to his people and does not insist that the news from Delphi remain only in the possession of political insiders (*OT* 91–98). This is in stark contrast to Jocasta (1060–68) and the shepherd (1152–54, 1165), both of whom attempt to prevent Oedipus from learning the truth about his identity.[39]

Creon's defense speech demonstrates that he does not feel envy or *phthonos* toward Oedipus. This makes him an exception to the rule concerning monarchs described by Herodotus' Otanes. As I discussed in Chapter 3.2.b, Otanes believes that even the best of humans can be affected negatively by absolute power. His many possessions lead him to become hybristic, while "envy (*phthonos*) is implanted in humanity." Being satiated, the ruler "does many reckless things, some from *hybris*, some from envy." Although "a *tyrannos* ought to be free of envy (*aphthonon*), having all good things, . . . he becomes the opposite of this in respect to his citizens" (*Hist.* 3.80). In Sophocles' play, neither Oedipus nor Creon fits Otanes' profile of an envious ruler.

We must also ask whether Oedipus exhibits any signs of *hybris*, even without being envious. And if he does act hybristically, does that allow us to view his enormous suffering as justified punishment? In the much-discussed second stasimon (*OT* 863–910), the chorus declares "*hybris* breeds the tyrant"[40]; explicit mentions of *hybris* appear only here. The chorus describes the tyrant as someone who is overfilled with many things in vain (874) and who acts disdainfully, without fear of justice or reverence for the seated statues of the *daimōnes* (884–86). Such a person should be seized by an evil *moira* for his ill-destined arrogant luxury (887–88).

Is the chorus implying that their king has committed *hybris*? Should the audience draw that conclusion? The majority of scholars do not believe that the chorus is accusing Oedipus of having behaved hybristically. As Winnington-Ingram points out, the chorus knows that Oedipus "did not kill the king to gain his throne." While some interpreters argue that Oedipus' act "was hubristic in its wholesale violence,"[41] the "conventional Greeks of the chorus would have seen it . . . as a "justified act of retaliation . . . by a man who found himself one among many and in danger of his life" (1980, 201). And even if it were "in the eyes of some, hubristic, this is not the *hubris* bred of *koros*[42] about which they sing." Winnington-Ingram grants that the chorus would find Oedipus' treatment of Tiresias and Creon to be "disquieting," but has he abused his power? Have the proverbial advantages of kingship have bred *hybris* in him? The answer is clear. The chorus members "characterize the arrogant man in terms of traditional excesses, impurities and impieties," but "Oedipus is not that kind of man at all" (Winnington-Ingram 1980, 202).

Similarly, Fisher notes that the chorus do not waver in their essential loyalty and affection towards Oedipus (1992, 340; cf. Segal 2001, 92; Hogan 1991, 54–56). He concludes that "there are no grounds for the assertion that they would describe his behaviour towards Creon as being a full case of *hybris*, though it does of course reveal him to be something less than a perfect judge of character and a perfect king." In Fisher's opinion, "no case can be made for seeing [Oedipus] significantly as a man of *hybris*." In fact, "it is largely because Oedipus fails to fit the picture of the hybristic villain of the song that his sufferings are so tragic" (1992, 340–42).[43]

While neither Apollo nor any other deity is said to feel—or exhibit—*phthonos* in the play, Cairns suggests that "the humbling of Oedipus" could perhaps be understood "in terms of a form of divine *phthonos*" which "vindicates Apollo's honour" (2013b, 156). This form of *phthonos* "is aroused by the failure to give appropriate credit to the role of divine favour in one's success," which "presupposes at least a minimal notion of offence, at least in the eyes of the gods themselves" (2013b, 157). For Cairns, Oedipus' "offense" involves ignoring the limited nature of human knowledge. Doing so involves "a degree of presumption, an arrogation to oneself of prerogatives that truly belong only to the gods." Cairns contends that the text provides "a degree of explicit support" for the idea that Oedipus is "implicated in status-rivalry with the gods." Prior to his fall, the king "could be seen as arrogating a kind of claim to efficacy and control that properly belongs only to a god" (2013b, 155), thereby provoking *phthonos* on the part of Apollo.

Cairns admits that there is a problem with this scenario: "effect would have to precede cause, the 'punishment' would be in place before any aspect, symbolic or otherwise, of the 'crime' had been perpetrated" (2013b, 157). Just as problematic is the unsupported assumption that Apollo feels "hostility" toward Oedipus (2013b, 158) and seeks to have his honor "vindicated" by Oedipus' downfall. Oedipus has done nothing which is said to have insulted Apollo or any other deity in the sense that Euripides' Hippolytus and Pentheus dishonor Aphrodite and Dionysus. While Oedipus naively (and grotesquely) exaggerates the degree of his own self-knowledge and insight,[44] he puts his supposed gifts to use as an ally of the god in an attempt to obey Apollo's order about rooting out the source of the city's pollution. He does not set himself up as the god's rival, let alone his equal.

If Oedipus is not guilty of *hybris* and has not called forth divine *phthonos* by dishonoring Apollo—and if his polluting acts of parricide and incest were done unwittingly—why does he have to suffer so "tragically"? As many commentators point out, *Oedipus Tyrannus* is not a tale of crime and punishment. Sophocles makes no mention of the tradition according to which Laius was cursed by Pelops for the kidnapping and rape of his son Chrysippus, who subsequently killed himself.[45] Lloyd-Jones (1983, 121) assumes that "Sophocles took it for granted that his audience would realise that a curse inherited from Laius rested on Oedipus," and concludes that "Apollo loathes the race of Laius" in the play (1983, 122). Similarly, Kovacs argues that Apollo must hate Oedipus "as the son of Laius," since he "has no reason to hate Oedipus *per se*" (2009, 367).

It is indeed probable that the original audience of *Oedipus Tyrannus* knew of this tradition from Aeschylus,[46] but that does not guarantee that they viewed the hero of this play as being the victim of divine revenge for his father's sin. It is equally possible that their knowledge of the Chrysippus story made them more sensitive to the fact that this tradition goes unmentioned in the *Oedipus*.[47] They might then ask why this seemingly good man has been destroyed in such a horrific manner. Allan (2013, 174–75) makes a similar point. He contends that Sophocles communicates "the opacity of divine motivation" by excluding any mention of the curse on Laius' descendants. This opacity "focuses the audience's attention on the chilling fact that terrible things can happen to basically sympathetic people." Of course, the fact remains that, sympathetic or not, Oedipus "*has* done deeds which were impure and impious; and to do such deeds was in fact his evil *moira*" (Winnington-Ingram 1980, 202).

Dodds (1966, 45) finds it "striking" that "after the catastrophe no one on the stage says a word either in justification of the gods or in criticism of them. Oedipus says 'These things were Apollo'—and that is all." This is in stark contrast to several plays by Euripides, two of which we will examine later. In *Hippolytus* and the *Bacchae* human voices question the justice or severity of divine punishment and express anger at the gods.[48] The gods in *Hippolytus* and *Bacchae* express emotions and make judgments about their human opponents. In Sophocles' *Oedipus* that is not the case. The audience is left with the somber fact that even the most gifted and well-meaning human being can be destroyed by a deity simply because it is his or her fate.

c. Herodotus' Adrastus and Sophocles' Oedipus

A number of scholars have noted parallels between the situation of Oedipus in Sophocles' play and the story of Adrastus and Atys in Herodotus. When Croesus is sleeping a dream appears to him, informing him that his son Atys will be struck by an iron spearpoint (*Hist.* 1.34). Croesus attempts to shield his son, in part by prohibiting Atys from engaging in military operations. During this period the Phrygian Adrastus arrives asking Croesus for purification, since he has unwittingly (ἀέκων) killed his brother and been expelled by his father. Croesus grants Adrastus' request and invites him to remain in his house (1.34–35). When a vicious boar wreaks havoc in the region, Croesus reluctantly allows Atys to participate in the hunt, assigning Adrastus to keep watch over him. Tragically,[49] when Adrastus attempts to kill the boar, his spear strikes and kills Atys. Croesus is disconsolate, since he gave food to his son's killer "unawares" (1.44). Adrastus asks Croesus to kill him but Croesus has pity for the young man, who has now inadvertently killed two men. Croesus views this misfortune as the work of "some god" (θεῶν κού τις), namely, the god who predicted Atys' death. Nevertheless, Adrastus cannot bear the burden of having killed these two young men. Realizing that he is most weighed down by ill-fortune of all the people he knows, he kills himself on Atys' grave (1.45).

According to Segal (2001, 121 n. 7), this tale "has a number of parallels with the *Oedipus*, especially the motif of trying to evade an oracle that is tragically fulfilled after all." Chiasson calls this "a striking parallel" (2003, 9). Dodds (1966, 44) believes that the Adrastus narrative is "the nearest parallel to the situation of Oedipus." He notes that Adrastus' involuntary slaying of Atys, "like the killing of Laius, fulfilled an oracle." Dodds contends that Adrastus kills himself "for the same reason that Oedipus blinds himself," namely, because both bore the heaviest burden of disaster. Dodds does concede that "even the case of Adrastus is not fully comparable," because "Oedipus is no ordinary homicide."

Even with Dodds' concession, the two situations are not as similar as he and the others imply.[50] While the deaths of Atys and Laius both fulfill oracles, in the former case the oracle was not received by the killer Adrastus, while in the latter Oedipus is told that he must kill his birth father (*OT* 795). Herodotus considers the fulfilled oracle against Croesus as a case of righteous anger (νέμεσις; *Hist.* 1.34), while Oedipus' slaying of Laius is not said to caused by any act of *hybris* or presumption on his part. In addition, Adrastus kills his brother accidentally, while Oedipus kills his adversary on the road in retaliation for a blow he received, arguably in self-defense. Adrastus knows that he has killed his brother, while Oedipus only learns many years later that the man he killed was his father. While Oedipus describes the incident on the road in some detail (*OT* 800–13), Herodotus gives readers no information about how and why Adrastus killed his brother. We can only take Adrastus' word for it that the killing was involuntary.

In addition, Croesus states that his son died because it was the will of some god, while Oedipus views his fate as willed by a specific deity, Apollo. We can concur with Dodds that Oedipus is not an ordinary homicide. The crimes of patricide and incest produce *miasma*, or pollution.[51] That pollution prompts the plague in Thebes, and the oracle implies that the only way to save the city from the plague is for the polluting agent, Oedipus, to be removed. This is a final difference between Oedipus' situation and that of Croesus' guest-friend[52] Adrastus, whose predicament does not involve bringing pollution either to his father's household or to his benefactor Croesus.

Comparing these two stories highlights the fact that Oedipus is legally innocent of having murdered the men on the road and morally innocent of having killed his birth-father. These factors do nothing to decrease the polluting force of his patricide and incest. Within the play itself, we cannot even conclude that Oedipus is made to suffer innocently because of his father's crimes against Pelops and Chrysippus. Laius and Jocasta exposed the infant Oedipus as a way of evading the oracle they received; their action is no more successful than Oedipus' later attempt to steer clear of his presumed parents in Corinth by heading toward Thebes. These characters freely choose how they want to react to Apollo's oracles, but no attempt is made to justify these oracles as ways of achieving justice for any crimes or sins. As Segal (2001, 54) puts it, "in contrast to Aeschylus, . . . Sophocles' oracles to Laius and Oedipus do not give commands or advice; they simply state the way things are." These characters inhabit a literary world in which divine care and empathy are no more present than divine envy.

d. Conclusions

In *Oedipus Tyrannus* the god Apollo is not presented as an anthropopathic deity who expresses, and acts on the basis of, negative feelings toward Oedipus. Oedipus initially views himself as Apollo's ally in unmasking the polluting killer but later sees himself as hated by the gods and destroyed by Apollo. We determined that Oedipus should not be considered guilty of *hybris* and that he has done nothing to offend or insult any deity. Finally, we noted that Sophocles omits mention of the curse against the family of Oedipus' father Laius. Taken together, these features of the play leave the protagonist—and the audience—in a state of uncertainty concerning the reasons this well-meaning monarch is made to suffer so terribly.

These aspects of the play are also part of the reason that some scholars view Oedipus' plight as an illustration of the "human condition" in general. According to Dodds (1966, 47–48), "the *Oedipus Rex* is a play about the blindness of man [*sic*] and the desperate insecurity of the human condition: in a sense every man must grope in the dark as Oedipus gropes, not knowing who he is or what he has to suffer; we all live in a world of appearance which hides from us who-knows-what dreadful reality." Segal (2001, 53) believes that "Oedipus embodies the human condition"[53] because the play shows that, paradoxically, "men and women . . . are both powerful and helpless, often at the same moment." Oedipus is "both free and determined, both able to choose and helpless in the face of choices that he has already made in the past or circumstances (like those of his birth) over which he had no power of choice." For Cairns, "Oedipus' story illustrates the fragility of human existence, . . . the unbridgeable gulf between the power of god and the insignificance of man [sic]" (2013b, 158).

The phrase "human condition" has, since its introduction in the late twelfth century CE, highlighted problematic features of human existence such as those mentioned by these commentators, that is, epistemological limitations, lack of control (including control over our fate), vulnerability to external forces, and mortality.[54] Dodds' emphasis on humans having to "grope in the dark" is especially important in this play. Sophocles presents the audience with a world in which characters cope with their cognitive uncertainty by predicating anthropomorphic forces both specific (Apollo) and more vague (the *daimōnes*).[55] Sophocles does not indicate whether he agrees with the characters' surmises about divinities.

Dodds quotes Odysseus' reason for pitying Ajax in *Aj*. 124–25: "In Ajax' condition . . . I recognize my own: I perceive that all men living are but appearance or unsubstantial shadow" (1966, 48). Dodds notes that the "view of the human condition which is made explicit in his earliest extant play is implicit . . . in the *Oedipus Rex*." Put another way, this very traditional Greek characterization of human life is told to the audience in *Ajax* but shown to the audience of *Oedipus* in a way which prompts that audience to experience their vulnerability and cognitive myopia along with the hero.

3. Envy and Revenge in Euripides' *Hippolytus*

a. Is Aphrodite's revenge against Hippolytus motivated by phthonos?

In the prologue, Aphrodite states her reasons for desiring the death of Artemis' devotee Hippolytus: "I honor those who reverence (σέβοντας) my power, but I lay low all those who have proud thoughts (φρονοῦσιν . . . μέγα) against me" (*Hipp*. 5–6). Hippolytus falls into the second category. Only he among the citizens of Trozen calls Aphrodite "the worst of divinities" (12–13). In addition, he has nothing to do with marriage (14). Instead, he has gained a companionship "greater than mortal" with the virgin goddess Artemis, whom he considers the greatest of divinities (16, 19). Aphrodite presents herself as a typical deity, in that all the gods, like humans, "enjoy receiving honor from mortals" (7–8). Sharing traits with humans does not seem to be a problem for her.[56]

Aphrodite insists that her desire to destroy Artemis' favorite Hippolytus is not motivated by *phthonos*: "To this pair I feel no envious ill-will (φθονῶ). Why should I?" (*Hipp*. 20). As Lefkowitz puts it, Aphrodite "would not resent the fact that Hippolytus honours Artemis, if he gave due honour also to her" (1989, 76). A "fundamental tenet" of Greek popular religion is that "the goodwill of the gods—of all the gods—must be maintained and that this is accomplished by giving them their due honor" (Mikalson 1991, 145). Since Hippolytus has failed to do so, the goddess will exact vengeance (τιμωρήσομαι) on him that very day for his wrongs against her (*Hipp*. 21–22). Hippolytus has become the goddess's enemy (49); in fact, he "wars against" her (43). As we discussed in Chapter 2.3.b.1, in ancient Greece revenge takes place "in a moral system that enjoins one to help one's friends and harm one's enemies" (Lefkowitz 1989, 76; cf. Kovacs 1980, 301). From the "standpoint of ancient Dike [justice], each god is perfectly within his [*sic*] rights" when punishing "a mortal who has refused him [or her] honour" (Lloyd-Jones 1983, 153).[57]

To accomplish her goal Aphrodite has kindled in Phaedra a desperate love for her step-son Hippolytus. While Phaedra has been fighting this illicit passion and remaining silent about it, Aphrodite will make sure that it becomes known to Hippolytus' father Theseus, who will utter a fatal curse against his son (*Hipp*. 42–46). The "highly regarded" Phaedra has to suffer and die because Phaedra's fate is not as important to Aphrodite as Hippolytus' demise (47–50).

Should the audience take Aphrodite as a trustworthy speaker in the prologue? Speaking to her mistress Phaedra, the Nurse echoes Aphrodite's statement of her policy toward humans: "Against those who yield to her demands, she comes in mildness, but the one whom she finds to be overly high and have big thoughts she takes and treats abusively (*Hipp*. 445; cf. 6)."[58] However, toward the end of the play Artemis refers to Aphrodite as a knave capable of anything (πανοῦργος; 1400) and alleges that Aphrodite was "vexed" by Hippolytus' moderation and self-control (1402). Artemis is hardly a disinterested party, however. She admits that Aphrodite is "the most hateful" goddess to those (such as herself) who take pleasure in virginity (1301–1302). It is also difficult for Artemis to take the high moral ground in relation to Aphrodite, since Artemis plans to exact vengeance on Aphrodite in exactly the same way as Aphrodite has done, by killing the mortal whom Aphrodite loves most (1421–22). In short, nothing in the play supports Artemis' allegations against Aphrodite or contradicts Aphrodite's self-description in the prologue.

Hippolytus' words and actions in the play corroborate Aphrodite's accusations against him. Hippolytus considers himself uniquely "reverent" (σεμνός) and self-controlled or moderate (σώφρων), but the text undermines both claims. Hippolytus is certainly not reverent toward Aphrodite. *Semnos* can also denote arrogance, haughtiness and pomposity. As Conacher observes, "he who is *semnos* in the bad sense cannot, . . . be *sôphrôn*" (1967, 32). Early on, a servant attempts to make Hippolytus aware that he is being *semnos* in the negative sense, especially in his scorn toward Aphrodite. The servant reminds Hippolytus of the law that one should hate what is *semnos* and not friendly to all. Hippolytus readily agrees, adding that haughty mortals are burdensome (*Hipp*. 93–94). After noting that there is charm in being affable and suggesting that the gods share these attitudes, the servant asks why his master will not address a revered divinity (σεμνὴν δαίμον'), referring to Aphrodite by using the positive sense of *semnos* (95–99). Hippolytus replies with a warning to the servant to be careful what he says. Nevertheless, the servant persists, observing that Aphrodite is a proud (σεμνός) goddess who is renowned among mortals (103) and that one should give the gods the honors due them (107). Once again, his wise advice falls of deaf ears.

When praying to Aphrodite the servant attempts to excuse Hippolytus' attitude toward the goddess by stressing his youth. Pointing to "the young" (τοὺς νέους)[59] in general, the servant grants that when they think in the manner which Hippolytus just displayed, they should not be imitated (*Hipp.* 114–15). And if because of youth someone's innermost parts are vehement and he speaks rashly about the goddess, she should pretend not to hear him (117–19).

Scholars such as Strauss do not agree that Hippolytus' youth excuses his behavior. Strauss (1993, 168) contends that Hippolytus is "an aristocratic snob" who "symbolically rejects the passage to manhood." He refuses to progress beyond the stage of an ephebe who engages in hunting during the transition from boy to man. Strauss notes that Hippolytus "claims to reject the normative Greek path of a political career" in *Hipp.* 986–89. He refers to large groups of his fellow citizens as a "mob" (987), which "was a standard oligarchic complaint about the assembly" (Strauss 1993, 172). He is only comfortable with his aristocratic "age-mates" (ἥλικας; 987; cf. 1098, 1180). Strauss also points out that Hippolytus' "emphatic chastity was a rejection of the normal male role" in founding and maintaining his own *oikos* (1993, 168).[60]

Hippolytus' judgments on sex, marriage, and women, as well as his proud confidence in his own superiority, show that he is far from moderate or self-controlled.[61] In addition, he is boastful. He brags that "he alone" is Artemis' companion, and can converse with her (*Hipp.* 84–85). He declares that "no man is more moderate or virtuous (σωφρονέστερος) than I" and "in the first place, I know how to reverence the gods" (994–96). When departing for exile, Hippolytus tells his companions that "you will never see another man more *sōphrōn*" (1100–1101). After being fatally injured by his horses, he refers to himself as "the best of men" (1242) and as "the reverent and god-revering one, the man who surpassed all in moderation and virtue (σωφροσύνη)" (1364–65).

Hippolytus' angry father Theseus also emphasizes these negative aspects of his son's personality after reading—and believing—Phaedra's accusation that Hippolytus sexually assaulted her. Theseus taunts his son as "the companion of the gods, as an extraordinary man" and as "*sōphrōn*, undefiled by evil," adding "I will never be persuaded by your boasting" (*Hipp.* 948–50). He even compares Hippolytus to those who hunt others down with their haughty (*semnois*) words while they are concocting disgraceful, shameful actions (956–57). Later Theseus declares that his son's being *semnos* will be the death of him (1064) and complains that Hippolytus practices "revering himself" more than showing piety to his parent (1080–81). Another issue is whether Hippolytus' insistence on his unparalleled virtue goes beyond normal human limits, and is therefore hybristic. If so, it might also invite divine envy, quite apart from his irreverent attitude toward Aphrodite.[62]

On the positive side, it is to Hippolytus' credit that he does not violate his oath of silence in order to vindicate himself and spare himself exile (*Hipp.* 1060–63), a fact that Artemis later points out to Theseus (1309). Artemis also wants to ensure that Hippolytus dies with a "good reputation" (1299), the same legacy that Phaedra wants for her name and that of her children. In general, scholars who recognize Hippolytus' shortcomings must also concede that he displays "an impressive piety and religious devotion" (Halleran 2004a, 274) as well as "ardent and tender devotion" to Artemis (Jaeger 1965, 352).[63]

b. What motivates Phaedra's accusation that Hippolytus raped her?

Phaedra is a much more complex character than Hippolytus. Scholarly opinion about Phaedra's personality and motivation is therefore more diverse than is the case with Hippolytus. This is especially true when it comes to Phaedra's reasons for leaving a note attached to her dead body claiming that Hippolytus had defiled Theseus' marriage bed by force (*Hipp.* 857–90).

Many readers believe that Phaedra falsely accuses Hippolytus in order to gain revenge. Some see her as driven by "vengeful rage" (L. Parker 2001, 47) or "outraged fury, crying for vengeance" (Reckford 1974, 325). Mueller (2011, 149) concedes that "most critics have . . . treated Phaedra's suicide and letter-writing as acts of punitive revenge," but she does not agree. Mueller argues that Phaedra "is preoccupied most of all with her own good name (*eukleia*) and Hippolytus' power to destroy it" (2011, 150). If Phaedra had regarded Hippolytus as an enemy, "we might have expected from her some proleptic expression of enjoyment as she anticipated his imminent destruction." Instead, in *Hipp.* 728–31 Phaedra "speaks of learning and self-restraint (*sophrosune*), eschewing the pleasure-infused rhetoric of revenge" (2011, 169). Blomqvist (1982, 403) agrees that Phaedra's "overall motive . . . is her concern for her own reputation and for the fate of her children." However, he disagrees with commentators who believe that Phaedra feels fury or rage against Hippolytus: "her anger is not directed against Hippolytus but against the Nurse."

Other scholars acknowledge that concern for her good reputation in a major motive for Phaedra, but add that other motives are also evident. Conacher cautions that "in emphasizing Phaedra's concern for *eukleia* . . . one should not . . . ignore the subtle admixture of other motives including revenge, anger and the venom of frustrated love which . . . influence Phaedra as well" (1967, 41 n. 19). Halleran cautions readers not to dismiss the fact that Phaedra wrote "the lying tablet" because "it is (at least in part) vindictive and destructive." At the same time, "the characterization of Hippolytus leavens judgment against Phaedra" (2004a, 274).[64]

One commentator suggests a novel motive for Phaedra's actions: envy. Sanders contends that "there is a trail of evidence that Phaidra . . . feels *phthonos* for Hippolytus" (2014, 125). Initially Phaedra "envies Hippolytus his lifestyle, . . . the emulative envy of *zêlos* rather than the destructive envy of *phthonos*" (2014, 126). Following Goldhill (1986, 124–25), Sanders asserts that Phaedra has a "transgressive desire to break out of the cloistered female world, and run free with Hippolytus." However, Hippolytus' later "threat to expose her turns her erotic love to anger." Phaedra now feels wounded pride, hatred, and rage, "the affects psychologists associate with envy scenarios" (2014, 126). Because "an important element of *phthonos* is the . . . 'if I can't have it, no one will' urge, . . . Phaidra's slander serves these twin purposes (punishment, and leveling down) of the begrudging envy she directs at Hippolytus" (2014, 127).

There are major problems with this reading of Phaedra's motivation. When we first encounter Phaedra she is seized with a frantic desire to be taken to mountain woods, in order to hunt and break in young horses (*Hipp*. 208–31). These are of course Hippolytus' favorite pastimes. Phaedra will not proclaim her passion for Hippolytus, so she expresses it obliquely by desiring to be where he spends his time. She may even be identifying with him at this moment. It is in this scene that we most directly witness the power of Aphrodite over this unfortunate woman. The fact that Phaedra seems to be on the edge of insanity in these speeches but still manages to suppress her passion in the rest of the play testifies to her self-control and strong will. Phaedra later tells the chorus and the Nurse that she had attempted to subdue her unwanted passion by being self-controlled and moderate (σωφρονεῖν; 399).[65] Her last words before dying express her hope that Hippolytus might become more humble and learn to be moderate (σωφρονεῖν; 731), Ironically, this wish echoes Hippolytus' statement that someone should teach women to be moderate or let him trample on them forever (667–68)!

Nor does Phaedra show any interest in fleeing to the woods and meadows or "leaving the city like a Bacchant" (Goldhill 1986, 125) after this first scene. Her evocation of Hippolytus' way of life does not reveal any dislike of a "cloistered" woman's life; it is within the social world of Trozen that she wants to retain her good reputation and status. As for Phaedra experiencing "begrudging envy" toward Hippolytus, Sanders' only evidence is the rage and hate he assumes Phaedra feels toward Hippolytus. As noted above, not all scholars believe that Phaedra is angry at her step-son. And not all cases of anger and hatred imply *phthonos*. Phaedra does not exhibit an "if I can't have him, nobody will" attitude toward the young man. She hopes that he will learn *sophrosune*, not that he will die so that no other woman can have him.

In her interactions with the Nurse, Phaedra repeatedly emphasizes the importance she attaches to having a good reputation (*Hipp*. 489; cf. 687, 717), and her dread of acting disgracefully. When the Nurse attempts to convince Phaedra to give in to her passion for Hippolytus, Phaedra chides her for speaking "disgracefully" or "shamefully," three times within seven lines.[66] The Nurse asks Phaedra if her pitiful condition is caused by an enemy. Phaedra answers that it is a "dear one" who is unwillingly destroying her (318–19). Later Hippolytus loudly condemns Phaedra—and all other women (616–68). This makes him, in effect, Phaedra's enemy, since he is in a position to destroy her good reputation if he reveals what the Nurse told him about Phaedra's illicit passion.

While the Nurse has expressed an accurate understanding of Aphrodite's nature and power (*Hipp*. 443–46), this does not mean that her advice to Phaedra is necessarily sound. Her specious arguments in favor of Phaedra consummating her desire for Hippolytus make Phaedra's self-sacrifice seem more laudable. For example, the Nurse suggests a remedy "without disgrace" for Phaedra; the fact that she is thinking of love-charms shows that she does not understand the depth of Phaedra's need to avoid disgrace. The Nurse finally betrays her mistress by propositioning Hippolytus on Phaedra's behalf, prompting Phaedra's desire to die as soon as possible (*Hipp.* 589–600).

Given the many ways in which Phaedra's actions have been assessed, is it possible to decide whether Phaedra writes her note charging Hippolytus with rape[67] in order to avenge herself against him? We cannot exclude the fact that she takes this action, in part, to prevent Hippolytus from ruining her good reputation—and the reputations of her children—if he decided to break his oath of silence and reveal her illicit passion for him. Phaedra also speaks of the possibility that her accusation might teach Hippolytus not to be prideful over her downfall and to be moderate. Yet she must surely know that her accusation will lead to Hippolytus' exile or death, and cause additional suffering for his father, her husband. In the prologue Aphrodite had forecast that Hippolytus would die that day, but later in the drama one gets the impression that it is entirely Phaedra's own idea to bring down Hippolytus in order to salvage her reputation, and thereby her children's reputation. In line 973 Theseus' impulse is to exile Hippolytus, which would leave room for Hippolytus to learn "life lessons" while in exile. But it would not fulfill Aphrodite's "prophecy" of Hippolytus dying this very day. Theseus' earlier curse did focus on Hippolytus' death that day ("make an end of my son, and may he not escape this day"; *Hipp.* 887–90; cf. 1167–68; 1241).

In the end, we can say that revenge does play a role in the actions of Aphrodite, Artemis, and Phaedra, but *phthonos* does not. Whether revenge plays a major role in Phaedra's case is up to each reader and audience member to decide. Even if one considers revenge Phaedra's primary motive, Kovacs (1980, 301) reminds us that "the bare fact that she causes the death of the young man she thinks is her enemy and the enemy of her good name would not in the fifth century have been regarded, without further encouragement from the poet, as evidence of moral failure."

4. Envy and revenge in Euripides' *Bacchae*

Euripides' *Hippolytus* and *Bacchae* have basic plot elements in common. In both cases a youthful male insults, and ultimately "wars against,"[68] a specific deity, who then punishes the offender with humiliation and death. In the *Bacchae* it is the young leader Pentheus who is the target of Dionysus' just revenge. In this section I will show that there are also crucial differences between the two situations. Hippolytus insults and denigrates the goddess Aphrodite, calling her the worst of the gods, while Pentheus refuses to acknowledge that Dionysus is a god at all. Hippolytus' fate is sealed when the play begins, while Dionysus gives Pentheus opportunities to recognize and acknowledge his divinity.[69] Hippolytus is satisfied with ignoring Aphrodite (although he does make disparaging remarks about her when she is mentioned to him), while Pentheus wants to eradicate Dionysian worship and kill the "Stranger" who is the god in disguise. While Hippolytus shows extreme devotion to another deity (Artemis), Pentheus is not described as having any patron deity. In addition, Aphrodite engineers her revenge against Hippolytus by involving an innocent third party, while Dionysus focuses his vengeance on the aggressive Pentheus and his family, although his ultimate goal is to teach all Thebans to worship him (*Bacch*. 39–40). Finally, we will find that while scholars differ in their evaluations of both young victims, the majority find that Euripides depicts Hippolytus in more sympathetic terms than he does Pentheus.

a. Is Dionysus' punishment of Pentheus motivated by phthonos?

Divine jealousy is a crucial part of Dionysus' history before the time when the *Bacchae* begins. Hera's jealousy of Zeus, and her resentment of the mortal women with whom Zeus has affairs, led to the destruction of Dionysus' mortal mother Semele. Semele's sisters deny this story, viewing it as a cover-up for Semele having been seduced by a mortal (*Bacch*. 26–31). In the prologue, Dionysus refers to Hera's "undying *hybris*" against his mother (9), but he does not say that the goddess was motivated by *phthonos*.[70]

Oranje is one of the few scholars who believes that Dionysus' actions toward Pentheus are motivated by *phthonos*. He points to the first choral staismon to show that Pentheus' hybristic behavior triggers the *phthonos* of Dionysus. Oranje notes that presumptuous people "are looked upon with hatred by Dionysus" and "that it is indeed Dionysus whose jealousy (*phthonos*) is aroused" (1984, 109). Oranje claims that "Pindar's general *athanaton phthonos* (jealousy of the gods) (I 7.39) is implicitly present in *Bacchae* 392–93."[71] In *Isthm*. 7.39–43 Pindar asks that "the immortals' envy (*phthonos*) not bring about disorder because I pursue the pleasure of the day and walk quietly towards old age and my fated span of life.... If a man gazes on faraway things he is nevertheless too weak to reach the bronze-floored house of the gods" (Verity 2007, 136). Oranje claims that "it is Euripides' specific application of this jealousy to Dionysus which provides an essential complement ... to the picture of Dionysiac euphrosyne in this play" (1984, 109). In fact, "the audience may be well aware that Pentheus' punishment originates precisely from Dionysus' envy" (1984, 165 n. 380).

In this staismon the chorus of Asian bacchants certainly highlights the calm and delight associated with Dionysian worship, as well as their distaste for "presumptuous" individuals such as Pentheus. They begin by invoking "Hosia" (holiness or purity) and charging Pentheus with *hybris* against Dionysus ("Bromius"; *Bacch*. 375). They contrast those who suffer misfortune due to their "unbridled mouths and lawless thoughtlessness" and those who live a calm life with unshaken thinking (386–91). The inhabitants of the upper sky look down on human affairs (393–94). Cleverness (τὸ σοφὸν) is not wisdom (σοφία).[72] Nor is it wise to think thoughts which are not mortal (395–96). Given our brief lifespan, one who pursues great things will lose what lies at hand. Such individuals are madmen and bad advisers (398–401). It is wise to steer clear of those who think themselves extraordinary (περισσῶν; cf. *Hipp.* 948), superior to common people (428–29). Clearly, the chorus is painting Pentheus' portrait in this poem.

Like the chorus in the *Bacchae*, Pindar links a peaceful, pleasant life with not "gazing on faraway things" and not thinking thoughts unsuited to mortals. But while Pindar views this way of life as a means of avoiding disturbance caused by divine *phthonos*, the chorus in the *Bacchae* does not make this connection. Nor does the chorus imply that it is *phthonos* which motivates Dionysus' plans for making Thebes acknowledge his divinity. Hybristic behavior does indeed trigger divine *phthonos* in some Greek texts, but the punishment endured by Pentheus is not said to have been caused by Dionysus' jealousy or envy.

Schechner attempts to prove that the Dionysus of the *Bacchae* is not only "jealous," but a "jealous God . . . cut from the same pattern" as the God of the Old Testament (1961, 126). Schechner makes the astounding claim that "Dionysus wholeheartedly adheres to [the] moral scheme" of the first three commandments of the "Mosaic Decalogue." He concedes that unlike Yahweh, "Dionysus recognizes other divinities," but adds that because Dionysus is a jealous god "he must be first in the Pantheon—not even Zeus deserves more reverence" (1961, 126–27), an assertion which is clearly not supported by the text. Schechner concludes that "in *The Bacchae* we have a capricious god enjoying jealous vengeance" (1961, 134).[73]

b. Is Pentheus shown to be irremediably stubborn and reckless?

There is a surprisingly wide spectrum of critical opinion concerning Pentheus.[74] For a few commentators Pentheus is "a consistently lovable character" (Pohlenz, qted. in Dodds 1960, xliii), a "warm-hearted," just, and "patriotic prince" who is "the finest character in the play" (Norwood 1908, 65–66). On the other end of the spectrum, Strauss (1993, 219) concludes that "it would be hard to imagine a more powerful or more scathing portrait of the vain and self-destructive pretensions of youth than the story of the protagonist Pentheus." Others compare Pentheus to Hippolytus. Dodds (1960, xliii) suggests that Euripides "could certainly have made him a second Hippolytus, fanatical, but with a touching and heroic fanaticism. . . . Instead, he has invested him with the traits of a typical tragedy-tyrant."[75] Mikalson (1991, 145) compares Hippolytus' neglect of Aphrodite to Pentheus' attitude toward Dionysus, "with the important exception that Hippolytus, unlike Pentheus, is moral and pious in other aspects of his life." Mikalson calls Pentheus "tragedy's most flagrant human mocker of a god" (1991, 151).

According to Dionysus, Pentheus "fights against God" (θεομαχεῖ; *Bacch.* 45; 1255; cf. 325). He warns the young ruler not to "take up arms against a god" (789) and advises him to sacrifice to the god rather than "kicking against the pricks in anger, a mortal against a god" (795). Pentheus refuses to heed these warnings. Mikalson wonders whether Euripides coined the verb *theomachein* "to suggest the exceptionally impious and heinous actions of Pentheus" (282 n. 78; cf. 159). Atkinson attempts to lessen the importance of the "stubborn impiety" often attributed to Pentheus in the play (2002, 10; cf. Burnett 1970, 28). He acknowledges that Pentheus does not accept the divinity of Dionysus but claims that "he is a true believer in the traditional gods of Thebes," citing *Bacch*. 45–46 and 247. There is scant evidence for such religiosity in the play.[76] In lines 45–46 Dionysus refers to Pentheus making drink offerings and praying, but Seaford (1996, 153) notes that this may refer to "community (not palace) rituals." And unlike Hippolytus, Pentheus is not said to be a devotee of a deity whom he considers the opposite of the god he attacks.

Some scholars believe that Pentheus' youth[77] should be taken into consideration when evaluating his character. Mills (2006, 61) suggests that because he is young, "his behavior could therefore also be understood to reflect the excess of enthusiasm combined with undeveloped judgment that was typical of young people in Greek eyes."[78] Strauss (1993, 217–19) believes that disenchantment with arrogant youthful leaders after the failure of the Sicilian expedition is reflected in the scathing portrayal of Pentheus in the *Bacchae*. In contrast, scholars such as Norwood are ready to excuse Pentheus' faults as "the weaknesses of immature greatness" (1908, 66). Winkler (1985, 27, 36) points to Xerxes in *Persians* and Pentheus in the *Bacchae* as examples of "youth at the first flowering of . . . adult vigor" who are "implicated in a catastrophe." He admits that "young males are the ones most likely to get it wrong." However, "it is not that Pentheus is overly harsh but that he displays admirable strictness at the wrong time and over the wrong persons" (1985, 36). McGinty is not so forgiving; he insists that "the *hybris* of Pentheus goes well beyond a youthful defensiveness; it is a rebellion against the ordained nature of the universe" (1978, 86).

The way in which Pentheus treats the prophet Tiresias can help the audience to assess his character. When Pentheus sees his grandfather Cadmus and Tiresias dressed in Bacchic garb, he says that he is ashamed at their laughable appearance (*Bacch*. 250–52). He then jumps to the conclusion that Tiresias has persuaded Cadmus to engage in this foolish behavior. Why? So that he could introduce a new *daimōn* to humankind and "have more birds to observe, more reward from burnt offerings" (255–57). Admittedly, Oedipus also accuses Tiresias of desiring profit when he joined Creon's alleged conspiracy against the king (*OT* 385–89).[79] However, Oedipus had first treated the prophet with great deference and respect. Only when Tiresias seems to be betraying Thebes by withholding vital information does Oedipus turn against him.

In contrast, Pentheus accuses Tiresias before the prophet can explain his motives to the young ruler. In addition, Pentheus orders the destruction and desecration of the site at which Tiresias engages in ornithomancy, actions which Pentheus assumes will hurt the prophet the most (*Bacch*. 346–51). Kirk (1970, 54) rightly comments that "there is a kind of spitefulness, a total lack of magnanimity, in Pentheus' proposed punishment of Tiresias and in the deliberate and complacent way in which he outlines it. This young man . . . is developing early some of the worst qualities of the tyrant."[80]

Oedipus had his most tyrannical moment when he accused Creon and Tiresias of conspiracy. While Oedipus had some grounds for suspecting the prophet,[81] there is no excuse for Pentheus' tyrannical behavior, either in the scene with

Envy and vengeance in Greek tragedy 127

Tiresias or his actions later in the play. In short, the repeated charge that Pentheus has committed *hybris* against Dionysus is justified by the young ruler's words and actions in the play.[82]

c. Dionysus' character in the Bacchae

In the prologue Dionysus clearly explains the reasons for what he has done and what he is about to do. He established his rites in Asian lands "so that" he might be seen as a divine being (*Bacch.* 22). He incited the females of Thebes to ecstasy "because" they had denied that his father was Zeus (26; cf. 32). He must therefore vindicate his mother Semele (41). His cousin Pentheus omits him from his drink offerings and prayers; "for this reason" Dionysus will show him and all Thebes that he is a god (45–48). If the Thebans attack the Bacchae in the mountains he will wage war on the city; "for this reason" he has changed his shape into that of a human (52–54).

Burnett (1970, 18–19) notes that "there is no fixed divine purpose attached to [Pentheus] when the play begins." In fact, Pentheus "begins his play before he has committed a decisive offense." Therefore, how the young ruler acts toward the divine "Stranger" determines his fate. Burnett shows that Dionysus offers Pentheus "a full sequence of instructions and demonstrations meant to reveal the nature of the divine enemy he would attack," in an "attempt to enlighten the 'victim'" (1970, 20). As early as lines 516–517 the Stranger warns the young ruler that Dionysus—the god Pentheus claims does not exist—will pursue him for his hybristic acts. Yet Pentheus refuses to learn. Dionysus exhibits forbearance: "the prince's continued impiety provokes no alteration in the manner of his adversary; there is no retaliation, only further instruction" (Burnett 1970, 21). The point of no return only occurs when Pentheus orders a divine attack on the bacchants, after the Stranger has offered to bring them back without using force (*Bacch.* 804).

Dionysus' treatment of Pentheus would seem to shed a positive light on the god's character. However, some readers wonder whether Dionysus' apparent attempts at educating and saving Pentheus are made in good faith. When the Stranger advises Pentheus to remain calm and not to take up arms against the god (*Bacch.* 788–95), Kirk asks, "'Is Dionysus serious in this advice, whose conciliatory tone is continued in the offer of 802 and 804?" (1970, 87). Kirk concedes that Dionysus' prediction in the prologue does not exclude this possibility, but he concludes that Euripides has the god act conciliatory merely "to make Pentheus' obstinate folly even plainer."[83] Mills also seems less than certain about Dionysus' motives. She believes that Euripides "leaves tantalizingly unclear what the deity really wants of Pentheus" (2006, 62), in spite of the fact that Dionysus consistently attempts to make Pentheus see the light.

In the end, we cannot determine whether Dionysus thought Pentheus capable of accepting his divinity. However, it is clear that Dionysus does not initially prevent the young ruler from acknowledging his status as a god. In the prologue Dionysus makes it clear that he intends to teach Thebes—and its young ruler—to acknowledge and respect his divinity: "this city must learn thoroughly, even if it does not want to, that it is not initiated into my Bacchic rites" (*Bacch.* 39–40). Dionysus will make plain to Pentheus and all the Thebans that he was born a god (47–48; cf. 859–60).

Dionysus' teaching technique with Pentheus bears some similarity to that employed by Yahweh with the Pharaoh in Exodus 5–14. In both cases the god offers the ruler the possibility of acknowledging the god's divinity after they have refused to do so. And in both cases the deity keeps the ruler (and therefore his land) on the road to destruction only after the ruler has chosen to remain obstinately impious toward the god.[84] The two situations also differ in crucial ways. In Exod 4:21–23 Yahweh makes it clear that he intends to destroy Pharaoh and the first-born of Egypt; in other words, he already knows that the final plague will occur. In contrast, Dionysus makes warring against Thebes contingent upon Pentheus and the Thebans continuing to deny his divinity and reject his rites. While Pharaoh had committed fatal sins against Yahweh's son Israel prior to the plagues, Pentheus only does so only after the play begins. In short, while Yahweh "toyed with" the Egyptians (Exod 10:2),[85] Dionysus is not toying with Pentheus when he issues the young man warnings and offers him good advice.[86]

One other aspect of Dionysus' character deserves mention. On a number of occasions Dionysus talks about his interactions with Pentheus causing him to suffer terribly[87] (*Bacch.* 492, 500, 788, 1376–77[88]). This implies that Dionysus endures suffering as a result of his attempts to show Pentheus the nature of his divinity. If we accept that these attempts are made in good faith, then the god's willingness to be endure this suffering speaks to the content of his character in the play.

d. Is Dionysus' vengeance excessive?

Given Pentheus' impiety and *hybris*, it is hardly surprising when the second messenger reports that Dionysus ordered the Theban maenads to "exact vengeance (τιμωρεῖσθέ) on him!" (*Bacch.* 1081; cf. 850). The guilt is not restricted to Pentheus. As Cadmus points out to Agave in line 1297, "you refused to believe he was a god," and thereby "insulted him with insult" (ὕβριν γ' ὑβρισθείς; Seaford 1996, 137). But is Dionysus' vengeance excessive or unnecessarily cruel? For Pentheus' grandfather Cadmus the answer is "yes"; he tells his daughter Agave that Dionysus has destroyed them "justly, but too severely," even though he too is a member of their family (1249–50). Later he tells Dionysus the same thing (1346), adding that gods should not be like mortals in their anger (1348). Dionysus responds by pointing out that he, a god, had been treated with *hybris* by all of them (1347) and that Zeus approved these things long ago (1349).

Characters in other tragedies also judge gods by human moral standards. In Sophocles' *Trachiniae* Heracles' son Hyllus asks for compassion from those helping him raise his suffering father's litter on the pyre, pointing out the "lack of feeling (ἀγνωμοσύνην) the Gods have shown" during a terrible series of events, even though they are called our fathers (*Trach.*1265–69). Hyllus concludes that there is nothing in these disasters "which is not Zeus" (1278). In Sophocles' *Philoctetes*, the protagonist accuses the gods of protecting the evil. While the divinities send away the just and productive, they delight in turning back from Hades those who are wicked and habitually knavish (πανοῦργα καὶ παλιντριβῆ; *Phil.* 446–50). Philoctetes then asks, "How am I to regard these things? How praise, when praising the gods, I find the gods evil" (*Phil.* 451–52). In Euripides' *Hippolytus* the servant tells Aphrodite that gods should be wiser than mortals (*Hipp.* 120). And in *Heracles*, the hero's human father Amphitrion tells Zeus that "you are either an ignorant, insensitive (ἀμαθής) god or you are by nature unjust" (*HF* 347).[89]

Modern critical opinion concerning Dionysus' actions depends on whether a given scholar views the god as a representation of a natural force or as a humanlike being. Those in the former group, such as Dodds, consider Dionysus "a 'person,' or moral agent, only by stage necessity. . . . In himself Dionysus is beyond good and evil" (Dodds 1960, xlv). Gods such as Dionysus and Aphrodite in *Hippolytus* represent universal laws; for them, "the human 'ought' has no meaning" (1960, 238). Yet Dodds still points to the "discrepancy between the moral standards implied in the myths and those of civilized morality and concludes that "the vengeance of Dionysus is as cruel and undiscriminating as the vengeance of Aphrodite in the *Hippolytus*" (1960, xlii). Similarly, Mills (2006, 64) believes that "through his very divinity [Dionysus] lacks the humanity which could forgive Pentheus' immaturity"; therefore "his vengeance inevitably seems excessive." At the same time, Mills lays more stress on Dionysus' presentation as a person in the *Bacchae*: "Dionysus is so anthropomorphized that it seems impossible to divorce his actions from all moral judgement." His acts "are those of an individual being, not some neutral symbol" (2006, 54, 89).

Other scholars view Dionysus' behavior as expectable and therefore justified by his status as a deity. Kirk, commenting on *Bacch.* 1347–49, notes that Dionysus is implying that "no punishment can be too great for insulting a god; and indeed this was a common view among men [*sic*]" (1970, 136). Given the way gods are presented in plays such as *Hippolytus* and *Bacchae*, "from the standpoint of ancient Dike, each god is perfectly within his rights; for a mortal to refuse a god his due honour is dangerous" (Lloyd-Jones 1983, 153). McGinty agrees: "the notion that gods will, as matter of course, punish those slighting their τιμή [honor] is perfectly congruent with Hellenic ideas" (1978, 83 n. 24). From this perspective, Dionysus' vengeance is not excessive.[90]

Notes

1 For an analysis of divine and human revenge in Euripides' *Hecuba*, see Chapter 2.3.b.2, above; on the same theme in Euripides' *Heracles*, see Chapter 8.1, below.
2 Hall points out that this is the "longest messenger scene in extant Athenian tragedy" (2007, 128).
3 According to (Garvie 2009, 177) the singular δαίμων "in the sense either of 'god' or of 'destiny,'" occurs eleven times in the play. Hall (2007, 15, 170) refers to the malevolent *daimōn* as "ubiquitous" in *Persians*. On the relationship between *daimōn* and *moira* (fate) in the play, see Winnington-Ingram, 1973, 212. On the role of *daimōnes* and *moira* in Sophocles' *Oedipus Tyrannus*, see Section 2.a, below.

130 *Envy and vengeance in Greek tragedy*

4 This term is an epithet of Odysseus in Homer (*Od.* 1.300); the so-called "Doloneia" (*Il.* 10) also illustrates the hero's wily-minded ability to deceive.
5 J. Barrett (1995, 541) argues that the speech "employs strategies designed to gain narrative authority for itself." These include the Messenger's use of a "twin perspective," describing events both in "fine detail" and in "broad strokes," while effacing himself in a way which "defuses" skepticism about his credibility (1995, 547, 550). Finally, Barrett contends that echoes of Homer in the Messenger's speeches lend him an aura of authority comparable to that of a Homeric bard (1995, 550–54).
6 See *Pers.* 158, 345, 354, 472, 515, 724, 725, 845, 911 and 921.
7 On this expression, see Garvie 2009, 223–24.
8 In Winnington-Ingram's phrase, "it was Xerxes—and not the gods—who was in a hurry. . . . it is when a man is himself bent upon an evil course that the ironical divine helper lends his aid" (1973, 216). The Rabbis make a similar point when justifying God's treatment of Balaam in Num 22:20–22: "a person (אדם) is led down the path s/he desires to go" (*Num. Rab.* 20.12; *Midr. Tanḥ*, Balak 8).
9 Darius does not describe the contents of these orders and messages. Could Darius have composed a "mirror for princes" for his sons? Garvie (2009, 306) suggests that Aeschylus might have invented these instructions in order to stress Xerxes' rashness in ignoring his wise father's advice. On "mirrors for princes" in the ancient world, see Lasine 2020, 74–78, 84–85.
10 Winnington-Ingram notes that Xerxes "attributes his disaster to the cruelty of a fickle *daimon*" who has turned against him. He describes his "hateful *moira*" as "'most unforeseen'" or "'most unforeseeable'," because he has failed "to understand the principles" upon which his failure is based (1973, 217–18).
11 See the discussion of divine envy as a "primitive" concept in Chapter 2.2, above.
12 Garvie cites the choral ode in *Agamemnon* 750–71 to show that "Aeschylus is able to describe the amoral view as the prevailing concept in 458 BC." In *Ag.* 750–56 the chorus refers to a saying expressed by mortals long ago, that from a person's good fortune there springs up unceasing misery (ἀκόρεστον οἰζύν).
13 In support, Garvie points to the story of Zeus' jars in *Iliad* 24.527–33 (2009, xxvii).
14 Cf. Queen Atossa's reference to an "abhorrent *daimōn*" (στυγνὲ δαῖμον) in *Pers.* 472, discussed previously.
15 See, for example, *OT* 5, 70–71, 86, 133, 242–43, 245, 305, 788, 965, 994, 1011, 1330.
16 According to Mikalson (1991, 28), "the *daimon* which afflicts Oedipus is increasingly personalized, increasingly recognized as peculiarly Oedipus', and is finally even identified as a specific cult deity."
17 As T. Gould (1970, 45) points out, *daimōn* in line 245 refers to Apollo.
18 It is not only "modern interpreters" who call this "fate"; *moira* is a factor acknowledged by characters within the drama, for example, in Tiresias' speech in lines 376–77. Μοῖρα appears six times in the play: *OT* 376, 713, 863, 887, 1302, and 1458. Only in the last case is Oedipus the speaker. T. Gould (1970, 162) notes that in this line "*moira* is almost equivalent to *daimōn*." In contrast, Kovacs (2019, 113) asserts that "in tragedy *moira* is not an independent agent but merely a way of talking about events retrospectively, emphasizing the divine control of them." In two instances (*OT* 376–77 and 711–14), "*moira* is merely a way of talking about what Apollo is going to bring about."
19 This is the reading in almost all modern translations. Knox (1971, 7–8) prefers the reading of all but one of the manuscripts, according to which Tiresias says that it is not his fate to fall at Oedipus' hands. Modern translations (with the exception of Knox and T. Gould [1970, 60]) follow the emended version, according to which Oedipus' fate is to fall through Apollo. While Hogan (1991, 39) is not persuaded by Knox's argument, he believes that even if we follow the emended version and take Tiresias literally, we do not need to "believe that he is exactly accurate in making Apollo the cause

of Oedipus' fate." According to Cairns (2013b, 135), Tiresias is saying that "Apollo had an interest in" Oedipus' downfall. He notes that in lines 376–77 "the main clause presents *moira* as a future state of affairs of which Tiresias has knowledge, but the subordinate clauses entail that that state of affairs is a product of deliberate divine activity" (2013b, 144).

20 While gods appear in the prologues to five plays by Euripides, Athena in the *Ajax* "is the only deity to appear on stage in extant Sophoclean tragedy" (Garvie 1998, 123).

21 Kennedy argues that Ajax and Athena have different understandings of what it means to be an "ally." Athena (as well as Menelaus) "conceive of allies as those under their direct command," while Ajax "looks to Athene as an equal because he conceives of an ally as equal and autonomous" (2009, 133, 128). According to Knox, Ajax "assumes not merely equality with Athena, but superiority to her. Athena mockingly recognizes this conception of their relationship by her use of the word 'ally' (σύμμαχος) to describe herself; the word in Athenian official parlance . . . suggests inferiority, and it is clear that this is how Ajax regards her" (1961, 8).

22 Esposito points out that "this is the only example in Sophocles where the verb 'love' [φιλέω] is used of the gods, who are not generally known for their 'love'" (2010a, 10 n. 53).

23 On this maxim, see Chapter 2.3.b.1, above.

24 While Ajax focuses on the leaders Agamemnon, Menelaus, and especially Odysseus, his vengeance is actually aimed at the entire army (see *Aj.* 44, 303–304, 843–44). The excessive nature of this desire for revenge becomes more clear when we recognize that the army's hostility toward Ajax "postdates" his nocturnal attack (Winnington-Ingram 1980, 45 n. 103; cf. Davidson 1975, 167).

25 This statement is part of what has been dubbed Ajax's *Trugrede* ("deception speech"). That is, some scholars doubt Ajax's sincerity in this speech.

26 To Hogan (1991, 180) Ajax's madness "seems the flowering of a deeper *hybris* that the Greeks identified with man's refusal to accept his mortal limits," while to Fisher (1992, 327) "Ajax's over-confident words involve a mild *hybris* against the gods." Within the play, Menelaus repeatedly accuses Ajax of acting hybristically and "thinking big" (*Aj.* 1061, 1081, 1088); at one point Menelaus calls him "a man of fiery *hybris*" (αἴθων ὑβριστής; 1088).

27 Even in the prologue, when he considers Athena his ally, Ajax rejects her request to stop mistreating "Odysseus" (actually a ram; *Aj.* 111–13; 241).

28 On *moira* and other Greek terms for "fate," see Winnington-Ingram 1980, 150–54.

29 As Knox points out (1971, 9–10), there is no suggestion that Apollo is responsible for the plague afflicting Thebes. Apollo *was*, however, held to be responsible for the plague in Athens in 430 BCE; see, for example, Thucydides 2.54.

30 Oedipus *does* claim that Apollo is the *daimōn* who fulfilled his own evil sufferings, including the blinding which Oedipus did with his own hand (*OT* 1330–31). From Oedipus' perspective, the blinding was "over-determined" (see Winnington-Ingram 1980, 177; Cairns 2013b, 136) or a case of "double-determination" (Blondell 2002, 129), in some sense.

31 Dawe (2006, 85) notes that "τιμωρεῖν is a strange word to use of action taken against an innocent party." He suggests that Oedipus might be "taking a vendetta against Laius and his family for granted."

32 Tiresias repeatedly evokes angry passion and temper in Oedipus (described with the related verbs ὀργαίνω, ὀργάζω, and ὀργίζω); see *OT* 335, 339, 344–45, 364; cf. 405 (using the noun ὀργή). The fact that both ancient and modern kings insist on being informed about matters touching their own security and that of the state makes Oedipus' anger at Tiresias more understandable; see Lasine 2001, 69. On "information loyalty" in other monarchical contexts, see Lasine 2001, xiv, 27 n. 37, 35–50, 83–89, 91, 245.

33 For examples, see Lasine 2001, 1–2, 81, 113–19.
34 The adjective πολυζήλῳ ("much emulated, intensely rivalrous") does not have the same connotation of resentment and ill-will as would be case if Oedipus had used a compound with the adjective φθονερός. Compare the use of ζῆλος in *OT* 1526.
35 There is another relevant appearance of φθονεῖν (and one of φθόνος, with emendation) during Oedipus' argument with Creon. However, there is too much scholarly disagreement about lines 590 and 624 for us to give full weight to these instances. Line 624 follows a gap after 623; commentators disagree about whether the speaker in line 624 is Creon or Oedipus. Jebb (1949, 72) contends that the speaker is Oedipus. He believes that if the line is read together with the preceding line spoken by Oedipus, it could mean "nothing but '*show forth* [by a terrible example] *what manner of thing it is to envy*,'—how dread a doom awaits him who plots to usurp a throne." If Creon is the speaker in line 624, and we also follow Dawe (2006, 124) in emending line 590 by replacing φόβου with φθόνου, Creon is saying that in his present position of power he can gain everything without envy rather than without fear. In other words, Creon is letting Oedipus know that he is not motivated by destructive envy or resentment and therefore has no desire to usurp the throne.
36 See Lasine 2001, 1–4, 16, 19, 56, 64, 77–79.
37 Winnington-Ingram (1980, 204 n. 72) confesses that he himself had "been led into an intemperate judgment upon Creon (who was a good man and behaves generously at the end of the play)." In fact, "in our prosaic lives, we shall be lucky if we behave as well as he did."
38 See Lasine 2001, 15–21, 40–44, 88–90, 113–17.
39 As I discuss elsewhere (Lasine 2001, 69), Oedipus has been kept ignorant of his true identity by his Corinthian foster parents, the Corinthian shepherd who accepted him as an infant, the Theban shepherd who handed him over, and now by Tiresias.
40 Some commentators accept the emendation "being tyrant breeds *hybris*." Winnington-Ingram (1980, 191) does so "with some reluctance."
41 For example, Allan (2013, 188 n. 12) refers to "Oedipus' (hybristic) killing of Laius." Allan lays great stress on Oedipus' description of his retaliation after he was struck on the head with a two-pronged goad by the older man on the road (2013, 176). Oedipus tells Jocasta that "not at all equal was the penalty he paid" (*OT* 810). For Allan, this means that Oedipus admits that his violence was excessive and disproportionate. This "marks him out as a potentially dangerous ruler." Allan's interpretation does not consider the context. Oedipus, recounting this youthful incident to his wife, may be bragging a bit about how he "paid the man back with interest," as a macho male might say nowadays—or as the biblical Samson actually does do. Many commentators note that according to Athenian law in Sophocles' time, if a highwayman strikes first, and is then killed by his victim acting in self-defense, the killer has to pay no penalty. See the sources cited in T. Gould 1970, 103. Gould also quotes Antiphon (*Tetralogies* 3b. 2): "the men who start the violence deserve to be answered, not with the same, but with more and worse than they gave."
42 *Koros* denotes excess, surfeit, or satiety. For *koros* breeding *hybris*, see Solon Fr. 6.3–4 (Gerber 1999, 122–23) and Theognis 153 (Gerber 1999, 194–95). For *koros* as the child of *hybris*, see Herodotus *Hist*. 8.77.
43 For a dissenting opinion see Conacher (1999, 43): "Oedipus' *hybris* (particularly in his treatment of Teiresias and of the old Shepherd) has been responsible for his tragic discovery of his identity and guilt." If Oedipus engaged in "status-rivalry" with the gods and arrogated divine prerogatives, as Cairns suggests, he may indeed have been acting hybristically. However, Cairns (2013b, 158) also points out that "if thinking we know what we are doing in running our lives, pursuing our ambitions, and trying to secure our own happiness is *hybris* then it is a *hybris* that tempts us all. Oedipus challenges the gods in the way that any successful human is a potential rival to the gods."

44 On Oedipus' abysmal ignorance concerning his own identity, see Lasine 2001, 67–71.
45 For this tradition, see Apollodorus 3.5.5; Athenaeus 13.79.
46 See Aeschylus' *Seven Against Thebes* 70, 689–92, 720–26, 742–52, 800–802.
47 Cf. Knox (1971, 101) "At point after point Sophocles remains silent on the question of Laius' responsibility, a silence all the more noticeable and emphatic because he was addressing an audience familiar with the Aeschylean handling of the material."
48 *Hipp.* 1146; *Bacch.* 1249–50, 1346, 1348; cf. *HF* 339–47, 1303–10. On these passages, see Section 4.d, below.
49 On the Croesus-Adrastus story as "tragic," see Chiasson 2003, 8–19. For Romm (1998, 69), the "final scene" (*Hist.* 1.44–45) "reads very much like the plot summary of a tragic drama."
50 The two situations are also similar in the sense that no family curse is mentioned in either case, thanks to Sophocles omitting the tradition concerning the curse on Laius' descendants.
51 On *miasma* in *Oedipus Tyrannus*, see R. Parker 1983, 316–21.
52 On Adrastus as a *xenos* or guest-friend (*Hist.* 1.43), see Vandiver 2012, 155–63. On the role of *xenia* in Euripides' *Hecuba*, see Chapter 2.3.b.2, above.
53 Cf. Kaufmann (1979, 126): "Sophocles' Oedipus is representative of the human condition."
54 See Chapter 1.1.a, above and Lasine 2019, 3–4, 10–15.
55 On the extent to which people anthropomorphize in order to cope with their human vulnerabilities, see Chapter 1.4, above.
56 Lefkowitz (1989, 79) points out that "Euripides' gods resemble mortals only in certain ways: they love their friends and hate their enemies; they like honour and recognition. In other respects they are very much unlike mortals: they do not feel pity; they do not act out of compassion for mortals." In contrast, Yahweh claims that mercy and compassion are two of his robust character traits (Exod 34:6–7), although he can also destroy both the guilty and the innocent "without pity" (לא חמל; e.g., Job 6:10; 16:13; Lam 2:2, 17, 21; 3:43). Lefkowitz also notes that the Greek gods' notion of justice may not include the "human notion"; for example, it may ensure the working out of a family curse or revenge for being dishonored (1989, 79). Lefkowitz does not add that the "human notion" may also include seeking revenge for being dishonored or disrespected.
57 Cf. Oineus in *Iliad* 9.535–37. He angers Artemis because she is the only god to whom he did not offer appropriate sacrifices, because "he had forgotten, or had not thought, in his hard delusion" (Lattimore 1961, 212). For Artemis the reason that she was ignored is irrelevant.
58 While the Nurse is not always a reliable speaker, as we shall see, nothing in the play contradicts her view.
59 Cf. *Hipp.* 967 and W. Barrett 1964, 181. On Hippolytus as a youth, see Strauss 1993, 170–71.
60 More generally, Strauss argues that "the social drama of Athens in the Peloponnesian War era is characterized by the rule of a stern father who is deposed and replaced by an over-indulged and rebellious son of tyrannical, dangerous, and seductive passions. . . . After giving the son great power, however, the people repent, destroy him, and attempt to reimpose the rule of a father" (1993, 177). On the so-called "generation gap" in Athens during the 420s, see Ostwald 1986, 229–40 and Strauss 1993, 136–48. Euripides' *Hippolytus* was performed in Athens in 428 BCE and the *Bacchae* after Euripides' death in 406 BCE.
61 Cf. Philostratus' *Life of Apollonius of Tyana* (6.3.5). Apollonius asks young Timasion whether he sacrifices to Aphrodite. Timasion answers in the affirmative, explaining that "she is a goddess who I think has great power in the affairs of humans and gods." Delighted at his reply, Apollonius declares, "Let us vote him a crown for modesty

134 *Envy and vengeance in Greek tragedy*

(σωφροσύνη) above even Hippolytus," who "insulted (ὕβρισε) Aphrodite. . . . I do not think it is a sign of modesty to be on bad terms with any of the gods, as Hippolytus was with Aphrodite. It is more modest (σωφρονέστερον) to speak well of every god" (C. Jones 2005, 100–101, slightly modified).

62 Ironically, the Nurse suggests that Phaedra might be committing *hybris* by trying to be better than gods such as Zeus and Eos, who *did* give in to their passion for inappropriate partners (*Hipp.* 451–76).

63 Mikalson (1991, 144) finds Hippolytus' "mystic communion with the goddess, the ascetic life of her devotees, and the beauty of the hymns in her honor" to be "immensely appealing." He describes such worship as "monotheistic, singleminded devotion." This is not monotheism; Hippolytus is not denying the reality or power of all other gods. His disdain is reserved for divinities who are worshipped at night (*Hipp.* 106), such as Aphrodite.

64 According to Kovacs (1980, 300), another "widely-held view of the play" is that Phaedra "fails because she is weak, conventional, and overly concerned with the opinions of others." Kovacs believes that this view is mistaken. I agree.

65 Kovacs (1980, 291) rightly concludes that in this long speech (*Hipp.* 373–430) Phaedra is "neither confessing to wrong-doing nor attempting to excuse it but rather explaining that she intends to do right and how and why." Doing right in her predicament means taking her own life.

66 *Hipp.* 499, 503, and 505; cf. 331 and 692.

67 Mueller (2011, 153–55) points out that the audience never learns the contents of Phaedra's tablet, because Theseus reads the tablet silently.

68 *Hipp.* 43; *Bacch.* 45; 325; 789; 1255. For more on Pentheus as a *theomachos*, see Section 4.b, below.

69 See, for example, Conacher 1967, 59: "in the *Hippolytus*, Aphrodite has already decided on the punishment of the offender; in [the *Bacchae*] the plan of Dionysus is conditional on Pentheus' continued resistance." Conacher finds it "surprising that several critics . . . tend to overlook this simple but important point" (1967, 59 n. 2; cf. Burnett 1970, 19; Mikalson 1991, 145).

70 Hera's desire to destroy the infant Dionysus is also referred to by the chorus (*Bacch.* 98) and by Tiresias (289–97).

71 Oranje asserts that this conclusion "lies naturally at the descriptive level in line with the dramatic facts" of the play (1984, 109).

72 Oranje takes the chorus's statement in *Bacch.* 1005 to mean "'I do not rejoice in pursuing, full of envy, clever thinking (*to sophon*)'." He believes that the chorus is "suggesting that Pentheus does pursue, full of envy, clever thinking (and therefore meets his doom)." Clever thinking is "denounced as a jealous state of mind, typical of a man like Pentheus." In fact, "he who supports clever thinking arouses the jealousy of Dionysus" (1984, 165). In *Bacch.* 820 Pentheus "begrudges" (φθονῶ) the Stranger any delay in going to watch the maenad women on the mountain.

73 Amzallag (2011, 399) also finds analogies between Yahweh and Dionysus. He claims that both gods require "the worship of everyone" in their respective lands, and that this worship leads to the god's recognition as the *exclusive* source of authority."

74 For examples of this wide range of opinion, see Versnel 1998, 97–98; Mills 2006, 84–85.

75 Among the traits listed by Dodds are absence of self-control, willingness to believe the worst on hearsay evidence or on none, brutality towards the helpless, a stupid reliance on physical force as a means of settling spiritual problems, foolish racial pride, and the sexual curiosity of a Peeping Tom (1960, xliii). Seaford (2003, 106; cf. 1996, 47) observes that "there is no indication anywhere of Pentheus representing the interests of the polis. He does illustrate the principle pronounced by the admirable Theseus in Euripides' *Suppliant Women* [429]: 'There is nothing more hostile to a polis than a tyrant'."

Envy and vengeance in Greek tragedy 135

76 *Bacch.* 247 says nothing about Pentheus believing in the "traditional gods of Thebes."
77 See *Bacch.* 274; 974–75; cf. *Bacch.* 1185–87.
78 Mills (2006, 61) acknowledges that Pentheus' failings include "the violence, impiety and arrogance typical of the tyrants . . . in tragedy" and that these are failings "which traditionally attract divine vengeance." However, she believes that Pentheus' youthful inexperience contributed to his "authoritarianism."
79 Tiresias is also abused by Creon in Sophocles' *Antigone* (1045–55).
80 While many commentators find satirical elements in Euripides' presentation of Tiresias and Cadmus in the *Bacchae* (see Seidensticker 2016, 281–82; cf. Conacher 1967, 62–64), the fact remains that when Tiresias finally has a chance to explain his motives to Pentheus, he gives the youth sound advice and crucial warnings, in addition to sophistical argumentation. See, for example, *Bacch.* 270–72, 309–10, 315, 325–26. In addition, the prophet wants to pray to Dionysus not to do anything sinister to Pentheus (360–62), just as the Servant in *Hippolytus* asks Aphrodite not to destroy Hippolytus after the young man had insulted her.
81 See Section 2.b, above.
82 The chorus of Asian bacchants levels this charge against Pentheus (*Bacch.* 374, 555), as does the god in his role as the Stranger (516). When Dionysus appears in his divinity, he accuses Thebes as a whole of *hybris* (1347), something which Cadmus had already acknowledged when speaking with Agave (1297).
83 In contrast, Seaford (1996, 212) believes that Dionysus' final offer to resolve the conflict peacefully is genuine (*Bacch.* 802–809).
84 Cf. the rabbinic saying, "a person is led down the path s/he desires to go" (see n. 8, above). Starting with the sixth plague, Yahweh is said to harden Pharaoh's heart (Exod 9:12), whereas earlier the king had either hardened his own heart or his heart was simply said to be hardened; see Propp 1998, 353.
85 This is Childs' felicitous rendering of Hebrew התעללתי (1974, 126; cf. 159).
86 Nor does Dionysus claim to be superior to other deities or that he is the only true god, as does Yahweh. The chorus leader merely insists "Dionysus is inferior to none of the gods" (*Bacch.* 777).
87 This leaves aside late traditions of Dionysus as a suffering god, for example, Pausanias 8.37.5.
88 I follow the one existing manuscript, which has Dionysus as the speaker in line 1377. Many scholars emend "I suffered" (ἔπασχον) to "he suffered" (ἔπασχεν), so that Cadmus becomes the speaker; see Dodds 1960, 241.
89 In the same play Heracles, referring to Hera, asks "who would pray to such a goddess?" (*HF* 1307). On this scene, see Chapter 8.1, below.
90 In contrast, a number of scholars believe that Euripides satirizes and criticizes the traditional "mythological" gods, who, in plays such as the *Hippolytus*, are motivated by "baser human reactions of pique, jealousy, and self-conceit" (Conacher 1967, 53 cf. Mikalson 1991, 235–36).

7 Comparing divine vengeance and envy in Hebrew and Greek texts

Now that we have investigated cases of divine envy, jealousy, and vengefulness in a variety of biblical and Greek texts, we are in a position to compare the ways in which these emotions and attitudes are presented in the two bodies of literature. I will begin by focusing on the issue of divine vengefulness. The Hebrew Bible and ancient Greek writings both offer examples of direct divine vengeance and cases in which the god or gods act through human agents to exact vengeance. Both include instances in which a deity achieves vengeance on behalf of a human being or group of humans, as well as situations in which humans attempt to take (sometimes excessive) vengeance on behalf of a god or gods. When we examine these general similarities more closely, we will find crucial differences in the ways that divine vengeance is depicted in biblical and Greek literature. In the second section of this chapter I will compare the Hebrew and Greek examples of divine jealousy and envy we discussed earlier in this study, as well as other cases that we have not yet considered.

1. Comparing varieties of divine vengeance

a. Deities directly taking vengeance

Both biblical and Greek deities are said to directly engage in vengeance. As we discussed in Chapter 2.3.a, Yahweh threatens to avenge those who might kill Cain. That Yahweh "returns vengeance on his adversaries" is asserted in the Song of Moses (Deut 32:43). Later on, Nahum calls Yahweh a jealous, avenging, and enraged God who takes vengeance on his adversaries, in this case, the Assyrians. Jeremiah 50–51 also includes several examples of Yahweh exacting vengeance on Babylon. We also noted passages in Jeremiah and Ezekiel in which Yahweh threatens to avenge himself on sinful Judah. Yahweh's people also implore him to end his anger against them and exact vengeance on their enemies (e.g., Ps 79:10). Those on whose behalf Yahweh has taken vengeance, such as King David, thank their God for having done so (2 Sam 22:48; cf. Ps 22:48).

If a casual reader of the Hebrew Bible were asked to give one example of Yahweh enacting vengeance against an enemy, the answer is likely to be the ten plagues inflicted on Pharaoh and the Egyptians in Exodus 7–12. The Hebrew

DOI: 10.4324/b23212-7

term for vengeance, *naqam*, does not appear in these chapters. The LXX version of Exod 12:12 does have Yahweh asserting that he will "execute vengeance" (ποιήσω τὴν ἐκδίκησιν) on all the gods of the Egyptians. In the later book of Jubilees vengeance becomes main theme of the plague narrative (Jub 48:5, 7–8).[1]

Even without the appearance of *naqam* in the MT, it is clear that Yahweh is engaging in "payback" against the Egyptian king. Before Moses returns to Egypt, Yahweh informs him that he, Yahweh, is going to do unto Pharaoh as Pharaoh did unto him. Pharaoh attempted to kill Yahweh's first-born son Israel, so Yahweh will kill Pharaoh's first-born son, as well as all the first-born males in Egypt, human and animal (Exod 4:22–23; 12:12, 29). Following the first-born plague and the exodus, Yahweh hardens Pharaoh's heart one more time, so that he and the Egyptians pursue the fleeing Israelites. When the refugees see the Egyptians coming toward them they panic, but Moses assures them that Yahweh will fight for them (Exod 14:4–14). At the critical moment Moses extends his hand over the sea, but it is Yahweh who parts the waters (14:21). Even the Egyptians recognize that Yahweh himself is fighting against them (14:25).[2]

In order to compare biblical examples of direct divine vengeance with those found in ancient Greek texts, we must take into account that the Greek gods and their activities are often described differently in epic, historical texts, and tragedy. We should therefore not expect uniformity in the ways in which divine vengeance is described in the Greek texts we have examined. As we discussed in Chapter 2.1, in Homeric epic the gods are mainly human-like persons, although they may also represent natural powers or forces in some situations. In Herodotus, unless an event is associated with a specific sanctuary or ritual, Herodotus refers to "the divine" (τὸ θεῖον), "divinity" (δαίμων; δαιμόνιον), "the gods," or "a god" (Mikalson 2003, 131, 139; cf. Linforth 1928, 222–23).[3] These terms are also attested in Homer[4] and tragedy;[5] in fact, Mikalson calls this usage "characteristically Greek, found in all genres of poetry and prose" (2003, 131; cf. Mikalson 1991, 18). In contrast, some of the tragedies we have examined include specific deities with strong personalities appearing on stage, addressing the audience or interacting with the human characters.

The first example of direct divine vengeance in Homer's *Iliad* comes in the epic's opening scene. Apollo's priest Chryses attempts to ransom his daughter, who had been taken by Agamemnon. Agamemnon insults, threatens, and refuses reciprocity with the old priest. Chryses then prays to Apollo, asking the god to avenge him by making the Greeks pay for (τίσειαν) his tears with the god's plague-bringing arrows. Apollo hears the prayer and immediately complies (*Il.* 1.35–52). Apollo, who backs the Trojans against the Greek army, is the enemy of Achilles. Toward the end of the epic, the half-divine but mortal hero Achilles expresses a desire to exact direct vengeance on the god. Achilles calls Apollo the most destructive of all gods after the god has robbed him of glory in battle (22.15). Achilles admits that the immortal Apollo has no retribution (*tisis*) to fear, but tells the deity "I would have taken vengeance (τισαίμην) on you, if I only had the power" (22.19–20).[6]

In *The Odyssey*, direct divine vengeance is triggered by Odysseus' companions eating the god Helios' cattle, an event alluded to at the very beginning of the epic

(*Od.* 1.7–9).[7] Hearing of this "evil recklessness" (12.300), the sun-god asks Zeus and the other Olympian deities to take vengeance on the companions, who had sworn an oath to Odysseus not to slaughter any cow or sheep they might find (12.299–303, 377–78). If they do not pay him fair compensation for the cattle, Helios threatens to go down to Hades and shine among the dead (12.382–83). Zeus responds by destroying the companions and their ship with a thunderbolt (12.385–419).[8]

The Hebrew Bible includes no parallel to a situation in which one deity asks another deity to seek vengeance on the first god's behalf.[9] However, we *can* compare Yahweh's role in backing an army in a war situation with that of individual Greek gods in Homer's account of the Trojan War. We have already discussed Yahweh fighting for Israel against the Egyptian army in Exodus and the Amorite coalition in the book of Joshua. We know exactly why the biblical God intervened on behalf of his covenant community. We also are told of battles in which Yahweh allows enemy armies to defeat the Israelites as punishment for his people's infidelity (for examples, see Section 7.1.b, below).

In contrast, we are not told why the principal deities in the *Iliad* are so hostile to one side or the other in the Trojan war. When Zeus asks Hera what the house of Priam had done to her to motivate her insatiable anger against them, Hera does not answer his question (*Il.* 4.31–67). Van Erp Taalman Kip (2000, 394) notes that while Zeus "sympathizes with the Trojans, [he] sacrifices Troy to Hera and Athena, whose hatred is either not motivated at all or perhaps—rather late in the poem—only by the judgement of Paris." Paris' choice of Aphrodite over Athena and Hera is only mentioned in the final book of the epic, and then for only three lines (24.28–30). Davies believes that Hera's and Athena's "apparently motiveless malignity" would be "reduced and trivialised if the Judgement of Paris were explicitly mentioned by her or the poet as the ultimate inspiration" of their hatred (1981, 56). He concludes that Homer postpones mention of the judgment in order to contrast the compassion exhibited by Achilles and Priam toward the slain Hector with the lack of compassion exhibited by Apollo, Hera, Poseidon, and Athena, "gods with rather less motives for their hatred than these two humans" (1981, 61).

Nor are we informed why Apollo favored the Trojan side and is so consistently antagonistic toward the Greek hero Achilles. Davies (1981, 60) concludes that Apollo's thwarting of Achilles in Book 22 and his role in the future killing of Achilles (*Il.* 21.277; 22.359–60) present us "with an apparently irrational, unmotivated and inextinguishable hatred of god for mortal." This unexplained animosity is so great that Nagy asks "whether the antipathy of the god toward the Achaeans [the Greeks] . . . has less to do . . . with his sympathy toward the Trojans and more with the theme of his antagonism toward the hero of the *Iliad*" (1979, 144). Thus, "there must have been something about Achilles that was particularly offensive to Apollo (1979, 61). Burkert helps Nagy to identify that "something." Burkert argues that the long-haired youthful Achilles is "almost a *Doppelgänger*" of the youthful, long-haired Apollo/Apellon (Burkert 1975, 19).[10] Here the hero is the "dim mirror-image of the god in indissoluble polarity to the sacrificial victim." Nagy affirms this notion, concluding that the god and hero "function as ritual antagonists" (1979, 62, 144–45).

There are also more general reasons for animosity between individuals (and nations) who are very similar to one another. Freud suggests that the cause of this phenomenon is "the narcissism of small differences" (1947b, 169; cf. Blok 1998, 34–36). Girard emphasizes that it is the loss of differences and distinctions which engenders rivalry and violence (Girard 1979, 49–51). Religious and ethnic minorities are reproached not for their difference from the majority, but "for not being as different as expected, and in the end for not differing at all" (Girard 1989, 22). Bourdieu points out that "social identity lies in difference, and difference is asserted against what is closest, which represents the greatest threat" (qted. in Blok 1998, 38). From this perspective, Freud's inclusion of "narcissism" in his label for this phenomenon is entirely appropriate. In these situations, one does not merely want to be different from others—including others who are almost one's *Doppelgänger*—but to be superior to that rival, if not altogether unique.

If this dynamic does apply to the antagonism between the half-divine Achilles and the god Apollo, is there any possible analogy to this phenomenon in Yahweh's behavior? Certainly readers of the Bible are not meant to conclude that the foreign gods mentioned in scripture are Yahweh's double. The contest on Mt. Carmel in 1 Kings 18, for example, functions to demonstrate that Yahweh and Baal have nothing in common. One is living, powerful, and awe-inspiring, while the other is lifeless, impotent, and ridiculous. Nevertheless, we have found ample evidence that Yahweh exhibits envy toward other gods, even though he insists that no other gods exist and that he is incomparable.[11] Yahweh as Israel's father does want his sons to mirror him, in the sense that their behavior might reflect positively on him (see Lasine 2002, 36–43). This does not mean that he wants his human children to be equal to him. He wants them to make dad proud. If they fail to reflect him adequately, he may smash these human mirrors, both individuals such as king Saul and entire communities such as the wilderness generation in Numbers 14.[12]

In both the Hebrew Bible and Homer's epics we are given access to the thoughts and speeches of the gods, including scenes taking place in the deities' own realm, although glimpses of Yahweh's heavenly court are fewer than scenes on Homer's Olympus.[13] When we turn to Herodotus, we lose all access to Olympus. As an historian, Herodotus can only speculate about divine influence in cases of vengeance witnessed on earth. At times he reports what specific groups or individuals take to be divine causation in events. In a smaller number of cases, Herodotus lets his audience know that he himself is certain of divine involvement.

An example of the latter is Herodotus' account of the two hundred Persian ships which are dispatched around the island of Euboea. Their mission is to prevent the retreat of the Greek ships from the strait when the rest of the Persian ships attack the Greeks from the front (*Hist.* 8.7). A violent and wild rainstorm overtakes the two hundred Persian ships, which drift and are then cast onto the rocks. Herodotus, in his own voice, comments that "all this was done by the god so that the Persian power might be reduced to a level with the Greeks and not much greater" (8.13).[14] Here the historian claims to know even the motive for the divine action. While vengeance does not play an explicit role in this particular incident, the war itself involves each side wanting vengeance against the other.[15]

We have already encountered cases in which Herodotus attributes a negative outcome to direct action by personified divine vengeance. After Oroetes is put to death, Herodotus comments that *tisis* caught up with Oroetes for Polycrates (*Hist.* 3.128; see Chapter 5.2, above). Similarly, while the historian observes that Hermotimus achieved the greatest *tisis* of any human against his foe Panionius, he concludes his account by saying that *tisis* and Hermotimus both overtook Panionius (8.105–106).[16] In other instances, such as the fate of the two hundred Persian ships, Herodotus gives his opinion about the gods' role in a series of events and even their motivation. Another clear example can be found earlier in the *Histories*. After arguing that the Trojans would have returned Helen to the Greeks if she were living with them, Herodotus declares that in his opinion "the divine (τὸ δαιμόνιον) provided that the Trojans' utter destruction make it clear to all humankind that retributive vengeances (τιμωρίαι) from the gods are great for great wrongdoings" (2.120).[17]

There are also cases in which Herodotus gives the opinion of others about divine causation for a dreadful event and then offers his own view. The clearest—and most complex—example involves Cleomenes' grisly suicide (*Hist.* 6.75). Being mad and violent, the Spartan king is held prisoner, but threatens his guard into giving him a knife. He then mutilates himself, working up from the shins to the belly, and finally dies. According to Herodotus, most Greeks say that his madness and death were due to him having persuaded the Pythia to lie about Cleomenes' foe Demaratus. The Athenians hold that it was because he had ravaged the precinct of the goddesses[18] in Eleusis. The Argives believe Cleomenes took Argive suppliants out of their sanctuary at Argos, killed them, and burned down the sacred grove. In other words, all three groups believe that Cleomenes' suffering is divine vengeance or punishment. The Spartans do not agree that the gods had anything to do with his madness; it was Cleomenes' un-Spartan-like heavy drinking in the Scythian manner which drove him mad (6.84).

After listing these differing views, Herodotus states that "it seems to me that Cleomenes paid *tisis* in full for Demaratus" (*Hist.* 6.84). While Herodotus does not mention anything about Cleomenes having persuaded the priestess to state a falsehood about Demaratus (the view of "most Greeks"), commentators tend to conclude that Herodotus agrees with the majority view (e.g., Boedeker 2003, 23). J. Gould (2003, 301) understands the historian to be saying "that the anger of divinity was responsible," although divine anger is not mentioned by any of those who suggest explanations for Cleomenes' madness and suicide, including Herodotus.

Is it possible that Herodotus' statement is intentionally vague, not simply because he has no direct access to the divine, but because Cleomenes is not a one-dimensional villain? Cartledge and Greenwood (2002, 357) suggest that Herodotus ultimately attributes Cleomenes' madness "to divine retribution for the latter's injustice towards his co-king Demaratus." This leaves out of account Demaratus' prior "injustice" towards Cleomenes. The two are co-kings of Sparta, a situation capable of inspiring rivalry and envy. We should therefore not be surprised when Herodotus reports that while Cleomenes was in Aegina "working in advance for the common good of Greece, Demaratus slandered him, not because he cared about the Aeginetans but out of envy and spite" (φθόνῳ καὶ ἄγῃ; 6.61; cf. 6.51).

It is for this (and other reasons) that Cleomenes became set on revenge against Demaratus (*Hist.* 6.65). The revenge took the form of the charge that Demaratus was not the son of Ariston and therefore not fit to reign in Sparta. The matter is ultimately submitted to the oracle at Delphi. Cleomenes, who on two previous occasions had refused bribes (3.148; 5.48–51), convinces an influential man named Cobon to persuade the priestess to say that Demaratus is not Ariston's son (6.66). On the first of the previous occasions Herodotus had called Cleomenes "a man of the highest integrity" (3.148). This is not to deny that Cleomenes committed impious and violent deeds as well (e.g., 6.78–81). Given the complexity of this figure, and the variety of ways in which divine retribution might have been involved, it is no wonder that Herodotus makes his own statement vague and open-ended, thereby inviting his audience to decide for themselves how to regard Cleomenes' horrific death.

As I discussed earlier, readers of the Hebrew Bible and Homer's *Iliad* have no difficulty determining which deity backs which side in a war.[19] The situation in the *Histories* is not so clear-cut. Earlier I mentioned Herodotus' view that "the god" sent the storm which attacked the two hundred Persian ships. Rather than taking this as a sign that the god was on the side of the Greeks, Herodotus concludes that divinity wanted the battle to be a fair fight.[20] Mikalson (2002, 188) points out that "the 'divine' and some gods, even Greek gods, ... helped Persians and their predecessors in earlier times."[21] However, "when the conflict became squarely between Persians and Greeks, the Greek divine world conceived of as a whole or in parts stood completely and solely behind the Greeks." In contrast, Romm believes that Herodotus' "recurring hints that the gods watch over or actually participate in the battles waged by men," in the form of portents and apparitions, "are meant not so much to show that the Greeks had God on their side ... as to add to the sense of destiny surrounding the entire course of the war" (1998, 194). It is also worth noting that divine activity in war is sometimes triggered by impious or hybristic actions committed by either side of the conflict.

The tragedies we have discussed also furnish striking examples of direct divine vengeance. In the opening scene of Euripides' *Hippolytus*, Aphrodite makes it clear that she will exact vengeance on her enemy Hippolytus that very day (*Hipp.* 21–22, 49). Later in the drama the goddess Artemis reveals that she will take vengeance on the mortal whom Aphrodite loves most (*Hipp.* 1418–22). In *The Bacchae*, after giving Pentheus opportunities to recognize Dionysus' divinity and end his war against the deity, Dionysus orders the Theban bacchants to wreak vengeance on Pentheus.

Earlier I rejected the claim that Dionysus and Yahweh are both jealous exclusivist deities (see Chapter 6.4.a, above). However, there is one sense in which the two deities *are* comparable. In Exodus 5, Pharaoh fails to acknowledge Yahweh as a deity and the same is true of Pentheus in regard to Dionysus. When Moses and Aaron tell the Egyptian king that Yahweh wants the Hebrews to hold a feast for him in the wilderness, Pharaoh replies, "I do not know Yahweh" and refuses the request (Exod 5:2). When Pentheus returns to Thebes and hears about the rituals honoring Dionysus, Pentheus dismisses him as "the new god, . . . whoever he is" (*Bacch.* 220; cf. 247).[22] Pentheus insists that Dionysus does not exist (333, 517). The Stranger, Dionysus in human form, is fully aware that in the end Pentheus "will come to know Dionysus, the son of Zeus" (859). Similarly, Yahweh uses the ten plagues to ensure that Pharaoh will "know that I am Yahweh" and that "there is none like me in all the earth" (Exod 9:14, 10:2; cf. 14:18). Unfortunately, neither Pentheus nor Pharaoh learns his lesson in time to save himself (Exod 14:27–28; Ps 136:15; *Bacch.* 1114–36).[23]

b. Deities indirectly taking vengeance

In both biblical and ancient Greek texts gods occasionally achieve vengeance through the agency of one or more human beings. As we discussed in Chapter 4.1.c, a young prophet quotes Yahweh commanding Jehu to "strike the house of Ahab your master, that I may avenge the blood of my servants the prophets, and the blood of all the servants of Yahweh from the hand of Jezebel" (2 Kgs 9:7). Even though this command singles out Jezebel as the one responsible for the deaths of Yahweh's prophets and servants, Yahweh's vengeance eradicates the entire house of Ahab. We also noted passages such as Ezek 25:14, in which Yahweh declares that he will lay his vengeance on Edom "by the hand of My people Israel," that is, using the Israelites as the instrument of his revenge.

In other cases Yahweh punishes his people Israel by "outsourcing" his vengeance, that is, using foreign armies. Earlier we discussed Jeremiah's claim that Yahweh roused the spirit of the kings of the Medes against Babylon (Jer 51:11; cf. 50:14, 51:2). In Isaiah, Yahweh famously calls Assyria the "rod of my anger" against his own people (Isa 10:5). Yahweh sends the Assyrians against his alienated, apostate nation (גוי חנף) and commands them against "the people of my fury" (עם עברתי; 10:6). Later, in besieged Jerusalem, the Assyrian king's representative, the Rabshakeh, quotes his master as saying that Yahweh himself told the king to go up against Judah and destroy it (Isa 36:10; cf. 2 Kgs 18:25). He assumes that his Judean audience could be persuaded by the prospect of Yahweh using a foreign nation to punish his people. The Rabshakeh, who may himself be an Israelite deported to Assyria at an earlier date, is a sophisticated propagandist, who is clearly familiar with Israelite theology. Nevertheless, his claim is shown to be false when Jerusalem is miraculously saved (Isa 37:36; 2 Kgs 19:35).

Similar pronouncements are made by Yahweh in relation to Jerusalem's eventual fall to the Babylonians. In Jeremiah, Yahweh declares that he will give many lands, including Judah, to his "servant" Nebuchadnezzar (Jer 27:5–7; cf. 25:9; 50:17). Later on, Yahweh will take vengeance against the "virgin daughter of Babylon" (Isa 47:1–3). He does so by grasping the right hand of Cyrus the Persian, whom Yahweh calls his "anointed one," his "shepherd" and "he whom Yahweh loves" (Isa 45:1; 44:28; 48:14). Yahweh declares that he is acting "for the sake of my servant Jacob," since, according to the Bible, Cyrus grants the Judeans the right to return home from exile (Ezra 1:1–4; 2 Chr 36:22–23).

Many biblical commentators have pointed out that the Bible is not the only ancient Near Eastern text which reports instances of divine abandonment and a deity directing a foreign nation to attack his own people. The examples most often cited in connection with passages in Isaiah and Jeremiah are the Sumerian *Curse of Agade*, Esarhaddon's Babylon inscriptions, and the so-called Cyrus Cylinder.[24] While these texts do have features in common with the prophetic passages we have just discussed, a brief review of these documents will reveal that they all differ from the biblical cases in one crucial respect.

According to the *Curse of Agade* (after 2100 BCE), the god Enlil withdraws his support for the city of Agade and its king Naram-Sin, for reasons left unexpressed.[25] This leads other deities to abandon the city. After mourning for seven years,[26] Naram-Sin twice seeks omens, but they say nothing about building the temple. The king then demolishes the Ekur, the god Enlil's temple in Nippur. The narrator does not explicitly state that Naram-Sin plans to build a new temple after razing the old one; however, seeking an omen about temple building strongly suggests that this is the case. Naram-Sin's destruction of the Ekur is likened to an assault by soldiers, athletes, or criminals (ll. 100–19; Black *et al.* 2006, 120–21; B. Foster 2016, 16, 353). The king's actions prompt Enlil to send the Gutians to destroy Agade.[27] This largely unhistorical text[28] was probably composed for a didactic purpose, using the name of this famous monarch to stress the importance of avoiding Enlil's displeasure. Scholars suggest a variety of settings for the document's composition.[29]

In the Babylon inscriptions of the Assyrian king Esarhaddon (ca. 678–670 BCE),[30] it is the god Marduk who brings disaster to Babylon. Marduk is worshiped in both Babylon and Assyria. In the versions of the inscription designed for a Babylonian audience,[31] it is Babylon's wrongful behavior which leads the furious Marduk to devastate Babylon. Once again the gods flee a city. The inscriptions highlight the flooding of the Arakhtu canal as the means of punishment, while remaining largely silent about the key role played by the Assyrian army under the command of Esarhaddon's own father Sennacherib, who goes unnamed in the inscriptions. The inscriptions are clearly pro-Esarhaddon propaganda. As Brinkman puts it, "the former debasement of the city and its abandonment by god and man acted as a perfect literary foil for its glorious resurrection under Esarhaddon and the restoration of its exiled deities and citizens" (1983, 42). Porter (1993, 100–101) points out that explaining a city's downfall as the result of its citizens' misdeeds is a strategy usually employed "by a defeated city to explain the failure of its gods to protect itself"; in this case, however, it is "used by the conqueror instead."

In the Cyrus Cylinder (after 539 BCE) it is again the god Marduk who orders a foreign king to go to Babylon. In this case it is not the citizens of Babylon who cause Marduk to become angry, but their sacrilegious king. Nabonidus had replaced Marduk with the moon god Sin as the city's patron deity and imposed the corvée on the citizenry (ll. 7–9; Cogan 2003, 315). As a result, the gods had abandoned their dwellings. Marduk then finds the righteous Persian king Cyrus and accompanies him to Babylon, without any need for fighting. In fact, everyone rejoices at Cyrus' kingship (ll. 17–19). Cyrus returns the gods to their cult centers, along with the people. This Akkadian foundation-text[32] was probably composed by priests in Babylon (Paul 2012, 15), or, as Goldingay (2001, 263) puts it, "ghost-written by Marduk's adherents."

None of these texts was composed by members of a devastated nation for an audience coping with the collapse of their country, as is the case in the biblical passages from Isaiah and Jeremiah. The *Curse of Agade* was written long after the fall of one city, perhaps as a paradigmatic illustration of what might happen if the god Enlil is not adequately honored. The scribes who composed Esarhaddon's Babylon inscriptions were associated with the victorious Assyrian king who has now become king of Babylon as well. The same can be said of the Cyrus Cylinder. Here a victorious Persian king announces his intention to be a righteous and fair ruler of Babylon.

In contrast, Isaiah 10, Jeremiah 27 and Isaiah 45 contend that Israel and Judah fell to foreign armies because of infidelity to Yahweh and rampant social injustice. Yahweh did not simply abandon his people, nor was he too weak to defend them against alien forces. On the contrary, Yahweh was so powerful that he could cause the pagan armies of Assyria and Babylon to devastate the promised land and put an end to kingship in Israel, whether the invaders knew they were following Yahweh's instructions or not.

These are astounding claims. Commenting on Isa 10:5–7, Kaiser notes that Israel, in its impotence and being at the mercy of the world powers of its time, recognized that these were Yahweh's tools for acting on behalf of his own people as well as his own glorification before the world. Kaiser finds this to be a "distinctive feature of the audacity (*Kühnheit*) of Israel's certainty of God" (1981, 223). I would suggest that it is the authors of these prophetic texts who are being "audacious" by asking their audience to accept that they are so sinful that their all-powerful paternal deity is justified in surrendering them to the tender mercies of pagan world powers. Habbakuk, for one, balks at this way of justifying the Babylonian destruction of Judah: "why are you [Yahweh] silent when the wicked swallows up one more righteous than he?" (Hab 1:13).

Goldingay (2001, 262) goes further when discussing Isa 45:1–8. After pointing out that the "revolution in Middle Eastern political affairs" initiated by Yahweh's support for Cyrus "is all brought about 'for the sake of Jacob my servant, of Israel my chosen' (v. 4a)," Goldingay observes that "the megalomania of this Poet would seem outrageous if history had not vindicated it by the fact that countless peoples for whom Cyrus means nothing recognize Jacob-Israel's significance." In other words, the only reason that the author's megalomania is not outrageous is that his ideology was successful in persuading later generations that Yahweh is as powerful and solicitous for Israel's welfare as he says he is in Second Isaiah. When this passage is viewed alongside the ANE texts just described, we can say that the biblical authors' audacious propaganda worked.

If the "Poets" of First and Second Isaiah are megalomaniacal, it may be in the sense of "childhood megalomania" described by psychologists. Bergler

(1957, 16–17) cites a scene from a novel by Romain Rolland to illustrate this phenomenon:

> The child commands the clouds. He wants them to go to the right, but they continued to the left. He scolds them, and repeats his command more urgently. . . . But they continue to move to the left. He stamps his feet, menaces them with his little stick, and changes his command. Now he wants them to go to the left, and this time the clouds obey. He is happy and proud of his power.

In the present case, Yahweh is unable to prevent the pagan armies from "going left" and attacking Israel and Judah. Therefore he commands the Assyrians and Babylonians to do what they were already doing, namely, devastating his people's land. Blaming the fall of Jerusalem on the sins of kings such as Manasseh and the infidelity of Yahweh's people also functions to obscure the actual powerlessness of Judah and its deity.

To accomplish this aim, Goldingay's "Poet" must depict the anthropomorphic Yahweh as making statements which might be deemed megalomaniacal if they were uttered by a human being. Yahweh repeatedly insists that "I am Yahweh and there is none else" and that "there is none but me" (Isa 45:5–6, 18, 22; 46:9). The Poet then quotes the "virgin daughter of Babylon" as making the very same claim: "I am, and there is none but me" (Isa 47:8, 10).[33] Paul calls Babylon's aspiration to godhood "megalomaniacal self-delusion" (2012, 295; cf. 287). Babylon's boasts are megalomaniacal because readers are aware that Babylon's self-definition is false. Yahweh's identical statements are to be accepted as true and therefore not megalomaniacal.

If one views Yahweh's quoted words in Second Isaiah as indicative of his personality, we may have to reconsider whether megalomania is really an inappropriate term to apply to this deity. After all, he is not making these declarations in a moment of triumph. On the contrary, he is speaking at a time when his Jerusalem temple has been destroyed and his chosen people have lost their promised land, with many being exiled to Babylon. Unable to order the "clouds" of Babylonians to go back east, he commands them to go west to Jerusalem and ravage it.

There are fewer examples of indirect divine vengeance in the Greek texts we have examined. At first glance it might seem that we have such an example at the very start of *The Odyssey*. The first quoted speech in the epic is about exacting vengeance. The god Zeus laments how mortals blame the gods for their own reckless acts. He points to Aegisthus, who murdered Agamemnon and was avenged by his victim's son, Orestes. Rather than claiming that he used Orestes to exact vengeance on his behalf, Zeus reminds his Olympian audience that he had sent the god Hermes to warn Aegisthus not to commit this crime, because vengeance (*tisis*) would be taken by Orestes. Aegisthus did not heed the warning and had to pay in full (ἀπέτισεν; *Od.* 1.32–43). In Herodotus, Hermotimus believes that the gods have brought his foe Panionius into his hands so that he could exact vengeance from him, but he does not say that he mutilated Panionius and his sons on behalf of the gods (*Hist.* 8.106).

In Euripides' *Hippolytus* and *Bacchae* deities do employ humans as agents of their vengeance. Aphrodite forces Phaedra to play a key role in the goddess' revenge against Hippolytus, and Dionysus uses the frenzied Theban maenads to destroy Pentheus. In Euripides' *Hecuba* the former queen Hecuba can also be considered an agent of divine justice when she causes the downfall of the murderous Polymestor. This does not surprise commentators such as Heath, who notes that "the gods habitually work through human intermediaries in such cases" (1987, 67). Finally, in *Oedipus Tyrannus*, king Oedipus believes that he is attempting to obtain vengeance on behalf of the god Apollo. In fact, he considers himself the god's "ally" in tracking down the regicide and thereby ending the plague which is destroying his city.[34] Oedipus achieves his goal, but only after recognizing that he himself is the polluted criminal against whom divine vengeance is directed.

At first glance, Sophocles' Oedipus and the biblical priest Phinehas may seem similar, in that both take action to stop a divinely-sent plague. However, the differences outweigh any similarities. We are not told Phinehas' motivation for killing Zimri and Cozbi; we only know that Yahweh interprets the priest's action as the result of Phinehas having identified with Yahweh's jealousy. In contrast, Oedipus' stated motivation is to act as the god's ally to save Thebes, at whatever cost to himself. In the end, Phinehas and his family line are rewarded greatly while Oedipus and his family remain cursed. Phinehas performs a violent cure to the plague, while polluted Oedipus cures Thebes by doing violence to himself and leaving his city.

We have also encountered instances in which a deity is willing (or perceived as willing) to exact vengeance on behalf of a human individual. Yahweh makes it clear that he will take vengeance sevenfold if anyone kills the killer Cain (Gen 4:15; see Chapter 2.3.b, above). Yahweh's role in Samson's suicide attack on the Philistines may be another example. Samson asks Yahweh to give him the strength to be avenged of his enemies one last time (Judg 16:28). Immediately after, he has the strength to collapse the pillars of a huge building, killing three thousand people as well as himself (Judg 16:27, 29–30). This suggests that Yahweh has heard Samson's plea and enabled him to exact vengeance on the Philistines. Fulfilling Samson's desire also allows Yahweh to accomplish his objective in choosing this Nazarite judge, which is to begin delivering Israel from the hand of the Philistines (Judg 13:5).

A character within the textual world may also assume that Yahweh has gained vengeance on behalf of a human being. For example, Jephthah's daughter encourages her father to go through with his vow to offer her as a sacrifice, because "Yahweh has done full vengeance for you (עשה לך יהוה נקמות) from your enemies" (Judg 11:36). Individuals may also ask Yahweh to exact vengeance on their own behalf. For example, Jeremiah begs Yahweh to "take vengeance for me (והנקם לי) on my persecutors" (Jer 15:15).[35]

Euripides' *Hippolytus* offers an example of a Greek deity planning to exact vengeance on behalf of a mortal. The goddess Artemis will not avenge Hippolytus while her most ardent devotee is still alive (*Hipp*. 1391–96, 1437–39). However, she assures Hippolytus that Aphrodite's anger against him will not go unavenged (1417). Artemis will take vengeance (τιμωρήσομαι) by attacking whichever of Aphrodite's followers that goddess loves the most (1418–22).

Finally, both literatures include instances in which humans believe (or act as though they believe) that they are exacting vengeance on behalf of a god or gods, but this is not the case. In 2 Sam 4:5–12, the brothers Rechab and Baanah kill Saul's son Ishbosheth while he is sleeping and then behead him. They bring the head to David and announce that Yahweh has taken full vengeance for their lord the king on Saul and his seed (4:8). David does not accept their self-presentation. In fact, he calls them wicked men and condemns them to death for having murdered a "righteous man in his house, on his bed" (4:11). If Rechab and Baanah had actually thought that they were Yahweh's agents in avenging the king—that is, if they are not merely seeking a reward from David—they would be akin to Herodotus' Apollonians, who blinded Euenius to avenge the shepherd's failure to protect sacred sheep (*Hist*. 9.93–94; see Chapter 5.3, above). The Apollonians were also punished for misreading their situation, because it was the gods themselves who had sent the wolves that killed the sheep.

2. Comparing divine envy and jealousy in biblical and Greek texts

In the Greek material we have examined, instances of divine jealousy and envy tend to be less frequent and less salient than instances of divine vengeance and revenge.[36] In the *Iliad* Hera's jealousy of her husband Zeus is certainly present, although Homer allows us to recognize that Hera's situation prompts her jealousy as much as (if not more than) any psychological predisposition toward jealousy. In contrast, Hera in *The Homeric Hymn to Apollo* and Euripides' *Heracles* comes much closer to Clay's characterization of the goddess as "*phthonos* itself."[37] In the play, the guiltless Heracles explicitly attributes his destruction to Hera's *phthonos* and neither the Chorus nor Theseus disputes his claim (*HF* 1309–10). Here, as in a number of other cases, Hera directs her jealous anger at the children whom Zeus fathered with one of his human lovers. Divine *phthonos* also plays a role in Aeschylus' *Persians*, when the Messenger attributes Xerxes' defeat to the gods' envy. However, not all commentators take the Messenger's perspective to be authoritative.[38] Finally, in Euripides' *Hecuba* the former queen implies that the Greek army will provoke divine *phthonos* if they sacrifice her daughter to the dead Achilles.[39]

While characters in Herodotus sometimes attribute others' failures to divine envy, they do not speak of a specific anthropopathic deity being driven by *phthonos*. Rather, the *phthonos* of the "gods" or "the divine" is triggered by acts which are viewed as exceeding human limits, whether that involves being too successful, engaging in excessive revenge, or usurping a divine prerogative. The actions prompted by divine envy tend to restore balance between the divine and human spheres.

Divine jealousy and envy in the Hebrew Bible are essentially different from the divine *phthonos* exhibited in Greek texts. The most fundamental difference stems from the fact that Yahweh in presented in the Bible as a multi-faceted, anthropopathic being who has a complex personality. Yahweh views himself as Israel's divine spouse, father, and sovereign, as well as the only true God and creator of the cosmos.[40] Yahweh's jealousy and envy can be aroused when he plays any of these roles, each of which demands that one and only one individual play that role at any given time. Yahweh's demand for exclusive and total devotion may also be an indicator of dispositional envy.[41] In Hazlitt's phrasing, if envy "does not occupy the whole space, [it] feels itself excluded" (1823, 7).

In return for their devotion to their divine husband, father, and king, Yahweh's followers are promised his care and protection. However, a number of biblical speakers express confusion or disappointment that Yahweh has not rescued them from danger or kept his promises of peace and plenty, in spite of their loyalty and obedience.[42] In contrast, the characters in the Greek texts we have studied do not have similar expectations about divine love, mercy, and protection (see, e.g., Lefkowitz 2019, 3, 49–50, 72–73).

When Yahweh's jealousy or envy is triggered he takes the perceived affront "personally," in a way which has no parallel among ancient Greek deities. In *Hippolytus* Aphrodite is not envious of the attention which Hippolytus bestows on Artemis; she merely wants to be honored in the same way as any other god. By insulting Aphrodite, Hippolytus makes her into his enemy. The same is true of Dionysus, who endures even more harsh insults from Pentheus. Israelites do not need to actively insult Yahweh in order to trigger their God's jealous wrath. Merely ignoring Yahweh, or assuming that Yahweh does not notice them, may be sufficient to arouse his jealousy. If one goes further and acknowledges or "bows down to" another god in addition to Yahweh, his jealousy, envy, and fury are sure to be ignited.

Another reason for the intensity of Yahweh's jealousy and envy is his identity as Israel's husband, a dimension totally absent from ancient Greek religion. Zeus may have intercourse with individual human women, but he is not said to be husband of the Greek people or any other nation. If Yahweh's wife Israel attempts to worship her divine husband along with other gods, she is cuckolding Yahweh. This threatens Yahweh's self-definition. And to the extent that Yahweh is portrayed as having a narcissistic disposition, being ignored, abandoned, and betrayed all become narcissistic wounds, to which Yahweh may respond with a variety of emotions. Yahweh may feel that he is being treated like a fool, treated with contempt, or hated by those who serve other gods and/or violate his statutes (see Chapter 3.2.c and 3.3.b, above). The Greek gods may want humans to honor and sacrifice to them, but none has the kind of narcissistic need for exclusive adoration exhibited by Yahweh, or the fear that their worshipers may abandon them for a rival deity.

Yahweh is also Israel's divine father. Zeus is viewed as a father as well. Homer and Hesiod repeatedly refer to Zeus as "father of men and gods."[43] Both Zeus and Yahweh are capable of feeling compassion for one or more of their human children. Yahweh declares that compassion is an essential part of his identity; he is a God of compassion (אֵל רַחוּם; Exod 34:6; cf. Deut 4:31). The most dramatic example of Zeus' compassion is his reaction to the impending death of his mortal son Sarpedon in the *Iliad*. When he finally agrees that he must let Sarpedon die, he "pours bloody drops to earth" honoring his dear son (*Il*. 16.459). Of course blood does not flow through the Olympian gods' veins. The uncanny image of the bloody drops serves an important function. As Lateiner points out, "Homer has Zeus merge human pre-battle propitiatory blood rituals and post-battle burial blood rituals with human grieving to express anthropomorphic parental agony.... He sorrows like a human" (2002, 47, 49).

Admittedly, Yahweh and the Greek deities do not always display compassion toward human beings, as we have seen throughout this study. Yahweh famously tells Hosea to name his daughter "No Compassion," because Yahweh will no longer have compassion on the house of Israel (Hos 1:6). In the *Iliad*, when Achilles treats Hector's corpse outrageously, not all the gods feel compassion for the fallen hero; Hera, Poseidon and Athene persist in their hatred. Typically, Zeus is a detached observer. His attitude is captured in Book 20, when he invites the other gods to join the battle on whichever side they prefer. Of the human combatants, Zeus declares "I care for them, though they perish." Yet he goes on to say that he will remain seated on Olympus gazing with delight (20.21–25).[44] Meanwhile the humans below suffer and die. According to Lynn-George (1996, 7), this is an example of "the *Iliad*'s tapestry of contrariety . . . the gods care and do not care."

There are also significant differences between the paternal behavior of Yahweh and Zeus. Yahweh as father to his human children demands obedience, while in Homeric religion "there is no obedience to god, just as there are scarcely any divine commands" (Burkert 1987, 189). Disobedience on the part of Yahweh's people is likely to provoke his jealousy and rage. In part, this is because in Yahweh's case it is crucial that his children reflect well on him and his success as a parent. Those who in his eyes have failed to mirror him, such as Saul and Jeroboam, have their family lines broken or eradicated. Even David, who is supposedly[45] a man according to Yahweh's heart (1 Sam 13:14), disappoints his God by breaking three of Yahweh's ten commandments, all in one incident (2 Samuel 11).[46] While Zeus exhibits love and pity toward humans such as Hector in the *Iliad*, it is difficult to imagine him saying that any mortal is a person according to his own heart, as Paul quotes God as saying about David in Acts 13:22.[47] Yahweh is also human beings' father in a more fundamental sense than Zeus, or any other Greek deity could be, since Yahweh created humans and did so "in his image."

Both Yahweh and Zeus are kings as well as fathers. As I noted earlier, Brueggemann claims that Yahweh will "brook no rival," for his intention is to be fully sovereign" (1997, 283). Similarly, W. Guthrie contends that Zeus is "a ruler who will brook no rivals," human or divine (1955, 39). Yahweh is Israel's divine king, but he cannot brook any divine rival for the simple reason that other gods do not exist, according to texts such as Deut 4:35 and Isa 44:6–8. Yet Yahweh elsewhere acknowledges the existence of other gods and reacts to them in a way which implies that they not only exist but are *too* real, because they too often attract his followers.

150 Comparing Hebrew and Greek texts

If Yahweh's subjects honor other gods as well as himself, he, Israel's divine king, feels rejected, abandoned, and scorned. This perception prompts Yahweh's envy and jealous wrath against both his disloyal subjects and their false gods.

In my final chapter I will ask whether Yahweh and the deities found in ancient Greek literature share another similarity: imperfection. If this is the case, I will ask what functions such imperfection might serve for the human characters who worship these gods.

Notes

1 According to Livneh (2011, 173), "Jub. 48:5a sets the language of vengeance drawn from prophecies against foreign nations in a new historical context, . . . namely, the Exodus."
2 For an example of a battle which illustrates both Yahweh's direct vengeance and the role of humans in taking vengeance for Yahweh's sake, see the discussion of Joshua 10 in Chapter 2.3.a, above.
3 According to Linforth (1928, 218), "though the multiplicity of gods is never called into question" in Herodotus, "there is a disposition to speak of the divine element in the world *as if* it were characterized by the indivisibility of the god of the pure monotheist." While some readers of Herodotus might have this "disposition," nothing in the *Histories* suggests the idea of an indivisible "god of the pure monotheist."
4 Redfield (1975, 77) notes that the poet also includes a reference to "god" [*theos*] without thinking of any particular deity (*Il.* 21.47).
5 See the discussion of Aeschylus' *Persians* in Chapter 6.1, above.
6 The most famous example of vengeance (*tisis*) in the *Iliad* is probably Achilles' revenge on Hector for having killed Achilles' dearest friend Patroclus; see Loney 2019, 35–39.
7 For a detailed study of vengeance and revenge in the *Odyssey*, see Loney 2019, 49–170.
8 We should keep in mind that the wily hero Odysseus is not necessarily a reliable narrator in the so-called "tale to Alcinous" (*Od.* 9–12; cf. Plato *Resp.* 614b). It is in the interest of this sole survivor to impress his Phaiacian hosts with tales of his courage, intelligence and discipline.
9 Admittedly, Homer portrays Helios as so human-like that no alteration would have been required if the situation had called for a human being to request that a deity seek vengeance on his or her behalf.
10 Burkert here uses the older Dorian spelling of Apollo's name.
11 See Chapter 3.2 and 3.3.b, above.
12 Even those individuals who seem to be among Yahweh's most successful and devoted "children," such as Moses, Elijah, Jonah, Jeremiah, and Job, suffer so much that they end up wanting to die or wishing that they had never been born (see Chapter 3.2.b, above). In Job's case, Yahweh's smashing of his human mirrors is almost literal: "I was at ease, but he smashed and smashed me (ויפרפרני); seized my neck then bashed me and bashed me (ויפצפצני)" (16:12; Habel 1985, 262, 264–65).
13 Yahweh's heavenly conversations in Job 1–2 are the most dramatic example in biblical narrative, although the prophet Micaiah claims to have had a vision of Yahweh on his heavenly throne, addressing the host of heaven and conversing with "the spirit" who stood before him (1 Kgs 22:19–23).
14 As noted by Mikalson (2002, 192), on two other occasions Greek speakers declare that they can win against the Persians if the gods give them equal treatment with their foes (*Hist.* 6.11, 109).
15 See *Hist.* 5.105 (Darius asks Zeus to grant him vengeance [τίσασθαι] against the Athenians for their part in burning Sardis) and 8.144 (the Athenians seek to avenge [τιμωρέειν] the burning and destroying of the gods' shrines and their images).

16　See Chapter 3.3.b.2 and 5.3, above.
17　Direct divine vengeance is also illustrated when Herodotus relates the words of the prophets at Dodona and Delphi who declare that the flocks and land of the Apollonians are infertile because the gods are avenging Euenius (*Hist.* 9.93); on this story, see Chapter 5.3, above.
18　The "goddesses" are Demeter and Kore (Persephone); see Hornblower and Pelling 2017:189.
19　In the HB a character can mistakenly attribute the outcome of a war to the wrong deity. For example, when the Chronicler's Ahaz is defeated by the Arameans, instead of realizing that the loss was due to punishment by Yahweh, the king "sacrificed to the gods of Damascus, who had struck him" (2 Chr 28:23).
20　Yahweh also reduces the number of combatants on one side prior to a battle. However, in this case it is the number of his own Israelite soldiers that is being reduced. The reason is not that he wants Gideon and Israel to lose to the Midianites and Amalekites but because he wants to show that it is he who is responsible for the victory, so that the Israelites do not brag that it was their own prowess which saved them (Judg 7:2).
21　As examples Mikalson cites *Hist.* 1.46–56, 1.85–91, l.124, 1.126, 1.209 and 9.122.
22　Pentheus assumes that newborn Dionysus burned to death along with his mother Semele (*Bacch.* 244–45).
23　For other similarities between Yahweh's attempts to teach the Pharaoh and Dionysus' efforts to teach Pentheus, see Chapter 6.4.c, above.
24　Block (2000, 34–42) argues that Ezekiel also adapted the ANE motif of divine abandonment in order to describe Yahweh's departure from the Jerusalem temple prior to the Babylonians' destruction of the city.
25　We are told that "the statement coming from the E-kur [Enlil's temple] was disquieting" (l. 57; Black *et al.* 2006, 120) or "like a ghastly hush" (B. Foster 2016, 352). We are not told the contents of that statement, but its effect on the populace and the other gods *is* reported: "because of Enlil (?) all Agade was reduced (?) to trembling, and terror befell Inana," who leaves the city (ll. 58–60; Black *et al.* 2006, 120). Franke asserts that Naram-Sin plans to rebuild Ekur, but Enlil rejects his proposal (1995, 838). This goes beyond the text, which mentions neither a proposal by the king to the god nor the reason for Enlil's displeasure.
26　The king has a nocturnal vision that Enlil "would not let the kingdom of Agade occupy a pleasant, lasting residence," but he is at a loss for words and keeps this knowledge to himself (ll. 83–87; Black *et al.* 2006, 120).
27　The other gods console Enlil by pointing out that he has achieved payback against Naram-Sin: "Enlil, may the city that destroyed your city, be treated as your city has been treated!" (l. 212; Black *et al.* 2006, 123).
28　The historical king Naram-Sin did not destroy the Ekur; in fact, he began to renovate it, according to his own inscriptions (Westenholz 1987, 28–29). In addition, the Gutians did not invade the country until after Naram-Sin's reign. Finally, scholars agree that *The Curse of Agade* was composed during the Ur III or OB period (e.g., Van De Mieroop 2016, 76).
29　Franke (1995, 838) believes that the text was written by "priests of Nippur and may have served as an object lesson to rulers who would favor any deity, including Inanna/Ishtar, over Nippur's god Enlil." Black *et al.* suggest that the story of the Ekur's destruction may have originated in a rebellion in southern Sumer which Naram-Sin quelled (2006, 117). B. Foster contends that the text was written by a "preservationist poet" who viewed "the lavish reconstruction of the temple . . . as an affront" (2016, 16, 267). For J. Cooper (1993, 17), the ending of the story stresses that only Naram-Sin's own city "should suffer for this sacrilege, not the entire land." And while the story ends without indicating Enlil's response to the consolation provided by the other gods, "the lifting of his anger against Babylonia would have been apparent to any reader/listener of the prosperous Ur III period" (1993, 17). In other words, the invasion of the Gutians, although orchestrated by Enlil, is limited to one sacrilegious city.

30 Novotny 2015, 161; cf. Frame 1992, 67.
31 These are commonly referred to as Babylon A, C, and E. See Porter 1993, 99–104. For the most recent edition of these inscriptions, see Leichty 2011, 193–217.
32 On the Cyrus Cylinder as a foundation-text, see Kuhrt 1983, 88–92.
33 This echoes Assyria's boast in Zeph 2:15.
34 *OT* 135–36; cf. 107, 244–45 and Chapter 6.2.b, above.
35 Peels argues that Jeremiah "does not pray that God will avenge him, . . . but that God will avenge himself, to Jeremiah's benefit" (1995, 230). This interpretation fits Jer 11:20, but not 15:15, in which Jeremiah is primarily concerned with Yahweh providing the prophet with relief from his tormentors.
36 In fact, in Euripides' *Hippolytus* Aphrodite makes a point of noting that her desire to kill Artemis' favorite Hippolytus is *not* driven by *phthonos* (*Hipp.* 20; see Chapter 6.3.a, above).
37 See Chapter 5.1, above and Chapter 8.1, below.
38 See Chapter 6.1.a, above.
39 See Chapter 2.3.b.2, above.
40 See Chapter 2.1, above; cf. Lasine 2010, 48–53; 2016, 467–75.
41 See Chapter 3, above.
42 See Chapter 2.1, above and Chapter 8.3, below.
43 For example, *Il*. 1.544, 4.68, 8.49, 8.132, 11.182, 16.458, 20.56, 22.167, 24.103; *Ody*. 1.28; Hesiod *Theog.* 47, 457 (each with the word order "father of gods and men"); cf. 542, 643, 838.
44 While P. Jones (2003, 272–73) contends that Zeus is referring to enjoying the *gods'* doing battle with each other, Zeus is actually replying to Poseidon's question about the battle between the Trojans and Achaeans. Moreover, the gods do not fight one another until Book 21.
45 This phrase in 1 Sam 13:14 is traditionally rendered "a man after his [Yahweh's] own heart." However, McCarter argues that "this has nothing to do with any great fondness of Yahweh's for David. . . . Rather it emphasizes the free divine selection of the heir to the throne" (1980, 229). Nor does it imply that David's heart resembles Yahweh's. In fact, when Samuel says this, he has no idea who the heir to the throne will be. Later, when he is sent by Yahweh to the house of Jesse, he mistakenly assumes that the eldest son Eliab is Yahweh's choice (1 Sam 16:6).
46 Yahweh's reaction to David's adultery with Bathsheba and cold-blooded murder of her husband does not include an explicit reference to Yahweh as David's father. Yahweh's disappointment is that of a benefactor or patron who has discovered that the man he has benefited is an ingrate; see Lasine 2016, 471. Nevertheless, far from extinguishing David's line, Yahweh continues to adopt David's sons as his own (2 Sam 7:14; Ps 89:27–30).
47 Paul adds that David will perform all God's wishes or desires (θελήματά).

8 The functions of divine imperfection

In both Greek and biblical writings there are cases in which a deity expresses anger and vengefulness in such a violent or unfair fashion that a character in the textual world (or a reader of that text) asks how that kind of god could be worshipped. Euripides presents an extreme form of Hera's jealousy in his tragedy *Heracles*. The goddess has sought the hero's destruction from the time he was an infant. As an adult Heracles saves his wife, Megara, and their children from the usurper Lycus. Hera and her minions then drive Heracles mad, so that he slaughters both Megara and the children. After returning to himself, Heracles imagines the goddess dancing on Olympus celebrating his downfall and asks "who would pray to such a goddess?" (*HF* 1307).[1]

Noll (1999, 39 n. 26) makes a similar point about Yahweh; he claims that "no sane reader would have worshiped the Yahweh of Samuel." Even King David is angry at his God when the angry Yahweh kills the innocent priest Uzzah (2 Sam 6:8).[2] The question "who would pray to such a deity?" could also be asked about the God of Job. After all, Yahweh torments Job and kills his children and workers precisely because Job has been incomparably obedient and loyal to him. Yahweh then justifies himself to the victim by trumpeting his immeasurable power (Job 1–2, 38–41).[3]

In spite of such divine behavior, characters in Greek tragedies do pray to gods such as Hera, and Israelites in the Bible do pray to Yahweh. Why? Both deities can be jealous and vindictive, if not envious. We have noted Yahweh's cruelty toward his wayward Israelite children, his failed leaders, and the adults and children of nations such as the Egyptians and Canaanites. We have also noted Hera's cruelty toward her son Hephaestus, as well as her attacks on Zeus' lovers and their children. Yet both gods believe that they have ample reason for their jealous anger, given the literal infidelities of Hera's husband, Zeus, and Yahweh's perception of his Israelite wife's metaphorical infidelity and his human children's disobedience. Clearly, we must investigate further if we want to understand why worshipers pray to such deities.

1. "Who would pray to such a deity"?

Euripides' *Heracles* acknowledges that individuals can entertain contradictory notions of a deity at the same time. The goddess Hera in this play is strikingly different from Homer's depiction of Hera in the *Iliad* (see Chapter 5.1, above).

DOI: 10.4324/b23212-8

154 *The functions of divine imperfection*

Heracles declares that Hera has persecuted him since "Zeus—whoever he is—begot me as an enemy for Hera." Even as an infant in the cradle, Hera sent fierce-eyed serpents to destroy him (*HF* 1262–63, 1265–68).[4] Hera's hatred of Heracles is motivated by jealousy and resentment (*phthonos*) stemming from Zeus having bedded the married human Alcmene and fathered Heracles (1309).

This drama portrays the goddess Hera as so extraordinarily vindictive and cruel that even Lyssa, who personifies madness, balks at the idea of inflicting madness on Heracles, who "alone restored the honors of the gods" when they were falling under unholy men (*HF* 852–53).[5] Hera's messenger Iris makes it clear that the purpose of making Heracles slaughter his beloved children is for him to recognize what Hera's anger is all about;[6] otherwise the gods are nothing (840–41). Lyssa makes it clear that she is following Hera's orders against her will (858). Hera is not the only deity viewed negatively in the play. Heracles' mortal father Amphitryon blames Zeus for not protecting his offspring Heracles. Amphitryon concludes that he has higher moral principles than Zeus, who is either ignorant or unjust (339–47). As noted above, Heracles also implicates Zeus in his sad fate.

While Heracles is fully aware of Hera's *phthonos* against him and Zeus' indifference to his plight, he expresses the belief that the gods do not engage in illicit love affairs or put chains on hands, nor is one god master (δεσπότης) over another. Heracles dismisses such depictions of deities as "the wretched tales of poets." A god who is truly god needs nothing (*HF* 1341–46). Yet even after expressing these beliefs Heracles continues to blame Hera for striking down him and his family with one miserable blow of fate (1392–93).

The clash between Heracles' beliefs in *HF* 1341–46 and his words elsewhere in the play has inspired many attempts to reconcile his contradictory attitudes (see Lawrence 1998, 129–39; A. Brown 1978, 22–27). I would suggest that Euripides is illustrating the fact that people adopt both anthropopathic and idealized non-anthropomorphic views of deities in order to cope with the misfortunes and injustices which are inescapable aspects of the human condition. The play as a whole envisions the gods as the direct cause of Heracles' unhappy and undeserved fate; Amphitryon and Heracles share this view. However, this reality has become too much for Heracles to endure. Heracles' friend Theseus had commented that like mortals, the gods are not untouched by fortune and engage in illicit unions, if the stories of the poets are not false (*HF* 1315). In lines 1345–46 Heracles responds: the poets are indeed false; a god who is truly god needs nothing. Yet at the same time Heracles blames Hera and her *phthonos* for his misfortunes.

Heracles is desperately attempting to cope with the fact that he has slaughtered his wife and children because of god-sent madness. His statement in *HF* 1341–46 does not cancel his view that jealous Hera and indifferent Zeus orchestrated his downfall. He is holding two contrary views simultaneously. As I discussed in Chapter 1.4, Hume contends that the more powerful a culture envisions its deity or deities to be, the more those gods are lacking in goodness and benevolence. At the same time, their worshipers simultaneously hold that their god is exalted and praiseworthy. This phenomenon has been also investigated by psychologists in recent years. In one study by Shtulman and Lindeman, most participants saw no contradiction in attributing to God both concrete, anthropomorphic properties and abstract, theological properties (2016, 665).[7] Heracles temporarily needs to retreat from the bitterly harsh realities which have characterized his life of toil and tragedy; the philosophic view[8] he expresses in lines 1340–46 gives him a temporary respite. He decides to go on living, not because he has become a religious optimist, but because it is the brave and honorable thing to do and because he recognizes that he is "a slave to fortune" (1357).

Heracles, a character in a work of poetry, has declared the falsity of poets' tales, but he remains rooted in his poetic world of anthropomorphic gods. A. Brown puts Heracles' words in *HF* 1341–46 in their proper context: "the lines which express the loftiest conception of divinity in all of Euripides occur in the play whose action does least to justify them" (1978, 27).

2. Divine perfection and Yahweh's imperfections

A number of Jewish theologians have frankly acknowledged that the God of the Hebrew Bible is imperfect. Blumenthal makes the flat statement that "God is powerful but not perfect" (1993, 16). He points to Yahweh making mistakes and then admitting those mistakes (e.g., after the Flood), being seduced by the *satan* in Job 1–2, being unnecessarily short-tempered with the Jewish people (e.g., in the Golden Calf story), and repenting on a number of occasions. Blumenthal points to the analogy between father and God to help describe God's imperfections: "we want God to be the ideal Father and we personally shape Him into this rather incoherent image, which is a mirror-image of our un-ideal fathers" (1993, 201).

Diamond contends that, within Judaism, ancient Greek notions of God's perfection "displaced a far more dominant and 'imperfect' portrait of a God depicted first in the Hebrew Bible" (2019, 43).[9] Such "philosophically laden theology denuded God of His vital biblical personality, leaving, in its place, a legacy of . . . divine omni-superlatives" (2018, 61). Like Blumenthal, Diamond points to the Flood narrative, this time to show that God's behavior belies each of the usual perfections. God's creation allows pervasive human wickedness (Gen 6:5). He then regrets having created humans, is saddened, and impulsively reacts by intending to eradicate all the life he had created (2018, 61–62). Finally, Margolin focuses both on God's role as creator and his emotions: "the Bible, time and again represents God as limited in power, as an imperfect creator, raging and jealous" (2020, 70).[10]

Clearly, the Hebrew Bible does not depict a god who lacks all human weakness and fallibility. What prevents Yahweh from attaining such "perfection"? Perhaps it is because he is in a relationship with his human children, his Israelite spouse, and his royal subjects. Once in relationship, there is no possibility for Yahweh to be self-sufficient and complete in himself. A perfect deity who is hermetically sealed in himself can be hailed as perfect and omni-everything, but such a deity cannot be in relationship with humans. Yahweh might not be married to another deity or to a mortal woman, but he perceives himself as father to his human children. The way in which Yahweh "raises" these children—and treats his "wife" Israel—reveals his predisposition toward jealousy, envy, and narcissism. And

156 *The functions of divine imperfection*

Yahweh is even in relationship with the "other gods" that he claims do not exist. Relationships include power imbalances. In extreme form, this can become the relationship between master and slave, or sadist and masochist.

The biblical God's negative and destructive emotions must be viewed together with his more positive traits and behaviors. If we do not do so, we will end up with a distorted image of his character. A good example of such distortion is provided by Mrs. Clennam, a character in Dickens' *Little Dorrit*. The novel's narrator echoes Hume in expressing wonder at the distorted images we humans project onto our God: "no human eyes have ever seen more daring, gross, and shocking images of the Divine nature than we creatures of the dust make in our own likenesses, of our own bad passions" (Dickens 2003, 808–809). His comment is prompted by the behavior of Mrs. Clennam. Her reading of the Old Testament focuses solely on passages involving human corruption (beginning with Adam) and the need for severity and punishment.[11] She views herself as "appointed" and "elected" by Jehovah to exact vengeance on sinners of her acquaintance, like those "who were appointed of old to go to wicked kings and accuse them" (2003, 809; cf. 379, 808, 810, 825). She prays that her enemies "be put to the edge of the sword, consumed by fire, smitten by plagues and leprosy, . . . [and] utterly exterminated" (2003, 51).[12]

Dickens makes it clear that Mrs. Clennam's appeals to scripture are being used to justify her desire to punish her husband, his former love, and their child. She interprets her husband's sin as infidelity (2003, 198, 809). He had been previously married[13] and fathered a child, a fact which Mrs. Clennam did not learn until she wed her husband in an arranged marriage. Her pose as an avenger appointed by Jehovah covers up her underlying motives of jealousy, spite, and vindictiveness, aspects of her character about which several characters are well aware (2003, 100, 162, 198, 815). One such character, the murderer Rigaud, describes her hypocrisy by charging that she is "full of anger, full of jealousy, full of vengeance, she forms . . . a scheme of retribution, the weight of which she ingeniously forces her crushed husband to bear himself, as well as execute upon her enemy" (2003, 806). Even after her husband and her rival are both dead, she inflicts suffering on the child borne by her rival, just as Euripides' Hera makes the "child" Heracles suffer for her husband's infidelity and biblical children are made to suffer for the sins of their fathers who were unfaithful to Yahweh.

Dickens clearly repudiates Mrs. Clennam's rigid and hypocritical religiosity, as well as her attempt to pass herself off as an agent of divine justice. According to his narrator, she "abided by her old impiety—still reversed the order of Creation, and breathed her own breath into a clay image of her Creator" (2003, 808; cf. 180). Earlier, the narrator characterized her attitude as an inversion of Matt 6:12. In Mrs. Clennam's mind forgiving her debtors becomes a desire to smite, wither, and crush them. Her prayer asks God to "do Thou as I would do, and Thou shalt have my worship" (2003, 61). In her way of reading scripture, God must do what she would do. In effect, he must imitate her rather than her imitating him. While Yahweh viewed Phinehas as jealous with his jealousy, Mrs. Clennam would have her Jehovah jealous with her jealousy. Mrs. Clennam would have done well to heed the rabbinic advice not to imitate four of God's behaviors: jealousy, revenge, exaltation, and acting deviously (Schechter 1961, 204). Instead, she views God's jealousy and revenge as resembling her own, distorting Yahweh's "imperfections" in the process.

Dickens does not contrast Mrs. Clennam's narrow focus on Jehovah's jealousy and vengeance with a more holistic and balanced view of the Old Testament deity, one which would also acknowledge his traits of compassion, mercy and patience. Instead, he opposes Mrs. Clennam's focus on Old Testament wrath and revenge with the superior message of the New Testament, as it is expressed by Dickens' heroine, Amy Dorrit.[14] For Amy, Jesus is "the patient Master who shed tears of compassion for our infirmities. . . . There is no vengeance and no infliction of suffering in His life" (2003, 826). *Little Dorrit* illustrates Mrs. Clennam's dysfunctional distortions of Jehovah and the Old Testament, but it cannot help us to determine the possible positive functions served by Yahweh's negative and destructive emotions, which form only part of his personality in the Bible.

3. Conclusion

A number of classicists have asserted that Greek tragedies present the gods "as they are." Lefkowitz contends that the gods described by Homer and Hesiod, the Greek dramatists, and later writers "exist to please themselves, not human beings." The tragedians "are saying that these are the kinds of gods that there *are*" (2019, 5–6). Kirk claims that Dionysus' vengeance is "needlessly cruel" in the *Bacchae*, and that in *Hippolytus* Aphrodite and Artemis are like Dionysus in this respect. Yet none of these deities is "held up to any kind of reprobation at the end of these plays. . . . That is how gods are" (1970, 9). Similarly, Dawe (2006, 4) observes that the gods in Sophocles' *Oedipus Tyrannus* are cruel to allow or cause terrible things to happen to someone like Oedipus, but "the Olympians are as they are." Commenting on the uncaring deities in Sophocles' *Trachiniae*, Jameson states that "the gods are 'the way things are'" (1967, 74). Finally, Winnington-Ingram concludes that in Sophocles "the gods represent—are responsible for—the world as it is and as it is governed" (1980, 322). In short, either the gods are the way they are because the world is as it is, or the world is as it is because the gods are the way they are. Both viewpoints alert believers not to expect divine compassion and care when they are suffering, and to expect divine violence and cruelty if they exceed human limitations or usurp a divine prerogative.

Lefkowitz goes beyond the other classicists just cited when she draws radical contrasts between Greek and biblical religion. In the former, "the separation between humankind and the gods made it possible for humans to complain to the gods without the guilt or fear of reprisal the deity of the Old Testament inspired." By "allowing mortals to ask hard questions, Greek theology encouraged them to learn, to seek all the possible causes of events." And unlike "the god of the Hebrews," the Greek gods "made life hard for humans, didn't seek to improve the human condition and allowed people to suffer and die" (Lefkowitz 2007 n. p.).[15]

None of these contrasts holds up under scrutiny. Many of Yahweh's favorite humans, such as Abraham, Moses, Elijah, Jeremiah, Jonah, and Job, complain to their God without guilt or fear (see Lasine 2019, 35–45). And among the many "hard questions" asked of Yahweh in the Bible are queries about why Yahweh is absent, inattentive, or hiding when his followers are in trouble or being persecuted by enemies.[16] His worshipers even ask why Yahweh has forgotten them, abandoned them, or cast them off when they need him most.[17] When the questioners feel that they have been rightly punished, they may still ask why the punishment is excessive or so long-lasting (e.g., Ps 79:5). Even his most loyal servants ask why the wicked prosper and are not punished in a timely fashion (Jer 12:1, 4; Job 21:7; 24:1). Finally, Yahweh not only "allows people to suffer and die," he causes profound suffering even to Job, the human being whom he considers his most loyal follower, and allows Job's innocent children to be killed.[18]

I would therefore argue that the Hebrew Bible presents the human world "as it is" just as fully as the Greek texts we have studied. In both cases the ruling deity or deities behave in a fashion which can explain why the human world is sometimes experienced as dangerous and unjust. In both Greek literature and the Hebrew Bible, negative and destructive emotions—including envy, jealousy, and associated dispositional traits—play a crucial role in this process.[19] As I mentioned earlier, Dover suggests that the Greeks needed their gods to have "a touchy and malevolent jealousy" in their attitude towards humanity in order to explain "the scale of human misfortune and the absence of any observable correlation between virtue and prosperity" (1994, 77). Can this also be one reason that the adherents of an ostensibly monotheistic religion would attribute jealousy, envy, and vengefulness to their deity as well?

We can rephrase this question if we recall S. Guthrie's notion that perceiving the world anthropomorphically is a "bet" which can yield more in occasional big successes than it costs in frequent little failures.[20] From this perspective we can ask why the Israelites "bet" on their god having a problematic personality. What was their "perceptual strategy"? According to Dover, only by perceiving the gods as human-like could the Greeks account for the suffering and injustice prevalent in their quotidian world. Yahweh, with his variety of character traits, can certainly account for the mass disasters and unfairness reported in the biblical world. But could he do so if he *lacked* the attributes of jealousy, envy, narcissism, and vengefulness? Would a deity who is a consistently benign and loving divine father or mother be able to explain the realities reported in the biblical world—and in our own life-worlds? If not, assigning negative traits to Yahweh may also function to explain the co-presence in our world of beauty, terror, innocent suffering, unpredictability, and paradox.

Notes

1 For other characters in Greek drama who question the gods' justice and intentions, see Chapter 6.4.d, above.
2 David is also understandably afraid of Yahweh in the aftermath of this killing (2 Sam 6:9). On this scene, see Lasine 2010, 41 n. 31. Narratives in 1 Samuel which might lead a reader to ask why Yahweh should be worshipped include the reports concerning the

priest Eli and king Saul, both of whom are treated harshly by Yahweh. On Yahweh's treatment of Saul, see Lasine 2001, 35–36, 40–44; on Eli, see Lasine 2016, 468–69.
3 We cannot entirely exclude divine envy as one possible motivation for Yahweh's torture of Job. In Chapter 3.2.b, I asked whether Yahweh might harbor a grudge against his favorite because Job is *too* good. For more on God's treatment of Job, see Lasine 1988, 29–47; 2001, 177–239; 2012, 57–61; 2016, 472–75.
4 Pindar describes Hera as "hasty in her temper" (σπερχθεῖσα θυμῷ; *Nem.* 1.40) when she sends the serpents immediately after Heracles and his twin brother receive their swaddling clothes.
5 As Barlow (1998, 8) puts it, Hera shows "gross vindictiveness toward a distinguished and innocent figure."
6 Halleran calls Iris "little more than an alter-Hera and her anger is simply Hera's transferred" (2004b, 291).
7 As Barrett and Keil point out, "even individuals who explicitly endorse the theological version of God might nonetheless implicitly embrace a very different version in most of their daily thoughts" (1996, 223).
8 Heracles' speech on the gods in poetry (*HF* 1341–46) is often compared to Xenophanes Fr. 11–12, as well as passages in Plato, Democritus, and Antiphon (see Lesher 1992, 82–84; Barlow 1998, 181; A. Brown 1978, 22). For the idea that the gods do not experience *phthonos*, see Chapter 3.2.a, above.
9 On the Greek origins of the idea of a perfect God, see, for example, Margolin 2020, 65, 71–72. Green notes that much of Abraham Heschel's theology is also "constituted by his sharp distinction between the deity posited by Greek philosophical thought and the living, feeling, speaking, commanding God of Hebrew Scripture." While "the God of the Greeks is dispassion and detachment itself," the God of the Bible "is one of passion and pathos" (2015, 248).
10 Robins (2015, 32) argues that Jewish pastoral care may benefit from acknowledging "the multifaceted face of God" in Jewish literary tradition, including God as "punishing, jealous, . . . authoritarian, and even abusive."
11 Walder describes the atmosphere in Mrs. Clennam's house—her "ungodly church"— as "charged with the cruelty and vengeance breathed by the bloodier portions of the Old Testament" (2007, 187). It is therefore appropriate that "the Plagues of Egypt" are framed and glazed upon the walls of her dining room (Dickens 2003, 48). Even Hablot Browne's illustration showing Mrs. Clennam at her desk features a well-known depiction of Josh 10:12–13, which reports the sun standing still until vengeance is exacted against Israel's enemies (Walder 2007, 188–89). On Josh 10:12–13 see Chapter 2.3.a, above.
12 Walder (2007, 35) assigns Mrs. Clennam to the Church of England, but most scholars consider her a Calvinist (e.g., Lenard 2014, 343, 353; Edgecombe 1996, 65).
13 Dickens leaves vague whether Mrs. Clennam's husband had married the young orphan singer who gave birth to the boy later taken by Mrs. Clennam to be her son. In his working notes, Dickens writes that when Mr. Clennam married Mrs. Clennam "he was already married, in a false name:—or as good as married" (2003, 903). In the novel itself, Mrs. Clennam, a very unreliable narrator, refers to the couple's "desecrated ceremony of marriage" (2003, 809).
14 As Edgecombe puts it, "Arthur [Clennam's] Calvinistic childhood, . . . is for Dickens a barbarous regression from the moral order of Christianity. To advert to Old Testament mores is in these terms to revert to them, and so to reinstate an unenlightened social and moral order" (1996, 65). In his working notes to the scene in which Mrs. Clennam confesses her wrongs to Amy Dorrit in the debtor's prison, Dickens reminds himself to "set the darkness and vengeance against the New Testament" (Dickens 2003, 905). On Dickens' esteem for the New Testament and criticism of the Old Testament, see, for example, Larson 1985, 10 and Walder 2007, 179.
15 Lefkowitz observes that "Zeus and his family of gods are not the kind of gods that humankind might have chosen, if anyone had offered them the choice." In reality,

160 *The functions of divine imperfection*

members of "humankind" such as Homer and Sophocles *did* choose to portray the Olympians as we find them in their works; it is therefore legitimate to ask what functions these portrayals are designed to perform, given that all the Greek texts we have studied agree that humans have severe cognitive limitations and need help negotiating their path through the dangers of life.

16 For example, Pss 10:1; 44:24–25; Hab 1:2–3; Job 13:24. On Yahweh feeling that he has been ignored (if not scorned or treated with contempt) by his people, see Chapter 3.2.c, above.
17 For example, Pss 10:1; 13:2; 22:2; 42:10; 43:2; 74:1. On Yahweh feeling that he has been abandoned or forsaken by his people, see Chapter 3.3.b, above.
18 Job himself cites many ways in which other people are made to suffer and die in the world created by his God; see Job 3:20–23; 7:17–18; 9:22–24; 12:14–25; 14:1–12; 21:23–26; 24:1–17.
19 Lefkowitz entirely omits this dimension of the biblical dynamic by vastly understating the degree to which Yahweh is presented as anthropomorphic and anthropopathic. She claims that "in the earlier books of the Hebrew Bible, God also *seems somewhat* anthropomorphic. . . . But in the later books of the Old Testament, God seems not to need anything" (2019, 2–3; emphasis added). Yet the only biblical texts she briefly cites in support of these generalizations are Genesis 2–9 and the frame narrative to Job (Job 1–2; 42).
20 See Chapter 1.4, above.

Bibliography

Albrecht, Jason E. and Edward J. O'Brien. 1993. "Updating a Mental Model: Maintaining Both Local and Global Coherence." *JEP:LMC* 19:1061–70.
Allan, William. 2013. "'Archaic' Guilt in Sophocles' *Oedipus Tyrannus* and *Oedipus Colonus*." Pages 173–91 in Cairns, 2013a.
Allison, Dale C., Jr. 1993. *The New Moses: A Matthean Typology*. Minneapolis: Fortress.
Allport, Gordon W. 1961. *Pattern and Growth in Personality*. New York: Holt, Rinehart and Winston.
Alter, Robert. 1981. *The Art of Biblical Narrative*. New York: Basic Books.
Amzallag, Nissim. 2011. "Was Yahweh Worshiped in the Aegean?" *JSOT* 35:387–415.
Armstrong, Karen. 1997. *In the Beginning: A New Interpretation of Genesis*. New York: Ballantine Books.
Ashley, Timothy R. 1993. *The Book of Numbers*. NICOT 4. Grand Rapids: Eerdmans.
Assmann, Jan. 2011. "What's Wrong with Images?" Pages 19–31 in *Idol Anxiety*. Edited by Josh Ellenbogen and Aaron Tugendhaft. Stanford: Stanford University Press.
Atkinson, J. 2002. "Euripides' *Bacchae* in Its Historical Context." *Akroterion* 47:5–15.
Augustine. 1995. *Confessions, Books I–IV*. Edited by Gillian Clark. Cambridge Greek and Latin Classics. Cambridge: Cambridge University Press.
Averill, James R. 1980. "A Constructivist View of Emotion." Pages 305–39 in *Emotion: Theory, Research and Experience. Vol. 1, Theories of Emotion*. Edited by Robert Plutchik and Henry Kellerman. New York: Academic Press.
Bacon, Francis. 1985. *The Essays*. Edited by John Pitcher. London: Penguin Books.
Baranger, Willy. 1991. "Narcissism in Freud." Pages 108–30 in Sandler *et al.*, 1991.
Barlow, Shirley A., ed. 1998. *Euripides: Heracles, with an Introduction, Translation and Commentary*. Warminster: Aris & Phillips.
Barrett, James. 1995. "Narrative and the Messenger in Aeschylus' *Persians*." *AJPh* 116:539–57.
Barrett, Justin L. and Frank C. Keil. 1996. "Conceptualizing a Nonnatural Entity: Anthropomorphism in God Concepts." *Cogn. Psychol.* 31:219–47.
Barrett, W. W., ed. 1964. *Euripides: Hippolytus. Edited with Introduction and Commentary*. Oxford: Clarendon.
Bartlett, Robert C. and Susan D. Collins, trans. 2012. *Aristotle's Nicomachean Ethics*. Chicago: University of Chicago Press.
Battezzato, Luigi, ed. 2018. *Euripides Hecuba*. Cambridge Greek and Latin Classics. Cambridge: Cambridge University Press.
Baumel, Amit and Ety Berant. 2015. "The Role of Attachment Styles in Malicious Envy." *J. Res. Pers.* 55:1–9.

Begg, Christopher. 2007. "Josephus' and Philo's Retelling of Numbers 31 Compared," *ETL* 83: 81–106.

Békés, Vera, J. Christopher Perry, and Brian M. Robertson. 2018. "Psychological Masochism: A Systematic Review of the Literature on Conflicts, Defenses, and Motives." *Psychother. Res.* 28:470–83.

Beldman, David J. H. 2017. *The Completion of Judges: Strategies of Ending in Judges 17–21*. Winona Lake, IN: Eisenbrauns.

Belfiore, Elizabeth. 1998. "Harming Friends: Problematic Reciprocity in Greek Tragedy." Pages 139–58 in *Reciprocity in Ancient Greece*. Edited by Christopher Gill, Norman Postlethwaite, and Richard Seaford. Oxford: Oxford University Press.

Belk, Russell W. 2008. "Marketing and Envy." Pages 211–26 in R. Smith, 2008b.

Bell, Richard H. 1994. *Provoked to Jealousy: The Origin and Purpose of the Jealousy Motif in Romans 9–11*. WUNT, 63. Mohr Siebeck: Tübingen.

Benjamin, Jessica. 1988. *The Bonds of Love: Psychoanalysis, Feminism, and the Problem of Domination*. New York: Pantheon.

Benjamin, Jessica. 1995. *Like Subjects, Love Objects: Essays on Recognition and Sexual Difference*. New York: Yale University Press.

Ben-Ze'ev, Aaron. 2000. *The Subtlety of Emotions*. Cambridge: The MIT Press.

Berger, Peter L. 1969. *The Sacred Canopy: Elements of a Sociological Theory of Religion*. Garden City: Anchor Books.

Bergler, Edmund. 1957. *The Psychology of Gambling*. New York: Hill and Wang.

Bergmann, Frithjof. 1978. Review of *The Passions*, by Robert C. Solomon. *J. Philos* 75:200–208.

Berke, Joseph H. 1988. *The Tyranny of Malice: Exploring the Dark Side of Character and Culture*. New York: Summit.

Besser, Avi and Beatriz Priel. 2009. "Emotional Responses to a Romantic Partner's Imaginary Rejection: The Roles of Attachment Anxiety, Covert Narcissism, and Self-Evaluation." *J Pers* 77:287–325.

Birky, Ian T. and Samuel Ball. 1988. "Parental Trait Influence on God as an Object Representation." *J. Psychol.* 122:133–37.

Black, Jeremy, Graham Cunningham, Eleanor Robson, and Gábor Zólyomi. 2006. *The Literature of Ancient Sumer*. Oxford: Oxford University Press.

Blenkinsopp, Joseph. 2003. *Isaiah 56–66: A New Translation with Introduction and Commentary*. AB 19b. New York: Doubleday.

Block, Daniel I. 1998. *The Book of Ezekiel, Chapters 25–48*. NICOT. Grand Rapids: Eerdmans.

Block, Daniel I. 1999. *Judges, Ruth: An Exegetical and Theological Exposition of Holy Scripture*. NAC, 6. Nashville: B & H Publishing Group.

Block, Daniel I. 2000. "Divine Abandonment: Ezekiel's Adaptation of an Ancient Near Eastern Motif." Pages 15–42 in *The Book of Ezekiel: Theological and Anthropological Perspectives*. SBLSymS, 9. Edited by Margaret S. Odell and John T. Strong. Atlanta: Society of Biblical Literature.

Blok, Anton. 1998. "The Narcissism of Minor Differences." *EJST* 1:33–56.

Blomqvist, Jerker. 1982. "Human and Divine Action in Euripides' Hippolytus." *Hermes* 110: 398–414.

Blondell, Ruby, ed. 2002. *Sophocles: King Oedipus*. Translation with Notes, Introduction and Essay. Newburyport: Focus.

Blumenthal, David R. 1993. *Facing the Abusing God: A Theology of Protest*. Louisville: Westminster/John Knox.

Blundell, Mary Whitlock. 1991. *Helping Friends and Harming Enemies: A Study in Sophocles and Greek Ethics*. Cambridge: Cambridge University Press.

Bodner, Keith and Benjamin J. M. Johnson, eds. 2020. *Characters and Characterization in the Book of Kings*. LHBOTS, 670. London: T & T Clark.

Boedeker, Deborah. 2003. "Pedestrian Fatalities: The Prosaics of Death in Herodotus." Pages 17–36 in *Herodotus and His World: Essays from a Conference in Memory of George Forrest*. Edited by Peter Derow and Robert Parker. Oxford: Oxford University Press.

Boström, Lennart. 2000. "Patriarchal Models for Piety." Pages 57–72 in Penchansky and Redditt, 2000.

Braund, Susanna and Glenn W. Most, eds. 2004. *Ancient Anger: Perspectives from Homer to Galen*. Yale Classical Studies, 32. Cambridge: Cambridge University Press.

Bremmer, Jan N. 1999. *Greek Religion. Greece and Rome*. New Surveys in the Classics, 24. Cambridge: Cambridge University Press.

Brinkman, J. A. 1983. "Through a Glass Darkly: Esarhaddon's Retrospects on the Downfall of Babylon." *JAOS* 103:35–42.

Broadhead, H. D., ed. 1960. *The Persae of Aeschylus. Edited with Introduction, Critical Notes, and Commentary*. Cambridge: Cambridge University Press.

Brown, A. L. 1978. "Wretched Tales of Poets: Euripides, *Heracles* 1340–6." *PCPS* 24:22–30.

Brown, Ken. 2015. "Vengeance and Vindication in Numbers 31." *JBL* 134:65–84.

Brueggemann, Walter A. 1997. *Theology of the Old Testament: Testimony, Dispute, Advocacy*. Minneapolis: Fortress Press.

Brueggemann, Walter A. 2000. "Texts That Linger, Not Yet Overcome." Pages 21–41 in Penchansky and Redditt, 2000.

Budd, Philip J. 1984. *Numbers*. WBC 5. Waco: Word.

Burkert, Walter. 1975. "Apellai und Apollon." *RhM* 118:1–21.

Burkert, Walter. 1987. *Greek Religion: Archaic and Classical*. Trans. John Raffan. Oxford: Blackwell.

Burnett, Anne Pippin. 1970. "Pentheus and Dionysus: Host and Guest." *CPh* 65:15–29.

Byron, John. 2011. *Cain and Abel in Text and Tradition: Jewish and Christian Interpretations of the First Sibling Rivalry*. Leiden: Brill.

Cairns, Douglas L. 1996."Hybris, Dishonour, and Thinking Big." *JHS* 116:1–32.

Cairns, Douglas L. 2003. "The Politics of Envy: Envy and Equality in Ancient Greece." Pages 235–52 in Konstan and Rutter, 2003.

Cairns, Douglas L. 2004. "Ethics, Ethology, Terminology: Iliadic Anger and the Cross-Cultural Study of Emotion." Pages 11–49 in Braund and Most.

Cairns, Douglas L. 2008. "Look Both Ways: Studying Emotion in Ancient Greek." *Critical Quarterly* 50:43–62.

Cairns, Douglas L, ed. 2013a. *Tragedy and Archaic Greek Thought*. Swansea: Classical Press of Wales.

Cairns, Douglas L. 2013b. "Divine and Human Action in the *Oedipus Tyrannus*." Pages 119–71 in Cairns, 2013a.

Cairns, Douglas L, ed. 2019a. *A Cultural History of the Emotions in Antiquity, Volume 1*. London: Bloomsbury Academic.

Cairns, Douglas L. 2019b. "Introduction: Emotion Theory and the Classics." Pages 1–15 in Cairns, 2019a.

Calvin, John. 1852. *Commentaries on the Four Last Books of Moses: Arranged in the Form of a Harmony, Volume I*. Translated by Charles W. Bingham. Edinburgh: Calvin Translation Society.

Carmichael, Calum. 2012. *The Book of Numbers: A Critique of Genesis*. New Haven: Yale University Press.

Carroll, Joseph. 2012. "The Extremes of Conflict in Literature: Violence, Homicide, and War." Pages 413–34 in *The Oxford Handbook of Evolutionary Perspectives on Violence, Homicide, and War*. Edited by Todd K. Shackelford and Viviana A. Weekes-Shackelford. Oxford: Oxford University Press.

Cartledge, Paul and Emily Greenwood. 2002. "Herodotus as a Critic: Truth, Fiction, Polarity." Pages 351–71 in *Brill's Companion to Herodotus*. Edited by Egbert J. Bakker, Irene J. F. de Jong, and Hans van Wees. Leiden: Brill.

Charmé, Stuart L. 1983. "Religion and the Theory of Masochism." *J. Relig. Health.* 22:221–33.

Chiasson, Charles C. 2003. "Herodotus' Use of Attic Tragedy in the Lydian Logos." *ClAnt* 22:5–35.

Chiasson, Charles C. 2016. "Solon's Poetry and Herodotean Historiography." *AJPh* 137:25–60.

Childs, Brevard S. 1974. *The Book of Exodus: A Critical Theological Commentary*. OTL. Philadelphia: Westminster.

Christ, Matthew R. 2007. Review of Gabriel Herman, *Morality and Behaviour in Democratic Athens: A Social History. BMCR* 2007.07.37. Available online: https://bmcr.brynmawr.edu/2007/2007.07.37/ (accessed January 12, 2021).

Clay, Diskin. 1972. "Socrates' Mulishness and Heroism." *Phronesis* 17:53–60.

Clines, David J. A. 1998. "Yahweh and the God of Christian Theology." Pages 498–507 in *On the Way to the Postmodern: Old Testament Essays 1967–1998, Volume 2*. Sheffield: Continuum.

Clines, David J. A. 2011. *Job 38–42*. WBC 18b. Nashville: Thomas Nelson.

Cogan, Mordechai. 2003. "Cyrus Cylinder (2.124)." Pages 314–16 in *The Context of Scripture: Monumental Inscriptions from the Biblical World, Volume II*. Edited by William W. Hallo. Leiden: Brill.

Cohen-Charash, Yochi and Elliott Larson. 2017. "What Is the Nature of Envy?" Pages 1–37 in *Envy at Work and in Organizations*. Edited by Richard H. Smith, Ugo Merlone, and Michelle K. Duffy. New York: Oxford University Press.

Cohen, Mariam C. 2007. Review of Gonen, *Yahweh versus Yahweh. Am. J. Psychoanal.* 67:397–401.

Colombetti, Giovanna. 2014. *The Feeling Body: Affective Science Meets the Enactive Mind*. Cambridge: MIT Press.

Colson, F. H., trans. 1966. "Moses I. and II." Pages 276–595 in *Philo VI*. LCL. Cambridge: Harvard University Press.

Conacher, D. J. 1967. *Euripidean Drama: Myth, Theme and Structure*. Toronto: University of Toronto Press.

Conacher, D. J. 1999. "Oedipus without Footnotes." *EMC/CV* 43:35–44.

Cooper, Arnold M. 2000. "Further Developments in the Clinical Diagnosis of NPD." Pages 53–74 in *Disorders of Narcissism: Diagnostic, Clinical and Empirical Implications*. Edited by Elsa F. Ronningstam. Northvale: Jason Aronson.

Cooper, Arnold M. 2009. "The Narcissistic-Masochistic Character." *Psychiatr. Ann.* 39:904–12.

Cooper, Jerrold S. 1993. "Paradigm and Propaganda: The Dynasty of Akkade in the 21st Century." Pages 11–23 in *Akkad, the First World Empire: Structure, Ideology, Traditions*. History of the Ancient Near East/Studies, V. Edited by Mario Liverani. Padova: Sargon srl.

Cottrill, Amy C. 2014. "A Reading of Ehud and Jael through the Lens of Affect Theory." *BibInt* 22:430–49.
Crenshaw, James L. 1983. "The Problem of Theodicy in Sirach: On Human Bondage." Pages 119–40 in *Theodicy in the Old Testament*. Issues in Religion & Theology, 4. Edited by James L. Crenshaw. Philadelphia: Fortress.
Crenshaw, James L. 1984. *A Whirlpool of Torment: Israelites Traditions of God as an Oppressive Presence*. Philadelphia: Fortress.
Crenshaw, James L. 2005. *Defending God: Biblical Responses to the Problem of Evil*. Oxford: Oxford University Press.
Davidson, J. F. 1975. "The Parodos of Sophocles' Ajax." *BICS* 22:163–77.
Davies, Malcolm. 1981. "The Judgement of Paris and Iliad Book XXIV." *JHS* 101:56–62.
Dawe, R. D., ed. 2006. *Sophocles: Oedipus Rex*. Cambridge: Cambridge University Press.
De Ste. Croix, G. E. M. 1977. "Herodotus." *G&R* 24:130–48.
DeYoung, Rebecca Konyndyk. 2014. *Vainglory: The Forgotten Vice*. Grand Rapids: Eerdmans.
Diamond, James A. 2018. *Jewish Theology Unbound*. Oxford: Oxford University Press.
Diamond, James A. 2019. "The Living God: On the Perfection of the Imperfect." Pages 43–62 in *The Question of God's Perfection: Jewish and Christian Essays on the God of the Bible and Talmud*. Edited by Yoram Hazony and Dru Johnson. Leiden: Brill Rodopi.
Dickens, Charles. 2003. *Little Dorrit*. Revised ed. Edited by Stephen Wall and Helen Small. London: Penguin.
Dickie, Jane R., Lindsey V. Ajega, Joy R. Kobylak and Kathryn M. Nixon. 2006. "Mother, Father, and Self: Sources of Young Adults' God Concepts." *JSSR* 45:57–71.
Dickie, Matthew W. 1993. "The Place of *Phthonos* in the Argument of Plato's *Phaedrus*." Pages 379–96 in *Nomodeiktes: Greek Studies in Honor of Martin Ostwald*. Edited by Ralph M. Rosen and Joseph Farrell. Ann Arbor: The University of Michigan Press.
Di Vito, Robert A. 1997. "Here One Need Not Be One's Self: The Concept of 'Self' in the Old Testament." Pages 49–88 in *The Whole and Divided Self: The Bible and Theological Anthropology*. Edited by David E. Aune and John McCarthy. New York: Crossroad.
Dodds, E. R., ed. 1960. *Euripides Bacchae*. 2nd ed. Oxford: Clarendon Press.
Dodds, E. R., ed. 1966. "On Misunderstanding the 'Oedipus Rex'." *G&R* 13:37–49.
Dodds, E. R., ed. 1968. *The Greeks and the Irrational*. Berkeley: University of California Press.
Dohe, Carrie B. 2016. *Jung's Wandering Archetype: Race and Religion in Analytical Psychology*. London: Routledge.
Dover, Kenneth J. 1994. *Greek Popular Morality in the Time of Plato and Aristotle*. Indianapolis: Hackett.
Dozeman, Thomas B. 1998. "The Book of Numbers." Pages 1–268 in *NIB*, Volume 2.
Driver, S. R. 1904. *The Book of Genesis*. London: Methuen.
Dumbrell, William J. 1975. "Midian: A Land or a League?" *VT* 25:323–37.
Easterling, P. E. 1985. "Greek Poetry and Greek Religion." Pages 34–49 in Easterling and Muir, 1985.
Easterling, P. E. and J. V. Muir, eds. 1985. *Greek Religion and Society*. Cambridge: Cambridge University Press.
Edgecombe, Rodney Stenning. 1996. "Reading through the Past: 'Archaeological' Conceits and Procedures in *Little Dorrit*." *The Yearbook of English Studies* 26:65–72.
Edwards, Catherine, trans. 2000. *Suetonius, Lives of the Caesars*. Oxford World's Classics. Oxford: Oxford University Press.

Eidinow, Esther. 2016. "Popular Theologies: The Gift of Divine Envy." Pages 205–32 in *Theologies of Ancient Greek Religion*. Edited by Esther Eidinow, Julia Kindt, and Robin Osborne. Cambridge: Cambridge University Press.

Ekman, Paul. 1992. "Are There Basic Emotions?" *Psychol. Rev.* 99:550–53.

Ekman, Paul. 1999. "Basic Emotions." Pages 45–60 in *Handbook of Cognition and Emotion*. Edited by Tim Dalgleish and Mick J. Power. Chichester: John Wiley and Sons.

Elias, Norbert. 1970. *Was ist Soziologie?* Grundlagen der Soziologie 1. Munich: Juventa.

Elias, Norbert. 1997. *Über den Prozeß der Zivilisation: Soziogenetische und psychogenetische Untersuchungen*. Band 1. Frankfurt: Suhrkamp Taschenbuch.

Elias, Norbert. 2002. *Die höfische Gesellschaft: Untersuchungen zur Soziologie des Königtums und der höfischen Aristokratie, mit einer Einleitung: Soziologie und Geschichtswissenschaft*. Gesammelte Schriften 2. Frankfurt: Suhrkamp.

Elliott, John H. 2007. "Envy, Jealousy, and Zeal in the Bible: Sorting Out the Social Differences and Theological Implications—No Envy for Yhwh." Pages 344–64 in *To Break Every Yoke: Essays in Honor of Marvin L. Chaney*. Edited by Robert B. Coote and Norman K. Gottwald. Sheffield: Sheffield Phoenix Press.

Elliott, John H. 2016a. *Beware the Evil Eye: The Evil Eye in the Bible and the Ancient World, Volume 2: Greece and Rome*. Eugene: Cascade Books.

Elliott, John H. 2016b. *Beware the Evil Eye: The Evil Eye in the Bible and the Ancient World, Volume 3: The Bible and Related Sources*. Eugene: Cascade Books.

Ellis, B. Anthony. 2015. "Proverbs in Herodotus' Dialogue Between Solon and Croesus (1.30–33): Methodology and 'Making Sense' in the Study of Greek Religion." *BICS* 58:83–106.

Ellis, B. Anthony. 2017. "The Jealous God of Ancient Greece: Interpreting the Classical Greek Notion of φθόνος θεῶν between Renaissance Humanism and *Altertumswissenschaft*." *Erud. Repub. Lett.* 2:1–55.

Elshout, Maartje, Rob M. A. Nelissen, and Ilja van Beest. 2015. "A Prototype Analysis of Vengeance." *Pers. Relatsh.* 22:502–23.

Enright. Robert D. 1994. "Piaget on the Moral Development of Forgiveness: Reciprocity or Identity?" *Hum. Dev.* 37:63–80.

Enright, Robert D., Maria J. D. Santos, and Radhi Al-Mabuk. 1989. "The Adolescent as Forgiver." *J. Adolesc.* 12:85–110.

Esposito, Stephen, ed. 2004. *Euripides: Medea, Hippolytus, Heracles, Bacchae*. Focus Classical Library. Newburyport: Focus.

Esposito, Stephen, ed. 2010a. *Odysseus at Troy: Ajax, Hecuba, and Trojan Women*. Focus Classical Library. Indianapolis: Hackett.

Esposito, Stephen. 2010b. "An Essay on Sophocles' *Ajax*." Pages 189–210 in Esposito, 2010a.

Feldman, Louis H. 2002. "The Portrayal of Phinehas by Philo, Pseudo-Philo, and Josephus." *JQR* 92:315–45.

Ferenczi, Sandor. 1950. "Stages in the Development of the Sense of Reality." Pages 213–39 in *Sex in Psychoanalysis: The Collected Papers of Sandor Ferenczi, M. D.* Volume 1. Translated by Ernest Jones. New York: Basic Books.

Fewell, Danna Nolan, ed. 1992. *Reading between Texts: Intertextuality and the Hebrew Bible*. Louisville: Westminster John Knox.

Finglass, P. J., ed. 2011. *Sophocles: Ajax. Edited with Introduction, Translation and Commentary*. Cambridge: Cambridge University Press.

Finley, M. I. 1985. "Forward." Pages xiii–xx in *Greek Religion and Society*. Edited by P. E. Easterling and J. V. Muir. Cambridge: Cambridge University Press.

Fishbane, Michael. 1998. *The Exegetical Imagination: On Jewish Thought and Theology.* Cambridge, MA: Harvard University Press.
Fisher, N. R. E. 1992. *Hybris: A Study in the Values of Honour and Shame in Ancient Greece.* Warminster: Aris and Phillips.
Forster, E. M. 1927. *Aspects of the Novel.* New York: Harcourt, Brace & Company.
Foster, Benjamin R. 2016. *The Age of Agade: Inventing Empire in Ancient Mesopotamia.* London: Routledge.
Foster, F. M. 1972. "The Anatomy of Envy: A Study in Symbolic Behavior." *CA* 13:165–202.
Frame, Grant. 1992. *Babylonia 689–627 B. C.: A Political History.* Istanbul/Leiden: Nederlands Historisch-Archaeologisch Instituut te Istanbul.
Franke, Sabina. 1995. "Kings of Akkad: Sargon and Naram-Sin." Pages 831–41 in *Civilizations of the Ancient Near East, Volumes I and II.* Edited by Jack M. Sasson. Hendrickson Publishers.
Fränkel, Hermann F. 1951. *Dichtung und Philosophie des Frühen Griechentums: Eine Geschichte der griechischen Literatur von Homer bis Pindar.* Philological Monographs, 13. New York: American Philological Association.
French, Peter A. 2001. *The Virtues of Vengeance.* Lawrence: University Press of Kansas.
Fretheim, Terence E. 1999. *First and Second Kings.* WBCom. Louisville: Westminster John Knox.
Freud, Sigmund. 1940. *Massenpsychologie und Ich-Analyse.* Pages 73–161 in vol. 13 of *GW*.
Freud, Sigmund. 1943a. "Eine Kindheitserinnerung des Leonardo da Vinci." Pages 128–211 in vol. 8 of *GW*.
Freud, Sigmund. 1943b. "Formulierungen über die zwei Prinzipien des psychischen Geschehens." Pages 230–38 in vol. 8 of *GW*.
Freud, Sigmund. 1944. *Totem und Tabu: Einige Übereinstimmungen im Seelenleben der Wilden und der Neurotiker,* in vol. 9 of GW.
Freud, Sigmund. 1946. "Zur Einführung des Narzissmus." Pages 137–70 in vol. 10 of *GW*.
Freud, Sigmund. 1947a. "Eine Kindheitserinnerung aus *Dichtung und Wahrheit*." Pages 15–26 in vol. 12 of *GW*.
Freud, Sigmund. 1947b. "Das Tabu der Virginität." Pages 161–80 in vol. 12 of *GW*.
Freud, Sigmund. 1948a. *Die Zukunft einer Illusion.* Pages 325–80 in vol. 14 of *GW*.
Freud, Sigmund. 1948b. *Das Unbehagen in der Kultur.* Pages 421–506 in vol. 14 of *GW*.
Freud, Sigmund. 1950. *Der Mann Moses und die monotheistische Religion.* Pages 103–246 in vol. 16 of *GW*.
Fromm, Erich H. 1994. *Escape from Freedom.* New York: Holt Paperbacks.
Furnham, Adrian. 1995. "The Relationship of Personality and Intelligence to Cognitive Learning Style and Achievement." Pages 397–413 in *International Handbook of Personality and Intelligence.* Edited by Donald H. Saklofske and Moshe Zeidner. New York: Plenum Press.
Gale, Raymond F. 1969. *Developmental Behavior: A Humanistic Approach.* London: Collier-Macmillan.
Gammie, John G. 1986. "Herodotus on Kings and Tyrants: Objective Historiography or Conventional Portraiture?" *JNES* 45:171–95.
García-Treto, Francisco O. 1992. "The Fall of the House: A Carnivalesque Reading of 2 Kings 9 and 10." Pages 153–71 in Fewell, 1992.
Garvie, A. F., ed. 1998. *Sophocles: Ajax.* Edited with an Introduction, Translation and Commentary. Aris & Phillips Classical Texts. Oxford: Aris & Phillips.
Garvie, A. F., ed. 2009. *Aeschylus: Persae.* With Introduction and Commentary. Oxford: Oxford University Press.

Bibliography

Geertz, Clifford. 1983. "'From the Native's Point of View'": On the Nature of Anthropological Understanding." Pages 55–70 in *Local Knowledge: Further Essays in Interpretive Anthropology*. New York: Basic Books.

Geller, Stephen A. 1996. *Sacred Enigmas: Literary Religion in the Hebrew Bible*. London: Routledge.

Gerber, Douglas E., ed. and trans. 1999. *Greek Elegiac Poetry, From the Seventh to Fifth Centuries BC*. LCL 258. Cambridge: Harvard University Press.

Gilbert, Daniel T. and Patrick S. Malone. 1995. "The Correspondence Bias." *Psychol. Bull.* 117:21–38.

Giner-Sorolla, Roger. 2019. "The Past Thirty Years of Emotion Research: Appraisal and Beyond." *Cogn. Emot.* 33:48–54.

Girard, René. 1979. *Violence and the Sacred*. Translated by Patrick Gregory. Baltimore: Johns Hopkins University Press.

Girard, René 1989. *The Scapegoat*. Translated by Yvonne Freccero. Baltimore: Johns Hopkins University Press.

Glatt-Gilad, David A. 2002. "Yahweh's Honor at Stake: A Divine Conundrum." *JSOT* 98:63–74.

Goldhill, Simon. 1986. *Reading Greek Tragedy*. Cambridge: Cambridge University Press.

Goldingay, John. 2001. *Isaiah*. NIBCOT. Peabody: Hendrickson.

Goldingay, John. 2007. *Psalms: Psalms 42–89*. Grand Rapids: Baker Academic.

Gonen, Jay Y. 2005. *Yahweh versus Yahweh: The Enigma of Jewish History*. Madison: University of Wisconsin Press.

Gould, John. 1985. "On Making Sense of Greek Religion." Pages 1–33 in Easterling and Muir, 1985.

Gould, John. 2003. "Herodotus and the 'Resurrection.'" Pages 297–304 in *Herodotus and his World: Essays from a Conference in Memory of George Forrest*. Edited by Peter Derow and Robert Parker. Oxford: Oxford University Press.

Gould, Thomas, trans. 1970. *Oedipus the King, by Sophocles*. Prentice-Hall Greek Drama Series. Englewood Cliffs, NJ: Prentice-Hall.

Gray, George Buchanan. 1906. *A Critical and Exegetical Commentary on Numbers*. New York: Charles Scribner's Sons.

Green, Arthur. 2015. "God's Need for Man: A Unitive Approach to the Writings of Abraham Joshua Heschel." *Mod. Juda.* 35:247–61.

Greenberg, Moshe. 1969. *Understanding Exodus*. Heritage of Biblical Israel. New York: Behrman House.

Gregory, Justina. 1999. *Euripides: Hecuba, Introduction, Text, and Commentary*. Atlanta: Scholars Press.

Gregory the Great. 1850. *Morals on the Book of Job, Volume 3, Part 2*. Translated by J. Bliss. Oxford: John Henry Parker.

Grene, David. 1988. "Introduction." Pages 1–32 in *Herodotus: The History*. Translated by David Grene. Chicago: The University of Chicago Press.

Grinberg, León. 1991. "Letter to Sigmund Freud." Pages 95–107 in Sandler *et al.*, 1991.

Grossman, Jonathan. 2007. "Divine Command and Human Initiative: A Literary View On Numbers 25–31." *BibInt* 15:54–79.

Grubrich-Simitis, Ilse. 1993. *Zurück zu Freuds Texten: Stumme Dokumente sprechen machen*. Frankfurt a. M.: S. Fischer.

Gunn, David M., and Danna Nolan Fewell. 1993. *Narrative in the Hebrew Bible*. Oxford Bible Series. New York: Oxford University Press.

Guthrie, Stewart Elliott. 1993. *Faces in the Clouds: A New Theory of Religion*. New York: Oxford University Press.

Guthrie, Stewart Elliott. 2015. "Religion and Art: A Cognitive and Evolutionary Approach." *JSRNC* 9:283–311.

Guthrie, W. K. C. 1955. *The Greeks and Their Gods*. Boston: Beacon Press.

Habel, Norman C. 1985. *The Book of Job: A Commentary*. OTL. Philadelphia, PA: Westminster Press.

Hackett, Jo Ann. 2004. "Violence and Women's Lives in the Book of Judges." *Int* 58:356–64.

Halbertal, Moshe and Avishai Margalit. 1992. *Idolatry*. Translated by Naomi Goldblum. Cambridge: Harvard University Press.

Hall, Edith, ed. 2007. *Aeschylus: Persians. Edited with an Introduction, Translation and Commentary*. Aris & Phillips Classical Texts. Oxford: Aris & Phillips.

Halleran, Michael R. 1992. Review of Ruth Padel, *In and Out of the Mind*. *BMCR* 03.06.14. Available online: http://bmcr.brynmawr.edu/1992/03.06.14.html (accessed January 7, 2010).

Halleran, Michael R. 2004a. "The *Hippolytus*: An Interpretation. Pages 269–83 in Esposito, 2004.

Halleran, Michael R. 2004b. "The *Heracles*: An Interpretation." Pages 284–98 in Esposito, 2004.

Halliwell, Stephen. 1990. "Traditional Greek Conceptions of Character." Pages 32–59 in Pelling, 1990a.

Hamilton, Victor P. 1990. *The Book of Genesis, Chapters 1–17*. NICOT. Grand Rapids: Eerdmans.

Hamilton, Victor P. 1995. *The Book of Genesis, Chapters 18–50*. NICOT. Grand Rapids: Eerdmans.

Hard, Robin, trans. 2014. *Epictetus: Discourses, Fragments, Handbook*. Oxford World's Classics. Oxford: Oxford University Press.

Harris, Christine R. and Peter Salovey. 2008. "Reflections on Envy." Pages 335–56 in Richard H. Smith, 2008b.

Harris, W. V. 1997. "Lysias III and Athenian Beliefs about Revenge." *CQ* 47:363–66.

Harris, W. V. 2004. "The Rage of Women." Pages 121–43 in Braund and Most, 2004.

Hazlitt, William. 1823. *Characteristics: in the Manner of Rochefoucault's Maxims*. London: W. Simpkin and R. Marshall.

Heath, Malcolm. 1987. "'*Jure Principem Locum Tenet*': Euripides' *Hecuba*." *BICS* 34:40–68.

Hegel, G. W. F. 1952. *Phänomenologie des Geistes*. Edited by Johannes Hoffmeister. 6th ed. Philosophische Bibliothek, 114. Hamburg: Felix Meiner.

Helson, Ravenna and Paul Wink. 1987. "Two Conceptions of Maturity Examined in the Findings of a Longitudinal Study." *J. Pers. Soc. Psychol.* 53:531–41.

Henniger, Nicole E. and Christine R. Harris. 2014. "Can Negative Social Emotions Have Positive Consequences? An Examination of Embarrassment, Shame, Guilt, Jealousy, and Envy." Pages 76–97 in *The Positive Side of Negative Emotions*. Edited by W. Gerrod Parrott. New York: Guilford Press.

Henniger, Nicole E. and Christine R. Harris. 2015. "Envy Across Adulthood: The What and the Who." *BASP* 37:303–18.

Herman, Gabriel. 2006. *Morality and Behaviour in Democratic Athens: A Social History*. Cambridge: Cambridge University Press.

Bibliography

Herodotus. 1988. *The History*. Translated by David Grene. Chicago: University of Chicago Press.

Hibbard, Stephen. 1992. "Narcissism, Shame, Masochism, and Object Relations: An Exploratory Correlational Study." *Psychoanal. Psychol.* 9:489–508.

Hobbs, T. R. 1985. *2 Kings*. WBC 13. Waco: Word.

Hogan, James C. 1991. *A Commentary on the Plays of Sophocles*. Carbondale: Southern Illinois University Press.

Hornblower, Simon and Christopher Pelling, eds. 2017. *Herodotus: Histories, Book VI*. Cambridge: Cambridge University Press.

Hossfeld, Frank Lothar and Erich Zenger. 2005. *Psalms 2: A Commentary on Psalms 51–100*. Edited by Klaus Baltzer. Translated by Linda M. Maloney. Hermeneia. Minneapolis: Fortress Press.

How, Walter W. and Joseph Wells. 1912. *A Commentary on Herodotus, Volume 2*. Oxford: Clarendon Press.

Hume, David. 1947. *Dialogues Concerning Natural Religion*. Edited by Norman Kemp Smith. The Library of Liberal Arts. Indianapolis: Bobbs-Merrill.

Hume, David. 2007. "The Natural History of Religion." Pages 34–87 in *A Dissertation on the Passions and the Natural History of Religion: A Critical Edition*. Edited by Tom L. Beauchamp. Oxford: Clarendon.

Humphreys, W. Lee. 2001. *The Character of God in the Book of Genesis: A Narrative Appraisal*. Louisville: Westminster John Knox.

Izre'el, Shlomo. 2001. *Adapa and the South Wind: Language Has the Power of Life and Death*. Winona Lake, IN: Eisenbrauns.

Jacob, Benno. 1942. "The Childhood and Youth of Moses, the Messenger of God." Pages 245–59 in *Essays in Honour of the Very Rev. Dr. J. H. Hertz*. Edited by I. Epstein, E. Levine and C. Roth. London: Edward Goldston.

Jaeger, Werner. 1965. *Paideia: The Ideal of Greek Culture, Vol. 1: Archaic Greece, The Mind of Athens*. 2nd ed. Translated by Gilbert Highet. New York: Galaxy.

Jameson, Michael. 1967. "Introduction to *The Women of Trachis*." Pages 68–75 in *Sophocles II: Ajax, The Women of Trachis, Electra, Philoctetes*. Edited by David Grene and Richmond Lattimore. New York: Washington Square Press.

Jebb, Richard, ed. 1949. *The Oedipus Tyrannus of Sophocles. Edited with Introduction and Notes*. Cambridge: Cambridge University Press.

Johnson, M. D., trans. 1985. The Life of Adam and Eve. Pages 258–95 in *The Old Testament Pseudepigrapha, Vol. 2*. Edited by James H. Charlesworth. Garden City: Doubleday.

Jones, Christopher P., trans. 2005. *The Life of Apollonius of Tyana, Books V-VIII*. LCL. Cambridge: Harvard University Press.

Jones, Gwilym H. 1984. *1 and 2 Kings, Volume 2*. NCBC. Grand Rapids: Eerdmans.

Jones, Peter. 2003. *Homer's Iliad: A Commentary on Three Translations*. London: Bristol Classical Press.

Joseph, Jane E., Caitlin A. J. Powell, Nathan F. Johnson, and Gayannée Kedia. 2008. "The Functional Neuroanatomy of Envy." Pages 245–63 in R. Smith, 2008b.

Josefsson, Kim, Markus Jokela, C. Robert Cloninger, Mirka Hintsanen, Johanna Salo, Taina Hintsa, Laura Pulkki-Raback, and Liisa Keltikangas-Järvinen. 2013. "Maturity and Change in Personality: Developmental Trends of Temperament and Character in Adulthood." *Dev. Psychopathol.* 25:713–27.

Jung, Carl Gustav. 1969. "Answer to Job." Pages 365–470 in *Psychology and Religion: West and East. The Collected Works of C. G. Jung, Volume 11*. 2nd ed. Edited and translated by Gerhard Adler and R. F. C. Hull. Princeton: Princeton University Press.

Justice, William G. and Warren Lambert. 1986. "A Comparative Study of the Language People Use to Describe the Personalities of God and their Earthly Parents." *JPC* 40:166–72.

Kaiser, Otto. 1981. *Das Buch des Propheten Jesaja, Kapital 1–12*. ATD 17. 5th ed. Göttingen: Vandenhoeck & Ruprecht.

Kantzios, Ippokrates. 2004. "The Politics of Fear in Aeschylus' *Persians*." *CW* 98:3–19.

Kastenbaum, Robert. 2000. *The Psychology of Death*. 3rd ed. New York: Springer.

Kaster, Robert A. 2003. "Invidia, νέμεσις, φθόνος, and the Roman Emotional Economy." Pages 253–76 in Konstan and Rutter, 2003.

Kaster, Robert A. 2005. *Emotion, Restraint, and Community in Ancient Rome*. Oxford: Oxford University Press.

Kaufman, Gordon D. 1981. *The Theological Imagination: Constructing the Concept of God*. Philadelphia: John Knox.

Kaufmann, Walter. 1979. *Tragedy and Philosophy*. Princeton: Princeton University Press.

Kearns, Emily. 2004. "The Gods in the Homeric Epics." Pages 59–73 in *The Cambridge Companion to Homer*. Edited by Robert Fowler. Cambridge: Cambridge University Press.

Kelly, Michael R. 2016. "Envy and *Ressentiment*, a Difference in Kind: A Critique and Renewal of Scheler's Phenomenological Account." Pages 49–66 in *Early Phenomenology: Metaphysics, Ethics, and the Philosophy of Religion*. Bloomsbury Studies in Continental Philosophy. Edited by Brian Harding and Michael R. Kelly. London: Bloomsbury.

Kennedy, Rebecca Futo. 2009. *Athena's Justice: Athena, Athens and the Concept of Justice in Greek Tragedy*. New York: Peter Lang.

Kirk, Geoffrey S. 1970. *The Bacchae by Euripides: A Translation with Commentary*. Englewood Cliffs: Prentice-Hall.

Kirsch, Jonathan. 1999. *Moses: A Life*. New York: Random House Ballantine.

Knox, Bernard M. W. 1961. "The *Ajax* of Sophocles." *HSPh* 65:1–37.

Knox, Bernard M. W. 1971. *Oedipus at Thebes: Sophocles' Tragic Hero and his Time*. New York: Norton.

Kok, Johnson Lim Teng. 1997. *The Sin of Moses and the Staff of God: A Narrative Approach*. Studia Semitica Neerlandica, 35. Assen: Van Gorcum.

Konstan, David. 2006. *The Emotions of the Ancient Greeks: Studies in Aristotle and Classical Literature*. Toronto: University of Toronto Press.

Konstan, David and N. Keith Rutter, eds. 2003. *Envy, Spite, and Jealousy: The Rivalrous Emotions in Ancient Greece*. Edinburgh Leventis Studies, 2. Edinburgh: Edinburgh University Press.

Kovacs, David. 1980. "Shame, Pleasure, and Honor in Phaedra's Great Speech (Euripides, *Hippolytus* 375–87)." *AjPh* 101:287–303.

Kovacs, David. 2009. "The Role of Apollo in *Oedipus Tyrannus*." Pages 357–68 in *The Play of Texts and Fragments: Essays in Honour of Martin Cropp*. Edited by J. R. C. Cousland and J. R. Hume. Leiden.

Kovacs, David. 2019. "On *Not* Misunderstanding *Oedipus Tyrannos*." *CQ* 69:107–18.

Kraus, Hans-Joachim. 1993. *Psalms 1–59: A Continental Commentary*. Trans. Hilton C. Oswald. Minneapolis: Fortress Press.

Krizan, Zlatan and Omesh Johar. 2012. "Envy Divides the Two Faces of Narcissism." *J. Pers.* 80:1415–51.

Kruger, Paul A. 2001. "A Cognitive Interpretation of the Emotion of Fear in the Hebrew Bible." *JNSL* 27:77–89.

Kruger, Paul A. 2015. "Emotions in the Hebrew Bible: A Few Observations on Prospects and Challenges." *OTE* 28:395–420.

Kucharski, Janek. 2012. "Vindictive Prosecution in Classical Athens: On Some Recent Theories." *GRBS* 52:167–97.
Kuhrt, Amélie. 1983. "The Cyrus Cylinder and Achaemenid Imperial Policy." *JSOT* 25:83–97.
Kutter, Mara Michelle. 2018. "Emotion in Politics: Envy, Jealousy, and Rulership in Archaic and Classical Greece." PhD diss., University of Michigan.
Lacan, Jacques. 2018. *The Four Fundamental Concepts of Psycho-Analysis*. Edited by Jacque-Alain Miller. Translated by Alan Sheridan. London: Routledge.
Lamb, David T. 2007. *Righteous Jehu and His Evil Heirs. The Deuteronomist's Negative Perspective on Dynastic Succession*. Oxford Theological Monographs. Oxford: Oxford University Press.
Langston, Scott M. 2006. *Exodus through the Centuries*. Blackwell Bible Commentaries. Oxford: Blackwell.
Lanzillotta, Lautaro Roig. 2010. "The So-Called Envy of the Gods: Revisiting a Dogma of Ancient Greek Religion." Pages 75–93 in *Myths, Martyrs, and Modernity: Studies in the History of Religions in Honour of Jan N. Bremmer*. Edited by Jitse Dijkstra, Justin Kroesen, and Yme Kuiper. Leiden: Brill.
Larson, Janet L. 1985. *Dickens and the Broken Scripture*. Athens: University of Georgia Press.
Lasine, Stuart. 1988. "Bird's-Eye and Worm's-Eye Views of Justice in the Book of Job." *JSOT* 42:29–53.
Lasine, Stuart. 1989. "The Riddle of Solomon's Judgment and the Riddle of Human Nature in the Hebrew Bible." *JSOT* 45:61–86.
Lasine, Stuart. 1992. "Reading Jeroboam's Intentions: Intertextuality, Rhetoric and History in 1 Kings 12." Pages 133–52 in Fewell, 1992.
Lasine, Stuart. 1994. "Levite Violence, Fratricide, and Sacrifice in the Bible and Later Revolutionary Rhetoric." Pages 204–29 in *Curing Violence*. Edited by Mark I. Wallace and Theophus H. Smith. Sonoma, CA: Polebridge Press.
Lasine, Stuart 2001. *Knowing Kings: Knowledge, Power and Narcissism in the Hebrew Bible*. SemeiaSt 40. Atlanta: Society of Biblical Literature.
Lasine, Stuart. 2002. "Divine Narcissism and Yahweh's Parenting Style." *BibInt* 10:36–56.
Lasine, Stuart. 2004. "Matters of Life and Death: The Story of Elijah and the Widow's Son in Comparative Perspective." *BibInt* 12:117–44.
Lasine, Stuart. 2010. "'Everything Belongs to Me': Holiness, Danger, and Divine Kingship in the Post-Genesis World." *JSOT* 35:31–62.
Lasine, Stuart. 2012. *Weighing Hearts: Character, Judgment and the Ethics of Reading the Bible*. LHBOTS, 568. New York: T&T Clark.
Lasine, Stuart. 2016. "Characterizing God in His/Our Own Image." Pages 465–77 in *The Oxford Handbook to Biblical Narrative*. Edited by Danna Nolan Fewell. New York: Oxford University Press.
Lasine, Stuart. 2019. *Jonah and the Human Condition: Life and Death in Yahweh's World*. LHBOTS, 688. New York: Bloomsbury/T & T Clark.
Lasine, Stuart. 2020. "Samuel-Kings as a Mirror for Princes: Parental Education and Judean Royal Families." *SJOT* 34:74–88.
Lateiner, Donald. 1980. "A Note on ΔΙΚΑΣ ΔΙΔΟΝΑΙ in Herodotus." *CQ* 30:30–32.
Lateiner, Donald. 1991. *The Historical Method of Herodotus*. Phoenix Supplementary Volume, 23. Toronto: University of Toronto Press.
Lateiner, Donald. 2002. "Pouring Bloody Drops (*Iliad* 16.459): The Grief of Zeus." *ColbyQ* 38:42–61.

Lattimore, Richmond. 1939. "The Wise Advisor in Herodotus." *CPh* 34:24–35.
Lattimore, Richmond. 1961. "Introduction." Pages 11–55 in *The Iliad of Homer*. Translated by Richmond Lattimore. Chicago: University of Chicago Press.
Lauterbach, Jacob Z. 1933. *Mekilta de-Rabbi Ishmael*, Volume 2. Philadelphia: Jewish Publication Society.
Lawrence, S. E. 1998. "The God That Is Truly God and the Universe of Euripides' *Heracles*." *Mnemosyne* 51:129–46.
Lazarus, Richard S. 1999. "The Cognition-Emotion Debate: A Bit of History." Pages 3–19 in *Handbook of Cognition and Emotion*. Edited by Tim Dalgleish and Mick J. Power. Chichester: John Wiley and Sons.
Leach, Colin Wayne. 2008. "Envy, Inferiority, and Justice: Three Bases of Anger About Inequality." Pages 94–116 in R. Smith, 2008b.
Leahy, Robert L. 2021. "Cognitive-Behavioral Therapy for Envy." *Cogn. Ther. Res.* 45:418–27.
Leavitt, John. 1996. "Meaning and Feeling in the Anthropology of Emotions." *Am. Ethnol.* 23:514–39.
Lefkowitz, Mary R. 1989. "'Impiety' and 'Atheism' in Euripides' Dramas." *CQ* 39:70–82.
Lefkowitz, Mary R. 2007. "Gods, or God?" *Los Angeles Times*, Oct. 23, 2007. Available online: www.latimes.com/archives/la-xpm-2007-oct-23-oe-lefkowitz23-story.html. (accessed April 28, 2021).
Lefkowitz, Mary R. 2019. *Euripides and the Gods*. New York: Oxford University Press.
Leichty, Erle. 2011. *The Royal Inscriptions of Esarhaddon, King of Assyria (680–669 BC)*. The Royal Inscriptions of the Neo-Assyrian Period, 4. Winona Lake, IN: Eisenbrauns.
Lenard, Mary. 2014. "The Gospel of Amy: Biblical Teaching and Learning in Charles Dickens' *Little Dorrit*." *Christ. Lit.* 63:337–55.
Lesher, J. H., ed. 1992. *Xenophanes of Colophon, Fragments: A Text and Translation with a Commentary*. Phoenix Supplementary Volume 30. Toronto: University of Toronto Press.
Levenson, Jon D. 1988. *Creation and the Persistence of Evil: The Jewish Drama of Divine Omnipotence*. San Francisco: Harper & Row.
Levine, Baruch A. 2000. *Numbers 21–36: A New Translation with Introduction and Commentary* AB 4A. New York: Doubleday.
Levy, Ken. 2014. "Why Retributivism Needs Consequentialism: The Rightful Place of Revenge in the Criminal Justice System." *Rut. Law Rev.* 66:629–84.
Lindholm, Charles. 2008. "Culture and Envy. Pages 227–44 in R. Smith, 2008b.
Linforth, Ivan M. 1928. "Named and Unnamed Gods in Herodotus." *UCPCP* 9:201–43.
Livneh, Atar. 2011. "Judgment and Revenge: The Exodus Account in *Jubilees* 48." *RevQ* 25:161–75.
Lloyd, Michael. 2013. "The Mutability of Fortune in Euripides." Pages 205–26 in Cairns, 2013a.
Lloyd-Jones, Hugh. 1983. *The Justice of Zeus*. 2nd ed. Sather Classical Lectures, 41. Berkeley: University of California Press.
Loney, Alexander C. 2019. *The Ethics of Revenge and the Meanings of the* Odyssey. Oxford: Oxford University Press.
Long, Burke O. 1991. *2 Kings*. FOTL, 10. Grand Rapids: Eerdmans.
Lundbom, Jack R. 2013. *Deuteronomy: A Commentary*. Grand Rapids: Eerdmans.
Lupfer, Michael, Matthew Weeks, and Susan Dupuis. 2000. "How Pervasive Is the Negativity Bias in Judgments Based on Character Appraisal?" *Pers. Soc. Psychol. Bull.* 26:1353–66.
Lutz, Catherine A. 1988. *Unnatural Emotions: Everyday Sentiments on a Micronesian Atoll and their Challenge to Western Theory*. Chicago: University of Chicago Press.

Lynn-George, K. 1996. "Structures of Care in the *Iliad*." *CQ* 46:1–26.
MacKenzie, R. A. F. 1955. "The Divine Soliloquies in Genesis." *CBQ* 17:157–66.
Maimonides. 1919. *The Guide for the Perplexed*. 2nd ed. Translated by M. Friedländer. London: George Routledge.
Margolin, Ron. 2020. "The Imperfect God." *EJPR* 12:65–87.
Matthiessen, Kjeld, ed. 2010. *Euripides "Hekabe": Edition und Kommentar*. Text und Kommentare, 34. Berlin: De Gruyter.
Maurer, Adah. 1966. "Maturation of Concepts of Death." *Br. J. Med Psychol.* 39:35–41.
Mbuwayesango, Dora Rudo. "Numbers." Pages 70–87 in *Postcolonial Commentary and the Old Testament*. Edited by Hemchand Gossai. London: T & T Clark.
McCann, J. Clinton. 2011. *Judges*. IBC. Louisville: Westminster John Knox.
McCarter, P. Kyle, Jr. 1980. *I Samuel*. AB 8. Garden City, N.Y.: Doubleday.
McGinty, Park. 1978. "Dionysos's Revenge and the Validation of the Hellenic World-View." *HTR* 71:77–94.
McHardy, Fiona. 2013. *Revenge in Athenian Culture*. London: Bloomsbury.
Mendenhall, George E. 1973. *The Tenth Generation: The Origins of Biblical Tradition*. Baltimore: Johns Hopkins University Press.
Mendenhall, George E. 1992. "Midian." Pages 815–18 in *ABD*, vol. 4.
Meridor, Ra'anana. 1978. "Hecuba's Revenge: Some Observations on Euripides' *Hecuba*." *AjPh* 99:28–35.
Mikalson, Jon D. 1991. *Honor Thy Gods: Popular Religion in Greek Tragedy*. Chapel Hill: University of North Carolina Press.
Mikalson, Jon D. 2002. "Religion in Herodotus." Pages 187–98 in *Brill's Companion to Herodotus*. Edited by Egbert J. Bakker, Irene J. F. de Jong, and Hans van Wees. Leiden: Brill.
Mikalson, Jon D. 2003. *Herodotus and Religion in the Persian Wars*. Chapel Hill: University of North Carolina Press.
Miles, Jack. 1996. *God: A Biography*. New York: Vintage.
Milgrom, Jacob. 1990. *Numbers* במדבר: *The Traditional Hebrew Text with the New JPS Translation*. JPS Torah Commentary. Philadelphia: Jewish Publication Society.
Miller, Andrew M. 1986. *From Delos to Delphi: A Literary Study of the Homeric Hymn to Apollo*. Leiden: Brill.
Mills, Sophie. 2006. *Euripides: Bacchae*. London: Duckworth.
Milton, John. 1935. *Paradise Lost*. New York: Odyssey Press.
Mirguet, Françoise. 2016. "What Is an 'Emotion' in the Hebrew Bible? An Experience That Exceeds Most Contemporary Concepts." *BibInt* 24:442–65.
Mirguet, Françoise and Dominika Kurek-Chomycz. 2016. "Introduction: Emotions in Ancient Jewish Literature." *BibInt* 24:435–41.
Mitchell-Boyask, Robin. 1996. Review of Mossman, *Wild Justice: A Study of Euripides'* Hecuba. *BMCR* 1996.03.04. Available online: https://bmcr.brynmawr.edu/1996/1996.03.04/ (accessed January 30, 2021).
Mitchell-Boyask, Robin. 2010. "The *Hecuba* of Euripides" and "An Essay of Euripides' *Hecuba*." Pages 78–129, 211–31 in Esposito, 2010a.
Momigliano, Arnaldo. 1985. "Marcel Mauss and the Quest for the Person in Greek Biography and Autobiography." Pages 83–92 in *The Category of the Person: Anthropology, Philosophy, History*. Edited by M. Carrithers, S. Collins, and S. Lukes. Cambridge: Cambridge University Press.
Montgomery, James A. and Henry Synder Gehman. 1951. *A Critical and Exegetical Commentary on the Books of Kings*. ICC. Edinburgh: T&T Clark.

Bibliography 175

Moore, Stephen D. 2019. "The Rage for Method and the Joy of Anachronism: When Biblical Scholars Do Affect Theory." Pages 187–211 in *Reading with Feeling: Affect Theory and the Bible*. Edited by Fiona C. Black and Jennifer L. Koosed. SemeiaSt, 95. Atlanta: SBL Press.

Morewedge, Carey K. and Michael E. Clear. 2008. "Anthropomorphic God Concepts Engender Moral Judgment." *Soc. Cogn.* 26:182–89.

Mossman, Judith. 1995. *Wild Justice: A Study of Euripides' Hecuba*. Oxford Classical Monographs. Oxford: Clarendon Press.

Most, Glenn. 2003. "Epinician Envies." Pages 123–42 in Konstan and Rutter, 2003.

Mueller, Melissa. 2011. "Phaedra's *Defixio*: Scripting *Sophrosune* in Euripides' *Hippolytus*." *ClAnt* 30:148–77.

Muffs, Yochanan. 1992. *Love & Joy: Law, Language and Religion in Ancient Israel*. New York: Jewish Theological Seminary of America.

Muffs, Yochanan. 2005. *The Personhood of God: Biblical Theology, Human Faith and the Divine Image*. Woodstock, VT: Jewish Lights Publishing.

Muir, J. V. 1985. "Religion and the New Education: The Challenge of the Sophists." Pages 191–218 in Easterling and Muir, 1985.

Mulder, Martin J. 1998. *I Kings, Volume 1: 1 Kings 1–11*. Historical Commentary on the Old Testament. Leuven: Peeters.

Munson, Rosaria Vignolo. 1988. "Artemesia in Herodotus." *ClAnt* 7:91–106.

Munson, Rosaria Vignolo. 2001. *Telling Wonders: Ethnographic and Political Discourse in the Work of Herodotus*. Ann Arbor, MI: University of Michigan Press.

Nagy, Gregory. 1979. *The Best of the Achaeans: Concepts of the Hero in Archaic Greek Poetry*. Baltimore: Johns Hopkins University Press.

Nelson, Richard D. 1987. *First and Second Kings*. IBC. Atlanta: John Knox.

Neufeld, Darren C. and Edward A. Johnson. 2016. "Burning With Envy? Dispositional and Situational Influences on Envy in Grandiose and Vulnerable Narcissism." *J. Pers.* 84:685–96.

Neusner, Jacob. 1989. *Lamentations Rabbah: An Analytical Translation*. BJS, 193. Atlanta: Scholars Press.

Newsom, Carol A. 2009. *The Book of Job: A Contest of Moral Imaginations*. Oxford: Oxford University Press.

Niditch, Susan. 1993a. "War, Women, and Defilement in Numbers 31." *Semeia* 61:39–57.

Niditch, Susan. 1993b. *War in the Hebrew Bible: A Study in the Ethics of Violence*. Oxford: Oxford University Press.

Niditch, Susan. 2011. *Judges: A Commentary*. OTL. Louisville: Westminster John Knox.

Nietzsche, Friedrich. 1887. *Zur Genealogie der Moral: Eine Streitschrift*. Leipzig: C. G. Naumann.

Nietzsche, Friedrich. 1999a. Der Antichrist. Pages 167–253 in *Der Fall Wagner, Götzen-Dämmerung, Der Antichrist, Ecce homo, Dionysos-Dithyramben, Nietzsche contra Wagner*. Kritische Studienausgabe. Edited by Giorgio Colli and Mazzino Montinari. Berlin: de Gruyter.

Nietzsche, Friedrich. 1999b. Morgenröthe. Pages 9–331 in *Morgenröthe, Idyllen aus Messina, Die fröhliche Wissenschaft*. Kritische Studienausgabe. Edited by Giorgio Colli and Mazzino Montinari. Berlin: de Gruyter.

Niskanen, Paul V. 2014. *Isaiah 56–66*. Berit Olam. Collegeville, MN: Liturgical Press.

Noll, K. L. 1999. "Is There a Text in This Tradition? Readers' Response and the Taming of Samuel's God." *JSOT* 83:31–51.

Noll, K. L. 2001. "The Kaleidoscopic Nature of the Divine Personality in the Hebrew Bible." *BibInt* 9:1–24.

Norwood, Gilbert. 1908. *The Riddle of the Bacchae: The Last Stage of Euripides' Religious Views*. Manchester: University of Manchester Press.

Novotny, Jamie. 2015. "New Proposed Chronological Sequence and Dates of Composition of Esarhaddon's Babylon Inscriptions." *JCS* 67:145–68.

O'Brien, Joan. 1991. "Homer's Savage Hera." *CJ* 86:105–25.

O'Brien, Julia M. 2008. *Challenging Prophetic Metaphor: Theology and Ideology in the Prophets*. Louisville: Westminster John Knox.

Oranje, Hans. 1984. *Euripides' Bacchae: The Play and Its Audience*. Leiden: Brill.

Organ, Barbara E. 2001. "Pursuing Phinehas: A Synchronic Reading." *CBQ* 63:203–18.

Ostwald, Martin. 1986. *From Popular Sovereignty to the Sovereignty of Law: Law, Society, and Politics in Fifth-Century Athens*. Berkeley: University of California Press.

Padel, Ruth. 1992. *In and Out of the Mind: Greek Images of the Tragic Self*. Princeton: Princeton University Press.

Palmer, Frank. 1992. *Literature and Moral Understanding: A Philosophical Essay on Ethics, Aesthetics, Education, and Culture*. Oxford: Clarendon.

Parker, L. P. E. 2001. "Where Is Phaedra?" *G&R* 48:45–52.

Parker, Robert. 1983. *Miasma: Pollution and Purification in Early Greek Religion*. Oxford: Clarendon Press.

Parrott, W. Gerrod. 1991. "The Emotional Experiences of Envy and Jealousy." Pages 3–30 in Salovey, 1991.

Parrott, W. Gerrod. 2002. "The Functional Utility of Negative Emotions." Pages 341–59 in *The Wisdom in Feeling: Psychological Processes in Emotional Intelligence*. Edited by Lisa Feldman Barrett and Peter Salovey. New York: Guilford Press.

Parrott, W. Gerrod and Richard H. Smith. 1993. "Distinguishing the Experiences of Envy and Jealousy." *J. Pers. Soc. Psychol.* 64:906–20.

Patrick, Dale. 1979. "Job's Address of God." *ZAW* 91:268–82.

Paul, Shalom M. 2012. *Isaiah 40–66: Translation and Commentary*. ECC. Grand Rapids: William B. Eerdmans Publishing.

Peat, Derek. 1984. "Responding Blindly? A Reading of a Scene in *King Lear*." *Syd. Stud. Eng.* 10:103–108.

Peels, H. G. L. 1995. *The Vengeance of God: The Meaning of the Root NQM and the Function of the NQM-Texts in the Context of Divine Revelation in the Old Testament*. OtSt 31. Leiden: Brill.

Pelling, Christopher, ed. 1990a. *Characterization and Individuality in Greek Literature*. Oxford: Clarendon.

Pelling, Christopher, ed. 1990b. "Conclusion." Pages 245–62 in Pelling, 1990a.

Pelling, Christopher, ed. 2006. "Speech and Narrative in the *Histories*." Pages 103–21 in *The Cambridge Companion to Herodotus*. Edited by Carolyn Dewald and John Marincola. Cambridge: Cambridge University Press.

Penchansky, David and Paul L. Redditt, eds. 2000. *Shall Not the Judge of All the Earth Do What Is Right? Studies on the Nature of God in Tribute to James L. Crenshaw*. Winona Lake, IN: Eisenbrauns.

Pironti, Gabriella. 2010. "Rethinking Aphrodite as a Goddess at Work." Pages 113–30 in *Brill's Companion to Aphrodite*. Edited by Amy C. Smith and Sadie Pickup. Leiden: Brill.

Pitard, Wayne T. 1982. "Amarna *ekēmu* and Hebrew *nāqam*." *Maarav* 3:5–25.

Pitkänen, Pekka. 2018. *A Commentary on Numbers: Narrative, Ritual, and Colonialism*. Routledge Studies in the Biblical World. London: Routledge.

Podlecki, A. J. 1980. "Ajax's Gods and the Gods of Sophocles." *Antiq. Class.* 49:45–86.
Pope, Marvin H. 1965. *Job: Introduction, Translation, and Notes*. AB, 15. Garden City: Doubleday.
Porter, Barbara Nevling. 1993. *Image, Power, Politics: Figurative Aspects of Esarhaddon's Babylonian Policy*. Philadelphia: American Philosophical Society.
Postlethwaite, Norman. 2000. *Homer's* Iliad*: A Commentary on the Translation of Richmond Lattimore*. Exeter: University of Exeter Press.
Postman, Neil. 1994. *The Disappearance of Childhood*. New York: Vintage Books.
Propp, William H. C. 1998 *Exodus 1–18*. AB, 2. New York: Doubleday.
Reckford, Kenneth J. 1974. "Phaedra and Pasiphae: The Pull Backward." *TAPA* 104:307–28.
Redfield, James M. 1975. *Nature and Culture in the* Iliad*: The Tragedy of Hector*. Chicago: University of Chicago Press.
Reeve, C. D. C., trans. 2018. *Aristotle Rhetoric*. Indianapolis: Hackett.
Reeve, C. D. C., trans. 2021. *Aristotle Eudemian Ethics*. Indianapolis: Hackett.
Reif, S. C. 1971. "What Enraged Phinehas?—A Study of Numbers 25:8." *JBL* 90:200–206.
Reinhardt, Karl. 1960. *Tradition und Geist: Gesammelte Essays zur Dichtung*. Edited by Carl Becker. Göttingen: Vandenhoeck & Ruprecht.
Rentzsch, Katrin and James J. Gross. 2015. "Who Turns Green with Envy? Conceptual and Empirical Perspectives on Dispositional Envy." *Eur. J. Pers.* 29:530–47.
Robins, Rochelle. 2015. "Complexity and Imperfection: A Theology of Jewish Pastoral Care." Pages 28–41 in *Jewish Pastoral Care: A Practical Handbook from Traditional and Contemporary Sources*. Edited by Dayle A. Friedman. Woodstock, VT: Jewish Lights Publishing.
Rofé, Alexander. 1988. *The Prophetical Stories: The Narratives about the Prophets in the Hebrew Bible, Their Literary Types and History*. Jerusalem: Magnes.
Rohmann, Elke, Eva Neumann, Michael Jürgen Herner, and Hans-Werner Bierhoff. 2012. "Grandiose and Vulnerable Narcissism: Self-Construal, Attachment, and Love in Romantic Relationships."*Eur. Psychol.* 17:279–90.
Romm, James. 1998. *Herodotus*. New Haven: Yale University Press.
Roncace, Mark. 2020. "He's Driving Like Jehu—Like a Madman: Humor and Violence in 2 Kings 9–10." Pages 167–81 in Bodner and Johnson, 2020.
Ronningstam, Elsa F. 2005. *Identifying and Understanding the Narcissistic Personality*. Oxford: Oxford University Press.
Rosegrant, John. 2012. "Narcissism and Sadomasochistic Relationships." *J. Clin. Psychol.: IS* 68:935–42.
Rubinkiewicz, R., trans. 1983. "Apocalypse of Abraham: A New Translation and Introduction." Translation revised by H. G. Lunt. Pages 681–705 in *The Old Testament Pseudepigrapha, Vol. 1*. Edited by James H. Charlesworth. Garden City, NY: Doubleday.
Sacher-Masoch, Leopold. 1980. *Venus im Pelz*. Frankfurt a. M.: Insel Taschenbuch.
Sackson, Adrian. 2017. *Joseph Ibn Kaspi: Portrait of a Hebrew Philosopher in Medieval Provence*. Études Sur Le Judaïsme Médiéval. Leiden: Brill.
Salovey, Peter, ed. 1991. *The Psychology of Jealousy and Envy*. New York: Guilford Press.
Salovey, Peter and Alexander Rothman. 1991. "Envy and Jealousy: Self and Society." Pages 271–86 in Salovey, 1991.
Sanders, Ed. 2014. *Envy and Jealousy in Classical Athens: A Socio-Psychological Approach*. Emotions of the Past. New York: Oxford University Press.
Sandler, J., E. S. Person, and P. Fonagy, eds. 1991. *Freud's "On Narcissism: An Introduction."* New Haven: Yale University Press.

Sandmel, Samuel. 1972. "The Ancient Mind and Ours." Pages 29–44 in *Understanding the Sacred Text: Essays in Honor of Morton S. Enslin on the Hebrew Bible and Christian Beginnings*. Edited by John Reumann. Valley Forge: Judson.

Sasson, Jack M. 1990. *Jonah: A New Translation with Introduction, Commentary, and Interpretation*. AB, 24B. New York: Doubleday

Schechner, Richard. 1961. "*The Bacchae*: A City Sacrificed to a Jealous God." *Tulane Drama Rev.* 5:124–34.

Schechter, Solomon. 1961. *Aspects of Rabbinic Theology: Major Concepts of the Talmud*. New York: Schocken.

Schein, Seth L, ed. 2013. *Sophocles Philoctetes*. Cambridge Greek and Latin Classics. Cambridge: Cambridge University Press.

Scheler, Max. 1955. Das Ressentiment im Aufbau der Moralen. Pages 35–147 in *Vom Umsturz der Werte: Abhandlungen und Aufsätze*. 4th ed. Edited by Maria Scheler. Bern: Francke Verlag.

Schimmel, Solomon. 2008. "Envy in Jewish Thought and Literature." Pages 17–38 in R. Smith, 2008b.

Schoeck, Helmut. 1987. *Envy: A Theory of Social Behaviour*. Indianapolis: Liberty Fund.

Schroeder, Jeanne L. 2005. "Envy and Outsider Trading: The Case of Martha Stewart." *Card. Law Rev.* 26:2023–79.

Schroer, Silvia and Thomas Staubli. 2007. "Biblische Emotionswelten." *KatBl* 132:44–49.

Scodel, Ruth. 2008. *Epic Facework: Self-presentation and Social Interaction in Homer*. Swansea: Classic Press of Wales.

Scodel, Ruth. 2009. *Listening to Homer: Tradition, Narrative, and Audience*. Ann Arbor: University of Michigan Press.

Scodel, Ruth and Ruth R. Caston. 2019. "Literature." Pages 109–24 in Cairns, 2019a.

Seaford, Richard. 1996. *Euripides: Bacchae, with an Introduction, Translation and Commentary*. Warminster: Aris & Phillips.

Seaford, Richard. 2003. "Tragic Tyranny." Pages 95–115 in *Popular Tyranny: Sovereignty and Its Discontents in Ancient Greece*. Edited by Kathryn A. Morgan. Austin: University of Texas Press.

Segal, Charles. 1990. "Violence and the Other: Greek, Female, and Barbarian in Euripides' *Hecuba*." *TAPA* 120:109–31.

Segal, Charles. 1993. *Euripides and the Poetics of Sorrow: Art, Gender, and Commemoration in Alcestis, Hippolytus, and Hecuba*. Durham: Duke University Press.

Segal, Charles. 2001. *Oedipus Tyrannus: Tragic Heroism and the Limits of Knowledge*. 2nd ed. New York: Oxford University Press.

Seidensticker, Bernd. 2016. "The Figure of Teiresias in Euripides' *Bacchae*." Pages 275–83 in *Wisdom and Folly in Euripides*. Trends in Classics—Supplementary Volumes, 31. Edited by Poulheria Kyriakou and Antonios Rengakos. Berlin: De Gruyter.

Shapiro, David. 2002. "Theoretical Reflections on Wilhelm Reich's *Character Analysis*." *Am. J. Psychother.* 56:338–46.

Shapiro, Susan O. 1996. "Herodotus and Solon." *ClAnt* 15:348–64.

Sharpsteen, Don J. 1991. "The Organization of Jealousy Knowledge: Romantic Jealousy as a Blended Emotion." Pages 31–51 in Salovey, 1991.

Shaviro, Steven. 2016. "Affect vs. Emotion." *The Cine-Files* 10:1–3. Available from www.thecine-files.com/shaviro2016/ (accessed November 18, 2021).

Shtulman, Andrew and Marjaana Lindeman. 2016. "Attributes of God: Conceptual Foundations of a Foundational Belief." *Cogn. Sci.* 40:635–70.

Sissa, Giulia and Marcel Detienne. 2000. *The Daily Life of the Greek Gods*. Translated by Janet Lloyd. Stanford: Stanford University Press.

Skinner, John. 1930. *A Critical and Exegetical Commentary on Genesis*. 2nd ed. ICC. Edinburgh: T. & T. Clark.

Slater, Humphrey R. 1947. *The Heretics: A Novel*. New York: Harcourt, Brace.

Slater, Philip E. 1992. *The Glory of Hera: Greek Mythology and the Greek Family*. Princeton: Princeton University Press.

Smith, Mark S. 2008. *God in Translation: Deities in Cross-Cultural Discourse in the Biblical World*. Grand Rapids, MI: Eerdmans.

Smith, Richard H. 1991. "Envy and the Sense of Injustice." Pages 79–99 in Salovey, 1991.

Smith, Richard H., ed. 2008b. *Envy: Theory and Research*. Oxford: Oxford University Press.

Smith, Richard H. and Sung Hee Kim. 2007. "Comprehending Envy." *Psychol. Bull.* 133:46–64.

Smith, Richard H., David J. Y. Combs, and Stephen M. Thielke. 2008a. "Envy and the Challenges to Good Health." Pages 290–314 in R. Smith, 2008b.

Smolewska, Kathy and Kenneth L. Dion. 2005. "Narcissism and Adult Attachment: A Multivariate Approach." *Self Ident*. 4:59–68.

Snell, Bruno. 1975. *Die Entdeckung des Geistes: Studien zur Entstehung des europäischen Denkens bei den Griechen*. 4th ed. Göttingen: Vandenhoeck und Ruprecht.

Solomon, Robert C. 1984. "Getting Angry: The Jamesian Theory of Emotion in Anthropology." Pages 238–54 in *Culture Theory: Essays on Mind, Self and Emotion*. Edited by Richard A. Shweder and Robert A. LeVine. New York: Cambridge University Press.

Solomon, Robert C. 1993. *The Passions: Emotions and the Meaning of Life*. Indianapolis: Hackett.

Solomon, Robert C. 1994. "Sympathy and Vengeance: The Role of Emotions in Justice." Pages 291–311 in *Emotions: Essays on Emotion Theory*. Edited by Stephanie H. M. Van Goozen, Nanne E. Van de Poll, and Joseph A. Sergeant. Hillsdale, NJ: Lawrence Erlbaum.

Sommer, Benjamin D. 1999. "Reflecting on Moses: The Redaction of Numbers 11." *JBL* 118:601–24.

Sourvinou-Inwood, Christiane. 2003. *Tragedy and Athenian Religion*. Lanham, MD: Lexington.

Spronk, Klaas. 1997. *Nahum*. HCOT. Leuven: Peeters.

Stanford, W. B. 1967. *The Odyssey of Homer, Vol. I (Books I–XII)*. 2nd ed. London: Macmillan.

Stanford, W. B. 1968. *The Ulysses Theme: A Study in the Adaptability of a Traditional Hero*. Ann Arbor: University of Michigan Press.

Stearns, Peter N. 2013. "Jealousy in Western History: From Past toward Present." Pages 7–26 in *Handbook of Jealousy: Theory, Research, and Multidisciplinary Approaches*. Edited by Sybil L. Hart and Maria Legerstee. Chichester: Wiley-Blackwell.

Steinberg, Naomi. 2018. "Social Death as Gendered Genocide: The Fate of Women and Children." *BibInt* 26:23–42.

Stern, David. 1992. "*Imitatio Hominis*: Anthropomorphism and the Character(s) of God in Rabbinic Literature." *Proof.* 12:151–74.

Stolorow, Robert D. 1975. "The Narcissistic Function of Masochism (and Sadism)." *IJP* 56:441–48.

Strauss, Barry S. 1993. *Fathers and Sons in Athens: Ideology and Society in the Era of the Peloponnesian War*. Princeton: Princeton University Press.

180 Bibliography

Stróżyński, Mateusz. 2013. "Love, Aggression, and Mourning in Euripides' *Heracles*." *Eos* 100:223–50.

Suthor, Nicola. 2018. *Rembrandt's Roughness*. Princeton: Princeton University Press.

Sweeney, Marvin A. 2007. *I & II Kings: A Commentary*. OTL. Louisville: Westminster John Knox.

Synodinou, Katerina. 1987. "The Threats of Physical Abuse of Hera by Zeus in the *Iliad*." *Wiener Studien* 100:13–22.

Taylor, Charles. 1989. *Sources of the Self: The Making of the Modern Identity*. Cambridge: Harvard University Press.

Thelle, Rannfrid I. 2015. "'Self as *Other*': Israel's Self-Designation as Adulterous Wife, a Self-Reflective Perspective on a Prophetic Metaphor." Pages 104–20 in *New Perspectives on Old Testament Prophecy and History: Essays in Honour of Hans M. Barstad*. VTSup, 168. Edited by Rannfrid I. Thelle, Terje Stordalen, and Mervyn E. J. Richardson. Leiden: Brill.

Tigay, Jeffrey H. 1996. *The JPS Torah Commentary: Deuteronomy*. Philadelphia, PA: Jewish Publication Society.

Tomkins, Silvan S. 1978. "Script Theory: Differential Magnification of Affects." *Neb. Symp. Motivat.* 26:201–36.

Tomkins, Silvan S. 1981. "The Quest for Primary Motives: Biography and Autobiography of an Idea." *J. Pers. Soc. Psychol.* 41:306–29.

Twain, Mark. 1996. "Letters from the Earth" Pages 218–60 in *The Bible According to Mark Twain: Irreverent Writings on Eden, Heaven, and the Flood by America's Master Satirist*. Edited by Howard G. Baetzhold and Joseph B. McCullough. New York: Touchstone.

Twersky, Geula. 2017. "Lamech's Song and the Cain Genealogy: An Examination of Gen 4,23–24 within its Narrative Context." *SJOT* 31:275–93.

Uniacke, Suzanne. 2000. "Why Is Revenge Wrong?" *J. Val. Inquiry* 34:61–69.

Van De Mieroop, Marc. 2016. *A History of the Ancient Near East, ca. 3000–323 BC*. 3rd ed. Blackwell History of the Ancient World. Chichester: Wiley Blackwell.

Van der Toorn, Karel. 1986. "Judges XVI 21 in the Light of the Akkadian Sources." *VT* 36:248–53.

Van Der Veen, J. E. 1993. "The Lord of the Ring: Narrative Technique in Herodotus' Story on Polycrates' Ring." *Mnemosyne* 46:433–57.

Vandiver, Elizabeth. 2012. "'Strangers are from Zeus': Homeric *Xenia* at the Courts of Proteus and Croesus." Pages 143–66 in *Myth, Truth and Narrative in Herodotus*. Edited by Emily Baragwanath and Mathieu de Bakker. Oxford: Oxford University Press.

Van Erp Taalman Kip, A. Maria. 2000. "The Gods of the *Iliad* and the Fate of Troy." *Mnemosyne* 53:385–402.

Verduyn, Philippe, Iven Van Mechelen, Francis Tuerlinckx, and Klaus Scherer. 2013. "The Relation between Appraised Mismatch and the Duration of Negative Emotions: Evidence for Universality." *Eur. J. Pers.* 27:481–94.

Verity, Anthony. 2007. *Pindar: The Complete Odes*. Oxford World's Classics. Oxford: Oxford University Press.

Vernant, Jean-Pierre. 1991. *Mortals and Immortals: Collected Essays*. Edited by Froma I. Zeitlin. Princeton: Princeton University Press.

Vernant, Jean-Pierre. 1996. *Myth and Society in Ancient Greece*. Translated by Janet Lloyd. New York: Zone Books.

Versnel, H. S. 1998. *Ter Unus: Isis, Dionysos, Hermes, Three Studies in Henotheism*. Inconsistencies in Greek and Roman Religion, 1.2nd ed. Leiden: Brill.

Vidaillet, Bénédicte. 2007. "Lacanian Theory's Contribution to the Study of Workplace Envy." *Hum. Relat.* 60:1669–1700.
Vidaillet, Bénédicte. 2008. "Psychoanalytic Contributions to Understanding Envy: Classic and Contemporary Perspectives." Pages 267–89 in R. Smith, 2008b.
Volz, Paul. 1924. *Das Dämonische in Jahwe*. Tübingen: Mohr (Paul Siebeck).
Von Rad, Gerhard. 1981. *Der erste Buch Mose: Genesis*. 11th ed. ATD. Göttingen: Vandenhoeck & Ruprecht.
Walcot, Peter. 1978. *Envy and the Greeks: A Study of Human Behaviour*. Warminster: Aris & Phillips.
Walder, Dennis. 2007. *Dickens and Religion*. New York: Routledge.
Waytz, Adam, John Cacioppo and Nicholas Epley. 2010. "Who Sees Human? The Stability and Importance of Individual Differences in Anthropomorphism." *Perspect. Psychol. Sci.* 5:219–32.
Webb, Barry G. 2012. *The Book of Judges*. NICOT. Grand Rapids: Eerdmans.
Weinfeld, Moshe. 1972. *Deuteronomy and the Deuteronomic School*. Oxford: Clarendon.
Wenham, Gordon J. 1981. *Numbers: An Introduction and Commentary*. TOTC. Downers Grove: InterVarsity Press.
Westenholz, Aage. 1987. *Old Sumerian and Old Akkadian Texts in Philadelphia, Part Two: The "Akkadian" Texts, the Enlilemaba Texts, and the Onion Archive*. Copenhagen: Museum Tusculanum Press.
White, Gregory L. and Paul E. Mullen. 1989. *Jealousy: Theory, Research, and Clinical Strategies*. New York: Guilford Press.
Whitehead, David. 2009. "Spiteful Heaven: Residual Belief in Divine *Phthonos* in Post-Fifth-Century Greece. *Acta Anti. Acad. Sci. Hungar.* 49:327–33.
Whitman, Cedric H. 1970. "Hera's Anvils." *HSPh* 74:37–42.
Whybray, R. N. 1981. *Isaiah 40–66*. NCBC. Grand Rapids: Eerdmans.
Wierzbicka, Anna. 1999. *Emotions Across Languages and Cultures: Diversity and Universals*. Paris: Cambridge University Press.
Williams, Bernard. 1993. *Shame and Necessity*. Berkeley: University of California Press.
Winkler, John J. 1985. "The Ephebes' Song: *Tragôidia* and *Polis*." *Representations* 11:26–62.
Winnicott, Donald W. 1958. *Collected Papers: Through Paediatrics to Psycho-Analysis*. New York: Basic Books.
Winnington-Ingram, R. P. 1973. "Zeus in the *Persae*." *JHS* 93:210–19.
Winnington-Ingram, R. P. 1980. *Sophocles: An Interpretation*. Cambridge: Cambridge University Press.
Wray Beal, Lissa M. 2007. *The Deuteronomist's Prophet: Narrative Control of Approval and Disapproval in the Story of Jehu (2 Kings 9 and 10)*. LHBOTS, 478. New York: T & T Clark.
Wray Beal, Lissa M. 2014. *1 & 2 Kings*. ApOTC 9. Downers Grove: InterVarsity Press.
Wray Beal, Lissa M. 2020. "Dancing with Death; Dancing with Life: Ahab between Jezebel and Elijah." Pages 103–20 in Bodner and Johnson, 2020.
Wright, Wilmer C., trans. 1923. *Julian: Against the Galilaeans*. Pages 318–427 in *Julian*, vol. *III*. LCL. Cambridge: Harvard University Press.
Zali, Vasiliki. 2013. "Themistocles' Exhortation Before Salamis: On Herodotus 8.83." *GRBS* 53:461–85.
Zanotti, Grace. 2019. "κυνὸς σῆμα: Euripides' *Hecuba* and the Uses of Revenge." *Arethusa* 52: 1–19.
Zivotofsky, Ari Z. 1994. "The Leadership Qualities of Moses." *Judaism* 43:258–69.

Index of ancient sources

HEBREW BIBLE

Genesis
1:26	45
3:22–23	45
4:1–15	26
4:5–6	14n14
4:6–7	40n34
4:8	40n34
4:12	26
4:13	40n33
4:14	26
4:15	26, 40n33, 146
4:24	40n33
5:3	45
6:5	155
18	21
19:16	21
22:11–12	77
27:35	81n21
29:31	49
29:33	49
34	73–4
34:30	73
37:2, 5–10, 23	14n14
37:11	14n14
39:21	21
40:7–8	4
49:5–7	73

Exodus
1:9–10	72
1:16	72
1:22	70, 71, 81n27
2:11–14	28, 74
2:12	28
4:21–23	128
4:22–23	137
5:2	142
6:25	62
8:5–9	71
9:12	135n84
9:14	142
10:2	128, 142
11:8	83n43
12:12	137
12:12 LXX	137
12:29	137
14:4–14	137
14:18	142
14:21	137
14:25	137
14:27–28	142
15:11	44
16:20	83n43
20:5	44, 49, 59n18, 59n20
32	75, 76, 83n45
32:19	75, 83n43
32:26–27	75
32:27	72
34:6	149
34:6–7	21
34:14	21, 48, 57n1, 62
34:14–16	62

Leviticus
10:16	83n43
19:17	15n22
19:18, 34	15n22, 25

Numbers
10:35	59n18, 59n27
11:10–11	83n43
11:10–12	83n43
11:28–29	64
11:29	76
12:2	75
12:3	71

12:6–8	76	31:17	72, 75, 81n27, 82n39
12:7–8	71	31:17–18	70–7
14:9	15n22	31:18	82n39
14:11	59n19		
14:23	59n19	Deuteronomy	
16:1–3	75	1:17	57n5
16:5	57n5	1:21	15n22
16:12–16	83n43	1:28	14n4
16:15	83n43	1:29	15n22
16:30	59n19	1:37	84n48
20:10	75	3:2	15n22
20:12	75, 84n48	3:23–28	84n48
20:14–21	75	3:26	76
20:27–28	75	4:3	76
21:1–3	75	4:21–22	84n48
21:8–9	75	4:23	60n41
21:21–31	75	4:24	57n1
21:25	62	4:31	60n43, 149
21:31	62	4:34	84n53
22:3	82n32	4:35	149
22:6	82n32	5:9	49, 59n18
22:20–22	130n8	6:5	52
25	39n19	6:12	60n41
25:1	62	6:15	57n1
25:2	62	7:10	59n18
25:3–4	75	8:14	60n41
25:3–5	63	8:19	60n41
25:4	63	9:17	83n43
25:4–5	71	10:14	57n5
25:5	63, 75	10:21	84n53
25:6	63	13:2–4	53
25:7–8	63, 75	13:13–16	73
25:8	79n3	20:13–14	82n31
25:9	63	26:8	84n53
25:10–13	76	28:20	60n39
25:11	49, 63, 75	29:18–19	49
25:11–13	39n19	29:19	49, 57n1
25:13	83n47	31:8	15n22
25:17	72	31:16	60n39
25:17–18	71	31:17	60n42
25:18	72	31:20	59n20
27:14	84n48	32:15–17	48
31:1–3	40n38	32:15	48
31:2	71–2, 74	32:16	27, 57n1, 62
31:2–3	74	32:17	47
31:3	72, 83n40	32:21	47, 48, 57n1
31:6	63	32:35	24
31:7–8	74	32:41	26, 49, 59n18
31:8	79n2, 82n32	32:43	25, 26, 80n12, 136
31:14–18	84n51	33:9	75
31:14	75, 83n43	33:26	44
31:16	72, 82n32	34:10	76
31:16–18	83n40, 84n51	34:12	76

184 *Index of ancient sources*

Joshua	
2:11	14n4
5:1	14n4
7:5	14n4
10:8	27
10:10	27
10:12–13	159n11
10:13	27
10:14	27
10:28–40	81n22
14:8	14n4
22:16–20	64

Judges	
5:4–5	52
7:2	151n20
9:50–54	103n50
11:27	39n30
11:36	26, 146
13:5	77, 146
14:4	77
14:5–6	77
15:3	78
15:7	78, 79
15:9	78
15:11	78
15:14	78
15:18	78
16:17	78
16:20	78
16:21	37, 78
16:27	146
16:28	78, 79, 146
16:29–30	146
16:30	78
17:6	73
18:7–10	74
18:27–28	74
20:18–25	73
20:18	82n38
20:23	82n38
20:27–28	64
20:46–48	73
21:1	73
21:3	82n38
21:5	73
21:10–11	73
21:10–12	72–4
21:11	82n39
21:12	82n39
21:25	73

1 Samuel	
2:25	56
13:14	149, 152n45
16:6	152n45

2 Samuel	
4:5–12	147
4:8	147
4:11	147
6:8	153
6:9	158n2
7:14	152n46
8:14	82n31
11	149
19:7	15n23
22:48	136

1 Kings	
1–2	102n35
3:26–28	101n18
3:23–27	4
5:8	61n51
5:10	61n51
9:11	61n51
10:13	61n51
11:14–22	71
11:17	82n31
11:18	81n24
11:40	77
14:10	67
14:10–12	69
14:11	68
14:22	57n1
14:22	LXX 58n14
15:25–27	81n23
15:27–28	69
16:1–4	69
16:2	69
16:2–4	68
16:4	68
16:7	69
16:8–10	81n23
16:11	68
16:18	69–70
18:1	81n26
18:19–40	81n26
18:20–38	52
18:20–39	64
18:21	48
18:30	65
18:31–32	65
18:36	65
18:39	65
18:40	64, 65, 67
19:1–8	64
19:10	64, 65

Index of ancient sources 185

19:14	64, 65	40:18	44
19:15–17	68	40:25	44
19:16–17	70	41:17	60n43
19:17	67	41:21–24	47
21:17–24	80n16	41:29	47
21:19	80n11, 80n12	42:13	57n1
21:21	67	42:16	60n43
21:21–22	67	44:6–8	149
21:21–24	70	44:9–20	101n27
21:23	66–7	44:28	142
21:24	68	45:1	142
22:19–23	150n13	45:1–8	144
		45:4	144
2 Kings		45:5–6	145
8:7–13	68	45:18	145
9:6–10	67, 80n19	45:22	145
9:7	25, 80n12, 142	46:5	44
9:8	67	46:9	145
9:10	67	47:1–3	142
9:22	80n11	47:8	145
9:23	81n21	47:10	145
9:25	69	48:14	142
9:25–26	80n12	49:14	60n42
9:26	80n12, 80n20	49:15	60n42
9:36–37	66	54	39n19
10:10	67	54:7	60n42
10:12–14	66, 70	59:15	27
10:13–14	68	59:15–16	27
10:15	66	59:15b–17	27
10:16	66	59:16	27–8
10:17	67	59:17	24, 28
10:19	81n21	59:17–19	28
10:30	69	59:18	28
13:23	21	61:2	40n44
17:15	47	63:1–2	27–8
18:25	142	63:1–6	52
19:35	142	63:3	28
25:7	42n68	63:4	28
		63:5	28
Isaiah		63:15	40n45
1:4	60n41	65:11	60n40, 60n41
1:28	60n41		
5:24	59n19	Jeremiah	
9:6	57n1	1:16	60n39
10:5	142	2:5	47
10:5–7	144	2:11	47
10:6	142	2:13	60n39
13:7	14n4	2:17	60n41
17:10	60n41	2:19	60n41
26:11	57n1	2:26–28	52
29:15	96	2:32	60n40
34:8	40n44	3:21	60n41
36:10	142	5:7	47, 60n39
37:36	142	5:9	26

186 Index of ancient sources

5:19	60n39	8:12	59n28, 60n42, 96
5:29	26	9:6	83n41
7:18	52	9:9	59n28, 60n42, 96
9:8	26	16	39n19, 54
9:12	60n39	16:38	57n1, 62
11:20	152n35	18:4	57n5
12:1	158	18:23	56
12:4	158	18:32	56
13:25	60n40	23:25	57n1
15:15	40n31, 59n21, 146, 152n35	24:8	26
16:11	60n39	25:12–17	40n37
17:13	60n41	25:12	26
18:12	59n29	25:13	26
18:15	60n40	25:14	25, 26, 142
19:4	60n39	36:5–6	57n1
22:9	60n41	36:5	57n1
23:17	59n19	38:19	57n1
23:27	60n40	39:25	57n1
25:9	142		
27:5–7	142	Hosea	
32:21	84n53	1–3	39n19
35:6–10	79n8	1:6	149
39:6–7	42n68	2:7	52, 53
44:17–19	52	2:9	53
44:20–27	53	2:10	53
50–51	25, 136	2:15	60n40
50:3	25	3:1	57n2
50:9	25	4:6	60n40
50:13	25	8:14	60n41
50:14	25, 142	13:6	60n40
50:15	25		
50:17	142	Joel	
50:24	25	2	25
50:25	25	2:17–18	25
50:28	25		
50:29	25	Nahum	
50:31	39n27	1:1	39n25
50:41	25	1:2	24
50:45	25	1:2–6	24
51:1	25	2:11	14n4
51:2	25, 142	2:14	39n27
51:6	25	3:1	24
51:11	142	3:5	39n27
51:24	25		
51:25	39n27	Habakkuk	
51:36	25	1:2–3	160n16
51:48	25	1:13	144
51:56	25, 39n23	1:13–17	56
52:10–11	42n68	3:3–12	52
52:11 LXX	84n57		
		Malachi	
Ezekiel		1:6	38n9
5:13	57n1	2:3	38n9

Index of ancient sources 187

Psalms		106:30	63
10	49	113:5	44
10:1	160n16, 160n17	135:5	57n4
10:3–4	59n20	136:15	142
10:3–6	96	139:20–21	59n18
10:3	59n19	139:21	59n27
10:11	59n20, 59n28, 96		
10:13	59n20	Proverbs	
13:2–3	56	6:34	79
13:2	160n17	20:22	25
14:1	49, 96	22:24–25	57
22:2	160n17	27:4	57, 84n60
22:28	57n5	29:11	57
22:48	136	29:22	57
24:1	57n5	30:8–9	49
37:8	57		
41:5	56	Job	
42:10	160n17	1–2	150n13, 153, 155, 160n19
43:2	160n17	1:1	27
44:10–27	56	1:8	27, 47
44:23	59n21	2:3	27, 47, 99
44:24–25	160n16	3:20–23	160n18
50:10–12	57n5	4:17–19	60n46
53	49	6:10	133n56
53:2	59n20	7:17–18	160n18
60:3	56	9:12	46
69	48–9	9:22–24	160n18
69:5	59n25	12:14–25	160n18
69:10	48, 59n24	13:15	54, 60n45
69:13	59.25	13:24	160n16
74:1	160n17	14:1–12	160n18
74:18	59n19	15:14–16	60n46
74:22	59n23	16:9	47
79:5	24, 56, 57n1, 158	16:12	150n12
79:9	56	16:13	133n56
79:10	25, 136	21:7	158
79:12	59n23	21:23–26	160n18
80:4	56	24:1	158
80:20	56	24:1–17	160n18
81:16	59n18	25:4–6	60n46
83:3	59n18, 59n27	28	45
89:7	44	32:2–5	57
89:27–30	152n46	32:19	57
89:39–52	56	38–41	54, 153
90:7–8	56	41:3	44
94:1	24	42:6	54, 60n45
94:6–7	96		
94:7	59n28	Lamentations	
95:3	57n4	2:2	133n56
96:4	57n4	2:17	133n56
97:9	57n4	2:21	133n56
106:6	56	3:30	60–1n50
106:16	58n14, 75	3:42	56

188 *Index of ancient sources*

3:42–50	56
3:43	133n56
5:20	56, 60n42

Qoheleth/Ecclesiastes
4:4	57n1
7:9	57
7:16	47
8:4	46
9:6	57n1
10:20	17n50

Esther
2:8–9	113

Ezra
1:1–4	142

Nehemiah
2:2–3	4

1 Chronicles
16:25	57n4

2 Chronicles
7:6	21
12:5	60n42
15:2	60n42
19:2	59n27
24:20	60n41, 60n42
28:23	151n19
36:22–23	142

APOCRYPHAL AND PSEUDEPIGRAPHAL BOOKS

Wisdom of Solomon
2:24	45

4 Maccabees
2:17	83n43

The Life of Adam and Eve
18:4	45

Apocalypse of Abraham
17:9–10	59n35

NEW TESTAMENT

Matthew
5:39	8
6:12	156

Luke
6:29	8

Acts
13:22	149

MISHNAH

Pirqe 'Abot
2.5	28

BABYLONIAN TALMUD

Yebamot
60b	82n37

'Abodah Zarah
54b–55a	48

MIDRASH AND OTHER JEWISH WORKS

Genesis Rabbah
21.5	68

Leviticus Rabbah
32:4	28

Lamentations Rabbah
Petichta 24	47

Mekilta
Baḥodesh 6	38n17

Seder 'Olam Rabbah
18–19	68

Josephus
Antiquities
4.159	64
4.162	71

Philo
On the Life of Moses (*De Vita Mosis*)
1.55	83n47
1.56	64, 83n47
1.311	71

ANCIENT GREEK WORKS

Aeschylus
Agamemnon
750–56	130n12
750–71	130n12

Index of ancient sources

Persians (Persae)

93	104
158	130n6
246–48	105
345	104, 130n6
345–47	104
354	104, 130n6
362	104, 105
362–63	104
373	105
454	105
472	130n6, 130n14
472–73	107
495–96	105
495–512	105
497–500	105
500–512	105
515	130n6
642	106
654	106
690–91	106
706	105
707–708	105
710–11	106
716–19	106
724	130n6
725	106, 130n6
738	105
742	106
744	106
749–51	106
783	106
801	106
804–808	106
809–13	106
820	106
820–22	106
821–22	108
827–28	106
829–31	106
845	130n6
857	106
911	130n6
921	130n6

Seven Against Thebes

70	133n46
689–92	133n46
720–26	133n46
742–52	133n46
800–802	133n46

Antiphon
Tetralogies

3b. 2	132n41

Aristotle
Eudemian Ethics (Ethica Eudemia)

1220b	41n50
1233b	41n49

Metaphysics (Metaphysica)

983a	46

Nicomachian Ethics (Ethica Nicomachea)

1108a–b	31

Rhetoric (Rhetorica)

1367a20–22	32
1370b28	32
1378b	8
1386b	8
1387b	8

Demosthenes
Against Nicostratus

53.1	32

Epictetus
Discourses

2.19.26	58n10

Euripides
Andromache

243–244	13n4

Bacchae

22	127
26	127
26–31	124
32	127
39–40	124, 128
41	127
45	125, 134n68
45–46	126
45–48	127
47–48	128
52–54	127
98	134n70
220	142
244–45	151n22
247	126, 142
250–52	126
255–57	126
270–72	135n80
274	135n77
289–97	134n70
309–310	135n80
315	135n80
325	125, 134n68
325–26	135n80

190 Index of ancient sources

333	142	749	41n57
346–51	126	749–50	33
360–62	135n80	756	41n57
374	135n82	774	33
375	124	775–76	32
386–91	124	781	33
392–93	124	789–90	41n57
393–94	124	790	33, 36
395–96	124	792	33, 36
398–401	124	799–801	33
428–29	125	803	33
492	128	803–805	33
500	128	834	33
516	135n82	842–43	41n57
516–17	127	850–58	33
517	142	852	33
555	135n82	859–60	33
777	135n86	869–74	33
788	128	882	41n57
788–95	127	890–1037	32
789	125, 134n68	902–904	33
795	125	1136–44	34
802	127	1160–72	42n68
802–809	135n83	1174–75	34
804	127	1205	34
820	134n72	1216	33, 34
850	128	1233–35	34
859–60	128	1234	33
859	142	1244–48	33
974	102n40	1244–45	34
974–75	135n77	1245	32
1005	134n72	1257–58	34
1081	128	1258	41n57
1114–36	142	1265	36
1185–87	135n77		
1249–50	128, 133n48	*Heracles*	
1255	125, 134n68	339–47	133n48, 154
1297	128, 135n82	347	129
1346	128, 133n48	840–41	154
1347–49	129	852–53	154
1347	128, 135n82	858	154
1348	128, 133n48	1262–63	154
1349	128	1265–68	154
1376–77	128	1303–10	133n48
		1307	135n89, 153
Hecuba		1309	154
25–27	32	1309–10	147
37–44	41n60	1315	154
49–50	34	1341–46	154
57–58	34	1357	155
177–437	41n60	1392–93	154
288–90	34		
715	33	*Hippolytus*	
716	32	5–6	118

Index of ancient sources   191

6	119	1064	120
7–8	118	1080–81	120
12–13	118	1098	120
14	118	1100–1101	120
16	118	1146	133n48
19	118	1167–68	123
20	23, 118, 152n36	1180	120
21–22	119, 141	1241	123
42–46	119	1242	120
43	119, 134n68	1299	121
47–50	119	1301–1302	119
49	119, 141	1309	121
84–85	120	1364–65	120
93–94	119	1391–96	147
95–99	120	1400	119
103	120	1402	119
106	143n63	1417	147
107	120	1418–22	141, 147
114–15	120	1421–22	119
120	129	1437–39	147
117–19	120		
172	120	*Suppliant Women*	
208–31	122	429	134n75
318–19	122		
331	134n66	**Herodotus**	
373–430	134n65	*Histories*	
399	122	1.32	90, 91, 98
428–29	125	1.33	92
443–46	122	1.34–35	116
445	119	1.34–42	92
451–76	134n62	1.34	92, 116
489	122	1.43	133n52
499	134n66	1.44–45	133n49
503	134n66	1.45	92
505	134n66	1.53	92
589–600	123	1.71	92
616–68	122	1.73	95
667–68	122	1.86–87	92
687	122	1.88–89	92
692	134n66	1.90–91	92
717	122	1.155–56	92
728–31	121	1.207–208	92
731	122	2.53	18
857–90	121	2.120	140
887–90	123	2.161–62	101–2n30
948	125	2.162	101n28
948–50	120	2.169	102n30
956–57	120	2.172	91–2
967	133n59	2.173–74	92
973	123	2.174	102n30
986–989	120	2.177	91
987	120	2.182	92
994–96	120	3.10	91
1060–63	121	3.16	101n25

192 *Index of ancient sources*

3.39	92	8.106	36–7, 96, 146
3.40	90, 91, 93	8.108–110	91
3.41	93	8.109	90, 91, 97
3.80	14n4, 38n16, 46, 114	8.112	91, 102n36
3.120	93, 102n37, 103n47	8.125	102n37
3.121–25	93	8.143	101n23
3.122	93	8.144	150n15
3.123	92	9.93–94	95–6, 147
3.126	93, 94, 102n38	9.93	151n17
3.127	93	9.108–13	94
3.128	94, 140		
3.148	141	**Hesiod**	
4.31	93	*Theogony*	
4.83	91	47	152n43
4.161–62	97	223	29
4.162–64	42n66, 97	457	152n43
4.164–67	97	542	152n43
4.200–202	97	643	152n43
4.205	97	838	152n43
5.48–51	141	924–28	100n15
5.105	150n15		
5.106–107	113	*Works and Days (Opera et Dies)*	
6.11	150n14	267	17n50
6.51	141		
6.61	141	**Homer**	
6.66	141	*Iliad*	
6.75	140	1.35–52	137
6.78–81	141	1.159	100n14
6.84	140	1.503–10	87
6.109	150n14	1.517–21	87
7.8–13	94	1.522–23	87
7.8]	95	1.536–50	87
7.10	90–1	1.544	152n43
7.10–11	91	1.560–63	87
7.10–18	102n34	1.565–68	87
7.35	94	1.572–89	88
7.46	91, 94	1.572	88
7.99	94	1.587	88
7.143–44	91	1.590–94	88
8.4–5	91	3.180	100n14
8.7	139	4.5–6	86
8.13	139	4.14–19	87
8.57–63	91	4.25–29	87
8.68	94	4.31–67	138
8.69	94	4.34–36	87
8.75–80	91	4.40–43	87
8.83	91	4.54–56	86
8.87–88	95	4.58–62	87
8.93	102n42	4.68	152n43
8.101	95	5.890	89
8.103–104	102n44	5.893	87
8.104–106	36, 140	6.414–34	14n16
8.105	36, 96	6.447–65	14n16

6.484–87	4
8.49	152n43
8.132	152n43
8.350–96	88
8.397–431	88
8.407–408	88
8.423–24	88
8.455–56	88
8.459–61	100n12
9.535–37	133n57
10	130n4
11.182	152n43
14.153–360	88
14.158	89
14.249–61	88
14.317–28	89
15.18–25	88
15.34	88
15.90–91	88
16.458	152n43
16.459	149
18.117–19	100n6
18.119	100n6
18.356–68	87
18.394–99	88
20.56	152n43
21.47	150n4
21.277]	138
22.15–20	137
22.167	152n43
22.359–60	138
24.25–30	89
24.103	152n43
24.527–33	130n13

Odyssey
1.7–9	137–8
1.32–43	145
1.300	130n4
1.346	100n3
1.346–50	29
4.145	100n14
4.181–82	85
8.318	100n15
8.319	100n14
9–12	150n8
12.299–419	138
21.285	40n47

Homeric Hymn to Apollo
100	89
300–69	4
307	89
309	89, 90
317	89, 101n15
323–25	90
325–30	90
331	89
356–62	90

Philostratus
Life of Apollonius of Tyana
6.3.5	133n61

Pindar
Isthmian Odes
7.39–43	124

Nemean Odes
1.40	159n4

Pythian Odes
10.20–21	29
10.41–42	29

Plato
Apology
28a–d	100n6

Lysis
215d	8

Republic (Respublica)
331e–332d	41n54
335e	41n54
614b	150n8

Phaedrus
247a	46

Timaeus
29e	46

Solon
Fr. 6.3–4	132n42
Fr. 13.5–6	32

Sophocles
Ajax
44	131n24
68	110
79	31, 110
90	110
105	31
111–13	131n27
116–17	110

194 *Index of ancient sources*

124–25	118	590	132n35
127–33	110	596–98	113
241	131n27	600	113
303–304	131n24	624	132n35
401–402	111	711–14	130n18
450	111	713	130n18
655	111	738	109
756–57	111	788	130n15
760–69	111	795	116
774–77	111	800–13	117
843–44	131n24	810	132n41
1061	131n26	816	108
1081	131n26	828	109
1088	131n26	863–910	114
		863	130n18
Antigone		874–88	114
1045–55	135n79	887	130n18
		965	130n15
Oedipus Tyrannus		994	130n15
5	130n15	1011	130n15
31–34	109	1065	112
70–71	130n15	1060–68	113
86	130n15	1152–54	113
91–98	113	1165	113
96–99	112	1170	112
106–107	109, 112	1301–1303	109
107	112, 152n34	1302	130n18
133	130n15	1330	130n15
135–36	109, 152n34	1330–31	131n30
136	112	1345–46	109
140	112	1458	130n18
242–43	130n15	1518	109
244–45	152n34	1526	132n34
245	130n15		
274–75	109	*Philoctetes*	
305	130n15	446–50	129
322–23	112	451–52	129
330–31	112	518	30
335	131n32	602	30
339	131n32	776–78	30
344–45	131n32		
364	131n32	*Trachiniae*	
376–77	109, 111, 130n18, 131n19	1265–69	128
376	130n18	1278	128
378	112		
380–82	112	**Theognis**	
385–89	112, 126	153	132n42
405	131n32		
443	112	**Thucydides**	
579–82	112	1.127	103n48
584–89	112	2.54	131n29
590–91	113	7.68	31

Xenophanes
Fr. 11 10
Fr. 11–12 159n8
Fr. 15 10

OTHER ANCIENT SOURCES

Curse of Agade
57 151n25
58–60 151n25
83–87 151n26
100–19 143
212 151n27

Cyrus Cylinder
7–9 143
17–19 144

Suetonius
Life of Augustus
§ 69 84n55

Index of authors

Albrecht, Jason E. 20
Allan, William 115, 132n41
Allison, Dale C. 75
Allport, Gordon W. 61n54
Alter, Robert 14n12
Amzallag, Nissim 134n73
Armstrong, Karen 54
Ashley, Timothy R. 74, 82n29
Assmann, Jan 75
Atkinson, J. 125
Augustine of Hippo 50–1
Averill, James R. 5

Bacon, Francis 44
Ball, Samuel 17n46
Baranger, Willy 59n30
Barlow, Shirley A. 41n54, 159n4, 159n8
Barrett, James 130n5
Barrett, Justin L. 12, 17n46, 159n7
Barrett, W. W. 133n59
Battezzato, Luigi 36, 41n61, 41n62
Baumel, Amit 51
Begg, Christopher 82n28
Békés, Vera, J. 60n48
Beldman, David J. H. 83n40
Belfiore, Elizabeth 33
Belk, Russell W. 7
Bell, Richard H. 22
Benjamin, Jessica 52
Ben-Ze'ev, Aaron 16n37, 58n17
Berant, Ety 51
Berger, Peter L. 54–6, 60n45
Bergler, Edmund 144–5
Bergmann, Frithjof 14n5
Berke, Joseph H. 50
Besser, Avi 51
Birky, Ian T. 17n46
Black, Jeremy 143, 151n25, 151n26, 151n27, 151n29

Blenkinsopp, Joseph 27
Block, Daniel I. 39n30, 40n36, 40n37, 151n24
Blok, Anton 139
Blomqvist, Jerker 121
Blondell, Ruby 113, 131n30
Blumenthal, David R. 155
Blundell, Mary Whitlock 41n54
Boedeker, Deborah 140
Boström, Lennart 54
Bremmer, Jan N. 19
Brinkman, J. A. 143
Broadhead, H. D. 108
Brown, A. L. 154, 155
Brown, Ken 73, 81n27, 82n34, 82n39, 83n40
Brueggemann, Walter A. 23, 48, 53, 149, 150n10
Budd, Philip J. 81n27
Burkert, Walter 18–19, 22, 86, 138, 149
Burnett, Anne Pippin 125, 127, 134n69
Byron, John 26, 40n33

Cairns, Douglas L. 1–2, 4–5, 7, 15n18, 15n19, 23, 31, 98–9, 103n54, 110, 114–15, 118, 130–1n19, 131n30, 132n43
Calvin, John 72
Carmichael, Calum 74
Carroll, Joseph 37
Cartledge, Paul 140
Caston, Ruth R. 4
Charmé, Stuart L. 54–5
Chiasson, Charles C. 98, 116, 133n49
Childs, Brevard S. 135n85
Christ, Matthew R. 41n56
Clay, Diskin 86, 100n6
Clear, Michael E. 12–13
Clines, David J. A. 21, 57n5, 60n45

Cogan, Mordechai 143
Cohen, Mariam C. 61n52
Cohen-Charash, Yochi 7, 14n14
Colombetti, Giovanna 1–2, 14n6
Conacher, D. J. 119, 121, 132n43, 134n69, 135n80, 135n90
Cooper, Arnold M. 50, 55
Cooper, Jerrold S. 151n29
Cottrill, Amy C. 15n30
Crenshaw, James L. 54, 59n28

Davies, Malcolm 138
Davidson, J. F. 131n24
Dawe, R. D. 113, 131n31, 132n35, 157
De Ste. Croix, G. E. M. 22, 24
Detienne, Marcel 89
DeYoung, Rebecca Konyndyk 50
Diamond, James A. 155
Dickens, Charles 156–7, 159n11, 159n13, 159n14
Dickie, Jane R. 12, 17n47
Dickie, Matthew W. 46
Dion, Kenneth L. 51, 53
Di Vito, Robert A. 3
Dodds, E. R. 22, 85, 115–18, 125, 129, 134n75, 135n88
Dohe, Carrie B. 56
Dover, Kenneth J. 22, 23, 31–2, 158
Dozeman, Thomas B. 81n27
Driver, S. R. 73
Dumbrell, William J. 81n24

Easterling, P. E. 18
Edgecombe, Rodney S. 159n12, 159n14
Eidinow, Esther 23, 86, 100n2
Ekman, Paul 1–2
Elias, Norbert 6, 15n28
Elliott, John H. 7, 39n19, 45, 47
Ellis, B. Anthony 22, 29, 38n11, 103n33
Elshout, Maartje 10, 16n36
Enright, Robert D. 57
Esposito, Stephen 110, 131n22

Feldman, Louis H. 83n47
Ferenczi, Sandor 50
Fewell, Danna Nolan 54
Finglass, P. J. 110
Finley, M. I. 18
Fishbane, Michael 19
Fisher, N. R. E. 107, 114, 131n26
Forster, E. M. 21
Foster, Benjamin R. 143, 151n25, 151n29
Foster, F. M. 6–8, 58n13

Frame, Grant 152n30
Franke, Sabina 151n25, 151n29
Fränkel, Hermann F. 2
French, Peter A. 8
Fretheim, Terence E. 67, 79n7
Freud, Sigmund 11–13, 16n44, 17n45, 50–1, 57, 59n33, 59–60n36, 139
Fromm, Erich H. 54–5
Furnham, Adrian 20

Gale, Raymond F. 57
Gammie, John G. 93, 101n26, 103n45
García-Treto, Francisco O. 68, 80n19
Garvie, A. F. 85, 100n2, 104–8, 129n3, 130n7, 130n9, 130n12, 130n13, 131n20
Geertz, Clifford 3
Gehman, Henry Synder 79n7
Geller, Stephen A. 14n12
Gilbert, Daniel T. 21
Giner-Sorolla, Roger 13n1
Girard, René 139
Glatt-Gilad, David A. 16n42, 39n26, 60n38
Goldhill, Simon 121–2
Goldingay, John 39n19, 40n42, 59n22, 144–5
Gonen, Jay Y. 56
Gould, John 20, 23, 109, 140
Gould, Thomas 130n17, 130n18, 130n19, 132n41
Gray, George Buchanan 82n29
Green, Arthur 159n9
Greenberg, Moshe 40n46
Greenwood, Emily 140
Gregory, Justina 35, 42n68
Gregory the Great 49–50
Grene, David 91
Grinberg, León 59n30
Gross, James J. 7
Grossman, Jonathan 75, 83n45
Grubrich-Simitis, Ilse 16n44
Gunn, David M. 54
Guthrie, Stewart Elliott 13, 158
Guthrie, W. K. C. 149

Habel, Norman C. 60n45
Hackett, Jo Ann 73
Halbertal, Moshe 48
Hall, Edith 105, 129n2, 129n3
Halleran, Michael R. 2, 121, 159n6
Halliwell, Stephen 3
Hamilton, Victor P. 14n14, 40n34, 73
Harris, Christine R. 6, 7, 15–16n32, 61n56
Harris, W. V. 35, 41n55

Index of authors

Hazlitt, William 148
Heath, Malcolm 34–5, 146
Hegel, G. W. F. 60n49
Helson, Ravenna 61n54
Henniger, Nicole E. 7, 15–16n32, 61n56
Herman, Gabriel 32, 41n54, 41n56
Hibbard, Stephen 60n48
Hobbs, T. R. 80n12
Hogan, James C. 30, 110–11, 113–14, 130–1n19, 131n26
Hossfeld, Frank Lothar 59n22, 59n24
How, Walter W. 102n40
Hume, David 10–11, 13, 16n42, 17n50, 23, 154, 156
Humphreys, W. Lee 54

Izre'el, Shlomo 14n8

Jacob, Benno 28, 40n46
Jaeger, Werner 121
Jameson, Michael 157
Jebb, Richard 132n35
Johar, Omesh 7, 50
Johnson, Edward A. 50
Johnson, M. D. 45
Jones, Christopher P. 134n61
Jones, Gwilym H. 66
Jones, Peter 100n10, 152n44
Joseph, Jane E. 16n34
Josefsson, Kim 61n54
Jung, Carl Gustav 56, 61n53
Justice, William G. 17n46

Kaiser, Otto 144
Kantzios, Ippokrates 106
Kastenbaum, Robert 57
Kaster, Robert A. 5, 15n19
Kaufman, Gordon D. 56
Kaufmann, Walter 133n53
Kearns, Emily 20
Keil, Frank C. 12, 17n46, 159n7
Kelly, Michael R. 7, 10
Kennedy, Rebecca Futo 110, 131n21
Kim, Sung Hee 7–9
Kirk, Geoffrey S. 126–7, 129, 157
Kirsch, Jonathan 84n51
Knox, Bernard M. W. 41n54, 110, 113, 130n19, 131n21, 131n29, 133n47
Kok, Johnson Lim Teng 83n44
Konstan, David 23, 28–31, 86, 100n7, 100n8
Kovacs, David 109–10, 115, 119, 123, 130n18, 134n64, 134n65
Kraus, Hans-Joachim 59n28

Krizan, Zlatan 7, 50
Kruger, Paul A. 14n4, 15n30
Kucharski, Janek 32
Kuhrt, Amélie 152n32
Kurek-Chomycz, Dominika 15n30
Kutter, Mara Michelle 4, 15n18, 15n21, 30–1, 90

Lacan, Jacques 50–1
Lamb, David T. 70
Lambert, Warren 17n46
Langston, Scott M. 84n52
Lanzillotta, Lautaro Roig 22, 38n14, 85
Larson, Elliott 7, 14n14
Larson, Janet L. 159n14
Lateiner, Donald 7, 58n11, 98–9, 103n49, 103n53, 149
Lattimore, Richmond 20, 102n31
Lawrence, S. E. 154
Lazarus, Richard S. 13n1
Leach, Colin Wayne 9
Leahy, Robert L. 6–7
Leavitt, John 2, 15n25
Lefkowitz, Mary R. 118–19, 133n56, 148, 157–8, 159–60n15, 160n19
Lenard, Mary 159n12
Lesher, J. H. 10, 16n41, 58n9, 159n8
Levenson, Jon D. 54
Levine, Baruch A. 79n3, 81n27
Levy, Ken 8
Lindeman, Marjaana 12, 154–5
Lindholm, Charles 7
Linforth, Ivan M. 137, 150n3
Livneh, Atar 150n1
Lloyd, Michael 22
Lloyd-Jones, Hugh 22, 108, 115, 119, 129
Loney, Alexander C. 150n6, 150n7
Long, Burke O. 67, 70, 80n16
Lundbom, Jack R. 59n29
Lupfer, Michael 20
Lynn-George, K. 149
Lutz, Catherine A. 4

MacKenzie, R. A. F. 38n17
Maimonides (Moses ben Maimon) 23, 39n18
Malone, Patrick S. 21
Margalit, Avishai 48
Margolin, Ron 155, 159n9
Matthiessen, Kjeld 35, 42n65, 42n68
Maurer, Adah 59n31
Mbuwayesango, Dora Rudo 82n29
McCann, J. Clinton 83n40
McCarter, P. Kyle, Jr. 152n45

Index of authors

McGinty, Park 126, 129
McHardy, Fiona 36, 42n66
Mendenhall, George E. 39n22, 81n24
Meridor, Ra'anana 35, 41n62
Mikalson, Jon D. 70, 119, 125, 130n16, 134n63, 134n69, 135n90, 137, 141, 150n14, 151n21
Miles, Jack 19
Miller, Andrew M. 90
Milgrom, Jacob 39n22, 63, 81n24, 81n27, 83n44
Mills, Sophie 126–7, 129, 134n74, 135n78
Milton, John 9
Mirguet, Françoise 15n22, 15n30
Mitchell-Boyask, Robin 41n61, 42n63, 42n69
Momigliano, Arnaldo 3
Montgomery, James A. 79n7
Moore, Stephen D. 15n30
Morewedge, Carey K. 12–13
Mossman, Judith 31, 35–6, 41n53, 42n64, 42n67, 42n68, 42n69, 98, 103n51, 103n52, 112
Most, Glenn 16n34, 44
Mueller, Melissa 121, 134n67
Muffs, Yochanan 19, 79n5
Muir, J. V. 18
Mulder, Martin J. 82n31
Mullen, Paul E. 6
Munson, Rosaria Vignolo 98–9, 102n41, 103n46

Nagy, Gregory 138
Nelson, Richard D. 80–1n20
Neufeld, Darren C. 50
Newsom, Carol A. 54, 60n46
Niditch, Susan 73–4, 82n29
Nietzsche, Friedrich 9–10, 16n33, 16n38, 16n39, 46
Niskanen, Paul V. 27–8
Noll, K. L. 19–20, 153
Norwood, Gilbert 125–6
Novotny, Jamie 152n30

O'Brien, Edward J. 20
O'Brien, Joan 86
O'Brien, Julia M. 38n9, 39n19
Oranje, Hans 124, 134n71, 134n72
Organ, Barbara E. 83n40
Ostwald, Martin 23, 133n60

Padel, Ruth 2, 14n9
Palmer, Frank 3

Parker, L. P. E. 121
Parker, Robert 31, 123n51
Parrott, W. Gerrod 7–8, 15n19, 15n20, 15n31, 16n34
Patrick, Dale 55
Paul, Shalom M. 27, 144–5
Peat, Derek 37, 43n72
Peels, H. G. L. 24, 28, 38n17, 40n33, 40n39, 40n40, 152n35
Pelling, Christopher 3, 98, 103n46, 151n18
Pironti, Gabriella 19, 37n3, 38n7
Pitard, Wayne T. 39n22
Pitkänen, Pekka 82n30
Podlecki, A. J. 30
Pope, Marvin H. 53
Porter, Barbara Nevling 143, 152n31
Postlethwaite, Norman 100n10
Postman, Neil 57
Priel, Beatriz 51
Propp, William H. C. 135n84

Reckford, Kenneth J. 121
Redfield, James M. 3, 14n11, 20, 38n6, 150n4
Reif, S. C. 79n3
Reinhardt, Karl 100n9
Rentzsch, Katrin 7
Robins, Rochelle 159n10
Rofé, Alexander 68–9, 80n12
Rohmann, Elke 51
Romm, James 37, 93, 98, 101n24, 101n28, 102n43, 133n49, 141
Roncace, Mark 68, 80n17
Ronningstam, Elsa F. 46
Rosegrant, John 60n48
Rothman, Alexander 6

Sacher-Masoch, Leopold 55
Sackson, Adrian 39n18
Salovey, Peter 6–7
Sanders, Ed 15n18, 29, 31, 40n47, 100n3, 100n4, 100n7, 101n17, 121–2
Sandmel, Samuel 3
Sasson, Jack M. 40n34
Schechner, Richard 125
Schechter, Solomon 157
Schein, Seth L. 30, 41n48
Scheler, Max 9–10, 16n40
Schimmel, Solomon 14n14
Schoeck, Helmut 7, 9
Schroeder, Jeanne L. 8, 44–5
Schroer, Silvia 13n2
Scodel, Ruth 4, 6, 100n13

Seaford, Richard 126, 128, 134n75, 135n83
Segal, Charles 34–6, 109, 112–14, 116–18
Seidensticker, Bernd 135n80
Shapiro, David 55
Shapiro, Susan O. 70, 98–9
Sharpsteen, Don J. 6
Shaviro, Steven 2, 15n30
Shtulman, Andrew 12, 154–5
Sissa, Giulia 89
Skinner, John 45
Slater, Humphrey R. 58n12
Slater, Philip E. 89
Smith, Mark S. 37n2
Smith, Richard H. 7–9, 16n34, 50
Smolewska, Kathy 51, 53
Snell, Bruno 2
Solomon, Robert C. 1, 8, 14n5
Sommer, Benjamin D. 83n43
Sourvinou-Inwood, Christiane 18
Spronk, Klaas 39n25, 39n27
Stanford, W. B. 100n15, 110
Staubli, Thomas 13n2
Stearns, Peter N. 57
Steinberg, Naomi 81n25, 82n35, 82n36
Stern, David 58n16
Stolorow, Robert D. 60n48
Strauss, Barry S. 102n40, 120, 125–6, 133n59, 133n60
Stróżyński, Mateusz 60n44
Suthor, Nicola 78
Sweeney, Marvin A. 66, 79n9
Synodinou, Katerina 87, 89

Taylor, Charles 3
Thelle, Rannfrid I. 79n1
Tigay, Jeffrey H. 49
Tomkins, Silvan S. 5, 15n24
Twain, Mark 58n6, 77
Twersky, Geula 40n33, 40n34

Uniacke, Suzanne 16n36, 31

Van De Mieroop, Marc 151n28
Van der Toorn, Karel 84n57
Van Der Veen, J. E. 93, 101n26, 101n29
Vandiver, Elizabeth 133n52
Van Erp Taalman Kip, A. Maria 138
Verduyn, Philippe 13n3
Vernant, Jean-Pierre 19
Versnel, H. S. 134n74
Vidaillet, Bénédicte 8, 50–1
Volz, Paul 38n5
Von Rad, Gerhard 26, 45, 58n8

Walcot, Peter 85–6, 99n1, 100n5
Walder, Dennis 159n11, 159n12, 159n14
Waytz, Adam 13, 17n50
Webb, Barry G. 84n58
Weinfeld, Moshe 57n2, 59n29
Wells, Joseph 102n40
Wenham, Gordon J. 81n27, 83n40
Westenholz, Aage 151n28
White, Gregory L. 6
Whitehead, David 22
Whitman, Cedric H. 100n11
Whybray, R. N. 27
Wierzbicka, Anna 1–2, 5
Williams, Bernard 3, 14n10
Wink, Paul 61n54
Winkler, John J. 126
Winnicott, Donald W. 51–2, 61n52
Winnington-Ingram, R. P. 106, 109, 111, 114–15, 129n3, 130n8, 130n10, 131n24, 131n28, 131n30, 132n37, 132n40, 157
Wray Beal, Lissa M. 80n12, 80n16, 80n18, 80n19

Zali, Vasiliki 101n24
Zanotti, Grace 35
Zenger, Erich 59n22, 59n24
Zivotofsky, Ari Z. 28

Printed and bound by CPI Group (UK) Ltd, Croydon, CR0 4YY
01/12/2024
01797780-0006